Engineering Asset Management Review

Volume 5

Engineering Asset Management Review (EAMR) is published under the auspices of the International Society of Engineering Asset Management (ISEAM). Engineering Asset Management focuses on life-cycle management of the physical assets required by a private or public firm, for the purpose of making products, and/or for providing services in a manner that satisfies various business performance rationales. In exploring the wide ranging issues involved in the management of engineered assets constituting our built environment, EAMR takes a broad view of the inter- and multi-disciplinary approach which combines science, engineering, and technology principles with human behavior and business practice. *Indexed in Scopus.*

Adolfo Crespo Márquez · Turuna Seecharan ·
Georges Abdul-Nour · Joe Amadi-Echendu ·
Antonio Sánchez Herguedas · Aitor Goti Elordi
Editors

Digital Maintenance and Asset Digitalization

Smart Strategies for Optimizing Asset Performance

Springer

Editors
Adolfo Crespo Márquez
Department of Industrial Management
University of Seville
Seville, Spain

Turuna Seecharan
Department of Mechanical and Industrial Engineering
University of Minnesota, Duluth
Duluth, MN, USA

Georges Abdul-Nour
Department of Industrial Engineering
Université du Québec à Trois-Rivières
Trois-Rivières, QC, Canada

Joe Amadi-Echendu
Department of Engineering and Technology Management
Graduate School of Technology Management
University of Pretoria
Pretoria, South Africa

Antonio Sánchez Herguedas
Department of Industrial Management
University of Seville
Seville, Spain

Aitor Goti Elordi
Department of Mechanics, Design and Industrial Management
University of Deusto
Bilbao, Spain

ISSN 2190-7846 ISSN 2190-7854 (electronic)
Engineering Asset Management Review
ISBN 978-3-032-21501-7 ISBN 978-3-032-21502-4 (eBook)
https://doi.org/10.1007/978-3-032-21502-4

This Springer imprint is published by the registered company Springer Nature Switzerland AG
The registered company address is: Gewerbestrasse 11, 6330 Cham, Switzerland

Preface I

The accelerating pace of industrial transformation is profoundly reshaping the way physical assets are conceived, operated, maintained, and renewed. Digital technologies are no longer peripheral enablers but have become structural elements of asset-intensive systems, influencing decision-making across the entire asset lifecycle. In this context, maintenance and asset management are evolving from predominantly reactive or preventive disciplines into data-driven, intelligent, and strategically integrated functions.

This volume, *Digital Maintenance and Asset Digitalization: Smart Strategies for Optimizing Asset Performance*, responds to this transformation by bringing together conceptual advances, methodological developments, and industrial applications that collectively define the emerging paradigm of digital maintenance.

This book constitutes Volume 5 of the *Engineering Asset Management Review* (EAMR) series and is closely aligned with the mission and activities of the Digital Maintenance and Asset Digitalization (DMAD) project group of ESReDA, coordinated by the two Guest Editors of this volume. The title intentionally mirrors the name of the project group, reflecting a shared vision and a consolidated research agenda. The DMAD project group was itself promoted within the framework of the DIGEST project (Digitalization as a Key Enabler for Asset Management), funded by the Spanish Research Agency. DIGEST aimed to adapt maintenance strategies and asset management practices to the realities of digital transformation, addressing not only technological advances but also organizational, methodological, and cultural dimensions.

Over recent years, the DMAD project group has served as a collaborative platform bringing together universities, research centers, and industrial organizations. A series of international meetings held in Bilbao, Gothenburg, and Madrid have played a key role in consolidating this community and fostering enduring academic–industrial partnerships. These interactions have catalyzed shared research directions, advances in AI-driven maintenance concepts, and the promotion of international scientific events.

As Guest Editors, we believe this volume captures both the intellectual maturity achieved by the community and the diversity of perspectives required to address digital maintenance as a systemic, multidisciplinary challenge. We hope it will stimulate further collaboration and contribute meaningfully to the evolution of engineering asset management in the digital era.

Seville, Spain — Antonio Sánchez Herguedas
Bilbao, Spain — Aitor Goti Elordi

Preface II

This volume brings together 15 chapters that reflect the breadth and depth of current research and practice in digital maintenance and asset digitalization. Collectively, the contributions address the representation of assets and maintenance processes in digital environments; the integration of heterogeneous data sources through semantic models, knowledge graphs, and digital twins; and the use of advanced analytics, artificial intelligence, and reasoning mechanisms to support decision-making across the asset lifecycle.

A recurring theme throughout the book is the transition from isolated digital tools toward coherent digital ecosystems. Digital twins, IoT-enabled monitoring, semantic interoperability, and distributed digital architectures are not treated as standalone solutions, but as interconnected components of integrated asset management systems. This systems-oriented perspective is complemented by contributions addressing reliability analysis, risk assessment, asset health indices, and life-cycle-oriented investment planning, highlighting how digitalization enhances—rather than replaces—established engineering and asset management principles.

Several chapters focus on safety-critical and high-complexity contexts, including energy infrastructures, transportation systems, fusion facilities, and industrial plants, where reliability, traceability, and transparency are paramount. Other contributions extend digital maintenance concepts beyond traditional industrial settings, demonstrating their applicability to perishable and logistics-intensive assets such as vaccine cold chains, where real-time monitoring, data integrity, and trust among stakeholders are critical.

Importantly, the volume also addresses organizational and strategic dimensions. Chapters devoted to maturity models, governance, skills, and operational excellence emphasize that successful digital transformation in maintenance is not purely a technological endeavor, but one that requires alignment with organizational readiness, process capability, and continuous improvement frameworks.

This book is intended for researchers, practitioners, and decision-makers involved in maintenance engineering, asset management, and industrial digitalization. By combining theoretical insights with practical case studies, it aims to support both academic inquiry and industrial implementation. Ultimately, the editors share the conviction that digital maintenance and asset digitalization are strategic levers for optimizing asset performance, enhancing sustainability, and supporting informed decision-making throughout the asset lifecycle.

Seville, Spain — Adolfo Crespo Márquez
Duluth, USA — Turuna Seecharan
Trois-Rivières, Canada — Georges Abdul-Nour
Pretoria, South Africa — Joe Amadi-Echendu
Seville, Spain — Antonio Sánchez Herguedas
Bilbao, Spain — Aitor Goti Elordi

Contents

Digital Twins, Semantic Models, and Interoperable Architectures

Industrial and Sectorial Applications of Digital Maintenance

Organizational Maturity, Strategy, and Operational Excellence

Foundations of Digital Maintenance and Asset Digitalization

The Digital Shift in Maintenance: Trends, Challenges, and Opportunities

Adolfo Crespo Márquez

Abstract The transition from traditional maintenance paradigms toward data-driven, intelligent asset management is redefining the role of maintenance in industrial strategy. This chapter introduces the digital shift in maintenance, positioning it as both a technological evolution and an organizational transformation. Building upon the foundations laid in *Digital Maintenance Management* (2022), it examines the accelerating convergence of operational technology (OT) and information technology (IT), and how emerging capabilities such as AI-driven diagnostics, digital twins, and cloud-edge architectures are reshaping decision-making and performance optimization. The chapter identifies key enablers—connectivity, standards, semantic interoperability, and governance frameworks—that support the scalable deployment of digital maintenance solutions. It also outlines persistent challenges including fragmented data ecosystems, skills gaps, cybersecurity threats, and the difficulty of aligning condition data with long-term investment decisions, the critical link between real-time condition monitoring and strategic asset value management. This introductory chapter serves to frame the structure of the book, offering a roadmap through the technological, organizational, and regulatory forces currently shaping maintenance transformation. It advocates for a layered, standards-based, and maturity-aligned approach to digitalization, recognizing that successful transformation is as much about culture and capability as it is about tools. By mapping key trends and tensions, the chapter sets the stage for deeper thematic analysis in subsequent contributions.

Keywords Predictive maintenance analytics · Cloud-to-edge computing architecture · Semantic interoperability · Data sovereignty in industrial systems · Intelligent asset management

A. Crespo Márquez (✉)
Department of Industrial Management, University of Seville, Seville, Spain
e-mail: adolfo@us.es

A. Crespo Márquez et al. (eds.), *Digital Maintenance and Asset Digitalization*, Engineering Asset Management Review 5,
https://doi.org/10.1007/978-3-032-21502-4_1

1 Introduction

Over the past two decades, maintenance has evolved from a cost-centered technical activity into a strategic function within industrial organizations. This transformation was first marked by the rise of operational reliability considerations when designing and analyzing maintenance, the use of condition monitoring, and the integration of maintenance into broader asset management systems. However, the current wave of digitalization represents a more fundamental shift: a redefinition of how asset health, risk, and value are assessed, managed, and optimized. It is not merely a question of adopting new tools, but of restructuring the very logic of maintenance within a connected, intelligent ecosystem.

In 2022 I published the book Digital Maintenance Management, (Crespo Márquez, 2022) the idea was to lay a groundwork for understanding how digital technologies—from new EAM-APM-AIP platforms to AI based predictive analytics—were reshaping practices and roles. Since then, this landscape has matured rapidly. Emerging technologies such as digital twins, edge computing, and artificial intelligence (AI) are no longer confined to pilot programs but are increasingly embedded in operational workflows. According to the Digital Twin Consortium (2022), digital twins are being adopted as core components of real-time diagnostics and simulation environments in asset-intensive sectors. At the same time, global disruptions—supply chain volatility, climate imperatives, energy constraints, and skills shortages—have forced organizations to reassess the resilience, agility, and intelligence of their maintenance strategies. As highlighted by the World Economic Forum (2023), these systemic pressures are accelerating digital transformation across industries, with maintenance playing a key role in operational resilience.

This chapter introduces the central thesis of the book: that digital maintenance is not an optional innovation but a necessary evolution to ensure sustainable performance, operational reliability, and value preservation in asset-intensive environments. It explores how the digital shift is underpinned by multiple interrelated forces. First, technological enablers (IIoT, AI/ML algorithms, etc.) provide the capability to acquire, contextualize, and act upon real-time data. Second, the growing importance of standards—such as ISO 55000 (ISO, 2014), IEC 81346 (IEC, 2022), RAMI 4.0, and ISO/IEC 42001 for AI governance (ISO/IEC, 2023)—ensures consistency, interoperability, and scalability. Third, decision-making is increasingly supported by integrated platforms that combine operational data with long-term planning, exemplified by the rising adoption of Asset Investment Planning (AIP) frameworks (Copperleaf Technologies, 2021).

Yet, the path toward digital maintenance excellence is neither linear nor uniform. Many organizations face challenges of fragmented data, incompatible systems, cybersecurity exposure, and workforce resistance or skill mismatches. Moreover, digital maturity varies widely across sectors and geographies, making it essential to consider cultural, organizational, and infrastructural readiness alongside technical capability. The Digital Readiness Framework developed by GFMAM (2021) emphasizes that successful transformation depends not only on technology, but also on leadership, governance, and integration capacity.

Lastly, as AI plays a growing role in predictive maintenance and anomaly detection, questions of transparency, classification, and responsible use become essential. The OECD Framework for the Classification of AI Systems (OECD, 2021) provides valuable guidelines to support ethical and traceable deployment of intelligent systems in industrial settings.

This introductory chapter sets the stage for a deeper exploration of the technologies, standards, case studies, and management approaches that define the digital maintenance frontier. It offers a roadmap for practitioners, researchers, and policymakers to understand not just what is changing, but why it matters—and how to respond strategically. The shift toward digital maintenance is not just about doing maintenance differently—it is about enabling organizations to think, decide, and adapt at a fundamentally new level of intelligence.

2 Methodological Approach and Scope of the Chapter

This chapter adopts a structured narrative and integrative review methodology. Rather than providing an empirical or quantitative analysis, it synthesizes developments from standards bodies, industry frameworks, and recent scientific literature to articulate the underlying logic of the digital transformation in maintenance. The method combines:

i *A narrative review,* to identify the conceptual foundations and evolution of digital maintenance strategies;

ii *A structured documentary analysis,* integrating recent standards (ISO/IEC 42001, IEC 62443, AAS, RAMI 4.0), industrial architectures, and reference frameworks published by international institutions; and

iii *An interpretative synthesis,* connecting technological, organizational, and governance developments into a coherent systemic perspective.

This methodological choice is aligned with the objectives of the chapter: to provide a holistic, multi-disciplinary framing of the digital shift in maintenance rather than a prescriptive technical guide. The approach also has limitations, including the absence of sector-specific empirical validation and the reliance on fast-evolving industrial guidelines that may evolve beyond the scope of this publication. Nonetheless, the method offers a robust foundation for interpreting the convergence of technologies, standards, and governance mechanisms shaping the digital maintenance landscape.

3 The Drivers of Digital Transformation in Maintenance

The digital transformation of maintenance is not an isolated phenomenon—it is the outcome of converging technological, economic, and organizational forces that are reshaping the way industrial assets are managed. While predictive maintenance and condition monitoring laid the groundwork for smarter operations, the current wave of innovation goes far beyond isolated technologies. It represents a systemic shift in how data, systems, and decision-making interact to deliver reliability, performance, and long-term value.

3.1 Technological Enablers: From Sensing to Intelligence

At the heart of digital maintenance lies the ability to capture, interpret, and act upon data. The emergence of the Industrial Internet of Things (IIoT) has enabled real-time data acquisition at scale, allowing sensors, actuators, and smart components to feed continuous streams of condition data into central systems. This has shifted the role of maintenance from reactive to predictive, and increasingly toward prescriptive models where interventions are optimized not only for technical risk but also for business impact.

Beyond connectivity, artificial intelligence (AI) and machine learning (ML) now play a critical role in detecting anomalies, forecasting failures, and recommending actions. These systems require large volumes of high-quality, contextualized data to generate insights—a capability supported by digital architectures that integrate IT and OT layers, including cloud-edge computing models and the use of asset data platforms.

Moreover, digital twins have become a cornerstone of advanced maintenance strategies. According to the Digital Twin Consortium (2022), digital twins provide a synchronized digital representation of a physical asset, enabling simulation, diagnostics, and performance optimization. Their growing deployment reflects a broader push toward model-based decision-making, where data is not only descriptive but actionable.

3.2 From Technical Standards to Semantic Interoperability

The scalability and reliability of digital maintenance systems depend heavily on the use of shared standards. The ISO 55000 series has established a common vocabulary and set of principles for asset management, including the alignment of maintenance activities with value creation. Complementary standards such as ISO 14224 (reliability data), IEC 81346 (system structuring), and ISO 10303 (product data exchange—STEP) provide foundational models for structuring, labeling, and exchanging asset information (ISO, 2022).

Recent frameworks such as RAMI 4.0 and the Industrial Internet Reference Architecture (IIRA) have extended this foundation (IIC, 2019) by describing how industrial systems should be modeled and integrated across their lifecycle stages. They also provide templates for layered digital architectures, connecting physical assets with logical representations, business processes, and platform services. These architectures are particularly important for ensuring interoperability across vendors and systems, and for enabling digital continuity over time.

The emergence of the Asset Administration Shell (AAS) as a standardized data model in Industrie 4.0 ecosystems reinforces this shift toward semantically interoperable and machine-readable maintenance data. The AAS defines how asset-related information can be described, stored, and exchanged across the value chain, allowing for more flexible, composable, and automated maintenance processes.

3.3 From Operational Constraints to Strategic Pressures

The push toward digital maintenance is also driven by macroeconomic and strategic pressures. Organizations face growing demands for asset availability, operational efficiency, cost control, and sustainability. In parallel, the complexity of asset portfolios and the consequences of unplanned downtime are increasing. These pressures have made it essential to move from reactive and time-based approaches to dynamic, data-informed strategies.

Sustainability goals and regulatory frameworks—such as the EU Green Deal or global ESG reporting standards—have further increased the focus on asset lifecycle management. Maintenance is no longer a purely technical function; it is part of an integrated strategy for extending asset life, reducing energy use, and minimizing environmental impact.

Furthermore, the COVID-19 pandemic and subsequent global disruptions exposed the vulnerabilities of traditional maintenance practices reliant on manual inspections and rigid schedules. Organizations have accelerated digital adoption not just for efficiency, but also for resilience and remote operability. As noted by the World Economic Forum (2023), maintenance digitalization is now seen as a core enabler of industrial transformation and competitiveness.

3.4 From Operational Optimization to Value-Driven Planning

The role of maintenance is increasingly shifting from operational support to strategic value generation. This evolution is enabled by platforms that link asset health with financial and risk-based planning. Asset Performance Management (APM) systems incorporate condition data, failure models, and reliability analytics to prioritize interventions and optimize maintenance plans. Meanwhile, Asset Investment Planning (AIP) platforms add a long-term dimension, enabling organizations to evaluate trade-offs between performance, risk, and cost over asset life cycles.

According to Copperleaf Technologies (2021), AIP systems help infrastructure managers align investment decisions with business objectives, incorporating maintenance insights into multi-year capital planning. This integration closes the loop between operational data and enterprise strategy, reflecting the maturity levels described in the GFMAM Digital Readiness Framework (GFMAM, 2021).

Ultimately, these capabilities support the transition from maintenance as a cost center to maintenance as a value enabler. They empower organizations to manage their asset base more intelligently, respond to uncertainty with agility, and drive transformation at both technical and managerial levels.

4 The Landscape in 2022—A Recap

When I published the book Digital Maintenance Management (Crespo Márquez, 2022), I did an effort in conceptualizing the evolution of maintenance practices within the digital era. Central to that work was the idea that maintenance was no longer a reactive or merely preventive activity—it was becoming connected, predictive, and more intelligent.

At the core of this shift was the integration of Enterprise Asset Management (EAM) platforms with Asset Performance Management (APM) tools. These technologies, coupled with sensorization and early applications of machine learning, offered unprecedented visibility into asset condition, enabling risk-informed decision-making and optimized maintenance scheduling. The book outlined a transition from traditional maintenance hierarchies toward data-driven ecosystems, where failure prediction, remote diagnostics, and lifecycle strategies could converge.

However, by 2022, several structural limitations were still evident:

- Fragmentation of digital tools: Many implementations remained siloed, unable to communicate across systems or scales.
- Low semantic interoperability: Standards existed but were inconsistently applied or too generic to bridge operational layers.
- Immature organizational alignment: Most digital initiatives were still IT-led, with little operational ownership or strategic governance.
- Unclear governance of AI and data ethics, especially in regulated environments.
- Pilot fatigue: Many initiatives stalled at proof-of-concept stage due to lack of scalability or integration planning.

These gaps highlighted the need for a more integrated, scalable, and sustainable approach to digital transformation in maintenance—one that is now taking shape through global developments in technology, standards, and industrial policy.

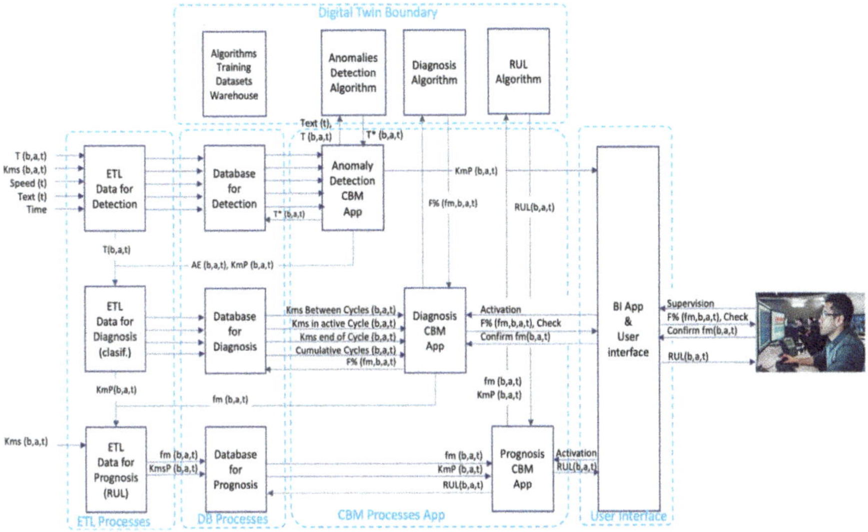

Fig. 1 Digital twins in condition-based maintenance apps (taken from Crespo Márquez et al., 2023)

5 Trends 2023–2025: What Has Evolved

Since 2022, several trends have gained momentum, reshaping the digital maintenance landscape, and addressing some of the limitations previously observed.

5.1 Maturity of Digital Twin Deployment

Digital twins, once confined to high-value, isolated assets, are now becoming part of scaled infrastructure strategies. The emergence of standards like the Asset Administration Shell (Platform Industrie 4.0, 2019) and taxonomy efforts by the Digital Twin Consortium (2022) have enabled a more structured approach to modeling, simulating, and orchestrating asset behavior across their lifecycle. These twins now link real-time data with operational logic, enabling what-if simulations, condition-based planning, and automated decision triggers (Fig. 1).

5.2 AI Governance and Ethical Deployment

The growing use of AI in maintenance—particularly for failure prediction, anomaly detection, and resource optimization—has led to an urgent need for governance. The publication of ISO/IEC 42001 (2023), the first standard for AI management systems,

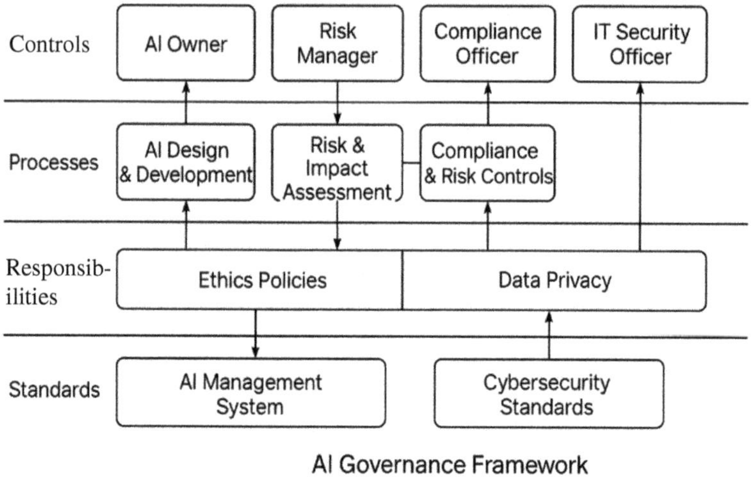

Fig. 2 Adapted governance cycle inspired by ISO/IEC 42001:2023 for AI systems in maintenance

marks a significant step toward ensuring transparency, accountability, and trust in algorithmic maintenance systems. Ethical concerns such as model bias, explainability, and workforce displacement are now on the radar of both regulators and industry bodies (OECD, 2021) (Fig. 2).

5.3 *Real-Time Diagnostics and Cloud-to-Edge Integration*

Recent studies confirm (Kelly, 2024) how edge computing is being able to transform real-time data processing by bringing computation closer to data sources, thus minimizing latency and enabling immediate response in critical sectors such as healthcare, industrial automation, and smart cities. Its decentralized architecture supports localized analytics, reducing reliance on centralized cloud infrastructure and improving both efficiency and resilience.

Edge computing also offers a scalable solution to manage the surge of data from IoT devices, overcoming the bandwidth and latency limitations of traditional cloud models. Additionally, edge systems strengthen data security and privacy by processing sensitive data locally. This is particularly importance in sectors like healthcare and finance.

Beyond operational benefits (Kurduban, 2024), these studies highlight edge computing's role in fostering innovation and economic growth (Premsankar et al. 2024). It enables applications such as real-time traffic optimization and predictive maintenance, reinforcing its value as a foundational technology in digital transformation (Fig. 3).

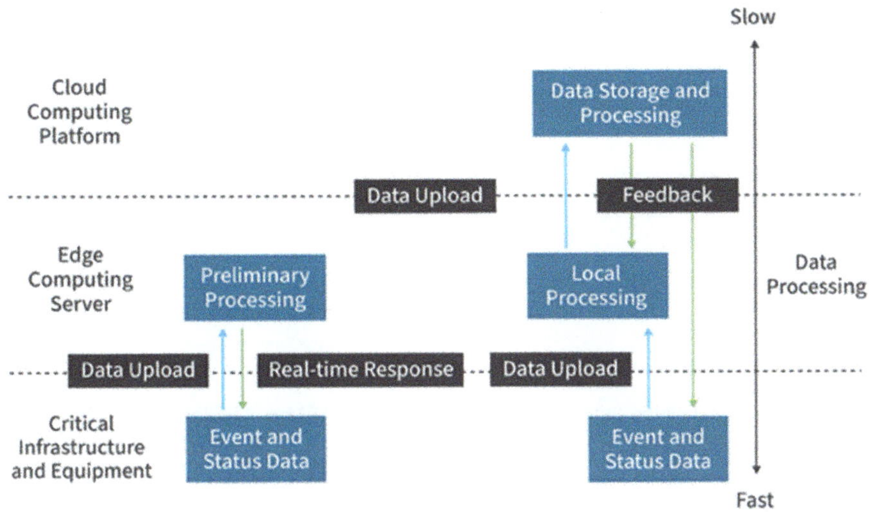

Fig. 3 The edge and cloud computing relationship (Kurduban, 2024)

The convergence of 5G connectivity, edge computing, and industrial IoT platforms has enabled diagnostics at scale. Assets can now be monitored in near real time, even in remote environments, allowing for autonomous fault detection and rapid response coordination. Cloud-to-edge architectures are becoming standard, with distributed intelligence enhancing system resilience and reducing latency (Gódor et al., 2022; Taleb et al., 2022).

5.4 Consolidation of EAM–APM–AIP Architecture

Perhaps the most strategic trend is the consolidation of Enterprise Asset Management (EAM), Asset Performance Management (APM), and Asset Investment Planning (AIP) capabilities into integrated platforms. Major software providers—such as SAP (2023), IBM (2023), Siemens Energy (2022), and GE Digital (2021)—have evolved their product ecosystems to support the full asset value chain.

- EAM continues to support operational and regulatory maintenance processes (e.g., work orders, asset hierarchies, spare parts),
- APM delivers condition analytics, reliability models, and risk-informed planning,
- AIP introduces multi-year investment optimization based on cost, risk, and performance trade-offs (Copperleaf Technologies, 2021).

This architectural integration fosters closed-loop control: from sensor data to risk-based maintenance, and from performance gaps to capital reallocation. It also enables scenario-based planning and alignment with ESG and resilience objectives (Fig. 4).

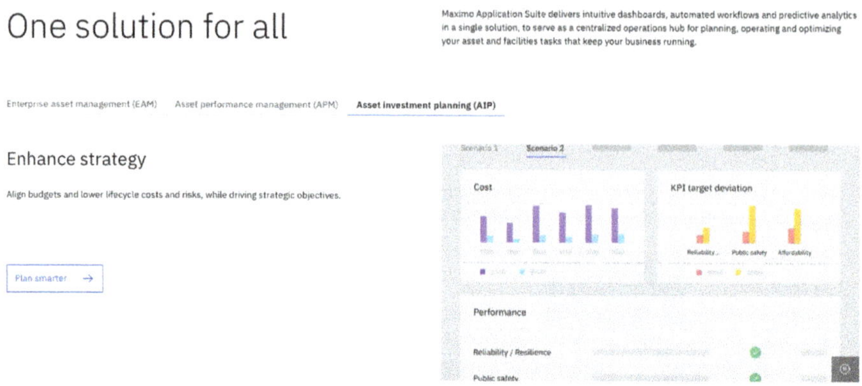

Fig. 4 Maximo application suite offering "features": AEM, APM & AIP. Taken 22.05.2025 from https://www.ibm.com/products/maximo

5.5 *Data Sovereignty and Secure Interoperability*

As maintenance ecosystems extend beyond single organizations, data sovereignty—the ability of data owners to control access, use, and governance—has become a critical requirement in digital infrastructure. Traditional centralized models fall short when handling multi-stakeholder operations that demand federated trust, such as in rail, aviation, and energy maintenance networks (Cavoukian & Naudts, 2023).

Initiatives like Gaia-X and the International Data Spaces Association (IDSA) have responded by establishing federated data-sharing frameworks that ensure technical interoperability, enforceable policies, and sovereign control over information flows. Gaia-X's 2023 Compliance Document formalizes the governance conditions under which services and platforms may participate in sovereign ecosystems, including identity verification, access control, and secure data flows (Gaia-X Association, 2023).

In parallel, the IDS Dataspace Protocol v2024-1 introduces detailed guidance for semantic compatibility, trust provisioning, and policy enforcement across distributed data infrastructures. These frameworks emphasize the importance of data usage control, whereby data providers can set and enforce conditions even after data has left their immediate domain (IDSA, 2024).

Diagram in Fig. 5, shows how data sovereignty and interoperability are supported through a federated, standards-based model. This makes data sharing in maintenance both secure and interoperable. Key elements of this model are presented in Table 1.

An illustrative initiative in this domain is Manufacturing-X, developed under the auspices of Platform Industrie 4.0, which places data sovereignty and interoperability at the core of future industrial architectures. Through its reference use cases—many of which address digital maintenance scenarios—Manufacturing-X showcases the increasing implementation of decentralized and federated data infrastructures to support real-world applications (Plattform Industrie 4.0, 2024). These developments

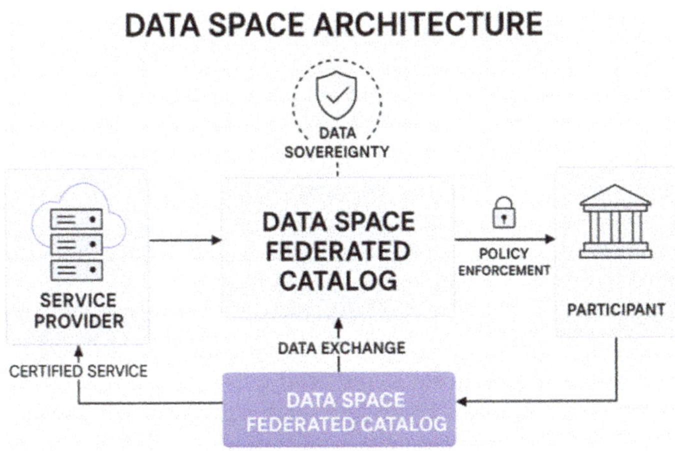

Fig. 5 Federated data space architecture for sovereign and interoperable maintenance ecosystems

Table 1 Basic elements in a federated data-sharing framework

Benefit	Description
Sovereign control	Asset owners retain legal and technical control over how their data is used
Secure federation	Credentials, compliance labels, and real-time policy checking enable trust in shared ecosystems
Semantic consistency	Use of ontologies and shared schemas ensures that data retains meaning when exchanged
Scalable architecture	The federation allows expansion without centralized bottlenecks

reflect a broader shift toward architectures that enable controlled, cross-enterprise data exchange in complex industrial ecosystems.

In parallel, international institutions such as the World Economic Forum have emphasized that embedding trust and sovereignty into digital infrastructure is a prerequisite for viable public–private data collaboration and long-term regulatory alignment (World Economic Forum, 2024). As industrial organizations progressively depend on shared maintenance platforms, the convergence of technical standards, semantic consistency, and enforceable governance frameworks becomes essential for achieving reliable and scalable interoperability.

A critical enabler of this interoperability is the advancement of shared ontologies and metadata schemas that enable the semantic interpretation of data across heterogeneous systems. For instance, Oliveira et al. (2024) introduce an ontology-based framework to support legal and semantic interoperability within international data spaces, addressing a key gap between operational needs and regulatory requirements. Similarly, Hodkiewicz et al. (2022) argue that semantic interoperability is foundational for effective cross-organizational data integration. Their interesting work maps ISO 14224 (ISO, 2016) maintenance data structures onto industrial knowledge graphs, enabling automated reasoning, improved data consistency, and decision support across digital twins and asset management platforms. This aligns with the goals of the Gaia-X and IDS initiatives by providing a structured and machine-readable foundation for federated sovereign data exchange.

In domains characterized by complex multi-stakeholder coordination—such as rail, aviation, and energy networks—these distributed and policy-enforced architectures provide resilience, maintain compliance with regulatory frameworks, and enable real-time, cross-organizational decision-making.

In conclusion, the architectural integration proposed by Gaia-X and IDS, underpinned by continuous governance, certification mechanisms, and semantic harmonization, constitutes a foundational step toward transforming maintenance ecosystems into secure, interoperable, and sovereign digital platforms capable of supporting scalable collaboration and innovation.

5.6 *Evolving Standards and Regulatory Alignment*

As digital maintenance systems grow more autonomous, connected, and data-driven, the regulatory and standardization landscape is undergoing a necessary evolution. This transformation is not only about creating new standards, but also about aligning existing frameworks to ensure semantic coherence, governance compatibility, and scalability.

Recent years have seen the publication of new normative references designed to address emerging needs in artificial intelligence, cybersecurity, and interoperability:

- ISO/IEC 42001 (2023) introduces the first formal requirements for AI management systems, covering algorithmic transparency, bias mitigation, and auditability in critical domains such as predictive maintenance and anomaly detection.
- IEC 62443, now in its 2024 revised edition, expands its cybersecurity controls to cover edge computing nodes, OT/IT convergence, and supply chain vulnerabilities, making it directly applicable to industrial maintenance platforms operating in federated or remote architectures.
- IEC 62264 (Edition 5, 2023) strengthens the enterprise–control system integration model, incorporating digital thread principles and updated mapping to ISA-95 Level 3/4 boundaries, which are essential for aligning condition monitoring systems with enterprise asset management (EAM) and asset investment planning (AIP) platforms.

Simultaneously, implementation guidance for established standards is being refined:

- New technical specifications and application guides for ISO 55001 focus on the integration of digital workflows and real-time asset data within asset management systems.

- The ISO 14224 community is extending the standard to include machine-readable schemas and compatibility with knowledge graph–based infrastructures, in line with initiatives like Asset Administration Shells (AAS) and IDSA-compliant data spaces.

The result is a gradual but necessary shift from framework proliferation to harmonization—a trend driven by the need to reduce fragmentation, improve interoperability, and support scalable implementations across sectors. This evolution supports organizations in deploying digital maintenance strategies that are not only technologically advanced but also regulatory-compliant, certifiable, and auditable.

By 2025, these developments are converging toward a layered ecosystem of standards where governance (ISO/IEC 42001), security (IEC 62443), semantic data exchange (ISO 14224 extensions) (ISO, 2026), and operational integration (IEC 62264) can interoperate to support secure, intelligent, and efficient maintenance operations across increasingly complex and distributed infrastructures.

6 Persisting Barriers and Structural Misalignments

Despite the rapid development of technological enablers and the proliferation of digital frameworks, significant challenges continue to constrain the full adoption of intelligent maintenance practices. Chief among these is the fragmentation of asset data across siloed systems, a legacy issue that resists harmonization despite the maturity of standards such as ISO 14224 and IEC 81346. In many organizations, enterprise asset management (EAM) platforms operate in isolation from condition monitoring tools, and even more so from financial planning environments. This disconnect undermines the ability to transition from predictive alerts to risk-informed investment decisions.

Another persistent limitation lies in the misalignment between digital ambitions and organizational readiness. Digital maturity assessments consistently reveal gaps in data governance, workforce capabilities, and change-management infrastructure. While cloud-native platforms, edge architectures, and AI-based diagnostics have matured, their integration into operational and decision-making processes remains uneven. Furthermore, cybersecurity concerns and unclear data ownership protocols—especially in multi-stakeholder environments such as rail and energy—compound the hesitation to move towards open, interoperable ecosystems. Initiatives such as Gaia-X and the International Data Spaces Association (IDSA) have responded to these challenges by proposing federated, sovereign data infrastructures, but adoption remains incipient.

7 Strategic Enablers and the Need for Institutional Models

Overcoming these limitations will require not only technological investment but also the reconfiguration of maintenance governance. A key enabler lies in adopting layered, standards-based architectures that provide a stable foundation for integration. Reference models such as RAMI 4.0, IIRA, and the Asset Administration Shell (AAS) now converge to offer a coherent structuring logic for intelligent asset systems. Their utility extends beyond interoperability: they anchor governance and foster cross-domain visibility.

The convergence of Asset Performance Management (APM) and Asset Investment Planning (AIP) also deserves special attention. When real-time health data is meaningfully linked to lifecycle cost projections, organizations can optimize asset strategies under uncertainty. This synergy moves maintenance from a purely operational function to a lever of financial performance and risk management. Such integration is increasingly facilitated by software platforms that natively support the AEM–APM–AIP logic—observable in market leaders like IBM, SAP, GE, and Copperleaf—suggesting an industry-wide shift toward architectural coherence.

Additionally, the expansion of open, standards-based platforms offers an alternative to proprietary vendor ecosystems. The Open Industry 4.0 Alliance and Digital Twin Consortium have promoted blueprints that emphasize semantic consistency, federated data access, and compliance-by-design. These ecosystems provide the scaffolding for shared maintenance services and cross-enterprise intelligence, particularly in industrial clusters and transportation corridors.

However, none of these technological trajectories will succeed without parallel investment in human capabilities. The upskilling of technicians, engineers, and analysts to work with data-driven tools is essential. Human-centric automation—where diagnostic technologies enhance, rather than replace, human expertise—must guide implementation. Leading organizations increasingly embed change agents, digital champions, and cross-functional task forces to support this transition.

8 Toward an Intelligent Maintenance Ecosystem

Looking ahead to 2030, the horizon for maintenance is not merely digital—it is intelligent, adaptive, and institutionalized. This vision demands a rethinking of asset management as a socio-technical ecosystem, where data is not just an operational artifact but a strategic asset. Holistic frameworks are needed to unify telemetry, simulation, financial planning, and regulatory compliance. These frameworks will be embedded in platforms that enable collaborative governance, traceability, and transparency.

Furthermore, data valorization will become a defining feature of the next phase. Maintenance data will be increasingly monetized or leveraged beyond its original operational context—whether to optimize supply chains, participate in data marketplaces, or train large-scale AI models. Semantic standards and secure data spaces will provide the conditions for this exchange, enabling maintenance organizations to capture value from their informational assets.

Ultimately, this evolution requires institutional change. The establishment of Digital Maintenance Centers of Excellence (DM-CoEs), cross-industry consortia, and embedded research and development functions will become critical. These structures will ensure that learning is codified, best practices are disseminated, and standards remain aligned with emerging technological and regulatory landscapes.

9 Conclusion: Redefining Maintenance in a Digital Age

This chapter has offered a structured overview of the ongoing digital transformation in maintenance, following a logical path from the foundations established in 2022 to the most recent developments shaping the period 2023–2025. At the time of the previous book, the focus was on the convergence of predictive maintenance with emerging digital tools and the early stages of integration across EAM, APM, and AIP platforms. That vision is now materializing in many industries, with increasing deployment of digital twins, cloud-to-edge architectures, and platform-based approaches that embed intelligence into maintenance ecosystems.

However, the progress made so far also highlights what remains unresolved. The consolidation of frameworks, the harmonization of standards, and the operational integration of asset data into strategic planning still face structural, organizational, and technological barriers. The promise of data-driven maintenance is no longer questioned—but the capacity to scale, govern, and extract value from that data across stakeholders is still a work in progress.

Throughout the chapter, we have emphasized that digital maintenance is not a collection of technologies, but a new paradigm—one that redefines how maintenance is understood, organized, and valued. Moving forward, the emphasis must shift from fragmented experimentation to systemic alignment. This will require not only tools and architectures, but new competencies, governance structures, and cross-functional strategies.

From a methodological standpoint, this chapter has relied on an integrative review of standards, architectures, and recent research to provide a coherent interpretation of current trends. While not exhaustive, this approach enables a structured understanding of how technological, organizational, and regulatory developments converge to shape the emerging paradigm of digital maintenance.

The road ahead points toward intelligent, collaborative, and sovereign maintenance environments. Maintenance will no longer be reactive or even merely predictive—it will be strategic, contextual, and embedded into the core of operational and financial decision-making. This chapter sets the tone for the rest of this volume, where these themes will be explored in depth through standards, technologies, applications, and emerging strategies.

References

Cavoukian, A., & Naudts, L. (2023). Sovereign data spaces: Toward a trustworthy and federated infrastructure in the age of AI. *Journal of Data Protection and Privacy, 6*(1), 34–49.

Copperleaf Technologies. (2021). *Asset investment planning in practice: a guide for infrastructure managers*. Retrieved from https://www.copperleaf.com (Visited on May 2025).

Crespo Márquez, A. (2022). *Digital maintenance management: From predictive maintenance to intelligent asset management*. Springer.

Crespo Márquez, A., Marcos Alberca, J. A., Guillén López, A. J., De La Fuente Carmona, A. (2023). Digital twins in condition-based maintenance apps: A case study for train axle bearings. *Computers in Industry, 151*, 103980.

Digital Twin Consortium. (2022). *Taxonomy and definitions for digital twins*. Retrieved from https://www.digitaltwinconsortium.org (Visited on May 2025).

Gaia-X European Association for Data and Cloud AISBL. (2023). Gaia-X compliance document (Rulebook, Version 2023). https://gaia-x.eu (Accessed: 2 April 2026).

GE Digital. (2021). *APM strategy: Asset performance management for predictive maintenance*. General Electric. Retrieved from https://www.ge.com/digital (Visited on May 2025).

GFMAM. (2021). *Digital readiness framework for asset management*. Global Forum on Maintenance and Asset Management. Retrieved from https://gfmam.org

Gódor, I., Luvisotto, M., Ruffini, S., et al. (2022). *A look inside 5G standards to support time synchronization for smart manufacturing*. arXiv preprint. https://arxiv.org/abs/2205.10154 (Visited on May 2025).

Hodkiewicz, M., Ng, A., Biehl, S., & Stirling, L. (2022). Towards semantic interoperability in asset management: Mapping ISO 14224 to an industrial knowledge graph. *Computers in Industry, 135*, 103564. https://doi.org/10.1016/j.compind.2022.103564 (Visited on May 2025).

IBM. (2023). *IBM Maximo application suite: Integrated EAM and APM platform*. Retrieved from https://www.ibm.com/products/maximo (Visited on May 2025).

IEC. (2022). *IEC 81346-1: Industrial systems—Structuring principles and reference designations—Part 1: Basic rules*. International Electrotechnical Commission.

IEC. (2023). *IEC 62264-1: Enterprise-control system integration—Part 1: models and terminology (Edition 5)*. International Electrotechnical Commission.

IEC. (2024). *IEC 62443: Security for industrial automation and control systems—Updated Edition*. International Electrotechnical Commission.

IIC. (2019). *The industrial internet reference architecture (IIRA), Version 1.9. industrial internet consortium*. Retrieved from https://www.iiconsortium.org/IIRA.htm (Visited on May 2025).

International Data Spaces Association (IDSA). (2024). *Dataspace Protocol Specification (Version 2024-1)*. IDS Knowledge Base.https://docs.internationaldataspaces.org/ids-knowledgebase/dataspace-protocol (Accessed: 2 April 2026).

ISO. (2014). *ISO 55001: Asset management—Management systems—Requirements*. International Organization for Standardization.

ISO. (2016). *ISO 14224: Petroleum, petrochemical and natural gas industries—Collection and exchange of reliability and maintenance data for equipment*. International Organization for Standardization.

ISO. (2022). *ISO 10303: Industrial automation systems and integration—Product data representation and exchange (STEP)*. International Organization for Standardization.

ISO. (2024). *ISO/NP 14224-2: Petroleum, petrochemical and natural gas industries—Linked data extension for reliability and maintenance data (draft proposal)*. International Organization for Standardization.

ISO/IEC. (2023). *ISO/IEC 42001: Artificial intelligence management system—Requirements*. International Organization for Standardization/International Electrotechnical Commission.

Kurduban, V. (2024). *Edge computing vs cloud computing: Differences and relationship*. Digi International. Retrieved from https://www.digi.com/blog/post/edge-computing-vs-cloud-computing (Visited on May 2025).

Kelly, B. (2024). The impact of edge computing on real-time data processing. *International Journal of Computing and Engineering, 5*(5), 44–58. https://doi.org/10.47941/ijce.2042 (Visited on May 2025).

Oliveira, D., Lemos, F., & Rocha, Á. (2024). An ontology-based framework to provide legal interoperability within international data spaces. In *Proceedings of FOIS 2024—International conference on formal ontology in information systems.* University of Twente.

Organisation for Economic Co-operation and Development (OECD). (2021). *OECD framework for the classification of AI systems.* OECD AI Policy Observatory. https://oecd.ai/en/classification (Accessed: 2 April 2026).

Plattform Industrie 4.0. (2019). *Details of the asset administration shell—Part 1: The exchange of information between partners in the value chain of Industrie 4.0 (Version 2.0).* Federal Ministry for Economic Affairs and Energy (BMWi). https://www.plattform-i40.de (Accessed: 2 April 2026).

Premsankar, C., Di Francesco, M., & Taleb, T. (2024). Leveraging edge computing for scalable real-time cloud systems. *International Journal of Future Manufacturing Research, 10*(6), 12–28.

SAP. (2023). *SAP intelligent asset management.* SAP SE. https://www.sap.com/products/scm/asset-management.html (Accessed: 2 April 2026).

Siemens Energy. (2022). *Navigator: Asset performance suite for digital maintenance.* Retrieved from https://new.siemens.com (Visited on May 2025).

Taleb, T., Afolabi, I., & Bagaa, M. (2022). *Orchestrating 5G network slices to support industrial internet and next generation smart factories.* arXiv preprint. https://arxiv.org/abs/2201.07185 (Visited on May 2025).

World Economic Forum. (2023). *Digital transformation of industries: Industrial clusters Outlook.* Retrieved from https://www.weforum.org (Visited on May 2025).

World Economic Forum. (2024). *Trustworthy data sharing and digital infrastructure.* https://www.weforum.org (Accessed: 2 April 2026).

From Traditional Maintenance to Smart Maintenance: A Narrative Review of Asset Digitalization Fundamentals

Aitor Goti Elordi, Aitor Oyarbide, Janire Gordon Isasi, and Elisabete Alberdi

Abstract This study summarizes the transformative influence of digitalization on maintenance, a key component of asset management, with particular emphasis on the transition from traditional maintenance practices to Smart Maintenance paradigms. For that, peer-reviewed and industrial research are analysed using a narrative review methodology, to identify how emerging digital technologies are reshaping maintenance processes, decision-making mechanisms, along with human and organizational dynamics. Methodologically, the review adopts a structured approach to map the historic evolution of digital maintenance, to classify the main technological and managerial enablers driving this transformation. It continues by exploring the challenges that hinder its large-scale implementation, such as data interoperability, cybersecurity, and workforce reskilling. Additionally, the research also presents some of the most relevant Smart Maintenance frameworks found in the literature, along with some implementation cases of different sectors. Thus, this research provides a comprehensive synthesis of current developments, highlights critical gaps in the literature, and outlines future research directions aimed at advancing the digital transformation of asset management and, within it, Smart Maintenance systems.

Keywords Smart maintenance · Asset digitalization · Cyber-physical systems · Generative AI in maintenance · Asset management analytics

A. Goti Elordi (✉) · A. Oyarbide · J. Gordon Isasi
Department of Mechanics, Design and Industrial Management, University of Deusto, Bilbao, Spain
e-mail: aitor.goti@deusto.es

A. Oyarbide
e-mail: aitor.oyarbide@deusto.es

J. Gordon Isasi
e-mail: janiregordon@deusto.es

E. Alberdi
Department of Applied Mathematics, University of the Basque Country (UPV/EHU), Bilbao, Spain
e-mail: elisabete.alberdi@ehu.eus

A. Crespo Márquez et al. (eds.), *Digital Maintenance and Asset Digitalization*, Engineering Asset Management Review 5,
https://doi.org/10.1007/978-3-032-21502-4_2

1 Introduction

Asset management, covering strategic planning, acquisition, utilization, maintenance, and disposal of physical assets, aims to maximize asset value, extend lifespan and optimize associated costs and risks. Within asset management, maintenance refers specifically to the set of activities aimed at preserving or restoring the function of assets, primarily during their operational phase. Maintenance ensures assets remain reliable, safe, and efficient, but it is just one part of the broader asset management process (Da Silva & Souza, 2020).

Historically, and as extended in Sect. 3, maintenance focused on the craftsman perspective, where manufacturers themselves performed the needed maintenance on their assets, evolving towards reactive and preventive strategies based on empirical observations and scheduled interventions (Baldin et al., 1982; Da Silva & Souza, 2020; Too, 2012). Evidently, this traditional approach did not integrate data-driven decision-making or advanced technologies. The 1970s marked a turning point with the emergence of microcomputers, which enabled the integration of technical, financial and optimization techniques into maintenance and pioneered as Terotechnology (Parkes, 1970). According to Lundgren et al. (2018), the Terotechnology model was developed for the industry in the UK with support from the government, receiving recognition from several experts (Baldin et al., 1982; Herguedas, 2002; Nakajima, 1988; Sherwin, 2000).

However, the pervasive digitalization across various industrial sectors has initiated a fundamental re-evaluation of these traditional approaches (Tugengold et al., 2019). So, it is necessary to revisit the whole historical trajectory of maintenance the asset management discipline, to foresee where it is going to evolve influenced by digitalization. To address this, the following research questions are proposed:

- RQ1: How has the maintenance paradigm evolved chronologically, and what are the specific characteristics that distinguish "Smart Maintenance" from traditional reactive and preventive approaches?
- RQ2: What are the primary managerial and technological drivers that act as enablers for the digital transformation of asset maintenance?
- RQ3: Which conceptual and architectural frameworks are currently established in the literature to support the integration of Smart Maintenance within broader asset management systems?
- RQ4: What are the critical implementation challenges and emerging risks—specifically regarding cybersecurity and Generative AI—that define the current research gaps in the field?

A literature review is proposed to respond to these research questions. It examines the foundational shift occurring in maintenance, within the discipline of asset management, due to digitalization. The review traces the trajectory from conventional maintenance practices, often characterized by fixed schedules or response to failures, to the sophisticated methodologies inherent in Smart Maintenance. The analysis considers the technological enablers, conceptual frameworks, and practical implications of this transformation, and provides a comprehensive overview for both academic discourse and industrial application.

1.1 Contributions and Structure of This Chapter

This review transcends a purely descriptive synthesis by providing several analytical contributions:

- Comparative Taxonomy: Rather than just listing historical milestones, the chapter develops a comparative taxonomy that maps the evolution of maintenance from artisanal to "next gen" autonomous systems, categorizing them by key characteristics, technologies, and inherent limitations.
- Dual-Driver Framework: It introduces a structured framework that identifies the synergy between managerial conditions (e.g., regulatory demands, economic constraints) and technological drivers (e.g., IoT, Digital Twins, AI), explaining why the shift to Smart Maintenance is occurring, not just that it is occurring.
- Organizational-Technological Synthesis: By categorizing Smart Maintenance frameworks into "organizational/managerial" and "technological/data-driven" types, the chapter provides a cohesive perspective on how these disparate models interact to support implementation.
- Emerging Risk Analysis: The chapter provides a novel analysis of contemporary risks, specifically identifying cybersecurity threats and operational vulnerabilities introduced by the integration of Generative AI and Agentic AI into maintenance optimization.
- Discussion on strategic implications: These analyses, together with a set of illustrative cases culminate in a structured discussion on elements affecting the research agenda in the field for future inquiry.

The review is structured as follows: Sect. 2 outlines the methodology employed for this literature review, detailing search strategies, selection criteria, and analytical approaches. Section 3 defines Smart Maintenance and shows how it evolved chronologically. After that, Sect. 4 expands on the context conditions supporting the evolution towards the 'smartization' of maintenance. Section 5 shows some of the most relevant Smart Maintenance frameworks available in the literature, along with the pillars supporting these frameworks. Then, Sect. 6 presents an analysis of application cases of Smart Maintenance, showcasing the validity of this evolution. Afterwards, in Sect. 7, the organizational, technical, and human dimensions of this transformation are explained. Finally, Sect. 8 discusses and highlights potential research gaps, theoretical debates, and future directions, culminating in a conclusive summary of the findings and their implications.

2 Methodology: Narrative Review

A Narrative Literature Review (NRL) was conducted to gather relevant academic and industrial literature about asset management, digitalization, and Smart Maintenance. Although not as rigorous as Systematic Literature Reviews (SLRs), NRLs are considered valid for, among others, rationales for future research, if they are done following some specific guidelines (see Ferrari, 2015, for further details).

Over 100 publications, articles, books and proceedings were analysed in this work. Key terms and their synonyms were identified, including "asset management," "physical asset management," "maintenance," "traditional maintenance," "Smart Maintenance," "digitalization," "digital transformation," "Industry 4.0," "Internet of Things (IoT)," "Artificial Intelligence (AI)," "Machine Learning (ML)," "Big Data," "predictive maintenance," "prescriptive maintenance," "digital twin," and "cyber-physical systems." Boolean operators (AND, OR) were utilized to construct search strings. The primary databases consulted included Scopus, Web of Science, IEEE Xplore, and Google Scholar, ensuring a broad coverage of engineering, computer science, and management disciplines. Publication dates were restricted to the last 12 years (2013–2025) to focus on all contemporary developments in digitalization providing, in comparison to other reviews related to Smart Maintenance, a wide focus but with a very specific time window.

Inclusion criteria for selected documents were as follows:

- Peer-reviewed journal articles, conference papers, and reputable academic books.
- Content directly addressing the integration of digital technologies in maintenance.
- Studies discussing the evolution from traditional to more digitally enabled maintenance paradigms.
- Papers providing conceptual frameworks, empirical studies, case studies, or architectural models relevant to Smart Maintenance.

The exclusion criteria were established to maintain methodological rigor and ensure alignment with the study's specific research objectives. Articles were systematically excluded if they fell into any of the following categories:

- Review articles synthesizing existing literature without contributing original empirical data, to prevent the introduction of derivative or duplicative information.
- Opinion pieces lacking systematic methodological frameworks or empirical validation, due to their inherently subjective nature.
- Non-relevant perspectives: Studies concentrating solely on perspectives of asset management not related to maintenance (e.g., financial instruments) or non-industrial applications were excluded to avoid conceptual ambiguity.

The selection process for this review followed a structured three-stage workflow to ensure both comprehensiveness and thematic relevance:

- Identification: An initial broad search was conducted across the following databases: Scopus, Web of Science, IEEE Xplore, and Google Scholar. This

Table 1 Summary of the literature selection process

Stage	Description	Number of articles
Retrieved	Total record identified through databases	148
Screened	Record screened based on title and abstract	148
Excluded	Records excluded after full text assessment and criteria established	87
Final included	Publications selected for the final narrative synthesis	61

Source Own elaboration

phase focused on capturing a wide range of studies related to maintenance and digitalization, resulting in 148 retrieved records.

- Screening: The resulting 148 retrieved records underwent a preliminary screening based on title and abstract. At this stage, duplicates were removed, and articles were excluded if they did not directly address the intersection of digital technologies and asset management (e.g., purely financial studies or non-industrial applications).
- Inclusion and Analysis: The remaining publications were subjected to a full-text eligibility assessment. After applying the exclusion criteria mentioned above, 87 records were excluded. This rigorous filtering resulted in the final selection of 61 publications (including peer-reviewed articles and key industrial reports) that form the basis of the current narrative synthesis.

Table 1 shows the details of each stage of the selection process, illustrating how the initial 148 records were refined to the final 61 sources used in this study.

3 Smart Maintenance: Definition and Chronological Evolution

Although Smart Maintenance is currently a sound concept, there has been an evolution marked by enablers pushing its spread, and it is not yet equally understood everywhere. This Section outlines its definition, the historical evolution for its appearance, the enabling technologies empowering it, and some architectural considerations where its applicability is scoped.

3.1 Defining Smart Maintenance Within Asset Management

Smart Maintenance represents the current advanced current stage of digitalization in asset management, integrating advanced technologies to achieve highly optimized, predictive, and autonomous maintenance operations. Smart Maintenance extends beyond traditional predictive maintenance by incorporating a broader array of digital technologies and analytical capabilities to foster proactive, adaptive, and highly efficient asset care. In 2020, it was "a transition towards new technologies", "with adjustment costs in the form of financial investments in both tangible and intangible assets" (Bokrantz et al., 2020a, 2020b). It originally embodies the principles of Industry 4.0, where interconnected systems, real-time data, and intelligent algorithms optimize the entire maintenance lifecycle. The concept is characterized by an emphasis on continuous monitoring, data-driven decision-making, and the automation of maintenance processes, often leading to self-optimizing systems (Nel & Jooste, 2016; Tugengold et al., 2019).

Key attributes of Smart Maintenance are:

- Prognostic Capabilities: Going beyond fault detection to predict when and how components may fail, including its remaining useful life (Cavalieri & Salafia, 2020).
- Prescriptive Actions: Not only forecasting failures but also recommending specific, optimized interventions, considering operational constraints, resource availability, and cost–benefit analysis (Carvalho et al., 2019; Liu et al., 2018).
- Interconnectivity: Ensuring s eamless data flow between machines, systems, and human operators, often facilitated by IoT platforms and cloud infrastructure (Lee et al., 2015; Wan et al., 2017).
- Adaptability: Dynamically adjusting maintenance strategies in real-time based on changing operational conditions, asset performance, and business objectives (Bokrantz et al., 2020a, 2020b).

Autonomy: Incorporating higher levels of automation in data collection, analysis, and even the execution of specific maintenance tasks or adjustments (Lee et al., 2018). It transforms maintenance from a cost centre scenario into a strategic value driver, which contributes directly to business profitability and sustainability (Cavalieri & Salafia, 2020). In the last years, and analysing the human-centrism, resilience, and sustainability orientations Smart Maintenance is tackling, it can be said that the concept is also evolving towards its integration of Industry and even Society 5.0 perspectives (Foresti et al., 2020).

3.2 The Evolution of Asset Maintenance: From Traditional to Smart

The evolution of asset maintenance reflects a fundamental shift from simple, reactive practices to integrated, intelligent systems powered by digital technologies and data analytics. This transition has been shaped by increasing industrial complexity, rising performance expectations, and the advent of Industry 4.0 paradigms.

Before the 1970s: Traditional Maintenance Era

- Characteristics: Maintenance was primarily reactive (addressing failures after breakdowns) and preventive (performed at scheduled intervals regardless of actual condition), often leading to unexpected downtime, excessive maintenance, and high repair costs (Moubray, 1997).
- Limitations: This period lacked condition monitoring or predictive capabilities. Manual inspections were common, prone to error, and inefficient. Maintenance data was often fragmented across departments, hindering integrated decision-making (Dhillon, 2006; Moubray, 1997).

1970s: Early Digitalization and Terotechnology

- Technological Milestone: The advent of microcomputers facilitated the first integration of technical, financial, and operational data in maintenance strategies (Kelly, 1997).
- Key Concept: This era marked the rise of Terotechnology, a UK-led initiative that promoted maintenance as a lifecycle cost discipline, integrating reliability, finance, and operations (British Standards Institute, 1970; Kelly, 1997).

2013–2023: Digital Transformation and Smart Maintenance Paradigms

- Paradigm Shift: This stage reflects a systemic transition toward data-driven, predictive, and autonomous maintenance systems. Traditional approaches are increasingly replaced by Smart Maintenance solutions that exploit real-time data and machine intelligence (Crespo Marquez et al., 2020).

Table 2 shows the chronological evolution of maintenance strategies, tracing the evolution from artisanal and reactive approaches to advanced smart and adaptive systems. This progression reflects significant technological, organizational, and methodological shifts, driven by the emergence of digital technologies. Table 2 synthesizes key characteristics, enabling technologies, and limitations across each stage, offering a clear timeline that contextualizes the ongoing digital transformation in asset maintenance. It highlights how maintenance has evolved from a cost-centred activity to a strategic, data-driven function essential for operational efficiency and sustainability (Cavalieri & Salafia, 2020).

4 Context Conditions Promoting Smart Maintenance in Companies

As summarized in the previous section, Smart Maintenance takes advantage of the application and integration of digital technologies related to first Industry 4.0 and now Society 5.0 to the area of maintenance. Nevertheless, as it happens with the adoption of other managerial frameworks, companies are pushed by both technological and managerial context conditions justifying the evolution towards Smart Maintenance.

Table 2 Chronological evolution of maintenance strategies

Stage	Decade	Maintenance type	Key characteristics	Enabling technologies	Limitations/Challenges
Artisanal	Before 1970s	Corrective Maintenance (Reactive)	Repairs only after failure; Experience-based decisions	None (manual practices)	High downtime; Unpredictable failures; No data use (Too, 2012)
Traditional	1970s–1990s	Preventive Maintenance	Time-based schedules; Periodic inspections; Terotechnology approach	Early CMMS, basic computing (Parkes, 1970)	Over-maintenance; Inefficient resource use; Data silos (Sherwin, 2000)
Early Digital	2000s–2010s	Predictive Maintenance	Condition monitoring; Sensor-based insights; Data-driven but static	IoT, SCADA, first analytics tools	Limited AI; Fragmented data systems (Campos et al., 2017)
Smart	2010s–Now	Smart Maintenance (Predictive + Prescriptive)	Real-time monitoring; AI/ML-based decisions; Integration with business systems	Real-Time IoT, AI, Big Data, Digital Twins, Blockchain (Cavalieri & Salafia, 2020)	Cybersecurity; Interoperability; Workforce adaptation
Next gen	2030s–(Expected)	Autonomous Adaptive Maintenance	Self-learning systems; Edge computing; Fully automated actions	Explainable and interactive AI, AR/VR, 5G, Cloud/Edge synergy	Ethical AI; Governance models; Standardization (Future Research Needs)

Source own elaboration

The following subsections expand on these (a) 5.0 related technological drivers and (b) managerial conditions promoting this change of paradigm.

4.1 Managerial Conditions Contextualizing the Evolution Towards Smart Maintenance

The change of paradigm of companies to move towards Smart Maintenance is accompanied by not only technical changes, but in relation to managerial context conditions, which are commented below.

Reliability, Maintainability, and Safety Shortcomings

Traditional maintenance approaches often struggled with accurately predicting equipment failures, leading to unexpected downtime and production losses. Existing traditional maintenance approaches, such as Reactive Maintenance (RM) and Preventive Maintenance (PM), are associated with high prevention and repair costs (Zhu et al., 2019). This approach also entailed higher repair costs and potential for secondary damage to equipment. Preventive maintenance, while reducing unexpected failures, introduced its own set of inefficiencies. Fixed-schedule maintenance often resulted in unnecessary interventions on healthy assets, leading to premature wear from intrusive maintenance, increased labour costs, and wasted resources (Cavalieri & Salafia, 2020). Such calendar-based schedules often did not account for actual asset condition or operational stress, meaning that maintenance could be performed too early, or critically, too late, missing the optimal window for intervention.

Furthermore, traditional methods presented challenges for maintainability and safety. Manual data collection and inspection processes were often labour-intensive, prone to human error, and could expose personnel to hazardous environments (Ariansyah et al., 2019). The absence of real-time insights into asset health hindered timely and precise fault diagnosis, prolonging repair times (García Marquez & Pedregal Tercero, 2011). Safety risks were amplified by the inability to anticipate failures of critical components, potentially leading to catastrophic events, particularly in high-risk industries such as energy or transportation infrastructure (Ismagilova & Sitnikova, 2017). The absence of comprehensive, integrated data prevented a holistic view of risk, making it difficult to prioritize safety–critical maintenance actions effectively.

Organizational and Economic Constraints

Beyond technical limitations, traditional maintenance was constrained by significant organizational and economic challenges. Information silos were widespread, with maintenance data often isolated from broader operational or financial systems. This fragmentation hindered holistic decision-making, making it difficult to evaluate the real cost of maintenance activities or their impact on overall business performance (von Petersdorff & Vlok, 2014). Manual record-keeping and paper-based processes limited data analysis capabilities, preventing the identification of long-term trends or root causes of recurring failures (Platfoot, 2014). Moreover, reliance on human expertise for diagnostics and scheduling, while valuable, was inherently subjective and difficult to scale across large asset portfolios (Kaito & Kobayashi, 2014).

From an economic perspective, traditional maintenance often generated higher overall costs due to inefficient resource allocation. Unplanned downtime resulted in production losses and missed revenue opportunities. Over-maintenance consumed excessive spare parts and labour, while under-maintenance accelerated asset degradation and necessitated costly capital expenditures for early replacement (Mobley, 2002). The lack of rigorous cost–benefit analysis for maintenance interventions meant that investment decisions were often made with incomplete information. Furthermore, the absence of robust data on asset performance hindered accountability and continuous improvement efforts, perpetuating inefficient practices (Too, 2012). Organizations found it challenging to justify maintenance budgets or demonstrate their return on investment without quantifiable performance metrics derived from integrated data. Collectively, these limitations underscored the necessity for a transformative shift in asset management paradigms.

Changing Regulatory and Market Demands

Beyond technological advancements, evolving regulatory frameworks and competitive market pressures are key drivers in the digitalization of asset management. Industries are subject to increasing scrutiny regarding safety, environmental impact, and operational resilience. Stricter regulations, particularly in energy, transportation, and manufacturing sectors, require more robust and auditable maintenance practices (Ismagilova & Sitnikova, 2017). Digital solutions provide the infrastructure to achieve higher levels of compliance, offering transparent data trails for regulatory reporting and demonstrating due diligence in asset integrity management. The capacity to continuously monitor and report on asset health, for instance, assists in meeting safety standards and reducing the likelihood of incidents.

At the same time, market demands also exert considerable pressure. Customers expect higher levels of service, product availability, and lower costs, which directly correlates with efficient asset performance. In a competitive environment, minimizing downtime, extending asset life, and optimizing operational costs become critical differentiators. Digitalization facilitates companies to achieve these efficiencies, translating into competitive advantages. The drive for sustainability and circular economy principles further reinforces the need for smart asset management (Arenkov et al., 2019) and, as a consequence, Smart Maintenance. By optimizing asset utilization and extending component lifespans through predictive maintenance, organizations can reduce waste, conserve resources, and lower their carbon footprint, aligning with broader corporate social responsibility objectives. The capability to offer 'asset-as-a-service' models, in which performance guarantees are tied to asset uptime and reliability, further highlights the necessity of advanced digital monitoring and maintenance capabilities.

Conceptualization of Digital Asset Management and Digital Maintenance Management Systems

The digital transformation of both asset management and maintenance fostered the development of integrated systems that leverage advanced technologies to enhance decision-making and operational efficiency (Gomaa, 2025). These systems extend beyond simple data collection to sophisticated modelling and analytical capabilities. As often these models and frameworks depend on architectures, the inter-relation among these models, frameworks, and architectures of Smart Maintenance is shown in Sect. 5.

4.2 Technological Drivers of Digital Transformation in the Management of Maintenance

The imperative for digital transformation in maintenance stems from a confluence of rapid technological advancements and evolving regulatory and market demands. The following drivers collectively push industries towards more sophisticated, data-intensive, and intelligent approaches to asset upkeep.

Internet of Things (IoT)

IoT devices, embedded with sensors and connectivity, enable real-time data acquisition from physical assets, capturing operational parameters, environmental conditions, and performance metrics (Taneja et al., 2019). This continuous stream of granular data, ranging from vibration and temperature to pressure and acoustic signatures, forms the bedrock for advanced analytical capabilities previously unattainable. The ability to wirelessly transmit this data to centralized or distributed platforms for analysis is a core enabler of Smart Maintenance (Rakshit & Sridhar, 2018), which feeds the Edge, Fog and Cloud computing paradigm.

Edge, Fog and Cloud computing

Edge computing enhances IoT by bringing computational power in close proximity to the data source. Instead of sending all raw sensor data to a centralized cloud for processing, or to a local server farm, the edge devices perform preliminary analysis, filtering, and aggregation directly at the asset level. It even acts before interacting with the rest of the assets, when real-time applications require it. This reduces data transmission latency, conserves network bandwidth, and enables faster decision-making for time-sensitive maintenance actions (Taneja et al., 2019). For example, an edge device might identify an abnormal vibration pattern and immediately trigger a local alert or initiate a partial shutdown before sending the data to the cloud for more comprehensive analysis. This distributed processing capability enhances the responsiveness and efficiency of Smart Maintenance systems.

Current cloud computing further supports this by offering scalable and flexible infrastructure for data storage and processing, accessible from anywhere (Gandhewar et al., 2019).

Blockchain

Finally, blockchain technologies, as decentralized assurance systems for a multi-attribute traceability helps facilitate a better understanding of the data and are considered as essential tools for maintenance intensive industries, such as the renewable energy sector (Arcelay et al., 2021), as it provides a secure, transparent and decentralized way of measuring and auditing situations and actions.

Integration of Digital Twins and Cyber-Physical Systems

A cornerstone of advanced digital asset management is the concept of the digital twin. A digital twin is a virtual representation of a physical asset, system, or process, updated in real-time with data from its physical counterpart (Gitelman et al., 2019). This dynamic linkage between the physical and virtual worlds provides a comprehensive, living model of the asset's current state, historical performance, and predicted future behaviour. Digital twins enable precise monitoring, simulation of various scenarios (e.g., the impact of different operational loads or maintenance strategies), and proactive problem identification without interfering with the physical asset (Giovannini et al., 2019). For maintenance, a digital twin allows for virtual testing of repair procedures, optimization of maintenance schedules, and identification of potential issues before they manifest physically, thereby minimizing downtime and maximizing efficiency (Tugengold et al., 2019).

Digital twins are integral components of Cyber-Physical Systems (CPS), which represent the deep integration of computation, networking, and physical processes. In the context of asset management, CPS involves a feedback loop where sensors collect data from physical assets. This data is analysed by computational systems (often leveraging AI/ML), and the insights generated then inform decisions that impact the physical asset, often through automated control mechanisms. This creates a highly responsive and adaptive system where physical operations are continuously optimized by digital intelligence (Nakajima, 2011). The interoperability between various components of a CPS, from sensors to control systems, is crucial for seamless data flow and effective operation (Cavalieri & Salafia, 2020). The integration of digital twins and CPS thus enables unprecedented levels of control and predictability in managing complex asset portfolios, moving from traditional reactive or preventive measures to truly intelligent asset lifecycle management.

Big data and the Role of Data Analytics in Maintenance Decision-Making

The concept of Big Data, characterized by its volume, velocity, and variety, underpins the ability to manage and extract value from the immense datasets generated by connected assets (Campos et al., 2017). Big Data analytics tools and platforms provide the infrastructure to store, process, and analyse this information, transforming raw data into actionable intelligence for maintenance decision-making (Elmeleegy et al., 2013). These data analytics tools form the backbone of modern maintenance decision-making by transforming raw operational data into actionable insights. With the advent of Big Data, asset management systems can now capture vast volumes of information from diverse sources, including sensors, operational logs, maintenance records, and external factors like weather or market conditions (Campos et al., 2017). The capacity to process and interpret this data is crucial for optimizing maintenance strategies (Elmeleegy et al., 2013).

The application of data analytics in maintenance evolves through several stages:

- Descriptive Analytics: Focused on understanding past events. This stage involves reporting on past performance, such as failure rates, repair times, and maintenance costs. Traditionally, computerized Maintenance Management Systems (CMMS) provided these insights (Takahashi, 2001).
- Diagnostic Analytics: Concerned with explaining why events occurred. This stage investigates the root causes of failures, often using statistical methods and correlation analysis (Adeyemi et al., 2022).
- Predictive Analytics: Aimed at anticipating future events. Leveraging AI/ML algorithms, this stage uses historical and real-time data to predict future asset behaviour, such as potential component failures or degradation trends. This is the core of predictive maintenance, enabling interventions just before a failure occurs (Sontakke & Zanke, 2024).
- Prescriptive Analytics: Focused on recommending the optimal maintenance actions considering factors like cost, risk, resource availability, and operational impact. For instance, it might recommend a specific repair, a part replacement, or a change in operational parameters to extend asset life (Giacotto et al., 2025).

Artificial Intelligence and Machine Learning Algorithms

Artificial Intelligence (AI) and Machine Learning (ML) serve as the analytical engines that transform raw sensor and operational data into actionable maintenance insights. These algorithms are trained on historical data, including failure records, operational parameters, and maintenance logs, to learn patterns indicative of asset degradation or impending failures (Cavalieri & Salafia, 2020).

Core applications of AI/ML in Smart Maintenance include:

- Anomaly Detection: Identifying unusual patterns in sensor data that deviate from normal operating conditions, signalling potential issues before they escalate.
- Fault Diagnosis: Automatically determining the root cause of an anomaly or failure based on observed symptoms and historical data.
- Prognostics and Health Management (PHM): Predicting the remaining useful life (RUL) of components and assets, allowing for optimal scheduling of maintenance interventions (Cavalieri & Salafia, 2020).
- Predictive and Prescriptive Maintenance Scheduling: Optimizing maintenance schedules dynamically based on predicted asset health, operational demands, and resource availability, moving beyond fixed intervals to condition-driven actions (Cavalieri & Salafia, 2020).

- Natural Language Processing (NLP): Analyzing unstructured text data from maintenance logs, technician notes, and incident reports to extract valuable insights on failure modes and maintenance effectiveness (Platfoot, 2014).

The iterative nature of ML allows these systems to continuously learn and improve their predictive accuracy as more data becomes available, making maintenance strategies increasingly precise and effective (Bokrantz et al., 2020b).

On top of the most popular year to date applications of AI, it is worth noting the rise of the Generative Artificial Intelligence (GAI). The capabilities of GAI, as indicated by Crespo Marquez & Pérez Oliver (2025), can drastically change the way of approaching maintenance optimization problems, particularly in single-unit systems, by dynamically modelling scenarios and improving decision making. In the last year, Agentic AI (GAI specifically trained for one purpose) opens a wide range of possibilities in the field of maintenance. What is more, its user-friendliness proposes technical and managerial application areas where its full potential and limitations are yet to be determined (Ćelić et al., 2024). Nevertheless, some authors (e.g. Mikołajewska et al., 2025) have already linked GAI with capabilities related to Industry 4.0, and even with Industry 5.0 or human-centred industry.

Cloud Computing and Data Infrastructure

Cloud computing provides the scalable and flexible infrastructure required to support the vast data storage, processing, and analytical demands of Smart Maintenance systems. The sheer volume of data generated by the aforementioned IoT devices and the computational intensity of AI/ML algorithms necessitate robust and adaptable computing resources, which cloud platforms readily offer (Taneja et al., 2019).

The key benefits of cloud computing for Smart Maintenance include:

- Scalability: The ability to easily expand or contract computing resources based on data volume and analytical needs, without significant upfront hardware investments.
- Accessibility: Data and analytical tools can be accessed from anywhere, facilitating remote monitoring, distributed teams, and collaboration across organizational boundaries.
- Cost-effectiveness: A pay-as-you-go model reduces capital expenditure and allows organizations to manage operational costs more efficiently.
- Data Integration: Cloud platforms often facilitate the integration of data from various sources (sensors, CMMS, ERP, etc.), creating a unified data lake for comprehensive analysis.
- Advanced Services: Cloud providers offer a wide array of ready-to-use AI/ML services, data visualization tools, and development environments that accelerate the deployment of Smart Maintenance solutions.

The underlying data infrastructure, whether cloud-based or hybrid, must be designed to handle high-velocity data streams and ensure data integrity, security, and accessibility for effective real-time decision-making in Smart Maintenance environments.

5 Smart Maintenance Architectural Bases and Frameworks

After presenting the chronological evolution towards Smart Maintenance and the technical plus managerial enablers for its promotion, this Section presents both the architectural bases to be taken into account for the creation of Smart Maintenance frameworks, and the set of main maintenance frameworks of this era, developed considering these bases.

5.1 Architectural Frames for Smart Maintenance Implementation

The implementation of Smart Maintenance requires carefully designed architectural frameworks that ensure seamless data flow, interoperability, and robust security across the entire ecosystem of connected assets and information systems. These frameworks provide the blueprint for integrating diverse technologies. Effective implementation of data analytics requires robust data governance, ensuring data quality, integration across disparate systems, and appropriate cybersecurity measures. These interoperability, data integration and cybersecurity considerations are expanded below.

Pillars of Interoperability and Data Integration

Interoperability is a critical pillar to implement Smart Maintenance successfully. It refers to the ability of different systems, devices, and applications to communicate, exchange data, and interpret that data meaningfully (Carvalho et al., 2014). In a Smart Maintenance context, this means that sensor data must be seamlessly integrated with enterprise resource planning (ERP) systems, computerized maintenance management systems (CMMS), supply chain platforms, and digital twin models (Cavalieri & Salafia, 2020; Crespo Marquez et al., 2020). Without robust interoperability, data remains siloed, hindering holistic analysis and automated decision-making.

Key enablers of interoperability and data integration include:

- Standardized Communication Protocols: Adoption of industry standards (e.g., OPC UA, MQTT) for data exchange between devices and platforms.
- Application Programming Interfaces (APIs): Providing interfaces for different software applications to interact and share data programmatically.
- Data Models and Semantics: Ensuring that data is consistently structured and interpreted across various systems. Reference architectures like RAMI 4.0 Asset Administration Shell (AAS) provide a means to achieve this by defining standardized interfaces and data models for assets (Cavalieri & Salafia, 2020).
- Data Lakes and Warehouses: Centralized repositories that can ingest and store diverse data types from multiple sources, facilitating comprehensive analytics.

- Middleware and Integration Platforms: Software layers that mediate communication and data transformation between disparate systems.

Effective data integration considering these points ensures that the appropriate information reaches the right stakeholders at the right time, enabling predictive analytics, optimized resource allocation, and informed strategic decisions for asset management.

Cybersecurity Considerations in Smart Maintenance Environments

The extensive connectivity and data exchange inherent in Smart Maintenance systems introduce significant cybersecurity risks. Protecting sensitive operational data, intellectual property, and ensuring the integrity of control systems are paramount. The increase of data exchanged in cloud environments, and the unconscious use of cloud-based aforementioned GAI increases the risk of major data breaches in companies. A breach could result in operational disruptions, data manipulation, safety hazards, and financial losses (Ageev, 2019). Towards Smart Maintenance, the following critical cybersecurity considerations should be considered:

- Network Segmentation: Separation of operational technology (OT) networks from information technology (IT) networks to prevent cyberattacks from spreading.
- Secure Communication: D ata encryption in transit and at rest, using secure protocols (e.g., TLS/SSL) to protect against eavesdropping and tampering.
- Authentication and Authorization: S trong identity management, multi-factor authentication, and granular access controls to ensure only authorized personnel and systems can access critical data and functions.
- Vulnerability Management: Regularly patching software, performing security audits, and conducting penetration testing to identify and remediate weaknesses.
- Incident Response Planning: Developing clear procedures for detecting, responding to, and recovering from cyber incidents, minimizing their impact.
- Supply Chain Security: Ensuring that all components and software from third-party vendors adhere to robust security standards.
- Data Privacy: Adhering to relevant data protection regulations, especially when handling personal or commercially sensitive information.

Cybersecurity must be embedded into the design of Smart Maintenance systems from the outset, rather than being an afterthought. A comprehensive security strategy is essential to build trust in these interconnected systems and safeguard operational continuity. Finally, on top of the technical suggestions provided herein, user awareness regarding data management is probably one of the top challenges not only in general, but also in maintenance, especially in the era of GAI. This GAI-related risk, in addition to the use of pseudo-optimal code generated automatically by GAI, is one of the new risks related to the cybersecurity in this new Smart Maintenance era.

The RAMI 4.0 Reference Model and its Dimensions in Maintenance Management

RAMI 4.0 functions as a three-dimensional model providing a shared terminology and structured approach for stakeholders involved in Industry 4.0 activities (Cavalieri & Salafia, 2020), based on hierarchy levels (derived from IEC 62264), life cycle value stream (based on IEC 62890) and using a virtual decomposition of equipment (consisting of six vertical layers).

The application of RAMI 4.0 in maintenance services is centred around the Asset Administration Shell (AAS), which acts as the digital container for all data and functionalities related to a specific asset (Cavalieri & Salafia, 2020). This structure, enforced by RAMI 4.0, is crucial because it ensures that all information—from real-time sensor measurements (Integration/Communication layers) of an operational Asset Instance (Hierarchy/Life Cycle axes) to the final cost optimization analysis (Business Layer)—is handled within a standardized framework (Cavalieri & Salafia, 2020; Ismagilova & Sitnikova, 2017). The architectural model thus transforms disparate maintenance solutions, often vendor-specific or internally tailor-made, into compatible components within a larger industrial ecosystem (Crespo Marquez et al., 2020). This enforcement of structured, layer-by-layer data exchange via an SOA makes RAMI 4.0 the enabling infrastructure that directly resolves the major technical challenge of data fragmentation and interoperability cited by industry leaders (Cavalieri & Salafia, 2020).

5.2 Smart Maintenance Frameworks

The previously commented foundations for the Smart Maintenance architectural bases have promoted the generation of several maintenance frameworks, which can be divided into (a) organizational and managerial, conceptual frameworks, and (b) technological and data-driven architectural frameworks. Some of the most common frameworks of both types are these:

Organizational and managerial, conceptual frameworks

The Smart Maintenance Organizational Design Framework (Bokrantz et al. 2020a, 2020b)

The organizational design framework developed by Bokrantz et al. (2020a, 2020b) is an empirically grounded model that defines Smart Maintenance as "an organizational design for managing maintenance of manufacturing plants in environments with pervasive digital technologies" (Bokrantz et al., 2020a, 2020b). Based on extensive input from industry experts, this framework provides a strategic perspective on implementing SM by focusing on four critical underlying dimensions that must be addressed concurrently with technology adoption (Bokrantz et al., 2020a, 2020b).

The four dimensions are:

1. Data-driven decision-making: This is the analytical core of SM, utilizing real-time asset data, AI, and Machine Learning (ML) algorithms to move beyond descriptive or diagnostic analytics toward prognosis and prescription (Bokrantz et al., 2020a, 2020b). This dimension requires the organizational capacity to derive predictive insights, such as Remaining Useful Life (RUL), and translate these into optimized maintenance schedules, fundamentally shifting decision-making from subjective experience to objective, adaptive optimization (Cavalieri & Salafia, 2020).
2. Human capital resource: This dimension addresses the inevitable organizational change and skill gap created by digitalization (Bokrantz et al., 2020a, 2020b). Pervasive digital tools demand that maintenance personnel possess competence in sensor technology, ICT systems, advanced data analysis, and the critical ability to interpret complex visualizations and predictive models (Bokrantz et al., 2020a, 2020b; Rakshit & Sridhar, 2018). Investment in workforce upskilling and knowledge development is recognized as essential to ensure that the technological gains are fully realized (Bokrantz et al., 2020a, 2020b).
3. Internal integration: This focuses on achieving seamless data flow and strategic collaboration within the enterprise (Bokrantz et al., 2020a, 2020b). The framework aims to eliminate traditional information silos, particularly between the maintenance function and production, planning, and operational departments (Bokrantz et al., 2020a, 2020b). Real-time data must be integrated to facilitate integrated scheduling, allowing maintenance interventions to be optimally aligned with production throughput and business goals (Bokrantz et al., 2020a, 2020b).
4. External integration: Acknowledging the complexity of modern supply chains, this dimension emphasizes the necessity of data sharing and collaboration with external partners, primarily equipment suppliers (OEMs) and service providers (Bokrantz et al., 2020a, 2020b). Suppliers often embed proprietary digital technologies in their offerings that hold valuable data for failure prediction, making external data crucial for comprehensive and accurate asset health management (Bokrantz et al., 2020a, 2020b; Gitelman et al., 2019).

This framework functions as a comprehensive contingency model, highlighting that technological adoption is constrained by organizational readiness. Successful implementation of Smart Maintenance requires parallel maturity across both technical capabilities (data) and human/organizational factors.

Strategic Integration via*Intelligent Asset Management Platforms* (IAMP; Crespo Marquez et al., 2020)

The Intelligent Asset Management Platform (IAMP) framework, presented by Crespo Marquez et al., (2020), is a strategic architecture focused on integrating maintenance management with overarching business and financial objectives, addressing the organizational challenge of translating maintenance technical value into quantifiable financial benefit (Crespo Marquez et al., 2020). This platform is particularly vital for organizations, such as utility companies, with extensive, dispersed, and capital-intensive asset portfolios (Crespo Marquez et al., 2020).

The IAMP architecture is structured as a three-level software pyramid utilizing cloud-based services, ensuring scalability and flexibility required for handling complex, multi-source industrial data (Crespo Marquez et al., 2020).

1. Bottom Level (Platform as a Service—PaaS): This foundational layer provides the critical infrastructure for data management. It supports essential services like Extract, Transform, Load (ETL) functions, scalable data storage, and the virtual machine environment required to handle Big Data generated by IoT devices (Crespo Marquez et al., 2020).
2. Middle Level (Software as a Service—SaaS): This level hosts the user-facing applications (Apps) designed for specific maintenance and asset management tasks (Crespo Marquez et al., 2020). These applications perform core functions such as assessing asset health and integrity, calculating lifecycle costs (LCC), developing Condition-Based Maintenance (CBM) programs, and analyzing process effectiveness (Crespo Marquez et al., 2020).
3. Data Model: Embedded within each SaaS application, the data model ensures standardization and configuration of databases, which is paramount for ensuring conceptual similarity and compatibility across diverse asset types and vendor-specific solutions (Crespo Marquez et al., 2020).

The IAMP framework is conceptually driven by the adoption of key digital enablers, including the Industrial IoT, predictive maintenance analytics leveraging Big Data, and Digital Twin simulations (Crespo Marquez et al., 2020). Its strategic value lies in its ability to facilitate better-balanced and more strategic decision-making by correlating technical asset status with financial and business constraints (Crespo Marquez et al., 2020). By integrating asset health with quantifiable financial metrics, the IAMP directly helps organizations justify maintenance budgets and demonstrate a return on investment (ROI), successfully positioning maintenance as a strategic value driver rather than merely a cost centre (Crespo Marquez et al., 2020).

The organizational readiness required for effective Smart Maintenance is therefore defined by a necessary duality. The Bokrantz framework establishes the requisite competencies and collaborative processes (Human/Integration), while the IAMP framework provides the mandatory strategic platform to collect, analyse, and translate the data into business results. The implementation of SM thus requires adopting both approaches: ensuring the technical structure (IAMP) is in place while cultivating the human capacity (Bokrantz's Human Capital) to leverage that integrated data for competitive advantage and maximizing financial performance indicators like Return on Assets (ROA; Bokrantz et al., 2020a, 2020b; Crespo Marquez et al., 2020).

Technological and data-driven architectural frameworks

The Digital Twin and Smart Big Data Predictive Maintenance Framework (Guc & Chen, 2022)

The Smart Predictive Maintenance framework proposed by Guc and Chen (2022) establishes the Digital Twin (DT) as the central analytical and control mechanism for maintenance in Industry 4.0 (Guc & Chen, 2022). A Digital Twin is defined as a virtual, real-time representation of a physical asset, system, or process, dynamically updated with data collected from its physical counterpart (Giovannini et al., 2019; Guc & Chen, 2022). This framework leverages the DT to execute several critical functions within a comprehensive Cyber-Physical System (CPS; Giovannini et al., 2019; Guc & Chen, 2022):

- Real-Time Data Ingestion: IoT sensors and devices continuously transmit high-velocity operational data (Smart Big Data) to the virtual space (Guc & Chen, 2022). The term "Smart Big Data" emphasizes the requirement for data to be pre-processed, filtered, and contextualized, ensuring data quality and utility for advanced analytics (Guc & Chen, 2022).
- Prognostics and Simulation: The DT utilizes this data feed to run sophisticated AI/ML models for Prognostics and Health Management (PHM), predicting failure modes and calculating the Remaining Useful Life (RUL) of components (Cavalieri & Salafia, 2020; Guc & Chen, 2022). Crucially, the virtual model allows maintenance planners and engineers to simulate various scenarios—such as the impact of different operational loads or maintenance procedures—without risk to the physical asset (Giovannini et al., 2019).
- Prescriptive Control: The framework progresses maintenance beyond simple fault prediction (Predictive Maintenance) to delivering prescriptive actions (Guc & Chen, 2022). The DT generates optimized recommendations, weighing factors like resource availability, operational constraints, cost–benefit analysis, and risk (Giacotto et al., 2025).
- Active Operational Regulation: The most advanced capability involves feeding the DT's output back into the physical asset's control system (Guc & Chen, 2022). For example, in managing wind turbines, the DT can recommend and execute real-time adjustments to the working load, actively reducing stress on components predicted to be nearing their degradation limit, thereby extending the asset's working cycle and minimizing maintenance needs (Guc & Chen, 2022).

The framework of Guc and Chen (2022) epitomizes the shift to true prescriptive maintenance. It provides unprecedented levels of control and predictability, ensuring that maintenance interventions are perfectly timed and that operational decisions are optimized based on the asset's predicted future health, leveraging the simulation power of the DT to maximize efficiency.

The Conceptual Framework for Smart Maintenance Based on Distributed Intelligence (Pulikottil et al., 2022)

The conceptual framework developed by Pulikottil et al. (2022) addresses the necessity for robust, rapid response in dynamic smart manufacturing environments by implementing distributed intelligence across the shop floor (Pulikottil et al., 2022). This design recognizes that centralized cloud computing is often inadequate for time-sensitive, mission-critical maintenance actions, thereby leveraging the capabilities of Edge and Fog computing paradigms (Taneja et al., 2019).

The architecture is structured into two fundamental blocks of intelligence (Pulikottil et al., 2022; Taneja et al., 2019):

- Innate Intelligence (Local/Edge): This block contains the intelligence embedded directly within the machine, sensor, or local edge device (Pulikottil et al., 2022). It is designed for robustness, high speed, and decentralized operation, enabling immediate preliminary analysis, data filtering, and local decision-making (Taneja et al., 2019). Innate intelligence can instantaneously identify abnormal vibration patterns, trigger local alerts, or initiate minor process adjustments without needing to communicate with the central cloud (Pulikottil et al., 2022). This local autonomy ensures safety, continuity, and system anti-fragility, particularly when network connectivity is intermittent or when real-time reaction is critical (Taneja et al., 2019).
- Adaptive Intelligence (Central/Cloud): This central block handles computationally intensive tasks that require a broader systemic context (Pulikottil et al., 2022). This includes large-scale data mining, complex Machine Learning model training, optimization of global maintenance schedules, long-term trend analysis, and learning from system-wide failure history (Pulikottil et al., 2022). The adaptive intelligence drives continuous improvement and strategic optimization, sending refined models and optimization routines back to the innate intelligence layer (Pulikottil et al., 2022).
- The distributed intelligence framework addresses limitations in traditional centralized systems by integrating technologies like Multi-Agent Systems and Ontology alongside Edge/Fog computing (Pulikottil et al., 2022). By dividing the computational load between rapid local action (innate) and complex global learning (adaptive), the framework ensures a highly responsive system, illustrated by its application in real-time condition monitoring, such as tool wear monitoring (Pulikottil et al., 2022).

The technological frameworks of Guc & Chen (Digital Twin) and Pulikottil et al. (Distributed Intelligence) are highly complementary within a functional Cyber-Physical System. The Distributed Intelligence framework dictates the optimal location for data processing (Edge for speed, Cloud for complexity), while the Digital Twin framework defines the content of that processing (simulation, RUL calculation, prescriptive control loop). This synergy moves maintenance capabilities beyond simple fault anticipation toward true prescriptive and adaptive action. The systems gain the ability to proactively modify asset operation (via DT feedback) and take immediate localized action (via innate intelligence), functionally bridging the gap between prescriptive maintenance and the expected long-term goal of fully Autonomous Adaptive Maintenance (Giacotto et al., 2025; Guc & Chen, 2022; Pulikottil et al., 2022).

6 Applications and Illustrative Examples Across Industries

The principles and technologies of Smart Maintenance are finding widespread application across a diverse range of industries, and demonstrating tangible benefits in terms of efficiency, reliability, and cost reduction. Actual illustrative cases exemplify the practical implementation and outcomes of these advanced strategies.

6.1 Smart Maintenance in High-Volume Discrete Manufacturing

In discrete manufacturing environments, characterized by high complexity and interdependence of machinery, Smart Maintenance is primarily utilized to monitor critical assets such as robotic arms, CNC machines, and complex assembly lines (Cavalieri & Salafia, 2020). Real-time data streams covering vibration, temperature, and power consumption feed into AI/ML models designed to anticipate component fatigue and tool wear.

CNH Industrial, a major global manufacturer, implemented a Digital Twin of its production lines, such as the Iveco plant in Suzzara, to enhance maintenance decision-making and support the rigorous demands of World Class Manufacturing (WCM) certification (Tugengold et al., 2019). The WCM initiative aims for continuous improvement and waste elimination, setting high standards for asset reliability. The Digital Twin provided a virtual, comprehensive representation of the line, allowing management to simulate various maintenance policies and scenarios without disrupting physical operations.

The simulation yields detailed information on total production throughput, required maintenance time, spare part costs, and maintenance labour costs. This analytical capability moves the maintenance team beyond merely predicting failure toward prescribing the optimal intervention—timing, scope, and resources—that maximizes operational efficiency while minimizing total cost (Giacotto et al., 2025). The utilization of this Digital Twin demonstrates that the value proposition of Smart Maintenance extends beyond mere operational cost savings to include non-financial benefits, such as achieving strategic industry qualifications. The efficacy of these prognostic systems is highlighted by related manufacturing deployments that utilize predictive maintenance to limit unplanned disruptions significantly, for example, reducing disruptions to 2.88% by preventing the failure of critical components, thereby guaranteeing production throughput (Zhu et al., 2019).

6.2 Leveraging AI/ML in Renewable Energy Operations

The energy sector, encompassing power generation and distribution, manages extensive, critical, and often remote assets (e.g., wind farms, transmission lines) where minimizing unplanned outages is essential for grid stability and profitability (Gitelman et al., 2019). Smart Maintenance provides the necessary framework for continuous, data-driven monitoring of these distributed assets.

Global power company AES launched a significant predictive maintenance initiative across its wind turbine farms, recognizing asset health management as a core strategic use case (Gitelman et al., 2019). By analyzing data collected via IoT sensors tracking pressure, temperature, and vibration, AI models were trained to predict component failures. These models achieved high prediction accuracy, exceeding 90% across dozens of critical wind turbine components (Arcelay et al., 2021).

This high degree of prognostic capability facilitated a decisive shift to prescriptive maintenance scheduling. The difference between planned, scheduled maintenance interventions (costing approximately $30,000) and emergency, unplanned maintenance (which costs upwards of $100,000 per repair) provides a highly persuasive financial validation of the prescriptive strategy (Gitelman et al., 2019). This disparity, which often exceeded $70,000 per avoided failure, resulted in millions of dollars of cost savings and improved consistency in power delivery. Furthermore, the use of predictive analytics optimized field operations by reducing non-essential technician travel, resulting in $1 million in annual savings by eliminating 3,000 unnecessary trips (Arcelay et al., 2021). This case demonstrates that intelligent maintenance is a vital pillar supporting the energy transition, providing the scalability and reliability required for distributed renewable infrastructure.

6.3 Advanced Asset Integrity Management (AIM) in Oil and Gas

In the oil and gas industry, Asset Integrity Management (AIM) is critical due to the high-risk, high-consequence nature of operations, where failures can lead to catastrophic environmental incidents, safety hazards, and massive regulatory penalties (Ismagilova & Sitnikova, 2017). Smart Maintenance solutions are deployed here primarily to enhance safety and ensure stringent compliance.

Oil and gas operators are increasingly deploying AI and Machine Learning (ML), combined with computer vision technology, to monitor the structural integrity of critical assets like pipelines and offshore platforms (Ariansyah et al., 2019). ML models are trained using labelled visual data to identify early signs of corrosion, coating breakdown, and structural defects, allowing proactive intervention before physical integrity is compromised (Ismagilova & Sitnikova, 2017). This methodology facilitates AI-enhanced Non-Destructive Testing (NDT), which examines materials and welds for internal flaws without requiring operational shutdown (Ariansyah et al., 2019).

This proactive approach drastically improves the efficiency of inspection processes and significantly reduces the reliance on manual, labour-intensive, and often dangerous field inspections (Ismagilova & Sitnikova, 2017). For these high-risk sectors, the primary strategic metric for Smart Maintenance shifts from maximizing mechanical availability to mitigating major safety and environmental risks. By enabling timely repairs and providing transparent data trails, the system ensures adherence to strict regulatory frameworks (Ariansyah et al., 2019), effectively making Smart Maintenance a tool for sophisticated risk management and the reduction of Mean Time to Incident (MTTI).

6.4 Prognostics and Health Management (PHM) in Aviation

The aviation sector requires impeccable safety standards and efficiency, driving the adoption of sophisticated Prognostics and Health Management (PHM) systems across complex aircraft components and entire fleets (Nakajima, 2011). The goal is to maximize airworthiness while minimizing costly Aircraft On Ground (AOG) events caused by unscheduled maintenance.

Lufthansa Technik's AVIATAR is a cloud-based digital platform that exemplifies the collaborative, ecosystem approach required for modern Smart Maintenance (Zhu et al., 2019). It integrates vast amounts of operational data from various sources, including aircraft sensors, airline operations, MRO providers, and Original Equipment Manufacturers (OEMs; Nakajima, 2011). By applying advanced analytical models to this consolidated data, the platform generates predictive insights and prescriptive recommendations, enabling airlines, such as United Airlines, to optimize their maintenance planning and resource allocation (Zhu et al., 2019).

The effectiveness of these centralized PHM systems is demonstrated by the achieved prediction accuracies, which range between 87.6 and 93.2% across critical aircraft systems (Zhu et al., 2019). This prognostic capability led to an average reduction in unscheduled maintenance events of 19.8%, resulting in an estimated annual cost avoidance of $328,000 per aircraft (Zhu et al., 2019). The requirement for such a platform to connect and manage data among multiple commercial stakeholders underscores the growing necessity for robust data governance, interoperability, and standardized data models within the Smart Maintenance architectural framework (Cavalieri & Salafia, 2020).

7 Discussion and Strategic Implications

The illustrative actual cases presented validate the technical feasibility and operational benefits of transitioning to Smart Maintenance. However, the successful large-scale implementation of these digital paradigms introduces significant organizational, human, and technological challenges that require a nuanced discussion on strategic management and risk mitigation.

7.1 Synthesizing the Shift: From Cost Centre to Strategic Value Driver

Smart Maintenance fundamentally alters the perception of the maintenance function, elevating it from a necessary cost centre to a critical strategic value driver for the enterprise (Cavalieri & Salafia, 2020). By providing data-driven insights, maintenance directly contributes to core business objectives, including maximizing asset value, extending asset lifespan, and optimizing costs and risks (Crespo Marquez et al., 2020).

The strategic significance of Smart Maintenance lies in its capacity for informed, long-term decision-making. The wealth of performance data generated guides capital expenditure and asset replacement strategies, ensuring that resources are allocated based on actual asset condition and projected Remaining Useful Life (RUL) rather than arbitrary schedules (Mobley, 2002). This capability also facilitates the implementation of circular economy principles by minimizing waste and optimizing component utilization.

Furthermore, the digital approach satisfies a dual imperative: operational efficiency and strategic risk management. Stricter regulatory frameworks across high-risk sectors (e.g., energy, oil and gas) demand auditable maintenance practices and enhanced safety standards (Ismagilova & Sitnikova, 2017). Smart Maintenance provides the necessary infrastructure to achieve higher levels of compliance, offering transparent data trails and reducing the risk of catastrophic incidents, which can be far more costly than mere production downtime. Evidence suggests that structured preventive maintenance, a precursor to smart practices, can reduce safety incident risk by as much as 87% (Zhu et al., 2019). Therefore, the strategic value proposition encompasses not only the reduction of unplanned downtime (up to 50%) but also the proactive avoidance of significant financial liability and reputational damage associated with regulatory non-compliance.

7.2 *Organizational and Human Dimensions: Navigating Implementation Barriers*

While the technological benefits are clear, the greatest obstacles to realizing the full Return on Investment (ROI) from Smart Maintenance are predominantly organizational, often rooted in human factors and systemic rigidity (Bokrantz et al., 2020a). The effective implementation requires a significant cultural shift, demanding new skills, overcoming ingrained resistance, and rigorous change management (Ariansyah et al., 2019).

A core challenge is widespread workforce resistance, reported to occur in 55–70% of implementations (Bokrantz et al., 2020a). This reluctance often stems from a lack of clarity regarding the technology's benefits, fear of job displacement, and inadequate training infrastructure (Ariansyah et al., 2019). Concurrently, a significant skills gap persists (65–80% occurrence), characterized by a shortage of personnel equipped with the necessary analytical thinking and data interpretation skills required to utilize predictive systems effectively (Bokrantz et al., 2020a). This deficit leads to delayed value realization and poor decision quality (Ariansyah et al., 2019).

Overcoming these organizational barriers requires a structured and intensive change management methodology (Ariansyah et al., 2019). The level of investment in human capital training serves as a direct predictor of success. Organizations achieving high technician adoption (80–90%) typically invest 60–80 h per person in structured, hands-on training, significantly higher than the 8–16 h typical of failed implementations (Bokrantz et al., 2020a). This difference reveals that organizational reluctance to invest adequately in soft infrastructure, specifically comprehensive training and communication, translates directly into a managerial resource allocation failure, severely undermining the potential ROI of the technological investment. By framing the adoption of these systems as empowering technicians—reducing unexpected failures and making maintenance more efficient—scepticism can be mitigated (Ariansyah et al., 2019).

Furthermore, technical challenges related to data quality (60–75% occurrence) and integration barriers (70–85% occurrence) prevent holistic analysis and compromise the credibility of predictive models (Bokrantz et al., 2020a). Without standardized communication protocols and robust integration platforms, information remains siloed, hindering the seamless flow of data required for prescriptive, automated decision-making (Cavalieri & Salafia, 2020; Taneja et al., 2019).

7.3 *Data Governance, Cybersecurity, and the (Generative) AI Vector*

The reliance on interconnected systems and cloud infrastructure in Smart Maintenance introduces profound cybersecurity and data governance challenges (Ageev, 2019). Data encryption, network segmentation (separating operational technology

(OT) from information technology (IT)), and strong identity management are non-negotiable requirements for safeguarding sensitive operational data and control systems (Ageev, 2019).

A critical emerging vector is the integration of Generative Artificial Intelligence (GAI). While GAI offers unprecedented opportunities for automating cognitive tasks (Ćelić et al., 2024), its use introduces novel security risks. When GAI, often leveraging cloud-based Large Language Models (LLMs), processes proprietary asset information, the risk of major data breaches or leakage of intellectual property is significantly heightened (Ageev, 2019).

Furthermore, GAI's capability to generate code or automated strategies (such as optimizing maintenance policies) poses a unique cyber-physical risk (Crespo Márquez & Pérez Oliver, 2025). If GAI produces "pseudo-optimal code" or flawed models that are subsequently integrated into the cyber-physical systems (CPS), the digital error can translate directly into physical asset instability, operational disruption, or safety hazards (Ageev, 2019). Because Smart Maintenance involves a continuous feedback loop between digital intelligence and physical operations, GAI acts as a multiplier of cyber-physical risk. Consequently, effective data governance and user awareness surrounding GAI usage are crucial, requiring immediate policy development to ensure rigorous human validation of all AI-generated strategies before physical deployment (Crespo Márquez & Pérez Oliver, 2025). The necessity for robust data provenance and integrity, particularly in collaborative environments, simultaneously reinforces the need for technologies like blockchain to provide secure and transparent traceability of actions and data (Arcelay et al., 2021).

These examples highlight the versatility of Smart Maintenance frameworks, adapting to the specific needs and challenges of different technological and organizational settings while consistently aiming for improved operational performance and reduced lifecycle costs through data-driven approaches.

8 Conclusion and Further Outlines

8.1 Concluding Summary of Findings

This analysis systematically investigated the transition from traditional to Smart Maintenance, confirming that digitalization constitutes a fundamental and strategic transformation in asset management. The evolution, driven by enabling technologies such as IoT, Big Data, Digital Twins, and AI/ML, successfully moves maintenance practices toward a highly optimized, prognostic, and prescriptive methodology. Illustrative examples across manufacturing, energy, oil and gas, and aviation demonstrate quantifiable benefits in enhanced reliability, reduced unplanned downtime (cost avoidance), and improved regulatory compliance, validating Smart Maintenance as a strategic value driver.

However, the analysis concludes that the realization of these technological benefits is fundamentally dependent upon organizational preparedness. The most pervasive barriers—workforce resistance, skills gaps, and data integration failures—are rooted in human and managerial deficiencies, often linked to insufficient investment in structured change management and training infrastructure. Looking forward, the introduction of Generative AI adds a new layer of complexity, simultaneously promising greater optimization and introducing novel cyber-physical risks related to data security and autonomous decision integrity.

8.2 Future Research Directions

The current maturity of predictive and prescriptive maintenance sets the foundation for the next phase of digital asset management—Autonomous Adaptive Maintenance (expected post-2030). Future academic research must focus on three interconnected streams to facilitate this transition and address the identified risks.

The Nexus of Generative AI and Prescriptive Maintenance Optimization

Research must focus intensely on integrating Generative AI (GAI) capabilities to scale and refine prescriptive decision-making. GAI, leveraging large language models and foundation models, holds the potential to automate complex, cognitive maintenance tasks.

Specific research efforts should investigate GAI's ability to dynamically model maintenance scenarios and optimize policies, especially in complex or single-unit systems, thereby accelerating decision support beyond the speed of traditional analytical models. Key avenues include validation of GAI-driven workflow automation, such as the generation of comprehensive work instructions, job plans, and asset-specific safety protocols derived from analysing vast amounts of unstructured text data and maintenance history. Furthermore, studies are required to rigorously test GAI's role in reliability engineering—using its analytical power to rapidly identify complex failure patterns and improve the speed and accuracy of diagnostic analysis, which are critical for increasing compliance efficacy and efficiency.

Towards Autonomous Adaptive Maintenance and Explainable AI (XAI)

Achieving truly autonomous adaptive maintenance requires overcoming the "black box" nature of current complex AI algorithms used for Prognostics and Health Management (PHM). The next generation of maintenance relies on fully automated, self-learning systems.

Consequently, significant research is paramount in developing and validating domain-specific methodologies for Explainable AI (XAI) in PHM. XAI systems must provide transparent, justifiable, and audit-ready reasoning behind their predictions (e.g., Remaining Useful Life estimates) and autonomous interventions. Establishing this transparency is essential for gaining the regulatory and ethical trust necessary for approving autonomous asset operation, particularly in high-risk, safety–critical applications where accountability is non-negotiable. Additionally, research is needed to define and validate the optimal distributed architecture—the synergy between Cloud, Fog, and Edge computing—to ensure low-latency, mission-critical autonomous actions can be executed effectively and securely at the asset level.

Governance, Standardisation, and Ethical Frameworks

The rapid advancement of digital technologies is creating a lag in the establishment of robust governance, ethical standards, and industrial protocols. Future research must proactively address this gap to ensure secure and responsible widespread adoption.

Research must focus on achieving universal standards for predictive maintenance (PdM) deployment, metrics, and data structures to ensure seamless interoperability across diverse Original Equipment Manufacturer (OEM) and vendor platforms. This is crucial for enabling large-scale, industry-wide data ecosystems. Furthermore, detailed investigation into blockchain assurance models is required to define its role as a trust layer for certifying the origin and integrity of asset data and maintenance records, thereby securing multi-stakeholder collaboration. Finally, rigorous efforts are needed to define ethical guidelines and governance models for AI, ML, and GAI applications in asset management to ensure that autonomous decisions adhere to human-centric principles, avoiding unintended bias and aligning with the principles of Industry 5.0. These foundational frameworks are essential to prevent technological fragmentation and build secure trust in future autonomous asset systems.

References

Abdelaty, A. (2017). *Data-driven algorithms for enhanced transportation infrastructure asset management* (Ph.D. thesis, Iowa State University). https://doi.org/10.31274/etd-180810-5097

Adeyemi, I. A., Rahman, M. S. A., & Adeyemi, A. (2022). Maintenance analytics for building decision-making: A literature review. *Journal of Information System and Technology Management, 7*(25), 127–138. https://doi.org/10.35631/jistm.725010

Ageev, A. I. (2019). Managing the digital future. *The World of New Economy, 12*(3), 6–23. https://doi.org/10.26794/2220-6469-2018-12-3-6-23

Arcelay, I., Goti, A., Oyarbide-Zubillaga, A., Akyazi, T., Alberdi, E., & Garcia-Bringas, P. (2021). Definition of the future skills needs of job profiles in the renewable energy sector. *Energies, 14*(9), 2609. https://doi.org/10.3390/en14092609

Arenkov, I., Tsenzharik, M., & Vetrova, M. (2019). Digital technologies in supply chain management. In *Proceedings of the international conference on digital technologies in logistics and infrastructure (ICDTLI 2019)*. Atlantis Press. https://doi.org/10.2991/icdtli-19.2019.78

Ariansyah, D., Rosa, F., & Colombo, G. (2019). Smart maintenance: A wearable augmented reality application integrated with CMMS to minimise unscheduled downtime. *Computer-Aided Design and Applications, 17*(4), 740–751. https://doi.org/10.14733/cadaps.2020.740-751

Baldin, A., Furlanetto, L., Roversi, A., & Turco, F. (1982). *Manual for maintenance of industrial facilities*. S. L. Gustavo Gili (Ed.)

Bokrantz, J., Skoogh, A., Berlin, C., & Stahre, J. (2020a). Smart maintenance: An empirically grounded conceptualization. *International Journal of Production Economics, 223*, 107534. https://doi.org/10.1016/j.ijpe.2019.107534

Bokrantz, J., Skoogh, A., Berlin, C., Wuest, T., & Stahre, J. (2020b). Smart Maintenance: A research agenda for industrial maintenance management. *International Journal of Production Economics, 224*, 107547. https://doi.org/10.1016/j.ijpe.2019.107547

British Standards Institute. (1970). *BS 3811: Glossary of terms used in Tero-technology*. BSI.

Campos, J., Sharma, P., Jantunen, E., Baglee, D., & Fumagalli, L. (2017). Business performance measurements in asset management with the support of big data technologies. *Management Systems in Production Engineering, 25*(3), 143–149. https://doi.org/10.1515/mspe-2017-0021

Carvalho, P., Hitzelberger, P., Otjacques, B., Bouali, F., & Venturini, G. (2014). Open data integration—Visualization as an asset. In *Proceedings of 3rd international conference on data management technologies and applications* (pp. 41–47). SCITEPRESS. https://doi.org/10.5220/0005000600410047

Carvalho, T. P., Soares, F. A. A. M. N., Vita, R., Francisco, R. P., Basto, J. P., & Alcalá, S. G. S. (2019). A systematic literature review of machine learning methods applied to predictive maintenance. *Computers & Industrial Engineering, 137*, 106024. https://doi.org/10.1016/j.cie.2019.106024

Cavalieri, S., & Salafia, M. G. (2020). A model for predictive maintenance based on asset administration shell. *Sensors, 20*(21), 6028. https://doi.org/10.3390/s20216028

Ćelić, J., et al. (2024). Generative AI in e-maintenance: Myth or reality? In *2024 47th MIPRO ICT and electronics convention (MIPRO)* (pp. 1911–1919). IEEE. https://doi.org/10.1109/MIPRO60963.2024.10569282.

Crespo Marquez, A., Gomez Fernandez, J. F., Martínez-Galán Fernández, P., & Guillen Lopez, A. (2020). Maintenance management through intelligent asset management platforms (IAMP). Emerging factors, key impact areas and data models. *Energies, 13*(15), 3762. https://doi.org/10.3390/en13153762

Crespo Márquez, A., & Pérez Oliver, D. (2025). Leveraging generative AI for modelling and optimization of maintenance policies in industrial systems. *Information, 16*(3), 217. https://doi.org/10.3390/info16030217

Da Silva, R., & Souza, G. (2020). Asset management system (ISO 55001) and total productive maintenance (TPM): A discussion of interfaces for maintenance management. *Revista Gestão da Produção Operações e Sistemas, 15*(2), 288–313. https://doi.org/10.15675/gepros.v15i2.2528

Dhillon, B. S. (2006). *Maintainability, maintenance, and reliability for engineers*. CRC Press.

Elmeleegy, H., et al. (2013). Overview of turn data management platform for digital advertising. *Proceedings of the VLDB Endowment, 6*(11), 1138–1149. https://doi.org/10.14778/2536222.2536238

Esekhaigbe, E., Kazan, E., & Usmen, M. (2020). Integration of digital technologies into underground utility asset management. *Open Journal of Civil Engineering, 10*(04), 403–428. https://doi.org/10.4236/ojce.2020.104030

Ferrari, R. (2015). Writing narrative style literature reviews. *Medical Writing, 24*(4), 230–235. https://doi.org/10.1179/2047480615Z.000000000329

Foresti, R., Rossi, S., Magnani, M., Bianco, C. G. L., & Delmonte, N. (2020). Smart society and artificial intelligence: Big data scheduling and the global standard method applied to smart maintenance. *Engineering, 6*(7), 835–846. https://doi.org/10.1016/j.eng.2019.11.014

Gandhewar, R., Gaurav, A., Kokate, K., Khetan, H., & Kamat, H. (2019). Cloud based framework for IIoT application with asset management. In *2019 3rd international conference on electronics, communication and aerospace technology (ICECA)* (pp. 920–925). IEEE. https://doi.org/10.1109/ICECA.2019.8821897.

Garcia Marquez, F. P., & Pedregal Tercero, D. J. (2011). Application of Kalman filter and fixed interval smoother to fault detection in railway turnouts. *Mechanical Systems and Signal Processing, 25*(6), 2139–2150. https://doi.org/10.1016/j.ymssp.2010.12.001

Giacotto, A., Marques, H. C., & Martinetti, A. (2025). Prescriptive maintenance: A comprehensive review of current research and future directions. *Journal of Quality in Maintenance Engineering, 31*(1), 129–173. https://doi.org/10.1108/jqme-07-2023-0064

Giovannini, E.C., Lo Turco, M., & Mafrici, N. (2019). Documenting historical research for a collection information modelling. A proposal for a digital asset management system. In *The international archives of the photogrammetry, remote sensing and spatial information sciences, XLII-2/W15* (pp. 519–525). https://doi.org/10.5194/isprs-archives-xlii-2-w15-519-2019

Gitelman, L. D., Kozhevnikov, M. V., & Kaplin, D. D. (2019). Asset management in grid companies using integrated diagnostic devices. *International Journal of Energy Production and Management, 4*(2), 230–243. https://doi.org/10.2495/eq-v4-n3-230-243

Gomaa, A. H. (2025). Maintenance 4.0: Optimizing asset integrity and reliability in modern manufacturing. *International Journal of Inventive Engineering and Sciences (IJIES), 12*, 18–26. https://doi.org/10.35940/ijies.B1098.12020225

Guc, A. F., & Chen, Y. (2022). Smart predictive maintenance enabled by digital twins and smart big data: A new framework. In *2022 IEEE 2nd International conference on digital twins and parallel intelligence (DTPI)*. https://doi.org/10.1109/DTPI55838.2022.9998937

Herguedas, A. (2002). *Modelos matemáticos para la obtención de políticas optimas de mantenimiento. Caracterización y aplicación práctica* (Ph.D. thesis, University of Seville).

Ismagilova, L., & Sitnikova, L. (2017). Organizational management technologies for maintenance and repair of power grid company facilities. In *Proceedings of the international conference on trends of technologies and innovations in economic and social studies 2017*. Atlantis Press. https://doi.org/10.2991/ttiess-17.2017.43.

Kaito, K., & Kobayashi, K. (2014). Big-data based infrastructure management: Towards asset metrics. *Journal of Japan Society of Civil Engineers, Ser. D3 (Infrastructure Planning and Management), 70*(5), I_21–I_30. https://doi.org/10.2208/jscejipm.70.i_21

Kelly, A. (1997). *Maintenance strategy*. Butterworth-Heinemann.

Lee, J., Bagheri, B., & Kao, H. A. (2015). A cyber-physical systems architecture for industry 4.0-based manufacturing systems. *Manufacturing Letters, 3*, 18–23. https://doi.org/10.1016/j.mfglet.2014.12.001

Lee, J., Davari, H., Singh, J., & Pandhare, V. (2018). Industrial artificial intelligence for industry 4.0-based manufacturing systems. *Manufacturing Letters, 18*, 20–23. https://doi.org/10.1016/j.mfglet.2018.09.002

Liu, R., Yang, B., Zio, E., & Chen, X. (2018). Artificial intelligence for fault diagnosis of rotating machinery: A review. *Mechanical Systems and Signal Processing, 108*, 33–47. https://doi.org/10.1016/j.ymssp.2018.02.016

Lundgren, C., Skoogh, A., & Bokrantz, J. (2018). Quantifying the effects of maintenance—A literature review of maintenance models. *Procedia CIRP, 72*, 1305–1310. https://doi.org/10.1016/j.procir.2018.03.175

Mikołajewska, E., Mikołajewski, D., Mikołajczyk, T., & Paczkowski, T. (2025). Generative AI in AI-based digital twins for fault diagnosis for predictive maintenance in Industry 4.0/5.0. *Applied Sciences, 15*(6), 3166. https://doi.org/10.3390/app15063166

Mobley, R. K. (2002). *An introduction to predictive maintenance* (2nd ed.). Butterworth-Heinemann.

Moon, B., Kim, J., & Lee, H. (2020). Development of smart pavement design sensitivity analysis software for asset management system. *Infrastructures, 5*(7), 56. https://doi.org/10.3390/infrastructures5070056

Moubray, J. (1997). *Reliability-centered maintenance*. Industrial Press Inc.

Nakajima, H. (2011). Smart health management technology. In *Health management—Different approaches and solutions*. InTech. https://doi.org/10.5772/22408

Nakajima, S. (1988). *Introduction to TPM*. Productivity Press Inc.

Nel, C. B. H., & Jooste, W. J. L. (2016). A technologically-driven asset management approach to managing physical assets—A literature review and research agenda for 'smart' asset management. *South African Journal of Industrial Engineering, 27*(4). https://doi.org/10.7166/27-4-1478

Parkes, D. (1970). In A. K. S. Jardine (Ed.), *Operational research in maintenance*. University of Manchester Press.

Platfoot, R. (2014). Practical analytics for maintenance teams using computerised maintenance management system work history. *Australian Journal of Multi-Disciplinary Engineering, 11*(1), 91–103. https://doi.org/10.7158/14488388.2014.11464886

Pogorelova, E. V., Efimova, T. B., & Haitbaev, V. A. (2019). Modernization of managing a "smart city" on the basis of digital platforms. In V. Mantulenko (ed.), *SHS Web of conferences*, Vol. 71. EDP Sciences. https://doi.org/10.1051/shsconf/20197104017

Popov, E., Semyachkov, K., & Popova, G. (2019). Digital technologies as a factor in the promotion of smart city leadership. In *Proceedings of the 5th international conference on social, economic, and academic leadership (ICSEALV 2019)*. Atlantis Press. https://doi.org/10.2991/assehr.k.191221.201

Pulikottil, T., Estrada-Jimenez, L. A., & Barata, J. (2022). Conceptual framework for smart maintenance based on distributed intelligence. *IFAC-PapersOnLine, 55*(19), 121–126.

Rakshit, S., & Sridhar, S. S. (2018). Asset management security system using RFID technology. *International Journal of Engineering & Technology, 7*(4.6), 391. https://doi.org/10.14419/ijet.v7i4.6.28448

Sherwin, D. (2000). A review of overall models for maintenance management. *Journal of Quality in Maintenance Engineering, 6*(3), 138–164. https://doi.org/10.1108/13552510010341171

Smyss, S., Vijesh, J. (2019). Big data business analytics as a strategic asset for health care industry. *Journal of ISMAC, 1*(2), 12–20. https://doi.org/10.36548/jismac.2019.2.002

Sontakke, D., & Zanke, M. P. (2024). *Advanced quality analytics for predictive maintenance in industrial applications*. Available at SSRN 4847933. https://doi.org/10.2139/ssrn.4847933

Takahashi, K. (2001). Application of computerized maintenance management system. *Japan Tappi Journal, 55*(3), 310–316. https://doi.org/10.2524/jtappij.55.310

Taneja, M., Jalodia, N., Byabazaire, J., Davy, A., & Olariu, C. (2019). SmartHerd management: A microservices-based fog computing–assisted IoT platform towards data-driven smart dairy farming. *Software: Practice and Experience, 49*(7), 1055–1078. https://doi.org/10.1002/spe.2704

Too, E. (2012). Infrastructure asset: Developing maintenance management capability. *Facilities, 30*(5/6), 234–253. https://doi.org/10.1108/02632771211208503

Tugengold, A. K., Voloshin, R. N., Yusupov, A. R., Kruglova, N. P. (2019). Production machines maintenance based on digitalization. *Vestnik of Don State Technical University, 19*(1), 74–80. https://doi.org/10.23947/1992-5980-2019-19-1-74-80

von Petersdorff, H., Vlok, P. (2014). Prioritising maintenance improvement opportunities in physical asset management. *South African Journal of Industrial Engineering, 25*(3). https://doi.org/10.7166/25-3-755

Wan, J., et al. (2017). A manufacturing big data solution for active preventive maintenance. *IEEE Transactions on Industrial Informatics, 13*(4), 2039–2047. https://doi.org/10.1109/TII.2017.2670505

Zhu, T., Ran, Y., Zhou, X., Wen, Y. (2019). *A survey of predictive maintenance: systems, purposes and approaches*. Available at: https://doi.org/10.48550/arXiv.1912.0738

Industrial Transformation Through Digital Maintenance Strategies

Gilberto Francisco Martha de Souza and Renan Favarão da Silva

Abstract Digital transformation is reshaping how maintenance is conceived and managed, particularly in asset-intensive industries. Rather than resulting from isolated technological initiatives, industrial transformation increasingly depends on the deployment of digital maintenance strategies aligned with organizational and physical asset management objectives. This chapter adopts a conceptual and process-oriented synthesis based on the ISO 55000 series and the Maintenance Management Framework for Asset Management (MMFAM) to examine how digital strategies in maintenance can systematically enable industrial transformation. The discussion analyzes how digital capabilities can be developed across the five maintenance management processes. Supported by enabling Industry 4.0 technologies such as AI, digital twins, cloud computing, and immersive technologies, digital maintenance strategies enhance and extend the established strategic role of maintenance by strengthening digital capabilities across the asset life cycle. Finally, the chapter highlights that, when digital capabilities are properly aligned with organizational and asset management objectives, digital maintenance strategies reinforce strategic integration and enable industrial transformation.

Keywords Digital maintenance strategy · Industrial transformation · Asset management alignment · Maintenance management framework · Industry 4.0 enablement

G. F. M. de Souza (✉)
Department of Mechatronics and Mechanical Systems Engineering, University of São Paulo, São Paulo, Brazil
e-mail: gfmsouza@usp.br

R. F. da Silva
Production Engineering Department, University of São Paulo, São Paulo, Brazil
e-mail: renanfavarao@usp.br

A. Crespo Márquez et al. (eds.), *Digital Maintenance and Asset Digitalization*, Engineering Asset Management Review 5,
https://doi.org/10.1007/978-3-032-21502-4_3

1 Introduction

The introduction of the digital transformation was initially effectively used by manufacturing process enabling the productivity increase associated with the improvement of production scheduling. Maintenance activities, which are one of the cornerstones of industrial operations management, can also benefit from digital transformation and collaborate with industrial transformation.

This chapter explore how industrial transformation can be systematically enabled through digitally driven maintenance strategies that are aligned with organizational and physical asset management objectives. Its main contribution lies in articulating a structured, strategy-oriented perspective in which digital maintenance is not treated as an isolated technological initiative, but as a coherent enabler of value creation across the asset life cycle. Based on the ISO 55000 series and the Maintenance Management Framework for Asset Management (MMFAM), the chapter demonstrates how digital capabilities, supported by Industry 4.0 technologies, can be purposefully developed and deployed to reinforce the strategic role of maintenance in asset-intensive industries.

Section 2 introduces the role of maintenance within the broader context of asset management and organizational strategy in the digital era, emphasizing the need for strategic alignment and governance of digital maintenance initiatives. Section 3 clarifies the concept of digital transformation as a strategic driver, distinguishing it from digitization and digitalization, and framing its implications for maintenance management. Section 4 presents a process-oriented analysis of digital maintenance strategies based on the MMFAM framework, discussing how digital capabilities can be developed across the five core maintenance management processes. Section 5 discusses how the systematic integration of digital maintenance strategies enables broader industrial transformation, reinforcing maintenance as a strategic function that supports organizational agility, performance, and long-term value creation. Finally, in the conclusions, the chapter reinforces that digital maintenance becomes a strategic lever for industrial transformation only when digital technologies are embedded within structured maintenance management processes and aligned with organizational and asset management objectives. It also highlights that such alignment strengthens decision-making across the asset life cycle, enabling sustainable performance improvements and competitive advantage in asset-intensive environments.

2 Strategy and Asset Management in the Digital Era

The growing interest in industrial digital transformation (DT) reflects a recent paradigm shift in how organizations manage operations, physical assets, and value delivery in complex environments. As digital technologies such as the Internet of Things (IoT), Artificial Intelligence (AI), Virtual and Augmented Reality (VR/AR), and digital twin become increasingly diffused in industrial systems, maintenance management emerges not only as a technical process but also as a critical enabler of strategic digital transformation in organizations.

As digitalization is going to change the way we conceive, develop, and industrialize maintenance, it should not be implemented all at once but must be consolidated quietly and safely (Crespo Márquez, 2022). Moreover, to ensure sustainable results, the digital transformation of maintenance processes shall be aligned with the organizational strategy and objectives within the Industry 4.0.

For enhance clarity, Fig. 1 illustrates how the digital transformation of maintenance management can be aligned with organizational strategy and objectives.

In this conceptual scheme of Fig. 1, the vertical axis represents the cascading of objectives from organizational strategy down to the maintenance plans, while the horizontal connectors on the right indicate the specific digital strategy artifacts, i.e. the digital objectives and deliverables generated at each hierarchical level.

Consequently, digital maintenance must not be treated as an isolated initiative. It integrates into the broader discipline of physical asset management, which is essentially strategic and lifecycle-based. As asset management enables an organization to realize value from assets in the achievement of its organizational objectives (ISO, 2014), the proper alignment is necessary to translate the digital strategy of the organization into physical asset management objectives and, subsequently, into maintenance management objectives.

Although maintenance represents only one phase within the asset life cycle, maintenance management plays a critical role in ensuring the efficient and effective management of physical assets throughout their entire life cycle (da Silva & de Souza, 2021). In other words, the maintenance stage is one of the main levers for achieving business results, since about two-thirds of the total life cycle cost of the asset is consumed in the operation and maintenance phases (GFMAN, 2016). Therefore, it plays a central role in enabling the industrial transformation through digital strategy in organizations, especially asset-intensive industries.

Accordingly, the strategic transformation of asset-intensive industries through digital technologies must recognize maintenance as a core organizational process. A well-structured strategy provides direction, prioritization, and governance for digital maintenance initiatives. Without this strategic foundation, digital maintenance risks becoming a fragmented collection of disconnected tools rather than a cohesive enabler of industrial transformation.

For instance, many organizations adopt isolated predictive analytics tools or IoT sensors in specific equipment but these technologies remain disconnected from maintenance planning and decision-making processes. As observed by Bokrantz et al. (2020), in many plants "the data are there, the systems are there, it is all there", yet the information is never actually used and no value is created out of it because it is not integrated into decision routines. In such cases, digitalization results only in isolated technical initiatives rather than a coherent, strategically aligned approach to maintenance transformation.

As can be seen in Fig. 1, the hierarchical alignment between organizational strategy, asset management, and maintenance management, emphasizing how

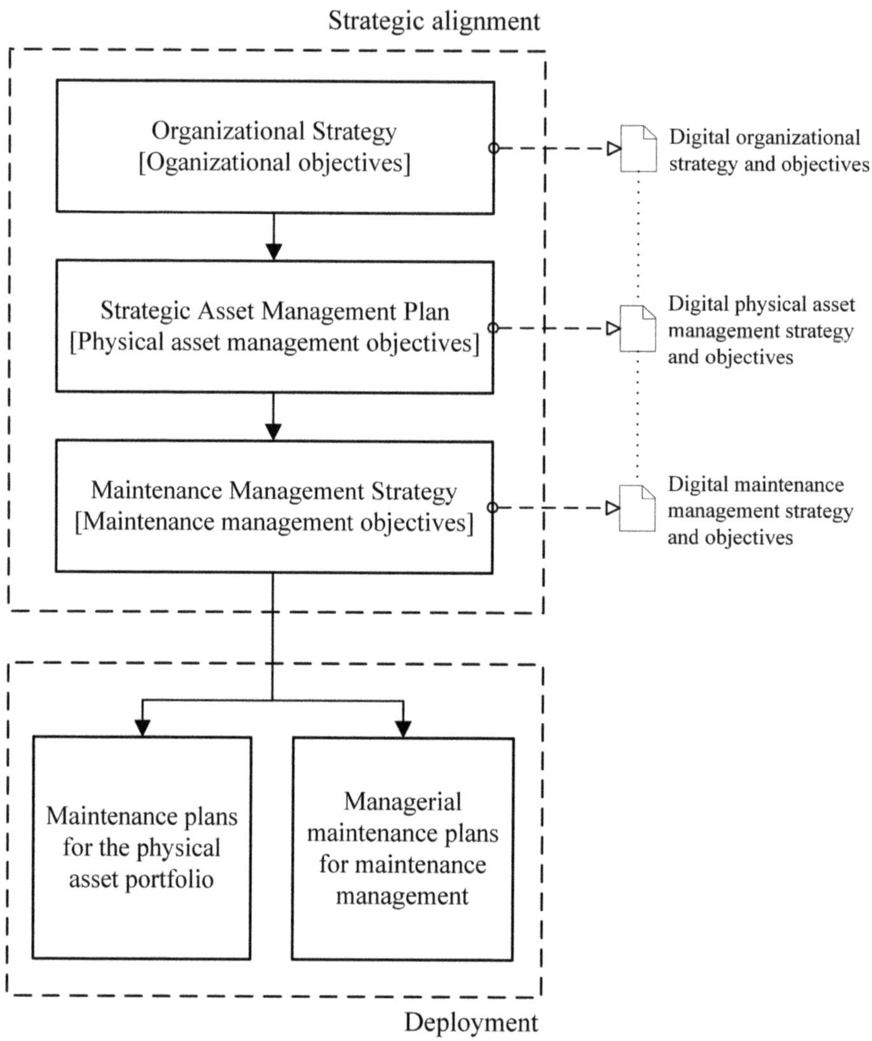

Fig. 1 Strategic alignment and deployment of digital maintenance strategies

strategic objectives are cascaded through different levels of planning and deployment. The diagram highlights that maintenance strategies must be derived from broader physical asset management plans, which in turn are informed by the organizational strategy. In addition, it is clear that the digital strategies and objectives integrate this approach as these aspects are part of the strategy and objectives in the three levels.

Finally, the deployment of these strategies is operationalized through maintenance plans targeting both the physical asset portfolio and the managerial dimensions of maintenance management. This structured alignment ensures that digital maintenance acts not as an isolated technological initiative, but as a coherent enabler of industrial transformation.

In this context, it is essential to broaden the discussion by considering the multidimensional nature of organizational strategy. Traditionally, strategy refers to a coordinated set of long-term decisions and actions designed to achieve competitive advantage in a dynamic environment. Michael Porter (1996) defines strategy as "choosing to perform activities differently or to perform different activities than rivals", emphasizing deliberate positioning, differentiation, and trade-offs. Accordingly, as shown in Fig. 1, a digital organizational strategy should guide the formulation of objectives for asset management and, consequently, maintenance management.

Additionally, Prahalad and Hamel (1990) argue that competitive advantage stems from the cultivation of core competencies, understood as collective learning and coordination mechanisms that enable firms to deliver unique value. In this sense, within the context of industrial transformation, digital maintenance can be viewed as a strategic competency that differentiates organizations in terms of reliability, responsiveness, and asset optimization.

In line with this strategic cascade, Kaplan and Norton (1996) propose the use of the Balanced Scorecard (BSC) and Strategy Maps as tools to translate an organization's vision and strategy into operational objectives and measurable outcomes. These tools support the articulation and alignment of objectives across different organizational levels, ensuring coherence and traceability throughout the strategic planning process.

In the digital era, strategic organizational planning increasingly incorporates the development of digital capabilities and the integration of emerging technologies across operational and managerial processes. When applied to physical asset management, this strategic deployment should include the definition of specific digital objectives for maintenance management. However, without such alignment digitalization efforts in maintenance may become fragmented or not in the desired direction with broader organizational goals.

Furthermore, organizations shall consider and understand both their internal and external contexts, as well as identify the needs and expectations of relevant stakeholders, in accordance with Sect. 4 ("Context of the organization") of the ISO 55001 standard (ISO, 2024), when establishing, for instance, a digital strategy for physical asset management. This approach enables the derivation of maintenance objectives and plans that are specific rather than generic, ensuring a tailored digitalization in organizations.

Finally, it is important to highlight the role of leadership and commitment from all managerial levels for the success of digital maintenance strategies. Leadership is one of the most critical human factors for asset management, as employee performance can be significantly influenced by the quality of leadership (Kriege & Vlok, 2015). Without it, asset management plans can fail due to insufficient or inappropriate asset provision or support (Hastings, 2015). In addition, leadership plays a central role in fostering a digital culture and enabling effective change management, both of which are essential for sustaining digital maintenance initiatives.

According to the ISO 55000 standard (ISO, 2014) leaders at all levels are involved in the planning, implementation and operation of the asset management system. Furthermore, the ISO 55001 standard (ISO, 2024) reinforces that top management must demonstrate leadership and commitment with respect to the asset management system. Therefore, in the digital context, this implies prioritizing the digitalization of maintenance activities and ensuring that these initiatives are aligned with organizational drivers such as availability, risk management, cost control, and sustainability.

The original contribution lies in articulating how industrial transformation can be systematically enabled through digital maintenance strategies derived from organizational digital objectives. While existing literature discusses digital technologies and smart maintenance practices in isolation, this perspective integrates these elements by demonstrating how digital strategy must cascade through asset management and into maintenance processes to generate coherent, organization-wide transformation.

From a methodological standpoint, the discussion is grounded in a conceptual synthesis based on the ISO 55000 series and the MMFAM framework, which serve as structured references to examine how digital strategies can reshape maintenance management and support industrial transformation. Accordingly, the chapter adopts an analytical narrative, combining established framework, standards, and recent literature to structure the discussion on digital maintenance strategies and their role in industrial transformation.

3 Digital Transformation as a Strategic Driver

Enabling industrial transformation through digital maintenance strategies requires a robust understanding of what digital transformation (DT) really means. According to Rogers (2016), "digital transformation is not about technology. It is about strategy and new ways of thinking. Transforming for the digital age requires your business to upgrade its strategic mindset much more than its IT infrastructure".

Therefore, industrial transformation through maintenance digitalization is not merely a matter of adopting enabling technologies or implementing Industry 4.0 solutions. It involves a coordinated shift in how organizations create value, interact with stakeholders, and structure maintenance management processes through digital capabilities in alignment with organizational objectives.

Rogers (2016) identifies five key domains of digital transformation: customers, competition, data, innovation, and value. This framework contributes to a broader understanding of the scope of digital transformation, particularly as it redefines strategic orientation. Similarly, the World Economic Forum (WEF, 2018) defines DT as the integration of digital technologies into all aspects of business and society, fundamentally changing how value is delivered. This view reinforces the notion that digital transformation is not just a technological effort, but also a business model shift encompassing cultural, structural, and collaborative dimensions.

Additionally, Gartner (2021) defines digital business transformation as "the process of exploiting digital technologies and supporting capabilities to create a robust new digital business model", highlighting the organizational capabilities required to achieve agility, innovation, and resilience. McKinsey & Company (2017) adds that successful DT initiatives are characterized by deep structural changes, strong leadership, and strategic alignment.

Regarding physical asset management, particularly in asset-intensive industries, digital transformation is reflected in the restructuring of maintenance management processes and activities. As proposed by da Silva e de Souza (2023), the Maintenance Management Framework for Asset Management (MMFAM), based on ISO 55000 series guidelines, comprises five core processes: defining scope, planning actions, implementing actions, evaluating performance, and improving the process. These five processes will be examined in detail later in this chapter. However, at this stage, it is first necessary to clarify key conceptual distinctions among digitization, digitalization, and digital transformation, which provide the theoretical foundation for understanding how these processes evolve in the digital context.

The first of these concepts is "digitization", which refers to the conversion of analog information into digital formats. In the maintenance context, for instance, this may include scanning paper-based maintenance logs, digitizing physical asset manuals, or creating digital records of work orders. Although essential as a foundation, digitization alone does not modify how decisions are made or how value is delivered.

The second concept is "digitalization", which involves the use of digital technologies to enhance or optimize existing processes and workflows. In maintenance management, this may include the implementation of a Computerized Maintenance Management System (CMMS) such as SAP or IBM Maximo, the use of mobile applications for work execution, or sensor-based condition monitoring. Besides, it can include the recent enabling Industry 4.0 technologies such as IIoT, augmented reality (AR) and virtual reality (VR), cloud computing, AI and analytics, digital twin, and others (Bona et al., 2021; Silvestri et al., 2020).

While digitization and digitalization are foundational to digital transformation, they represent only partial dimensions of the broader strategic and organizational shift that true DT provides. This hierarchy can be represented as concentric concepts, where digital transformation encompasses and transcends both digitization and digitalization, as illustrated in Fig. 2. In this layered view, digitization provides the technical foundation upon which digitalization builds process improvements, whereas digital transformation integrates and extends both to enable industrial transformation through digitally enhanced maintenance strategies.

Thus, digital transformation represents a broader and more strategic paradigm. It involves a systemic redefinition of how an organization operates, creates value, and competes. As a result, it directly influences how physical asset management is approached. This transformation encompasses not only the implementation of digital tools, but also changes in business models, organizational culture, governance structures, and performance metrics.

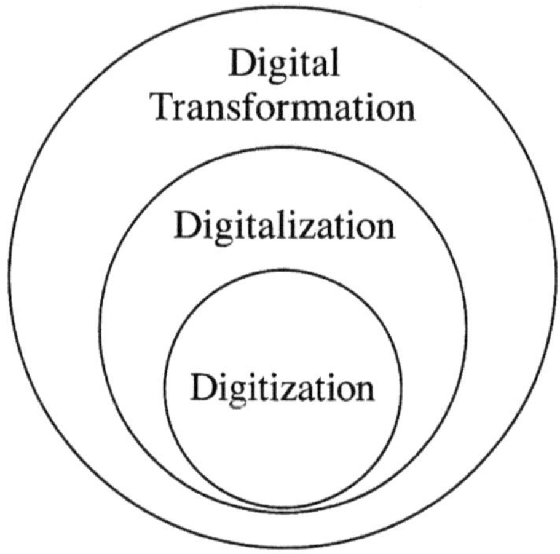

Fig. 2 Conceptual hierarchy of digitization, digitalization, and DT

In other words, although digitization and digitalization are important steps, industrial transformation through digital transformation requires strategic integration across the entire organization, as previously illustrated in Fig. 1. Aligning with the digital organizational strategy enables a clearer translation of asset management objectives and, consequently, maintenance objectives, which are in line with the digital maintenance strategies.

4 Digital Transformation Strategies for Maintenance Management

The successful implementation of digital transformation in asset-intensive industries requires more than the adoption of isolated technological solutions. It depends on the strategic alignment of maintenance management with the organization's digital objectives. In this context, digital maintenance strategies can be formulated by deriving specific objectives that may require changes in maintenance management processes, supported by enabling digital technologies and the development of human and organizational capabilities.

To structure this discussion, the chapter adopts a process-oriented perspective based on the MMFAM framework, through which the analysis is systematically organized across maintenance management processes. From a practical perspective, strategy deployment begins with the translation of organizational objectives, such as safety, profitability, sustainability, resilience, and customer satisfaction, into specific and measurable objectives for the physical asset management. These may include maximizing asset availability, reducing total cost of ownership, improving operational response time, or ensuring regulatory compliance. For instance, an organizational objective such as achieving "zero unplanned downtime" may lead to a physical asset management strategy focused on condition-based monitoring and predictive diagnostics capabilities.

Building on this strategic cascade, the formulation of digital maintenance strategies must derive from the organization's digital objectives, ensuring that maintenance processes are oriented toward the broader direction established at higher strategic levels. As a result, the role of maintenance management becomes inherently strategic and increasingly digital.

It no longer can be viewed merely as a reactive support function, instead maintenance now acts as a central enabler of industrial transformation through digital strategies. This perspective is consistent with findings from Bokrantz et al. (2020), who show that modern maintenance, characterized by data-driven decision-making, enhanced human capabilities, and strong internal and external integration, assumes a proactive and strategic role in digitalized industrial environments. For that, maintenance processes and activities should be redefined and conducted with the support of digital capabilities and enabling technologies.

To provide a clearer understanding of digital maintenance strategies, this section discusses the development of digital capabilities through technological tools and enablers across each one of the five processes of maintenance management, as defined in the MMFAM and in alignment with ISO 55000 series (da Silva & de Souza, 2021).

The first process, defining scope, involves establishing the boundaries and scope of maintenance management in accordance with ISO 55001 requirements. Subsequently, the planning action process is the stage in which the organization formulates both the maintenance plans for the physical asset portfolio and the managerial supporting plans for maintenance management. Additionally, this process includes the planning of actions aimed at controlling and correcting nonconformities and undesirable events, addressing their consequences and root causes, mitigating non-tolerated risks, and exploring opportunities for improvement (da Silva & de Souza, 2023).

Digital transformation, through digitalization and application of digital technologies of Industry 4.0, enhances both of these processes of maintenance management by enabling data-driven decision-making. For instance, cloud-based CMMS and integrated Enterprise Asset Management (EAM) platforms provide centralized access to asset information, historical records, and real-time condition indicators, supporting more accurate forecasting and scenario simulation.

Moreover, technologies such as digital twins and cyber-physical systems further enrich the planning process by modeling physical asset behavior and maintenance needs under varying operational conditions. Planners can simulate degradation trends, different failure modes, and the effects of maintenance interventions, enabling risk-informed maintenance planning aligned with reliability targets and lifecycle cost optimization.

The implementation action process is the stage in which all planned actions are formally assigned and executed. It encompasses not only work orders related to physical assets, but also administrative, contractual, and training activities that address aspects beyond the assets themselves. For instance, this process includes the identification and prioritization of actions derived from maintenance plans for the physical asset portfolio and from maintenance management plans. It involves actions to control and correct nonconformities and undesirable events, mitigate their consequences and root causes, address non-tolerated risks. Finally, it includes the scheduling, assignment, and monitoring of all planned actions to ensure their effective implementation (da Silva & de Souza, 2023).

The digital transformation of this implementation process relies on integrating enabling technologies that enhance the execution, control, and adaptability of maintenance activities. Industrial Internet of Things (IIoT) platforms allow for real-time condition monitoring through embedded sensors, which transmit operational data to cloud-based maintenance systems. These platforms have the potential to automatically generate, assign, and update work orders based on predefined thresholds or intelligent anomaly detection algorithms powered by machine learning within Artificial Intelligence (AI).

Furthermore, technologies such as AR and VR are increasingly being used to transform to transform maintenance execution and inspection by providing hands-free access to technical documentation, guided procedures, and remote expert support directly in the field. Additionally, VR can be applied in technical training programs to simulate high-risk maintenance activities, supporting skill development and contributing to the improvements in human reliability.

Regarding the evaluation performance process, its primary focus is the assessment of maintenance management performance based on aligned performance indicators and compliance with applicable standards and regulations. In this context, the process involves, for instance, the evaluation of physical asset conditions, the performance of maintenance management activities, and the effectiveness of risk and opportunity management within the asset management system. It also includes conducting internal audits and management reviews and identifying opportunities for improvement and non-tolerated risks (da Silva & de Souza, 2023).

The digital transformation of the evaluation performance process can be enabled by the integration of Industry 4.0 technologies that enhance data collection, analysis, and visualization. Advanced sensor networks and IIoT platforms facilitate the continuous monitoring of asset health and operational conditions, feeding real-time data into maintenance management systems. This can contribute to implementing maintenance performance indicators can be calculated and updated dynamically, increasing accuracy and responsiveness.

Additionally, big data analytics and machine learning techniques allow organizations to detect hidden patterns, predict failures, and identify root causes based on historical and real-time data. Cloud-based dashboards and Business Intelligence (BI) platforms aggregate data across vertical (operational) and horizontal (interdepartmental) systems. These tools support strategic decision-making, compliance monitoring, and the identification of opportunities for continuous improvement. The insights generated by these analytical tools directly inform the improvement process, linking performance evaluation with targeted actions for continuous enhancement.

Finally, the improve process encompasses the activities aimed at analyzing performance results and developing actions to enhance the previous processes in order to drive continuous improvement. This process includes, for instance, the formulation of actions to control and correct undesirable incidents, mitigate their consequences, address non-tolerated risks, and explore improvement opportunities. It also involves root cause analysis and the development of corrective or preventive actions. Once defined, these actions are forwarded to the appropriate processes ensuring that lessons learned and feedback loops effectively enhance the overall maintenance management (da Silva & de Souza, 2023).

The digital transformation of this last maintenance management process can be driven by advanced analytics and closed-loop feedback systems that support evidence-based decision-making. Moreover, the integration of cloud computing platforms ensures secure storage and accessibility of structured maintenance records, facilitating iterative refinement of strategies.

To support a clearer understanding of how digital strategies for maintenance management can be effectively implemented, the Table 1 summarizes examples of how digital capabilities can be developed across each maintenance management process defined in the MMFAM. These examples demonstrate the potential of digitalization to enhance planning, execution, evaluation, and improvement of maintenance management processes and their activities towards digital transformation.

To support practical application, the structure summarized in Table 1 can serve as a foundation for developing a digital maintenance roadmap. One useful approach is to combine the MMFAM processes with a maturity assessment model, such as the maturity principles presented by the GFMAM in the "Position Statement on Asset Management Maturity" (GFMAM, 2021), in order to evaluate the organization's current state and identify priority areas for development. By mapping existing practices, technological enablers, and data readiness across the maintenance management

Table 1 Examples of digital capabilities by maintenance management process

Maintenance management process	Digital enablers or technologies	Digital capabilities developed
Defining scope and planning actions	Cloud-based CMMS, Integrated EAM platforms, Digital twins, and Cyber-physical systems	Centralized data access, forecasting, scenario simulation, and risk-informed planning
Implementing actions	IIoT platforms, AI for anomaly detection, and AR/VR for execution support and training	Real-time monitoring, automated work order generation, hands-free guidance, and immersive training
Evaluating performance	IIoT, Advanced sensors, big data analytics, and Machine learning, BI platforms	Dynamic KPI monitoring, failure prediction, root cause analysis, and strategic decision support
Improving process	AI-based analytics, Cloud platforms, and Closed-loop feedback systems	Continuous improvement, knowledge retention, and iterative strategy refinement

processes, organizations can more clearly identify capability gaps, sequence implementation steps, and align digital investments with strategic objectives. This type of assessment supports a more coherent and phased digital transformation journey, ensuring that technological adoption is both feasible and strategically oriented.

Nevertheless, these capabilities do not represent an exhaustive set of solutions, nor do they constitute guidelines. As previously discussed, the pathway to digital transformation shall be guided by the organization's digital maintenance strategy, which, in turn, should be aligned with the broader objectives of physical asset management and organizational strategy. Each organization operates within a unique context, characterized by distinct priorities, technological maturity, and resource availability. Therefore, the design and implementation of digital maintenance strategies should be flexible and tailored for the organization, reflecting its strategic intent, operational needs, and technological readiness.

5 Industrial Transformation Enabled by Digital Maintenance

Digital transformation is reshaping how maintenance is conceived and executed. According to the GFMAM (2024), "digital technologies are at a point where their application makes sense for most industries", a perspective that underscores the growing relevance of maintenance and asset management within this new technological landscape. However, digital maintenance is not an end in itself, but rather a strategic enabler of broader, integrated, and sustainable industrial transformation. As discussed throughout this chapter, the integration of digitalization and enabling technologies into maintenance management processes only makes sense when aligned with the organization's digital strategy and strategic objectives. This alignment is what justifies and gives direction to the efforts toward digital transformation in maintenance.

When digital strategies are effectively cascaded into physical asset management objectives and implemented in maintenance management processes and activities, they establish the foundations for a new industrial paradigm. Digital maintenance becomes a key enabler of this industrial transformation by redefining how physical assets are monitored, controlled, and optimized across their entire life cycle.

Technologies such as the IIoT, cyber-physical systems, digital twins, augmented and virtual reality (AR/VR), and cloud-based analytics platforms are able to facilitate the continuous collection and analysis of condition data. For instance, O'Sullivan et al. (2020) describe the introduction of a maintenance-oriented digital twin in a large-scale manufacturing facility, showing how sensor data, IoT platforms and smart analytics can be integrated to predict issues before they occur and support better-informed maintenance decisions.

Most of the data that is collected through new digital technologies can be used.

to increase the effectiveness of asset management decision-making (Crespo Márquez, 2022). By enabling real-time monitoring and advanced analytics, organizations gain predictive and prescriptive insights that support proactive maintenance planning, improved reliability, and optimized resource allocation.

It is important to note that this integration of digital maintenance does not imply a rupture with established engineering and management practices. On the contrary, it builds upon foundational tools and techniques that have long supported maintenance and reliability engineering. Traditional approaches such as Reliability-Centered Maintenance (RCM), Failure Mode and Effects Analysis (FMEA), Life Data Analysis (LDA), Risk-Based Maintenance (RBM), Multicriteria Decision-Making (MCDM) methods, and others remain essential in structuring and guiding technical decisions.

As illustrated in Fig. 3, digital maintenance management must be supported by a robust maintenance management framework for asset management, which in turn relies on both traditional methodologies and digital enablers.

Accordingly, the integrated and strategic shift for digital maintenance management does not eliminate the use of technical and well-known maintenance, reliability and risk support tools, techniques, methods. In fact, the digitalization of activities

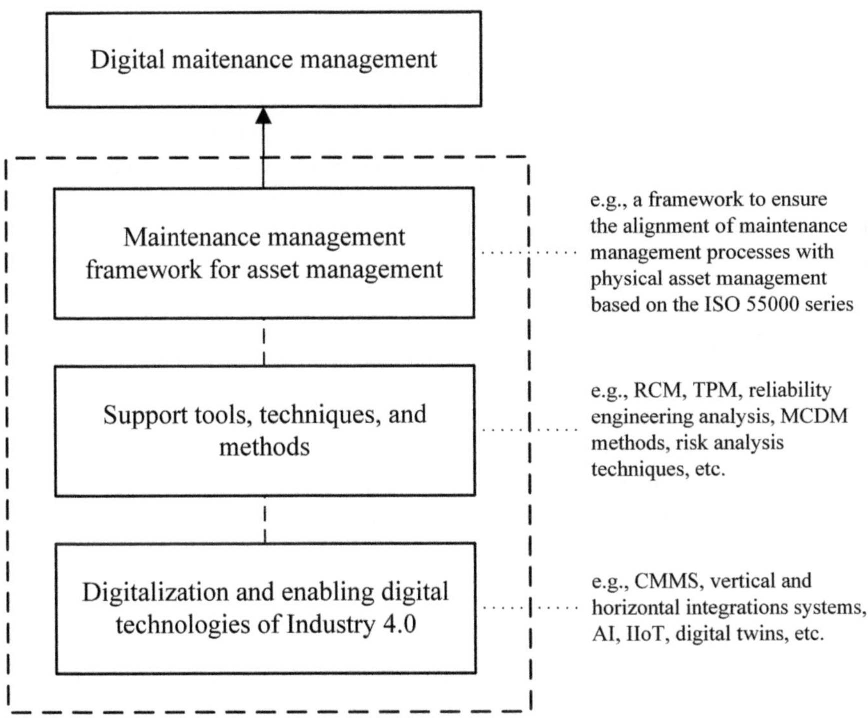

Fig. 3 Integrated structure for digital maintenance management

and the implementation of enabling Industry 4.0 can potentialize them in deriving value.

In this context, digital maintenance should not be seen as a disruptive force that replaces traditional maintenance, reliability, and risk engineering, but rather as a transformative layer that integrates, amplifies, and arranges these established practices within data-driven and digitalized processes. However, the decision to move toward digital maintenance is not merely technological. It is strategic, as extensively discussed throughout this chapter.

As presented in Fig. 1, such transformation requires alignment with organizational vision and objectives, cascading through asset management and ultimately shaping maintenance processes and activities. Consequently, different organizations will incorporate digitalization and enabling technologies at varying levels and speeds, depending on their strategic priorities, resource availability, and digital maturity.

Within this integrated and aligned approach, the benefits of digital maintenance extend across all three levels of maintenance management. At the operational level, it can enhance asset availability, reduce unplanned downtime, and improve workforce productivity. At the tactical level, it can support adaptive planning, process standardization, and continuous information flow across maintenance, production, and engineering. Finally, at the strategic level, digital maintenance could contribute to organizational agility and responsiveness.

When digital capabilities are embedded within structured maintenance management processes and systematically aligned with asset management and organizational objectives, the strategic role of maintenance is reinforced and expanded. In this integrated perspective, digital maintenance enhances the coordination of decisions across the asset life cycle, enabling maintenance management to more effectively connect operational execution with tactical planning and strategic objectives, and thereby support broader industrial transformation.

6 Conclusions

In asset-intensive industries, where physical assets represent the core of value creation, maintenance plays a critical role throughout the asset life cycle. When maintenance management is digitally transformed, it not only improves performance indicators but also enables a systemic transformation of industrial processes. In this sense, digital maintenance acts as a strategic lever for broader industrial transformation, reinforcing maintenance as a central agent of change and a source of competitive advantage in the digital era.

This chapter examined how digital maintenance strategies can systematically support industrial transformation when derived from organizational digital objectives and deployed through asset management structures. To organize this discussion, a process-oriented perspective grounded in the MMFAM framework was adopted. This approach allowed the analysis to be consistently structured across the five maintenance management processes in alignment with ISO 55000 series.

In summary, industrial transformation is not achieved simply by adopting digital technologies, but by deploying coherent digital maintenance strategies that reshape how organizations plan, execute, and improve maintenance across the asset life cycle. The strategic digitalization of maintenance strengthens decision-making, reinforces established engineering practices, and enables new data-driven and digital capabilities. When these capabilities are aligned with organizational objectives, digital maintenance becomes a lever that extends beyond the maintenance function itself, driving broader industrial transformation and supporting competitive advantage in asset-intensive environments.

Although this work offers a conceptual and strategic perspective, it does not attempt to exhaust all technological, organizational, or sector-specific dimensions involved in digital maintenance strategies. The proposed conceptual representations and structures discussed are intended to support strategic reasoning and alignment rather than prescribe detailed implementation pathways. Future developments may extend these ideas through empirical studies, sector-specific applications, and implementation frameworks adapted to different industrial contexts.

References

Bokrantz, J., Skoogh, A., Berlin, C., Wuest, T., & Stahre, J. (2020). Smart Maintenance: an empirically grounded conceptualization. *Internantional Journal of Production Economics, 223*, 107534 (Online). Available at: https://doi.org/10.1016/j.ijpe.2019.107534

Bona, G., Cesarotti, V., Arcese, G., & Gallo, T. (2021). Implementation of Industry 4.0 technology: New opportunities and challenges for maintenance strategy. In *International conference on Industry 4.0 and smart manufacturing. Procedia computer science*, vol. 180, pp. 424–429 (Online). Available at: https://doi.org/10.1016/j.procs.2021.01.258

Crespo Márquez, A. (2022). *Digital maintenance management: Guiding digital transformation in maintenance* (1st ed.). Springer (Online). Available at: https://doi.org/10.1007/978-3-030-97660-6

Da Silva, R. F., & de Souza, G. F. M. (2021). Modeling a maintenance management framework for asset management based on ISO 55000 series guidelines. *Journal of Quality in Maintenance Engineering, 28*(4), 915–937 (Online). Available at: https://doi.org/10.1108/JQME-08-2020-0082

Da Silva, R. F., & de Souza, G. F. M. (2023). Discussing the applicability of the maintenance management framework for asset management (MMFAM): a hydroelectric power plant case study. *Journal of Quality in Maintenance Engineering, 30*(1), 1–25 (Online). Available at: https://doi.org/10.1108/JQME-06-2022-0038

Gartner (2021). Glossary: Digital transformation. *Gartner IT Glossary* (Online). Available at: https://www.gartner.com/en/information-technology/glossary/digital-transformation. Accessed 28 June 2025.

GFMAN. (2016). *The Maintenance framework* (1st ed.). GFMAN.

GFMAN. (2021). *The asset management maturity: A position statement* (2nd ed.). GFMAN.

GFMAN. (2024). *Digital transformation in maintenance and asset management* (1st ed.). GFMAN.

Hastings, N. A. J. (2015). *Physical asset management* (1st ed.). Springer (Online). Available at: https://doi.org/10.1007/978-3-319-14777-2

International Organization for Standardization (ISO). (2014). *ISO 55000:2014—Asset management—Overview, principles and terminology* (1st ed.). ISO.

International Organization for Standardization (ISO). (2024). *ISO 55001:2024—Asset management—Management systems—Requirements* (2nd ed.). ISO.
Kaplan, R. S., & Norton, D. P. (1996). *The balanced scorecard: Translating strategy into action.* Harvard Business School.
Kriege, L., & Vlok, P. J. (2015). Human resources within ISO 55000—The hidden backbone to the asset management system. In: *Proceedings of the 10th world congress on engineering asset management (WCEAM 2015)* (pp. 435–446). Springer (Online). Available at: https://doi.org/10.1007/978-3-319-15536-4_34
McKinsey & Company (2017). *Unlocking success in digital transformations.* McKinsey Digital (Online). Available at: https://www.mckinsey.com/business-functions/mckinsey-digital/our-insights/unlocking-success-in-digital-transformations. Accessed 28 June 2025.
O'Sullivan, J., O'Sullivan, D., & Bruton, K. (2020). A case-study in the introduction of a digital twin in a large-scale smart manufacturing facility. *Procedia Manufacturing, 51*, 1523–1530 (Online). Available at: https://doi.org/10.1016/j.promfg.2020.10.212
Prahalad, C. K., & Hamel, G. (1990). The core competence of the corporation. *Harvard Business Review, 68*(3), 79–91 (Online). Available at: https://hbr.org/1990/05/the-core-competence-of-the-corporation
Porter, M. E. (1996). What is strategy? *Harvard Business Review, 74*(6), 61–78 (Online). Available at: https://hbr.org/1996/11/what-is-strategy
Rogers, D. L. (2016). *The digital transformation playbook: Rethink your business for the digital age.* Columbia Business School Publishing.
Silvestri, L., Forcina, A., Introna, V., Santolamazza, A., & Cesarotti, V. (2020). Maintenance transformation through Industry 4.0 technologies: A systematic literature review. *Computers in Industry, 123*, 103335 (Online). Available at: https://doi.org/10.1016/j.compind.2020.103335
World Economic Forum & Accenture (2018). *Digital transformation initiative: Unlocking $100 trillion for business and society from digital transformation.* World Economic Forum.

Data, Models, and Intelligence for Smart Asset Management

Cybersecurity Challenges and Solutions in Digital Asset Management

Carmen Elena Patino Rodriguez and Fernando Jesús Guevara Carazas

Abstract This chapter delivers a systematic literature review (SLR) of cybersecurity in digital asset management, moving from methodological grounding to thematic synthesis. A rigorous research design, targeted literature selection, and structured analytical process establish the basis for reliable and coherent findings. The analysis integrates conceptual, geographical, and temporal perspectives, examining the interaction between foundational technologies and systemic concerns, regional disparities in research activity, and the thematic diversification accelerated by recent socio-economic changes. The review identifies key challenges: technological risk vectors, lifecycle misalignments, governance and compliance gaps, disciplinary fragmentation, and sector-specific vulnerabilities. These issues are framed within the dynamics of innovation, regulatory adaptation, and institutional capacity, underscoring the need for integrated approaches. The chapter concludes by advocating adaptive, context-aware frameworks to strengthen digital asset resilience, aligning scholarly insights with the operational demands of interconnected infrastructures.

Keywords Cybersecurity in digital asset management · Asset lifecycle security · Cyber-physical infrastructure protection · Cyber risk governance · Systematic literature review

C. E. Patino Rodriguez (✉)
Universidad de Antioquia, Medellín, Colombia
e-mail: elena.patino@udea.edu.co

F. J. Guevara Carazas
Universidad Nacional de Colombia Sede Medellín, Medellín, Colombia
e-mail: fjguevarac@unal.edu.co

A. Crespo Márquez et al. (eds.), *Digital Maintenance and Asset Digitalization*, Engineering Asset Management Review 5,
https://doi.org/10.1007/978-3-032-21502-4_4

1 Introduction

The progressive digitalization of asset management and maintenance has reshaped how organizations monitor, operate, and govern asset-intensive systems. The adoption of data-driven approaches supported by connected sensors, industrial data platforms, and digital representations of physical assets has enabled a transition from reactive and preventive maintenance to predictive and condition-based strategies. These strategies improve asset availability, enhance performance monitoring, and support lifecycle-oriented decision-making in sectors such as energy, transportation, manufacturing, and critical infrastructure (Brandín & Abrishami, 2021; Firouzi et al., 2022; Turk et al., 2022).

At the same time, the increasing dependence on interconnected digital infrastructures has introduced new cybersecurity risks into asset management systems. The convergence of information technology (IT) and operational technology (OT), together with continuous data exchange across distributed environments, has expanded the attack surface of digital asset ecosystems. Cyber incidents affecting maintenance platforms, monitoring systems, or asset lifecycle data repositories can compromise data integrity, disrupt operational continuity, and undermine confidence in decision-support systems (Lawal & Nawari, 2023; Li et al., 2025). Consequently, cybersecurity has evolved from a supporting technical function into a core requirement for reliable digital asset management.

Digital asset management systems typically operate within complex ecosystems that involve cloud services, external vendors, industrial platforms, and third-party software. Their security therefore depends not only on conventional information security controls, but also on governance mechanisms, lifecycle coordination, and system resilience under real-time operational constraints. Prior studies report vulnerabilities associated with misconfigured networks, software dependencies, embedded devices, and organizational practices, as well as the increasing prevalence of ransomware, insider threats, and persistent attacks in asset-intensive environments (Li et al., 2025; Pakseresht et al., 2023; Turk et al., 2022). These risks highlight the need to examine cybersecurity as a systemic and lifecycle-oriented challenge rather than as an isolated technical issue.

Although cybersecurity in industrial and digital environments has been widely investigated, existing literature reviews often focus on specific technologies, individual sectors, or regulatory perspectives. As a result, current knowledge remains fragmented, and there is limited synthesis that integrates cybersecurity challenges and solution approaches across the full digital asset lifecycle. This fragmentation hinders the identification of recurring risk patterns, dominant mitigation strategies, and persistent research gaps at a consolidated level.

To overcome this limitation, this chapter performs a SLR of cybersecurity challenges and solutions in digital asset management within Industry 4.0 contexts. A structured and transparent methodological framework is applied so that peer-reviewed studies on cybersecurity risks, governance mechanisms, and mitigation approaches related to digital assets can be identified, screened, and analysed.

The review uses systematic selection procedures combined with bibliometric and thematic analyses to map the intellectual structure of the field, trace the evolution of themes over time, and identify areas of concentrated and underrepresented research (Booth et al., 2016; Donthu et al., 2021).

The contribution of this chapter lies in providing an integrated synthesis that connects technological, organizational, and governance perspectives on cybersecurity in digital asset management. Rather than proposing new technical solutions, the chapter consolidates existing evidence to support a structured understanding of current challenges, recurring vulnerabilities, and emerging solution frameworks. The findings are intended to inform researchers and practitioners involved in asset management, maintenance engineering, and cybersecurity, and to provide a coherent foundation for developing more resilient and secure digital asset ecosystems.

Based on this motivation, the review is guided by the following research questions:

RQ1: What cybersecurity challenges and risk factors associated with digital asset management systems are reported in academic literature?
RQ2: What technological, procedural, and organizational solutions have been proposed to mitigate cybersecurity risks across the digital asset lifecycle?
RQ3: How has the research on cybersecurity in digital asset management evolved in terms of thematic focus, application domains, and analytical approaches?

2 Systematic Review Methodology

This chapter adopts a SLR as its primary methodological approach to ensure transparency, replicability, and analytical rigor in synthesizing existing knowledge on cybersecurity challenges and solutions in digital asset management. The design and execution of the review follow established methodological guidelines for SLR in engineering, management, and information systems research threat vectors (Booth et al., 2016; Keele, 2007; Petticrew & Roberts, 2008). This structure ensures methodological coherence and minimizes selection bias, while supporting the exploration of thematic patterns, research gaps, and conceptual trends (see Fig. 1).

An SLR is especially appropriate for this research domain due to its interdisciplinary character, the rapid evolution of Industry 4.0 technologies, and the fragmentation of cybersecurity research across technical, organizational, and governance-oriented streams. Unlike narrative literature reviews, the SLR applies explicit, rule-based procedures for identifying, selecting, appraising, and synthesizing prior studies, thereby reducing selection bias and increasing the reliability of cumulative findings.

The SLR was designed to identify and synthesize academic related to technological, procedural, and organizational challenges in securing digital assets across their lifecycle. Figure 1 shows the transition from raw bibliographic data to strategic research insights. methodological workflow consisting of four sequential stages: Identification, Screening, Eligibility, and Inclusion. The structured protocol ensures

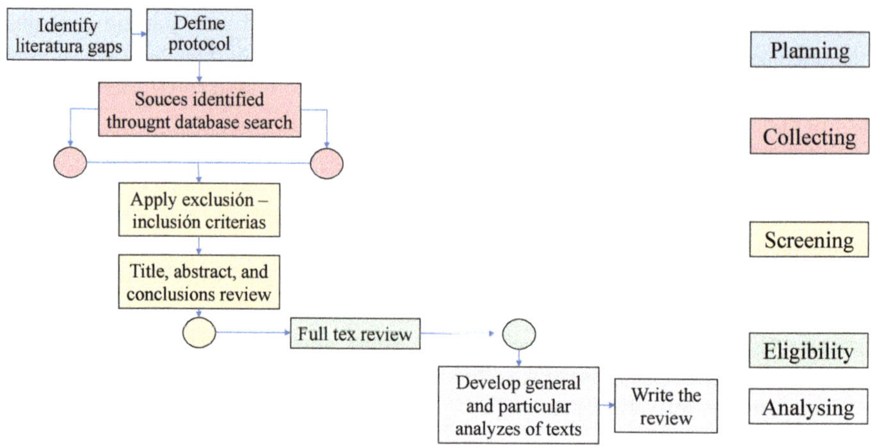

Fig. 1 Conceptual methodological framework

transparency, replicability, and analytical depth, which are essential in fields characterized by rapid innovation and shifting threat vectors (Booth et al., 2016; Keele, 2007; Petticrew & Roberts, 2008). This structure ensures methodological coherence and minimizes selection bias, while supporting the exploration of thematic patterns, research gaps, and conceptual trends.

Before detailing the specific objectives and scope of the review, it is important to contextualize the rationale behind the research design. In domains where digital infrastructures are rapidly evolving and cybersecurity threats emerge unpredictably, the choice of a structured and evidence-based methodological approach is not merely procedural—it is essential (Bolbot et al., 2020; Booth et al., 2016; Clavijo Mesa et al., 2024; Liberati et al., 2009). The integration of bibliometric tools with a SLR allows for the simultaneous exploration of both the volume and the substance of scholarly contributions. This approach ensures that the resulting insights are not only comprehensive and current but also grounded in methodological rigor, enabling a deeper understanding of how cybersecurity concerns are being conceptualized and operationalized within digital asset ecosystems. This formulation was refined through test queries, expert validation, and noise reduction procedures to ensure an adequate balance between precision and recall, allowing the retrieval of relevant documents while minimizing noise (Sicari et al., 2015). The final corpus was subjected to both descriptive and inferential bibliometric analyses.

The SLR approach enables a structured examination of how cybersecurity challenges and solutions are conceptualized across technological, organizational, and governance dimensions. Given the convergence of Industry 4.0 principles, distributed architectures, and lifecycle-oriented asset management, a systematic method is essential to capture both the breadth and structure of the field while minimizing subjective interpretation. To complement the qualitative synthesis, bibliometric analysis was integrated to provide an objective mapping of thematic evolution, research concentration, and intellectual structure.

2.1 Identification

The identification of search terms followed a theory-driven and concept-oriented approach, consistent with established guidelines for conducting systematic literature reviews in interdisciplinary domains (Booth et al., 2016; Donthu et al., 2021). Rather than relying on ad hoc or frequency-based term selection, the keyword strategy was grounded in consolidated conceptual frameworks from cybersecurity, digital asset management, and industrial digitalization literature.

The search logic is based on the intersection of cybersecurity and asset management systems operating in digitally intensive environments. The foundational definitions and terminologies were derived from internationally recognized standards and seminal studies that focus on asset lifecycle management and information security, particularly ISO 55000 and ISO/IEC 27001, which establish cybersecurity as a governance and risk management function embedded in asset-intensive organizations (Anon, 2014; ISO, 2009, ISO 22514-7:2021, 2021) These standards provide a stable conceptual anchor for distinguishing cybersecurity in digital asset contexts from general IT security.

Based on this foundation, the keyword set was structured around two primary conceptual domains:

1. Cybersecurity and information security, capturing threats, vulnerabilities, and protection mechanisms in digital and cyber–physical systems (Boyes et al., 2018);
2. Digital asset management and lifecycle governance, examining the management of physical and digital assets across their lifecycle, including maintenance, reliability, and data integrity (Parn & Edwards, 2019; Turk et al., 2022).

Boolean operators applied hierarchically to operationalize this logic. The operator AND was used to connect the cybersecurity and digital asset management groups, enforcing the simultaneous presence of both conceptual dimensions in each retrieved document. Within each group, the operator OR was employed to accommodate terminological diversity and disciplinary variation, thereby improving recall while preserving semantic coherence (Booth et al., 2016; Keele, 2007; Petticrew & Roberts, 2008). Table 1 presents the keywords utilized for the search.

The inclusion of the lifecycle constraint was deliberate, as it ensures that retrieved studies explicitly engage with asset governance, maintenance, or risk management

Table 1 Keywords used in the search

Cybersecurity dimension	Digital asset management dimension
Cybersecurity	Digital asset management
Cyber risk	Asset lifecycle management
Cyber threats	Maintenance management
Information security	Predictive maintenances
Governance and compliance	Asset-intensive systems
Data integrity	Industrial assets

over time, which is a defining characteristic of digital asset management in Industry 4.0 environments. Conversely, the exclusion of technology-specific terms such as IoT or Digital Twin were intentionally excluded from the search equation to avoid a technology-biased corpus and prioritize studies on cybersecurity at the systemic, managerial, and governance levels.

2.2 Screening

Retrieved records were exported with complete metadata fields, including titles, abstracts, keywords, author, affiliations, sources, publication year, and references. The datasets were then merged and processed using the Bibliometrix package in R (Aria & Cuccurullo, 2017; R Core Team, 2025) which supports standardized handling of multi-source bibliographic data. Deduplication procedures were applied to eliminate overlapping records across databases. Data cleaning included normalization of author names, institutional affiliations, keywords, and source titles to reduce inconsistencies arising from formatting differences. This step was critical to ensure analytical consistency in subsequent bibliometric mapping. Throughout the process, emphasis was placed on data integrity and traceability, ensuring that each record could be tracked back to its source database and inclusion decision.

During the screening phase, duplicate records were removed, and titles and abstracts were reviewed to assess thematic relevance. This step serves as a preliminary filter to exclude studies that do not address cybersecurity issues related to the management, protection, or lifecycle governance of digital assets. Screening criteria were applied consistently to reduce selection bias and to maintain alignment with the defined research scope.

During this phase, strict criteria were carefully applied to filter the 1566 papers initially identified—81% from Web of Science and 19% from Scopus—to ensure their relevance and quality for inclusion in this SLR. Only studies published in English were retained to ensure consistency in scholarly communication and to facilitate comparability across international research outputs. This criterion was met by 99.6% of the retrieved records, indicating a strong alignment between the search strategy and the dominant language of publication in this research domain. The review prioritized contributions published in peer-reviewed academic outlets to guarantee scientific validity and editorial quality.

Subsequent filtering based on document type further reduced the dataset, as only records classified as journal articles were retained for analysis. This step resulted in the selection of 702 articles, representing 44.83% of the consolidated corpus, while other document types (e.g., editorials, notes, book chapters, and non-research items) were excluded to maintain methodological rigor and comparability.

Each remaining article was then subjected to a relevance assessment based on title, abstract, and keyword content to ensure explicit alignment with the scope of cybersecurity challenges and solutions in digital asset management. This structured filtering process ensured that the final dataset was both thematically coherent and methodologically robust, forming a reliable foundation for subsequent bibliometric and thematic analyses.

2.3 Eligibility

The eligibility phase involved a full-text assessment of the screened studies. Inclusion and exclusion criteria were applied to evaluate methodological relevance, contextual alignment, and academic quality. Only peer-reviewed publications explicitly addressing cybersecurity mechanisms, threats, frameworks, or governance aspects in digital asset environments were retained. Studies focusing solely on unrelated IT security domains or lacking a clear asset management perspective were excluded. This phase ensures conceptual coherence and methodological consistency across the final corpus.

To ensure methodological rigor, transparency, and direct alignment with the research objectives, explicit inclusion and exclusion criteria were defined and systematically applied according to the guiding research questions (RQs). This procedure follows established systematic review protocols, which emphasize the alignment between research questions, search logic, and screening decisions to reduce selection bias and enhance reproducibility (Booth et al., 2016). Studies were included in the review if they satisfied all the following conditions:

- IC1. Thematic relevance: The study explicitly addressed cybersecurity challenges, threats, vulnerabilities, or protection mechanisms in the context of digital asset management, asset lifecycle management, or digital maintenance systems.
- IC2. Contextual alignment: The study was situated within Industry 4.0—related environments, including but not limited to predictive maintenance, digital twins, industrial IoT, cyber-physical systems, or distributed digital infrastructures.
- IC3. Scientific quality: Only peer-reviewed journal articles were considered, ensuring methodological soundness and academic validation.
- IC4. Language: Publications were written in English, facilitating consistent interpretation and international comparability.
- IC5. Empirical or conceptual contribution: The study provided empirical evidence, analytical frameworks, taxonomies, models, or systematic conceptual discussions relevant to cybersecurity in digital asset ecosystems.

Studies were excluded if any of the following conditions applied:

- EC1. Domain misalignment: The study focused exclusively on cryptocurrency trading, pure cryptographic algorithms, or general IT security without explicit linkage to digital asset management or asset lifecycle contexts.
- EC2. Technological isolation: Papers addressing Industry 4.0 technologies (e.g., IoT, blockchain, digital twins) solely from a functional or performance perspective, without examining cybersecurity implications, were excluded.

- EC3. Non-academic sources: grey literature, including technical reports, white papers, standards documents, theses, editorials, and opinion pieces, were excluded to maintain academic consistency.
- EC4. Redundancy and data quality: Duplicate records across databases and publications lacking sufficient methodological detail were removed.
- EC5. Peripheral relevance: Studies addressing cybersecurity in unrelated sectors or contexts, with no transferable implications for digital asset management, were excluded during full-text screening.

Foundational guidance on SLR was drawn from established protocols (Keele, 2007; Petticrew & Roberts, 2008), enabling a structured filtering of sources. Applied works such as those by (Arsecularatne et al., 2024; Lezzi et al., 2025; Moreaux & Mitrea, 2023) illustrate the practical convergence of cybersecurity with digital asset lifecycle management. Conversely, studies limited to cryptographic theory or traditional IT security lacking contextual application were excluded, as seen in filtering decisions aligned with the review's focus on Industry 4.0 scenarios (Friday et al., 2024; Fyshchuk et al., 2025; Riesco et al., 2020).

The inclusion and exclusion criteria were applied sequentially during the screening and eligibility stages of the review. Titles and abstracts were first evaluated to remove clearly irrelevant records, resulting 254 articles to apply analytical Pathways. This structured filtering process ensured that the final corpus was both thematically coherent and methodologically robust, providing a reliable foundation for subsequent bibliometric and qualitative analyses.

2.4 Analytical Procedures

For this purpose, the study integrates a SLR with bibliometric analysis, allowing both qualitative interpretation and quantitative mapping of the research landscape. Tools such as the Bibliometrix R package (Aria & Cuccurullo, 2017; R Core Team, 2025) and its Biblioshiny interface were employed for their capacity to extract multivariate insights from bibliographic metadata. These tools allow mapping of intellectual, conceptual, and social structures, providing evidence-based support for both researchers and practitioners navigating the cybersecurity landscape of digital infrastructures (Aria & Cuccurullo, 2017; Keele, 2007).

The analytical phase combined quantitative bibliometric techniques with qualitative thematic synthesis. Bibliometric analysis was used to examine publication trends, keyword co-occurrence networks, thematic clusters, and citation structures. These methods enable objective identification of dominant research streams, emerging topics, and structural relationships within literature (Mousavi et al., 2024).

Keyword co-occurrence analysis supported the identification of conceptual groupings related to cybersecurity risks, mitigation strategies, governance mechanisms, and lifecycle concerns. Thematic evolution analysis was employed to observe shifts in research focus over time, particularly in relation to Industry 4.0 adoption. Network mapping techniques were used to visualize relationships among themes and research domains. To avoid over-reliance on algorithmic outputs, bibliometric findings were complemented with qualitative review of central and high-impact studies within each cluster. This triangulation ensured contextual interpretation of results and mitigated the limitations of purely quantitative analysis. The combined analytical approach supports a structured and evidence-based synthesis, providing a robust foundation for the results presented in subsequent sections.

3 Descriptive and Thematic Results

This section reports the descriptive and thematic outcomes derived from the SLR. In line with the methodology described in Sect. 2, the results focus on observable patterns in scientific production, without advancing interpretative or causal claims. The analysis combines descriptive statistics and thematic mapping to characterize the structure of research on cybersecurity in digital asset management.

The results are organized along three complementary analytical dimensions commonly used in systematic and bibliometric studies: (i) descriptive characteristics of the corpus, (ii) temporal and geographical distribution of research activity, and (iii) thematic structures emerging from keyword co-occurrence and clustering. This structure supports the identification of dominant research trends, concentration areas, and structural gaps, providing an empirical basis for the analytical discussion developed in Sect. 4

3.1 Descriptive Analysis for Cybersecurity in Digital Asset Management Documents

The systematic review examines cybersecurity challenges associated with digital asset management and identifies solution strategies proposed in academic literature. This enables the classification of threats and responses at technological, procedural, and organizational levels (Xu et al., 2018; Núñez-Merino et al., 2020).

presents the distribution of document types and academic fields included in the review. Research articles dominate the corpus (44.84%), while Computer Science represents the largest disciplinary contribution (33.33%). This composition indicates that the analyzed literature is largely based on peer-reviewed and methodologically robust research, reinforcing the reliability of the findings. The prevalence of journal articles suggests sustained scientific activity, while the presence of review papers reflects increasing efforts to consolidate knowledge in this domain.

Additional disciplinary analysis shows a strong concentration in Computer Science and Engineering, with comparatively lower representation from Social Sciences, Environmental Sciences, and Business & Economics. This imbalance suggests a predominant focus on technical perspectives, while organizational, social, and governance-related dimensions remain comparatively underexplored.

Figure 2 presents the distribution of document types and academic fields included in the review. Research articles dominate the corpus (44.84%), while Computer Science represents the largest disciplinary contribution (33.33%). This composition indicates that the analyzed literature is largely based on peer-reviewed and methodologically robust research, reinforcing the reliability of the findings. The prevalence of journal articles suggests sustained scientific activity, while the presence of review papers reflects increasing efforts to consolidate knowledge in this domain.

Additional disciplinary analysis shows a strong concentration in Computer Science and Engineering, with comparatively lower representation from Social Sciences, Environmental Sciences, and Business & Economics. This imbalance suggests a predominant focus on technical perspectives, while organizational, social, and governance-related dimensions remain comparatively underexplored.

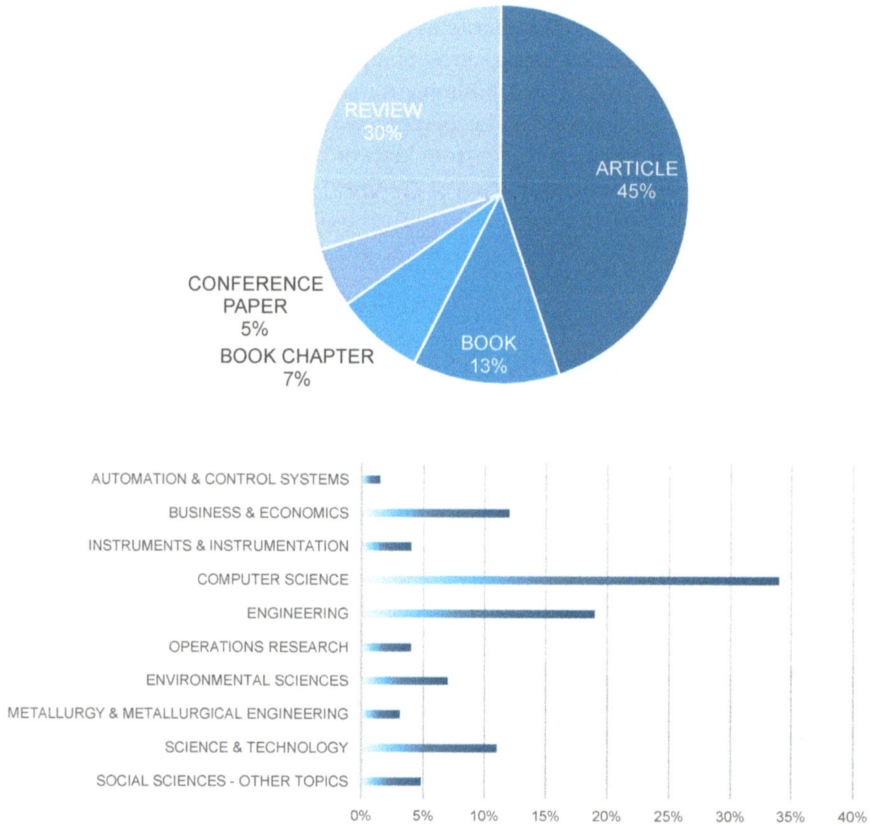

Fig. 2 Document types and academic fields

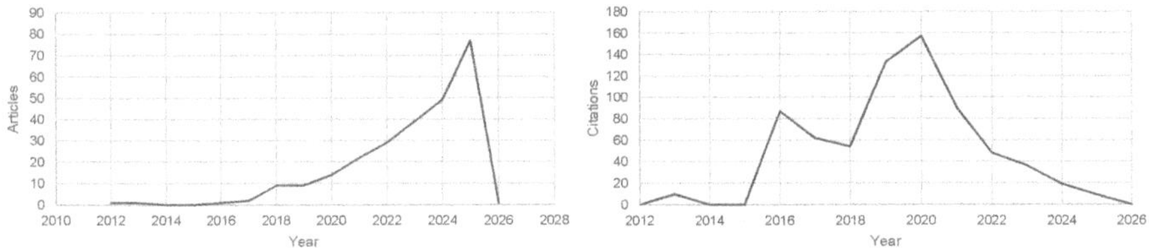

Fig. 3 Annual scientific production and citations

3.2 Temporal Evolution of Cybersecurity in Digital Asset Management

The temporal analysis reveals sustained growth in scholarly output addressing cybersecurity in digital asset management, with a marked acceleration after 2015. Early studies focused on isolated security controls, whereas more recent research reflects the increasing complexity of interconnected digital assets and lifecycle-oriented platforms (See Fig. 3). A pronounced inflection occurs after 2020, coinciding with the COVID-19 pandemic, which accelerated the adoption of remote operations, cloud platforms, and digitally mediated asset management systems. These shifts exposed latent cybersecurity vulnerabilities and intensified academic attention to data integrity, system availability, and operational resilience.

This growth parallels the wider adoption of Industry 4.0 principles, including cyber–physical integration and data-driven maintenance. Peaks in publication activity follow major cybersecurity incidents and regulatory developments, indicating partially reactive research dynamics. Overall, the temporal pattern reflects a transition from exploratory research to structured frameworks addressing systemic risks, governance, and resilience.

This trend is evident in studies focused on cybersecurity risks in construction (Awan & Al Ghamdi, 2019), smart contract vulnerabilities (Ly et al., 2024), and integrated frameworks for information security in asset management (Li et al., 2025; Rafique & Qadir, 2024; Turk et al., 2022). Recent contributions also include proposals for secure data traceability (Riesco et al., 2020), distributed ledger integration (Samuel et al., 2023), and real-time cyber-physical resilience architectures (Friday et al., 2024; Hanif & Yaqoob, 2025).

3.3 Geographical Distribution of Cybersecurity in Digital Asset Management

Figure 4 illustrates the geographical distribution of scientific production. Countries such as the UK, USA, and China exhibit high output dominated by single-country publications, indicating strong internal research capacity. In contrast, countries with

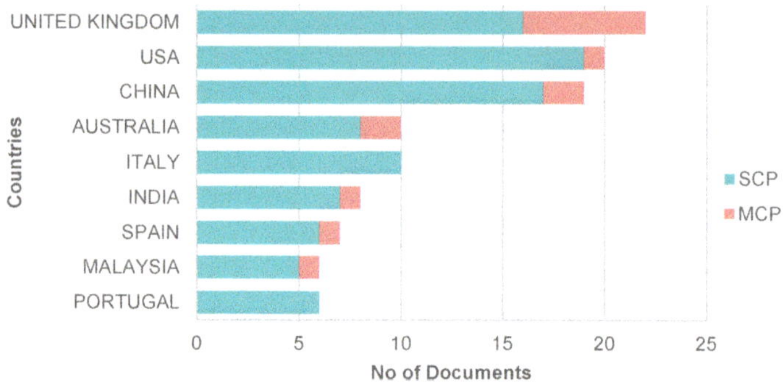

Fig. 4 Most productive countries

lower output rely more heavily on international collaboration, reflecting structural dependence on transnational research networks.

Research activity is concentrated in regions with advanced industrial digitalization and robust research infrastructure, particularly Europe, North America, and East Asia. European studies emphasize regulatory alignment and lifecycle governance, North American research focuses on technical architectures and resilience, and Asian contributions increasingly address scalability, blockchain-based solutions, and data integrity. Limited representation from developing regions highlights a gap between global exposure to cyber risks and research production capacity.

4 Emerging Trends in Cybersecurity for Digital Assets

Digital asset management systems are now fundamental across diverse sectors including infrastructure, finance, energy, and agri-food (Awan & Al Ghamdi, 2019; Goyal, 2025; Pakseresht et al., 2023; Rafique & Qadir, 2024). Their growing reliance on interconnected architectures has intensified cybersecurity risks related to governance fragmentation, system complexity, and inconsistent standards (Toapanta et al., 2019; Turk et al., 2022).

Applied studies demonstrate the convergence of cybersecurity with digital asset lifecycle management, while works limited to cryptographic theory or conventional IT security were excluded to maintain alignment with Industry 4.0 contexts. Bibliometric findings are complemented by qualitative analysis of high-impact studies, enabling a nuanced interpretation of conceptual evolution beyond algorithmic metrics alone (Keele, 2007; Zupic & Čater, 2015).

4.1 Integration of Foundational and Systemic Themes

Thematic trajectories reveal that early research centered on digital security protocols and smart contracts has progressively evolved to address more complex constructions such as data governance, lifecycle risks, and supply chain integrity. This transition is not merely terminological—it reflects a deepening systemic understanding, as evidenced by frameworks that integrate data integrity with lifecycle and governance mechanisms (Hijazi et al., 2023; Moreaux & Mitrea, 2023). The broadening of thematic scope suggests a pivot from purely technological to governance- and resilience-oriented inquiries, driven by the increasing complexity of cyber-physical infrastructures.

Moreover, co-authorship networks and citation analyses highlight the interdisciplinary nature of the field. International collaborations and institutional linkages are particularly pronounced, revealing a globalized epistemic community that incorporates engineering, management, and legal expertise (Jaskula et al., 2025; Nazir et al., 2025). These interconnections enhance both the credibility and applicability of proposed solutions, enabling them to address challenges that transcend disciplinary and national boundaries.

4.2 Geographical Asymmetries and Strategic Positioning

As shown in Figure, scientific production is disproportionately concentrated in China, India, Italy, the United Kingdom, and the United States. This distribution reflects not only their advanced digital infrastructures but also their proactive cybersecurity strategies and investment in national research systems (Aggarwal & Kumar, 2021; Jørgensen & Ma, 2025; Zhang, 2021). China and India were early leaders, fueled by state-led digitalization initiatives and industrial modernization agendas. Italy and the UK gained traction post-2022, driven by EU-level policy alignment and cross-sectoral adoption cybersecurity technologies (Arcos-Argudo & Gutiérrez, 2024; Dong et al., 2023; Ghadiminia et al., 2022; Mousavi et al., 2024; Turk et al., 2022).

These disparities are shaped by structural factors such as regulatory maturity, funding availability, and institutional coordination. Countries with dedicated frameworks for cybersecurity governance exhibit greater thematic diversification and methodological innovation (Jovovic et al., 2017; Delso-Vicente et al., 2025; Friday et al., 2024; Toapanta et al., 2019).Conversely, nations lacking strategic direction risk exclusion from global standard-setting processes, resulting in dependency on foreign technologies and limited influence on international policy debates (Alves et al., 2025; Fyshchuk et al., 2025; Mishra & Tripathi, 2020) (Fig. 5).

The international collaboration network reveals a concentrated yet uneven structure, where India, USA, and China act as central hubs. The strong India-USA

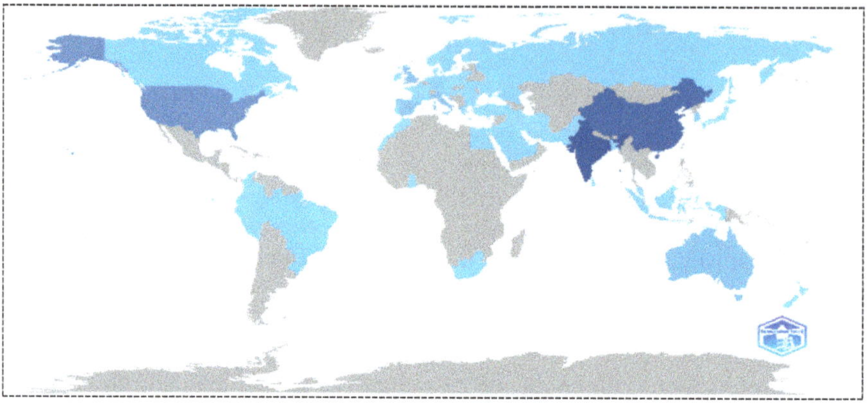

Fig. 5 Country scientific production

linkage underscores their leadership in cybersecurity research. These countries bridge multiple regions, reinforcing their influence on global research agendas.

Distinct clusters emerge: the blue cluster, with India, USA, and UK, suggests dense transcontinental collaboration. The red cluster, led by Italy and Germany, reflects European-Pacific cooperation (Lezzi et al., 2025). Meanwhile, China forms a more self-contained orange cluster, consistent with previous observations on its limited international co-authorships (see Fig. 6) (Toapanta et al., 2019; Mousavi et al., 2024).

Peripheral clusters, such as the purple (e.g., Spain, Colombia) and green (Pakistan, Saudi Arabia), reveal emerging but isolated collaborations, possibly due to institutional or policy limitations (Booth et al., 2016; Brandín & Abrishami, 2021). These

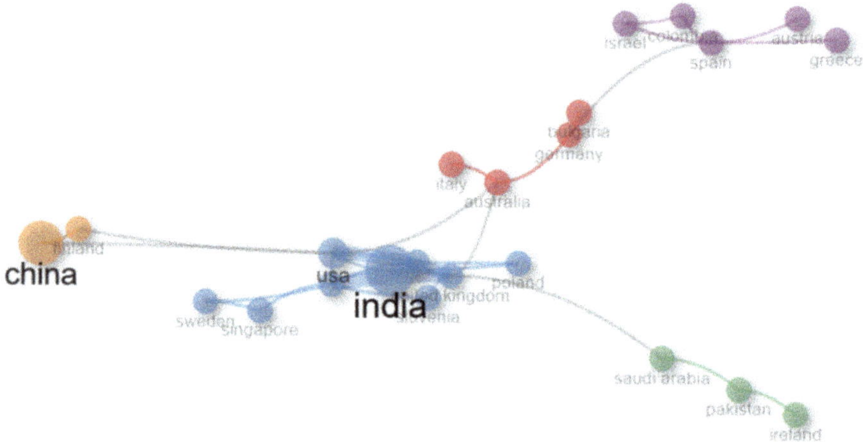

Fig. 6 Countries' occurrences network

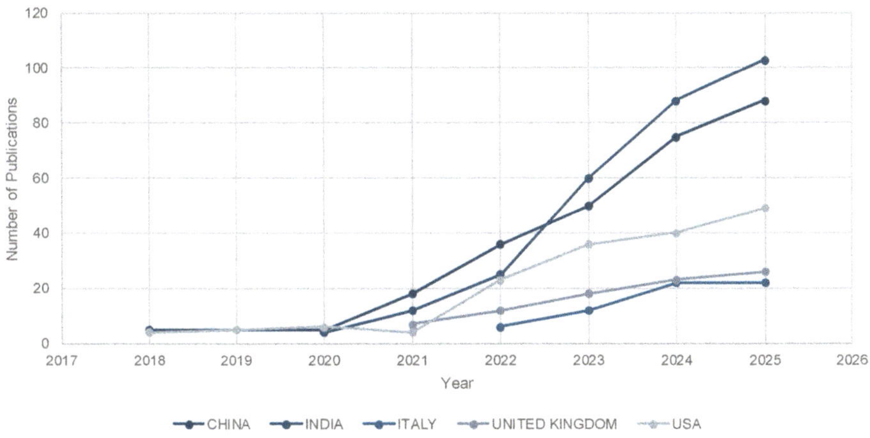

Fig. 7 Temporal evolution of scientific production by country

asymmetries may hinder the integration of diverse regional concerns into global cybersecurity frameworks.

4.3 Temporal Patterns and Post-pandemic Acceleration

The longitudinal evolution of scientific output (see Fig. 7) uncovers three distinct phases. The period from 2008 to 2015 is characterized by foundational and exploratory studies, reflecting the nascent status of digital asset technologies and limited cybersecurity integration (Hanif & Yaqoob, 2025; Lezzi et al., 2025). Between 2016 and 2019, the field experiences thematic consolidation around enabling technologies such as blockchain (Gol & Gondaliya, 2024; Moreaux & Mitrea, 2023), and smart asset tracking (Brandín & Abrishami, 2021; Dong et al., 2023; Ly et al., 2024; Moreaux & Mitrea, 2023).

A sharp acceleration occurs after 2020, the crisis catalyzed digital transformation and highlighted vulnerabilities in remote asset governance, prompting increased investment in cyber-resilient infrastructures (Alves et al., 2025; Manzoor et al., 2024; Zhang, 2021). As a result, by 2025 the field exhibits an average annual growth rate of 26.42%, signaling both a quantitative boom and a qualitative pivot toward operational, systemic, and integrative concerns.

4.4 Thematic Diversification and Conceptual Maturation

The keyword evolution (see Fig. 8) offers empirical insight into the field's intellectual trajectory. Early focus on technical constructs like blockchain and smart contracts has

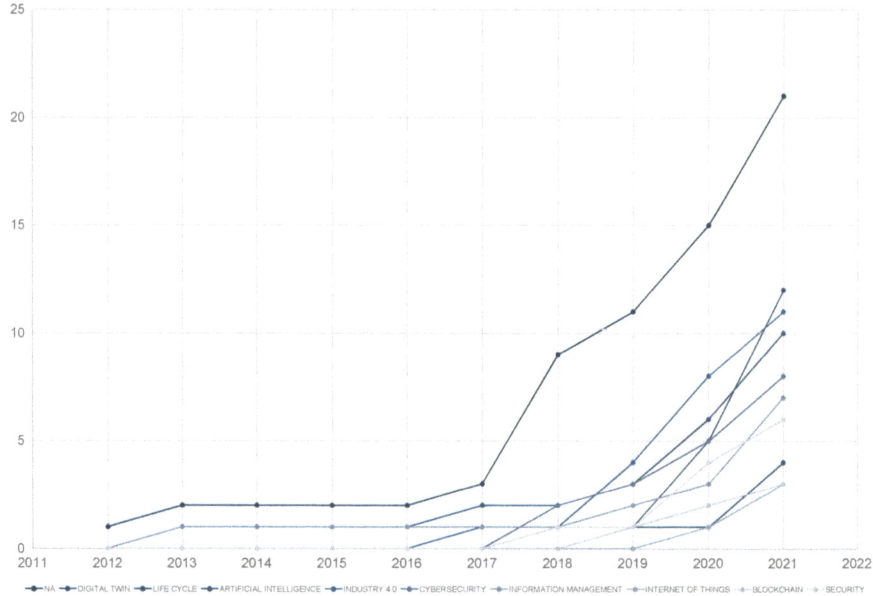

Fig. 8 Distribution of keywords over time

given way to broader terms such as data governance, Digital Twin integration, and lifecycle management (Alves et al., 2025; Brandín & Abrishami, 2021; Kaplinsky, 2017; Moreaux & Mitrea, 2023). This shift implies not only thematic diversification but also conceptual maturation, as cybersecurity is increasingly framed within holistic digital asset strategies.

The comparison of "Author Keywords," "Keywords Plus," and "All Keywords" reveals rising lexical complexity, indicating greater intentionality in defining conceptual boundaries. This pattern affirms the emergence of a cohesive academic field grounded in interdisciplinary dialogue, with engineering, information systems, and policy domains converging to address shared concerns (Delso-Vicente et al., 2025; Dong et al., 2023; Li & Kassem, 2021; Salami Pargoo & Ilbeigi, 2023).

4.5 National Thematic Convergence and Strategic Reorientation

The country-specific analysis in Fig. 9 reveals how thematic priorities have evolved across leading nations. A bifurcation persists between China–India and Italy–UK, shaped by divergent policy instruments and technological capacities. The United

States consistently occupies a central thematic position, bridging governance, technical, and procedural domains (Friday et al., 2024; Parn & Edwards, 2019; Salami Pargoo & Ilbeigi, 2023; Turk et al., 2022).

Italy's recent surge in themes such as Assets, Data, Blockchain, and Management—surpassing the UK by 2024—suggests a deliberate strategic shift, possibly spurred by EU cybersecurity directives and national investments in Industry 4.0 enablers (Arseculiaratne et al., 2024; Gol & Gondaliya, 2024; Moreaux & Mitrea, 2023). This repositioning may elevate Italy's standing in European research leadership and foster innovative public–private collaborations in lifecycle security, AI-enabled asset tracking, and decentralized governance (Alves et al., 2025; Hijazi et al., 2023; Kaplinsky, 2017).

In contrast, the UK shows signs of thematic plateauing, likely due to shifting post-Brexit funding and research agendas. Meanwhile, the US continues to shape global epistemic trends, acting as a stable integrator of diverse thematic concerns.

The observed evolution in thematic complexity, geographical participation, and keyword diversification reflects the consolidation of cybersecurity in digital asset environments as a mature, interdisciplinary field. The global convergence around shared research priorities, particularly after 2020, suggests an emergent consensus on the centrality of cybersecurity to resilient digital governance.

More than tracking technological adoption, the literature reveals a strategic reconfiguration of epistemic priorities aligned with operational imperatives and real-world vulnerabilities. These developments set the stage for a more granular exploration of cybersecurity challenges, including risk typologies, mitigation frameworks, and domain-specific threats. Accordingly, the following section—Cybersecurity Challenges in Literature—shifts from descriptive mapping to analytical engagement with the core risks and barriers identified across the scholarly corpus.

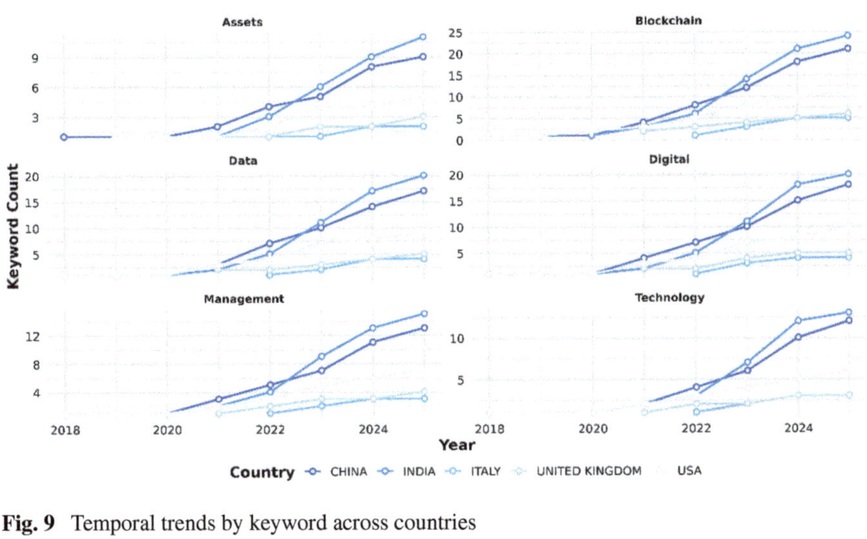

Fig. 9 Temporal trends by keyword across countries

5 Cybersecurity Challenges

Based on the longitudinal and structural patterns previously examined, this section explores the cybersecurity challenges that have emerged in the literature on digital asset management. The thematic diversification identified earlier indicates a maturing discourse that has evolved from isolated technical discussions into a multidimensional research domain. Cyber risk is now understood as a complex interaction between enabling technologies, governance structures, and institutional dynamics, rather than solely due to system malfunction. This broader understanding reflects the systemic nature of cybersecurity threats in digital ecosystems and underscores the necessity of adopting an integrated approach that considers not only vulnerabilities, but also the socio-technical contexts in which they emerge (Aggarwal & Kumar, 2021; Dong et al., 2023; Gol & Gondaliya, 2024; Santa Barletta et al., 2024).

The lack of integrated frameworks that consider technical, organizational, and regulatory dimensions suggests an intellectual dispersion that limits the field's ability to offer comprehensive solutions (Casillo et al., 2022; Delso-Vicente et al., 2025). In response, this section organizes the literature into five critical challenge areas derived from conceptual clustering and co-occurrence patterns, synthesizing them to support both theoretical consolidation and practical application.

5.1 *Technological Risk Vectors and Enabling Infrastructures*

A consistent concern in the literature is the emergence of new risk vectors resulting from the deployment of advanced digital technologies (see Fig. 10). The integration of technology, governance, and smart contracts has increased the complexity of digital infrastructures. Instead of merely creating isolated vulnerabilities, these technologies reshape entire operational environments, introducing new dependencies and failure points (Aggarwal & Kumar, 2021; Gol & Gondaliya, 2024; Hanif & Yaqoob, 2025; Salami Pargoo & Ilbeigi, 2023).

Although blockchain is praised for its decentralization and immutability, it remains vulnerable to consensus attacks, key mismanagement, and smart contract misconfigurations (Aggarwal & Kumar, 2021; Hanif & Yaqoob, 2025). Digital technologies, which are being adopted more in sectors like manufacturing and smart cities, are susceptible to data desynchronization, unauthorized access, and manipulation of simulation parameters (Fig. 11). This can potentially compromise physical operations (Arsecularatne et al., 2024; Gol & Gondaliya, 2024). The proliferation of devices further magnifies risks by multiplying endpoints, many of which lack robust security configurations or updating protocols (Santa Barletta et al., 2024).

These threats are often addressed in isolation. Research streams on blockchain or IoT rarely intersect to address shared vulnerabilities. As a result, conceptual clusters remain disconnected, and mitigation strategies become fragmented. This lack of epistemological integration hinders anticipatory risk management and promotes reactive

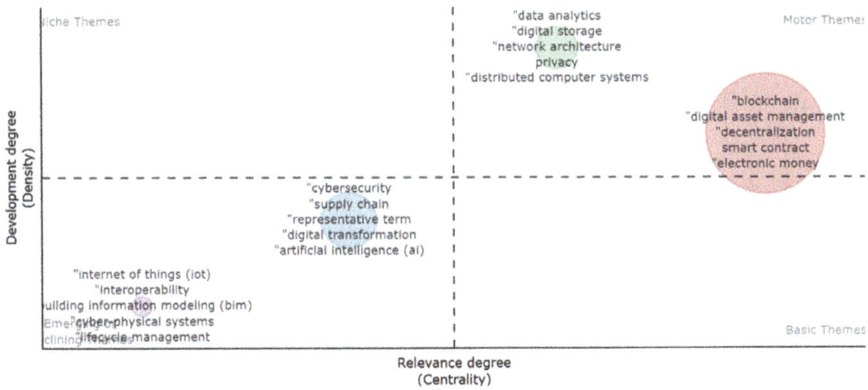

Fig. 10 Strategic diagram represented the thematic importance

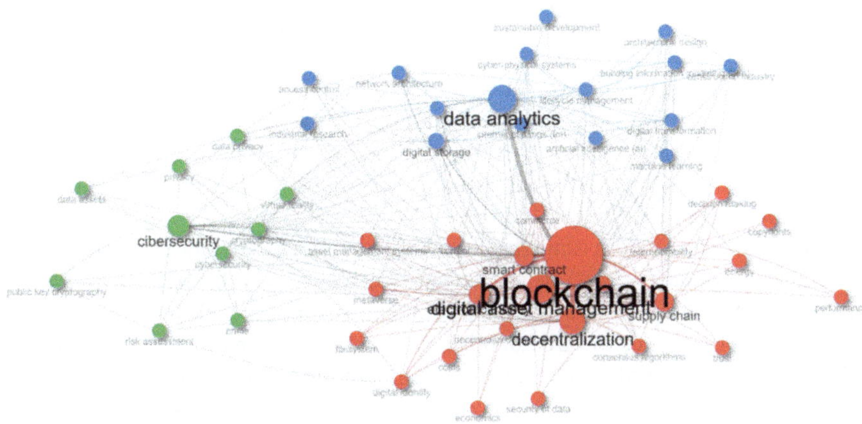

Fig. 11 Keywords network

security approaches (Hanif & Yaqoob, 2025; Salami Pargoo & Ilbeigi, 2023). For instance, cryptographic solutions designed for blockchain are seldom evaluated for compatibility with IoT-based asset environments or smart contract execution under dynamic conditions (Gol & Gondaliya, 2024; Santa Barletta et al., 2024).

Furthermore, the literature emphasizes that, despite being designed to automate secure transactions, smart contracts are often implemented with logic flaws or in volatile operational contexts. This renders them susceptible to exploitation through malicious input or unforeseen external triggers (Aggarwal & Kumar, 2021; Hanif & Yaqoob, 2025). Without a unified framework linking these technological vectors, the ability to predict systemic risks and design adaptive infrastructures is limited.

The analysis reveals that conceptual clusters around terms like blockchain vulnerability, IoT exploits, and smart contract misconfigurations tend to appear disconnected

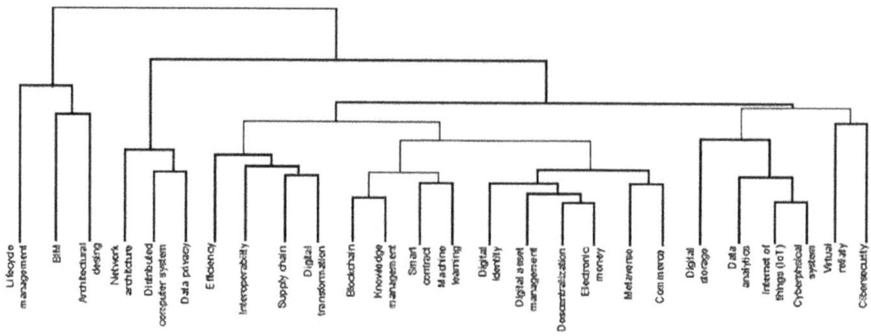

Fig. 12 Conceptual cluster (Dendogram)

in the literature (see Fig. 12). This fragmentation reflects a lack of unified frameworks capable of situating these risks within broader system logics. For example, while blockchain is often hailed as inherently secure, misaligned protocols, consensus manipulation, and cross-chain bridging errors expose assets to integrity and authentication breaches (Aggarwal & Kumar, 2021; Gol & Gondaliya, 2024; Hanif & Yaqoob, 2025). Similarly, IoT devices embedded in industrial assets offer rich functionality but also introduce uncontrollable entry points, especially when deployed without robust firmware updating mechanisms or network segmentation (Arsecularatne et al., 2024; Salami Pargoo & Ilbeigi, 2023).

Moving forward, addressing these technological risk vectors demands cross-disciplinary approaches that do not isolate the technology from its governance, deployment environment, and operational context. Security models must evolve from perimeter defense logics toward adaptive architectures that recognize the fluid and embedded nature of digital assets in critical infrastructures. Only through such integration can the field advance from documenting vulnerabilities to shaping resilient, technology-aligned defense frameworks.

5.2 *Lifecycle-Oriented Cybersecurity Gaps*

The literature highlights a critical gap during the maintenance phase, where limited resources and fragmented monitoring practices hinder the early detection and mitigation of threats. The decommissioning stage is even more neglected, with outdated systems often left operational or accessible, creating residual risks that are difficult to detect and neutralize (Adu-Amankwa et al., 2023). These lifecycle misalignments not only weaken security but also create governance ambiguities, as responsibility for risk management shifts between design teams, operational units, and external partners. Scholars have proposed embedding traceability mechanisms—such as distributed logs and persistent digital identifiers—across all lifecycle phases to support proactive interventions and accountability (Adu-Amankwa et al., 2023; Dong et al., 2023).

Others emphasize the need for governance frameworks that assign clear security roles and protocols for each stage, including secure disposal and asset transition strategies (Kaplinsky, 2017).

The study conducted a mapping about the relationship between contributing countries, dominant keywords, and publication outlets reinforces these observations. In this mapping was established than the concentration of topics such as blockchain, smart contracts, digital assets, supply chain management, and information management in research hubs—particularly India, China, and the USA—indicates a disproportionate scholarly focus on design and deployment stages. In contrast, maintenance, secure decommissioning, and post-operational management remain underrepresented, perpetuating security blind spots. This imbalance reflects the fragmented adoption of security-by-design principles and the absence of longitudinal frameworks ensuring continuity of protection from asset inception to retirement. Furthermore, the diversity of publication outlets, spanning computer science, engineering, business, and industrial applications, underscores the difficulty of establishing cohesive lifecycle-oriented governance. Disciplinary silos limit the cross-stage knowledge transfer required for adaptive and resilient cybersecurity strategies (Arsecularatne et al., 2024; Lezzi et al., 2025; Prasanth et al., 2025; Riesco et al., 2020).

Overall, the fragmented treatment of the digital asset lifecycle creates persistent vulnerabilities, highlighting the need for integrated, forward-looking frameworks that embed cybersecurity considerations from conception to decommissioning, enabling proactive rather than reactive responses to evolving threats.

5.3 Governance, Compliance, and Organizational Challenges

A significant barrier to effective cybersecurity in digital asset environments lies in the absence of standardized governance structures and uneven compliance mechanisms. This institutional fragmentation is particularly problematic in cross-border digital ecosystems, where multiple actors share cybersecurity responsibilities without clear accountability (Friday et al., 2024; Li & Kassem, 2021).

One of the primary causes of this challenge is the disparity in regulatory adoption across jurisdictions. While some countries have introduced comprehensive cybersecurity frameworks, others lag behind or implement sector-specific norms that lack interoperability. This results in legal uncertainty and compliance asymmetries that elevate operational and reputational risks for organizations operating across regions (Parn & Edwards, 2019).

Internally, organizations frequently treat cybersecurity as an operational expense rather than a strategic asset. This perception, coupled with limited awareness and inadequate digital training, leads to resistance against implementing security protocols—especially in traditional industries such as manufacturing or construction (Moreaux & Mitrea, 2023). Furthermore, underinvestment in institutional capacity, insufficient incident response strategies, and siloed decision-making processes reduce organizational adaptability in the face of evolving threats (Jaskula et al., 2025).

Therefore, even technically robust systems can remain vulnerable due to poor organizational preparedness. Authors emphasize the need for cross-functional governance models, dynamic policy frameworks, and cultural shifts that embed security into strategic decision-making, not just IT operations (Friday et al., 2024; Li & Kassem, 2021).

5.4 Interdisciplinary Gaps and Conceptual Fragmentation

Despite the inherently interdisciplinary nature of cybersecurity in digital asset contexts, the literature continues to exhibit conceptual fragmentation. Technical, legal, and managerial perspectives often operate in parallel, with limited cross-referencing and methodological convergence (Delso-Vicente et al., 2025).

Engineering research tends to focus on technological risk vectors, while legal and organizational studies explore regulatory frameworks and institutional dynamics. However, few works bridge these domains to develop unified models or transferable practices that support cross-sectoral integration (Brandín & Abrishami, 2021; Casillo et al., 2022). This epistemic separation leads to duplicated efforts and underutilization of critical insights, impeding the development of scalable and context-sensitive strategies.

Additionally, as a result, research findings often remain confined within disciplinary silos, limiting their visibility and policy impact. Bridging these divides requires coordinated efforts to foster interdisciplinary collaboration, encourage joint authorship, and build knowledge platforms that integrate insights from engineering, policy, and management studies (Delso-Vicente et al., 2025).

5.5 Sector-Specific Risk Frameworks

Although digital asset cybersecurity is frequently treated as a generic challenge, evidence reveals that sector-specific dynamics significantly shape risk exposure, mitigation capacity, and governance responses (Fig. 13). Literature focused on industrial sectors such as energy, construction, finance, and healthcare highlights distinctive vulnerabilities and solution pathways (Mishra & Tripathi, 2020; Radanović & Likić, 2018).

In manufacturing and energy, cybersecurity concerns revolve around real-time control systems, Digital Twin synchronization, and asset traceability under high operational loads (Ghadiminia et al., 2022; Zhang, 2021). In contrast, financial systems face challenges linked to the transparency and legal enforceability of smart contracts, cross-jurisdictional data flows, and decentralized transaction architectures (Turk et al., 2022).

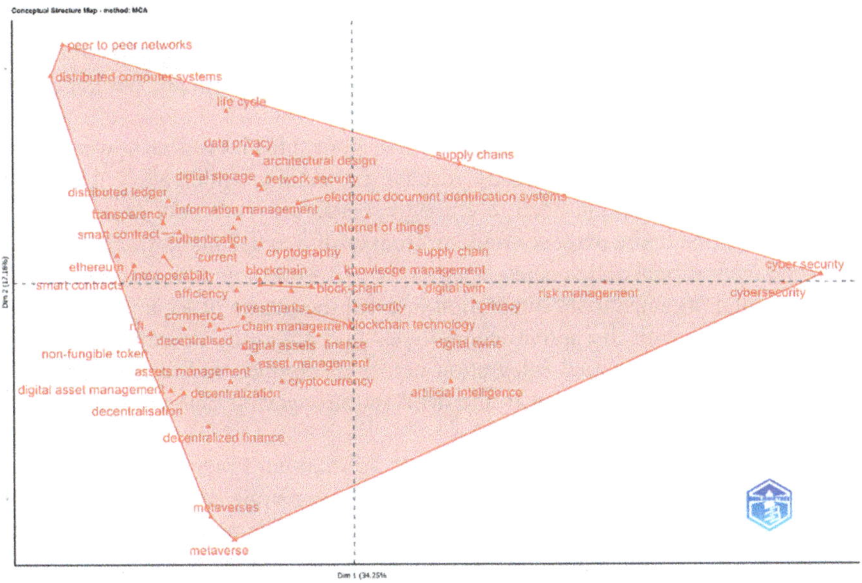

Fig. 13 Factorial analysis

Healthcare infrastructures introduce another layer of complexity, with vulnerabilities stemming from outdated equipment, fragmented data systems, and the criticality of uninterrupted service delivery. The COVID-19 pandemic amplified these risks, prompting urgent calls for sector-specific resilience frameworks (Bocayuva, 2021; Shang et al., 2025).

Smart city environments and the construction sector also present unique cybersecurity needs, particularly regarding IoT deployment, decentralized governance, and real-time decision-making across multiple stakeholders (Hijazi et al., 2023; Zhang, 2021). These conditions require flexible risk management strategies that accommodate dynamic operational contexts and shifting regulatory expectations.

The absence of harmonized taxonomies and context-aware frameworks prevents the effective transfer of lessons across sectors and undermines benchmarking. As highlighted by (Moreaux & Mitrea, 2023), effective cybersecurity must be grounded in institutional specificity and operational pragmatism, avoiding the oversimplification of diverse risk landscapes.

6 Conclusions

The analysis of cybersecurity challenges in digital asset management reveals a fragmented yet increasingly convergent research landscape. Across the five thematic dimensions examined—technological vulnerabilities, lifecycle gaps, governance and organizational barriers, interdisciplinary fragmentation, and sector-specific risk frameworks—a consistent pattern emerges: while the field is clearly maturing, cybersecurity risks remain unevenly addressed across conceptual, temporal, and geographical dimensions.

Technological risk vectors continue to evolve alongside innovation; however, their identification remains predominantly reactive rather than anticipatory. Lifecycle-related gaps underscore the need to embed cybersecurity not only at deployment but throughout the entire asset continuum, from design to decommissioning. Governance and institutional deficiencies—particularly in workforce training, compliance alignment, and organizational integration—reveal the inertia of legacy frameworks when confronted with disruptive technologies and emerging operational models. Similarly, limited conceptual integration across disciplines and uneven treatment of sector-specific contexts point to the need for stronger epistemic alignment and methodological pluralism.

The implications of these deficiencies are substantial. Fragmented governance undermines systemic resilience, sectoral blind spots constrain adaptive capacity, and conceptual silos restrict innovation and cross-domain learning. Without addressing these foundational challenges, digital asset ecosystems risk becoming more vulnerable precisely as they grow more interconnected and strategically critical to organizational and national infrastructures.

At the same time, the thematic patterns identified in this review indicate encouraging signs of convergence. Increasing density in keyword co-occurrence networks, the rising prominence of governance-oriented concepts, and growing interdisciplinarity in high-impact publications suggest an epistemological shift toward integrative and system-level thinking. These developments point to an emerging research phase that moves beyond the diagnosis of isolated threats toward the design of holistic frameworks capable of reconciling security, functionality, and sustainability in digital asset management.

Future research on cybersecurity in digital asset management should therefore prioritize integrated, lifecycle-oriented, and governance-driven security frameworks rather than isolated threat identification. Emerging trajectories highlight the convergence of cybersecurity with digital governance, regulatory compliance, and asset intelligence platforms. Nonetheless, significant challenges persist in operationalizing security across the full asset lifecycle, particularly during early design and end-of-life stages. Further research is also needed to address sector-specific vulnerabilities, especially within critical infrastructures where cybersecurity failures may trigger cascading systemic effects. From a methodological standpoint, advancing the field requires stronger interdisciplinary collaboration that integrates engineering, information security, organizational sciences, and regulatory studies. Finally, greater emphasis should be placed on longitudinal and empirical validation, shifting from predominantly conceptual models toward tested, scalable, and decision-support-oriented solutions that enhance the resilience of digital asset ecosystems in Industry 4.0 and emerging Industry 5.0 contexts.

References

Adu-Amankwa, N. A. N., Pour Rahimian, F., Dawood, N., & Park, C. (2023). Digital Twins and Blockchain technologies for building lifecycle management. *Automation in Construction, 155*, 105064. https://doi.org/10.1016/j.autcon.2023.105064

Aggarwal, S., & Kumar, N. (2021). Transportation system. In *Advances in Computers, 121*, 431–454.

Alves, R., da Silva, J., Junior, L., & Nunes, R. (2025). Enhancing cybersecurity in the judiciary: Integrating additional controls into the CIS framework. *Computers & Security*, 104584.

Anon (2014). *Asset management—Overview, principles and terminology*. Available at: https://www.iso.org/standard/55088.html

Arcos-Argudo, M. and Gutiérrez, D. (2024). Cybersecurity: Comparative study of data protection legislation in Ecuador and Chile. In: *International conference on business and technology* (pp. 208–216). Springer.

Aria, M., & Cuccurullo, C. (2017). Bibliometrix : An R-tool for comprehensive science mapping analysis. *Journal of Informetrics, 11*(4), 959–975. https://doi.org/10.1016/j.joi.2017.08.007

Arsecularatne, B., Rodrigo, N., & Chang, R. (2024). Digital twins for reducing energy consumption in buildings: A Review. *Sustainability, 16*(21), 9275.

Awan, M. S. K., & Al Ghamdi, M. A. (2019). Understanding the vulnerabilities in digital components of an integrated bridge system (IBS). *Journal of Marine Science and Engineering, 7*(10), 350. https://doi.org/10.3390/jmse7100350

Bocayuva, M. (2021). Cybersecurity in the European Union port sector in light of the digital transformation and the COVID-19 pandemic. *WMU Journal of Maritime Affairs*. https://doi.org/10.1007/s13437-021-00240-4

Bolbot, V., Theotokatos, G., Boulougouris, E., & Vassalos, D. (2020). A novel cyber-risk assessment method for ship systems. *Safety Science, 131*, 104908. https://doi.org/10.1016/j.ssci.2020.104908

Booth, A., Sutton, A., & Papaioannou, D. (2016). Systematic approaches to a successful literature review. *Journal of the Canadian Health Libraries Association/Journal de l'Association des bibliothèques de la santé du Canada*. https://doi.org/10.5596/c13-009

Boyes, H., Hallaq, B., Cunningham, J., & Watson, T. (2018). The industrial internet of things (IIoT): An analysis framework. *Computers in industry*, 101, 1-12. https://doi.org/10.1016/j.compind.2018.04.015

Brandín, R., & Abrishami, S. (2021). Information traceability platforms for asset data lifecycle: Blockchain-based technologies. *Smart and Sustainable Built Environment, 10*(3), 364–386.

Casillo, M., Colace, F., Gupta, B. B., Lorusso, A., Marongiu, F., & Santaniello, D. (2022). Blockchain and NFT: A novel approach to support BIM and architectural design. In: *2022 International conference on innovation and intelligence for informatics, computing, and technologies (3ICT)* (pp.16–620). IEEE.

Clavijo Mesa, M. V., Patino-Rodriguez, C. E., & Guevara Carazas, F. J. (2024). Cybersecurity at sea: A literature review of cyber-attack impacts and defenses in maritime supply chains. *Information, 15*(11), 710. https://doi.org/10.3390/info15110710

Delso-Vicente, A.-T., Diaz-Marcos, L., Aguado-Tevar, O., & De Blanes-Sebastián, M. G. (2025). Factors influencing employee compliance with information security policies: A systematic literature review of behavioral and technological aspects in cybersecurity. *Future Business Journal, 11*(1), 28. https://doi.org/10.1186/s43093-025-00452-7

Dong, Y., Hu, Y., Li, S., Cai, J., & Han, Z. (2023). Bim and blockchain-based automatic asset tracking in digital twins for modular construction. *Computing in Civil Engineering, 2023*, 501–508.

Donthu, N., Kumar, S., Mukherjee, D., Pandey, N., & Lim, W. M. (2021). How to conduct a bibliometric analysis: An overview and guidelines. *Journal of Business Research, 133*, 285–296.

Firouzi, F., Farahani, B., Barzegari, M., & Daneshmand, M. (2022). AI-driven data monetization: The other face of data in IoT-based smart and connected health. *IEEE Internet of Things Journal, 9*(8), 5581–5599. https://doi.org/10.1109/JIOT.2020.3027971

Friday, D., Melnyk, S. A., Altman, M., Harrison, N., & Ryan, S. (2024). An inductive analysis of collaborative cybersecurity management capabilities, relational antecedents and supply chain cybersecurity parameters. *International Journal of Physical Distribution & Logistics Management, 54*(5), 476–500. https://doi.org/10.1108/IJPDLM-01-2023-0034

Fyshchuk, I., Noesgaard, M. S., & Nielsen, J. A. (2025). Managing cyberattacks in wartime: The case of Ukraine. *Public Administration Review, 85*(3), 619–627.

Ghadiminia, N., Mayouf, M., Cox, S., & Krasniewicz, J. (2022). BIM-enabled facilities management (FM): A scrutiny of risks resulting from cyber attacks. *Journal of Facilities Management, 20*(3), 326–349.

Gol, D. A., & Gondaliya, N. (2024). Blockchain: A comparative analysis of hybrid consensus algorithm and performance evaluation. *Computers and Electrical Engineering, 117*, 108934.

Goyal, S. R. (2025). Real-world examples of data science and blockchain synergies. In *Human-centric integration of next-generation data science and blockchain technology* (online) (pp. 257–263). Elsevier. https://doi.org/10.1016/B978-0-443-33498-6.00013-3.

Hanif, M. Z., & Yaqoob, N. (2025). Prioritized decision support system for cybersecurity selection based on extended symmetrical linear Diophantine Fuzzy Hamacher aggregation operators. *Symmetry, 17*(1), 70. https://doi.org/10.3390/sym17010070

Hijazi, A. A., Perera, S., Calheiros, R. N., & Alashwal, A. (2023). A data model for integrating BIM and blockchain to enable a single source of truth for the construction supply chain data delivery. *Engineering, Construction and Architectural Management, 30*(10), 4645–4664.

ISO. (2009). Risk management—principles and guidelines: BS ISO 31000:2009. *British Standard International Organization for Standarization, 1*, 1–34.

ISO 22514-7:2021, 2021. *ISO 22514-7:2021 Statistical methods in process management—Capability and performance*. International Organization for Standardization and International Electrotechnical Commission.

Jaskula, K., Kifokeris, D., Papadonikolaki, E., & Rovas, D. (2025). Blockchain-based decentralized common data environment: User requirements and conceptual framework. *Journal of Construction Engineering and Management, 151*(9), 04025112.

Jørgensen, B. N., & Ma, Z. G. (2025). Digital twin of the European electricity grid: A review of regulatory barriers, technological challenges, and economic opportunities. *Applied Sciences, 15*(12), 6475. https://doi.org/10.3390/app15126475

Jovovic, R., Draskovic, M., Delibasic, M., & Jovovic, M. (2017). The concept of sustainable regional development—Institutional aspects, policies and prospects. *Journal of International Studies*. https://doi.org/10.14254/2071-8330.2017/10-1/18

Kaplinsky, H. (2017). Collections management on the blockchain: A return to the principles of the Museum. In *Artists Re: Thinking the blockchain* (pp. 261–274). Torque Editions & Furtherfield.

Keele, S. (2007). *Guidelines for performing systematic literature reviews in software engineering*. Technical report, ver. 2.3 ebse technical report. ebse.

Lawal, O., & Nawari, N. O. (2023). Blockchain and city information modeling (CIM): A new approach of transparency and efficiency. *Journal of Information Technology in Construction, 28*.

Lezzi, M., Corallo, A., Lazoi, M., & Nimis, A. (2025). Measuring cyber resilience in industrial IoT: a systematic literature review. *Management Review Quarterly*, 1–55.

Li, B., Jin, X., Ba, T., Pan, T., Wang, E., & Gu, Z. (2025). Deceptive cyber-resilience in PV grids: Digital twin-assisted optimization against cyber-physical attacks. *Energies, 18*(12), 3145.

Li, J., & Kassem, M. (2021). Applications of distributed ledger technology (DLT) and blockchain-enabled smart contracts in construction. *Automation in Construction, 132*, 103955.

Liberati, A., Altman, D.G., Tetzlaff, J., Mulrow, C., Gøtzsche, P.C., Ioannidis, J.P.A., Clarke, M., Devereaux, P.J., Kleijnen, J., & Moher, D. (2009). The PRISMA statement for reporting systematic reviews and meta-analyses of studies that evaluate health care interventions: explanation and elaboration. *Journal of clinical epidemiology*. https://doi.org/10.1016/j.jclinepi.2009.06.006

Ly, R., Shojaei, A., & Naderi, H. (2024). DT-DAO: Digital twin and blockchain-based DAO integration framework for smart building facility management. In *Construction research congress*

2024 (online) (pp. 96–805). American Society of Civil Engineers. https://doi.org/10.1061/9780784485262.081

Manzoor, J., Waleed, A., Jamali, A. F., & Masood, A. (2024). Cybersecurity on a budget: Evaluating security and performance of open-source SIEM solutions for SMEs. *PLoS ONE, 19*(3), e0301183.

Mishra, S., & Tripathi, A. R. (2020). Platform business model on state-of-the-art business learning use case. *International Journal of Financial Engineering, 07*(02), 2050015. https://doi.org/10.1142/S2424786320500152

Moreaux, A. C., & Mitrea, M. P. (2023). Blockchain asset lifecycle management for visual content tracking. *IEEE Access, 11*, 100518–100539.

Mousavi, Y., Gharineiat, Z., Karimi, A. A., McDougall, K., Rossi, A., & Gonizzi Barsanti, S. (2024). Digital twin technology in built environment: A review of applications, Capabilities and Challenges. *Smart Cities, 7*(5), 2594–2615. https://doi.org/10.3390/smartcities7050101

Nazir, M. A., Roomi, M. A., & Khan, M. R. (2025). Entrepreneurial firms in the crypto era: Adoption trajectories and innovation dynamics. *Journal of Small Business and Enterprise Development, 32*(8), 18–53.

Núñez-Merino, M., Maqueira-Marín, J. M., Moyano-Fuentes, J., & Martínez-Jurado, P. J. (2020). Information and digital technologies of Industry 4.0 and Lean supply chain management: a systematic literature review. *International Journal of Production Research, 58*(16), 5034–5061. https://doi.org/10.1080/00207543.2020.1743896

Pakseresht, A., Yavari, A., Kaliji, S. A., & Hakelius, K. (2023). The intersection of blockchain technology and circular economy in the agri-food sector. *Sustainable Production and Consumption, 35*, 260–274. https://doi.org/10.1016/j.spc.2022.11.002

Parn, E. A., & Edwards, D. (2019). Cyber threats confronting the digital built environment: Common data environment vulnerabilities and block chain deterrence. *Engineering, Construction and Architectural Management, 26*(2), 245–266. https://doi.org/10.1108/ECAM-03-2018-0101

Petticrew, M., & Roberts, H. (2008). *Systematic reviews in the social sciences: A practical guide*. Wiley.

Prasanth, A., Sharma, V., Dhanaraj, R. K., Raj, P. (Eds.) (2025). *Blockchain-based digital twins: research trends and challenges* (1st edn). Apple Academic Press, Inc.

R Core Team (2025). *R: A language and environment for statistical computing*. Available at: https://www.r-project.org/.

Radanović, I., & Likić, R. (2018). Opportunities for use of blockchain technology in medicine. *Applied Health Economics and Health Policy, 16*(5), 583–590.

Rafique, W., & Qadir, J. (2024). Internet of everything meets the metaverse: Bridging physical and virtual worlds with blockchain. *Computer Science Review, 54*, 100678. https://doi.org/10.1016/j.cosrev.2024.100678

Riesco, R., Larriva-Novo, X., & Villagra, V. A. (2020). Cybersecurity threat intelligence knowledge exchange based on blockchain: Proposal of a new incentive model based on blockchain and Smart contracts to foster the cyber threat and risk intelligence exchange of information. *Telecommunication Systems, 73*(2), 259–288. https://doi.org/10.1007/s11235-019-00613-4

Salami Pargoo, N., & Ilbeigi, M. (2023). A scoping review for cybersecurity in the construction industry. *Journal of Management in Engineering, 39*(2), 03122003.

Samuel, R., Lakhanpal, V., & Kumar, K. (2023). Blockchain supercharges digital well program towards cyber-physical drilling system. In *SPE/IADC Middle East drilling technology conference and exhibition* (online) (p. D011S001R001). SPE. https://doi.org/10.2118/214536-MS

Santa Barletta, V., Caivano, D., De Vincentiis, M., Pal, A., & Scalera, M. (2024). Hybrid quantum architecture for smart city security. *Journal of Systems and Software, 217*, 112161.

Shang, W., Li, H., Ni, X., Chen, T., & Liu, T. (2025). BlockGuard: Advancing digital copyright integrity with blockchain technique. *Computers and Electrical Engineering, 122*, 109897.

Sicari, S., Rizzardi, A., Grieco, L. A., & Coen-Porisini, A. (2015). Security, privacy and trust in internet of things: The road ahead. *Computer Networks, 76*, 146–164.

Toapanta, S. M. T., Gurumendi, A. J., & Gallegos, L. E. M. (2019). An approach of national and international cybersecurity laws and standards to mitigate information risks in public organizations of Ecuador. In: *Proceedings of the 2019 2nd international conference on education technology management (*ICETM 2019*)* (online) (pp 61–66). ACM. https://doi.org/10.1145/3375900.3375909

Turk, Ž, García De Soto, B., Mantha, B. R. K., Maciel, A., & Georgescu, A. (2022). A systemic framework for addressing cybersecurity in construction. *Automation in Construction, 133*, 103988. https://doi.org/10.1016/j.autcon.2021.103988

Xu, L. D., Xu, E. L., & Li, L. (2018). Industry 4.0: state of the art and future trends. *International Journal of Production Research, 56*(8), 2941–2962. https://doi.org/10.1080/00207543.2018.1444806

Zhang, Y. (2021). Distributed energy intelligent transaction model and credit risk management based on energy blockchain. *Journal of Information Science & Engineering, 37*(1).

Zupic, I., & Čater, T. (2015). Bibliometric methods in management and organization. *Organizational Research Methods, 18*(3), 429–472.

Reliability and Risk Assessment in Compressors: Impact of the Asset Health Index (AHI) on Maintenance Management and Investment Planning

Sonia Liñán García, Antonio De la Fuente Carmona, Javier Serra Parajes, and Adolfo Crespo Márquez

Abstract This research investigates the impact of aging critical assets on operational reliability and investment planning within energy infrastructure, with a specific focus on the boil-off gas (BOG) compression system at a liquefied natural gas (LNG) regasification facility. The Asset Health Index (AHI) methodology is employed to evaluate compressor degradation and its influence on the probability of failure (PoF) and overall system reliability. A case study involving four BOG compressors is presented, in which thirteen operational scenarios—representative of the plant's actual operating modes—are modeled to assess system performance under real-world conditions. The integration of AHI with probabilistic modeling and decision-support tools such as the Asset Investment Project (AIP) enables more effective maintenance strategies and investment prioritization, thereby supporting service continuity and long-term economic viability. Our results highlight how this approach helps anticipate failures, justifying timely interventions, and enhancing life cycle cost (LCC) analysis frameworks.

Keywords System reliability · Asset health index (AHI) · BOG compressors · Probability of failure (PoF) · Asset investment planning (AIP) · Asset life cycle (LCC)

S. Liñán García (✉) · J. Serra Parajes
Enagás Transporte S.A.U., Madrid, Spain
e-mail: aslinan@enagas.es

J. Serra Parajes
e-mail: jserra@enagas.es

A. De la Fuente Carmona · A. Crespo Márquez
Department of Industrial Management, Universidad de Seville, Seville, Spain
e-mail: antoniodela84@gmail.com

A. Crespo Márquez
e-mail: adolfo@us.es

A. Crespo Márquez et al. (eds.), *Digital Maintenance and Asset Digitalization*, Engineering Asset Management Review 5,
https://doi.org/10.1007/978-3-032-21502-4_5

1 Introduction

Enagás is a leading company in the development, operation, and maintenance of energy infrastructure, with a solid track record in ensuring supply reliability and service performance. Its commitment to operational efficiency and sustainability is reflected in the continuous evolution of its asset management and maintenance methodologies, based on a management model certified under ISO 55001. This framework establishes a systematic approach to maximizing asset value throughout their life cycle by enabling risk-based, performance-driven, and sustainability-oriented decision-making (ISO 55001, 2024).

Currently, Enagás faces a strategically significant challenge: a substantial portion of its high-value assets—critical infrastructure with considerable capital investment—is approaching the end of its useful life. This scenario calls for timely and well-supported decisions regarding the continued operation of these assets, either through reinvestment in their renewal or via intensive maintenance strategies that extend their service life without compromising reliability.

Given this challenge, analyzing how asset aging affects system reliability becomes crucial, as well as the incremental costs associated with maintaining current service levels. Tools such as the Asset Health Index (AHI) and Asset Investment Planning (AIP) methodologies enable the estimation of failure probability and the determination of optimal replacement or intervention points, thereby ensuring efficient life cycle management of equipment. Here, we examine how these strategies shape the reliability of Enagás' services and the economic sustainability of its operations through the application of these methodologies in a practical case study involving an LNG regasification facility.

2 Literature Review

Asset management in critical infrastructure has evolved toward models that integrate reliability, risk, and sustainability as core pillars for decision-making. Within this context, the Asset Health Index (AHI) has become a key tool for assessing the degradation state of equipment throughout its life cycle. Its origin lies in the Health Index developed by UK network operators and standardized by Ofgem (Office of Gas and Electricity Markets [Ofgem], 2017) through the Common Network Asset Indices Methodology (CNAIM, 2017), which several authors, including Crespo Márquez and De la Fuente, have successfully adapted to industrial environments (Crespo Márquez & De la Fuente, 2021).

In engineering terms, the reliability of compression systems has been addressed using classical probabilistic models such as Weibull and exponential distributions, which are widely used in maintenance engineering to estimate the Probability of Failure (PoF) and the reliability function R(t) of assets. Standards such as ISO 14224 (ISO, 14224, 2016) provide guidelines for the collection and analysis of reliability data in industrial equipment, while specific standards like API 617 and ISO 20815 (American Petroleum Institute [API] 617, 2014; ISO, 20815, 2008) govern the design and maintenance of compressors in cryogenic environments (Fernández et al., 2020; Zhou & Li, 2021).

Regarding system architecture, k-out-of-n redundancy models stand out, allowing for the evaluation of overall system reliability based on the operational configuration of equipment. These models have been applied in studies such as that of Musa (Musa, 2018), who analyzed the impact of asset arrangements (series, parallel, partial redundancy) on system availability.

This review highlights the convergence of reliability theory, asset management practices, and technical standards, and supports the use of the AHI as an integrative tool for risk assessment and investment planning in critical systems such as BOG compressors.

3 Methodology and Case Study

3.1 Reliability Study of the Boil-Off Gas Recovery System

The GB-113 compressor and its smaller counterparts—GB-103A/B/C—form the core of the boil-off gas (BOG) recovery system. The function of a compressor is to receive low-pressure gas and, through one or more stages (each with one or more cylinders), increase its pressure to the required level—approximately 5 bars so it can be reinjected into the circuit or storage tank. Each stage operates with a defined pressure ratio, and an intermediate heat exchanger cools the gas to restore density and prevent overheating (Schultz & Paulus, 2015).

In LNG plants, Fig. 1, these units operate under cryogenic conditions, which significantly influence their specialized maintenance requirements. They are equipped with special lubrication systems and "dry" seals that prevent liquefied gas leakage, in compliance with standards such as API 617 and ISO 20815 (API 617, 2014; ISO, 20815, 2008).

Although our compressors are manufactured by DRESSER RAND, the only available reliability reference comes from similar compressors produced by Atlas Copco (Atlas Copco, n.d.), which report reliability levels exceeding 98%. At Enagás, we operate ten Atlas Copco compressors across various compression stations, where technical specialists have confirmed this reliability.

Let us begin by clarifying the concepts of asset reliability and system reliability:

- **Asset reliability**: refers to the probability that a single compressor will operate without failure over a specified period under defined conditions. It is typically measured using metrics such as Mean Time Between Failures (MTBF) or the reliability function R(t), which can be modeled using distributions such as Weibull or exponential (ISO, 14224, 2016).

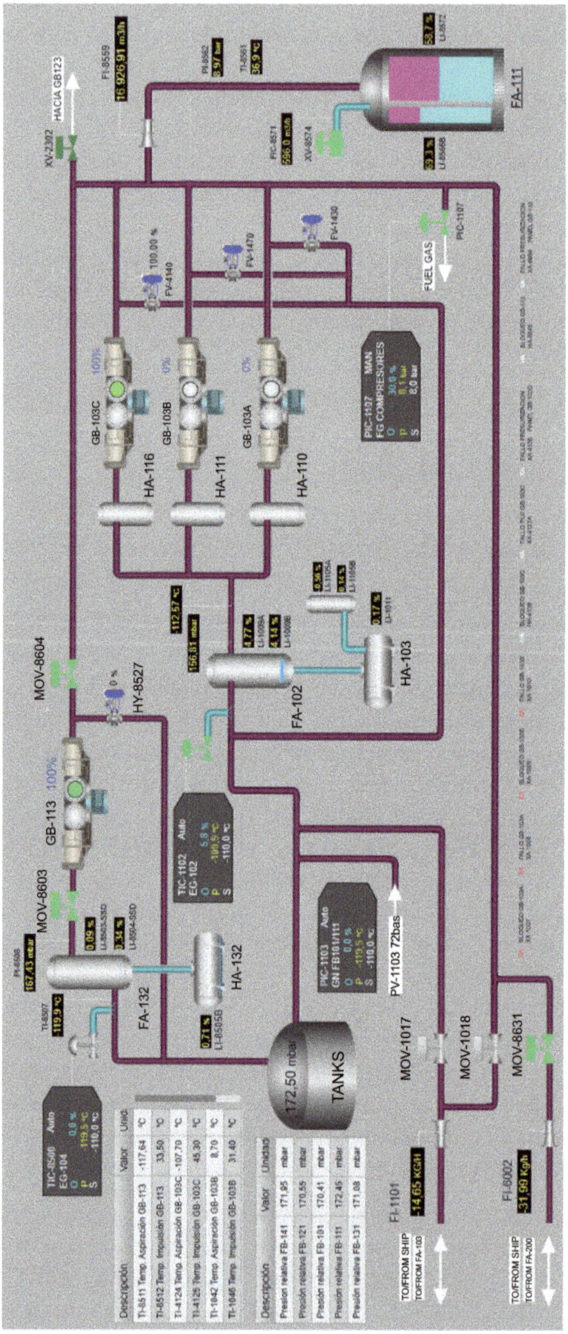

Fig. 1 General schematic of the BOG system with GB-103ABC, GB-113 compressors and storage tanks

- **System reliability**: refers to the probability that the entire set of compressors will fulfill its mission—recovering all boil-off gas (BOG)—without interruptions. This leads us to consider possible configurations such as series, parallel, or k-out-of-n redundancy models (Musa, 2018).

The overall system behavior depends both on the reliability of each individual compressor and on the redundancy strategy or configuration employed. In maintenance engineering, these models are used to estimate system-level reliability based on the reliability of individual assets.

The reliability formulas are as follows:

$$\text{Series}: \mathrm{R}_{\text{series}} = \prod_i \mathrm{R}_\mathrm{i} \tag{1}$$

$$\text{Parallel}: \mathrm{R}_{\text{Parallel}} = 1 - \prod_i (1 - \mathrm{R}_\mathrm{i}) \tag{2}$$

$$\text{k-out-of-n}: R_{k-n} = \sum_k^n \binom{n}{i} R^i (1 - R)^{n-i} \tag{3}$$

Applied Use Case: Compression System Reliability

The objective of this study is to determine the required reliability of each boil-off gas (BOG) compressor under optimal conditions, based on a target reliability for the overall compression system. This is done for each of the plant's operational modes (or scenarios) and subsequently adjusted to account for equipment degradation using the Asset Health Index (AHI). The following assumptions are made:

- **Target system reliability of 98%**: Literature references were consulted to estimate a realistic reliability target for the BOG compression system. According to the manufacturer Atlas Copco, the reliability of their BOG compressors exceeds 98% (Atlas Copco, n.d.).
- **Identical compressor reliability**: Since the compressors are identical, it is assumed that each has the same reliability: RGB-103A = RGB-103B = RGB-103C = RGB-103.

Given a required reliability for the BOG compression system, the goal is to calculate the necessary reliability of each individual compressor across the various operational modes of a liquefied natural gas (LNG) regasification plant.

The BOG compression system consists of one large compressor, GB-113, and three smaller compressors of equal capacity: GB-103A, GB-103B, and GB-103C; are shown in Table 1.

This compression system operates continuously, although it is not necessary for all compressors to run simultaneously. This is because, under any plant operating mode, all generated BOG must be recovered. The plant's operating modes and the

Table 1 Available BOG compressor capacities

Compressor	Capacity (kg/h)	Capacity (Nm^3/h)
GB-103A	3800	4978
GB-103B	3800	4978
GB-103C	3800	4978
GB-113	9120	11,947

Table 2 Plant operating scenarios and BOG generation (annual averages)

Scenario	% Time	Boil off gas (kg/h)
Idle (No loading)	81	14,993
XL Unloading	13	12,264
Loading 7000–12,000	5	17,942
Ship Loading > 35,000	1	21,192

corresponding BOG generation rates, expressed in kg/h as annual averages, are shown in Table 2.

Analysis of Each Scenario Using Annual Average Data, Table 3—Compressor Combinations by Scenario (CCS): It is important to note that each scenario occurs for a specific percentage of the year.

a. Similar conditions for: E01, E02 y E03 Idle /E08, E09, E10 XL Unloading, Table 4.

   It is evident that compressor GB-113 is indispensable for system operation, while among the three smaller units, one consistently remains in standby mode. Under this configuration, it is appropriate to conceptualize GB-113 as forming a dedicated subsystem (S1), and compressors GB-103A, GB-103B, and GB-103C as constituting a second subsystem (S2), characterized by partial redundancy—where one unit is reserved as backup to ensure operational continuity, Fig. 2.

The overall system reliability can be expressed as follows:

$$RSystem = RS1*RS2 \tag{4}$$

where:

- RS1 = RGB-113, since this compressor operates without redundancy.
- RS2 corresponds to a partially redundant configuration, specifically a 2-out-of-3 system, in which two of the three smaller compressors (GB-103A/B/C) are required to be operational.

The results of the calculations are shown in Table 5: Knowing that the system's reliability is required to be 98%, the reliability of subsystems 1 and 2, which we consider identical, is the square root of 0.98 = 0.989949494.

Table 3 Compressor combinations by scenario (CCS)

CCS	Scenario	Boil off gas (kg/h)	Compressors used	Total capacity (kg/h)
E01	Idle	14,993	GB-103A, GB-103B, GB-113	16,720
E02	Idle	14,993	GB-103A, GB-103C, GB-113	16,720
E03	Idle	14,993	GB-103B, GB-103C, GB-113	16,720
E04	Idle	14,993	GB-103A, GB-103B, GB-103C, GB-113	20,520
E05	XL unloading	12,264	GB-103A, GB-113	12,920
E06	XL unloading	12,264	GB-103B, GB-113	12,920
E07	XL unloading	12,264	GB-103C, GB-113	12,920
E08	XL unloading	12,264	GB-103A, GB-103B, GB-113	16,720
E09	XL unloading	12,264	GB-103A, GB-103C, GB-113	16,720
E10	XL unloading	12,264	GB-103B, GB-103C, GB-113	16,720
E11	XL unloading	12,264	GB-103A, GB-103B, GB-103C, GB-113	20,520
E12	Loading 7000–12,000	17,942	GB-103A, GB-103B, GB-103C, GB-113	20,520
E13	Loading > 35,000	21,192	No feasible combination	

Table 4 Compressor configuration in scenarios E01 and E08

E01	BOG (kg/h)	Compressors used	Capacity (kg/h)
Idle	14,993	GB-103A	3800
		GB-103B	3800
		GB-103C	Back-up
		GB-113	9120
		Total	16,720
E08	BOG (kg/h)	Compressors used	Capacity (kg/h)
XL unloading	12,264	GB-103A	3800
		GB-103B	3800
		GB-103C	Back-up
		GB-113	9120
		Total	16,720

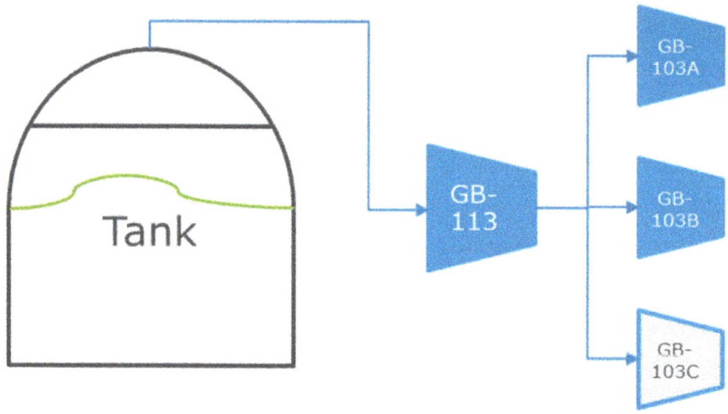

Fig. 2 Configuration of subsystems S1 and S2 with one backup compressor

Table 5 Individual reliabilities and subsystem reliabilities in Scenario E01

E01	Subsystem reliability	Compressor	Compressor reliability
Subsystem 2	0.989949494	GB-103A	0.94
		GB-103B	0.94
		GB-103C	0.94
Subsystem 1	0.989949494	GB-113	0.989

3.1.1 .

b. Similar conditions for E05, E06 y E07: XL Unloading, Table 6.

   Compressor GB-113 plays a pivotal role in maintaining system functionality, whereas among the three smaller compressors, one is consistently kept in reserve to safeguard operational continuity.

This architecture corresponds to a 1-out-of-3 configuration in Subsystem S2, where any one of the smaller compressors can fulfill the required capacity, while the remaining two serve as backups. Such a configuration enhances system resilience and

Table 6 Compressor configuration in Scenario E05

E05	BOG (kg/h)	Compressor used	Capacity (kg/h)
XL Unloading	12,264	GB-103A	3800
		GB-103B	Back-up
		GB-103C	Back-up
		GB-113	9120
12,920			

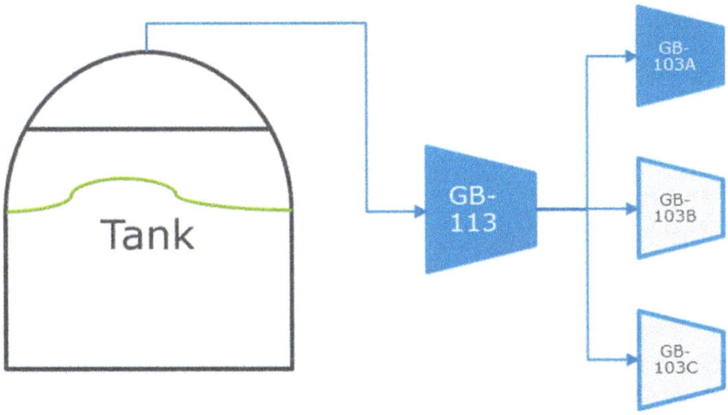

Fig. 3 Configuration of subsystems S1 and S2 with two backup compressors

ensures operational continuity even in the presence of multiple component failures, Fig. 3.

The overall system reliability can be expressed as follows:

$$RSystem = RS1 * RS2 \tag{5}$$

where:

- RS1 = RGB-113, since this compressor operates without redundancy.
- RS2 corresponds to a partially redundant configuration, specifically a 1-out-of-3 system, in which two of the three smaller compressors (GB-103A/B/C) are required to be operational.

The results of the calculations are shown in Table 7.

c. Similar conditions for E04 Idle/ E11 XL Unloading/E12 Unloading 7000–12,000, Table 8.

In this case, all compressors are used simultaneously to recover the full boil-off gas (BOG) flow.

Table 7 Individual reliabilities and subsystem reliabilities in Scenario E05

E05	Subsystem reliability	Compressor	Compressor reliability
Subsystem 2	0.989949494	GB-103A	0.785
		GB-103B	0.785
		GB-103C	0.785
Subsystem 1	0.989949494	GB-113	0.989

Table 8 Compressor configuration in Scenarios E04, E11 y E12

E04	BOG (kg/h)	Compressors Used	Capacity (kg/h)
Idle	14,993	GB-103A	3800
		GB-103B	3800
		GB-103C	3800
		GB-113	9120
		Total	20,520
E11	BOG (kg/h)	Compressors used	Capacity (kg/h)
XL Unloading	12,264	GB-103A	3800
		GB-103B	3800
		GB-103C	3800
		GB-113	9120
		Total	20,520
E12	BOG (kg/h)	Compressors used	Capacity (kg/h)
Unloading 7000–12,000	17,942	GB-103A	3800
		GB-103B	3800
		GB-103C	3800
		GB-113	9120
		Total	20,520

Configuration A

Under these conditions, compressor GB-113 can be modeled as forming a dedicated subsystem (S1), while compressors GB-103A, GB-103B, and GB-103C constitute a second subsystem (S2). These two subsystems are assumed to operate in parallel, contributing jointly to the system's total capacity, Fig. 4.

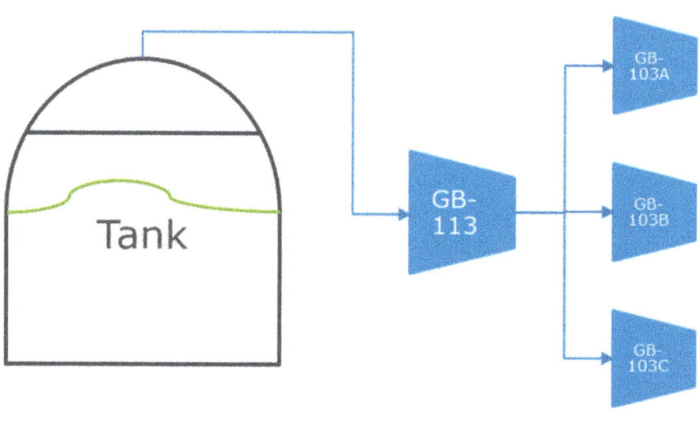

Fig. 4 Configuration of subsystems S1 and S2 without back-up

The overall system reliability can be expressed as follows:

$$RSystem = RS1 * RS2 \tag{6}$$

where:

- RS1 = RGB-113
- RGB-103A = RGB-103B = RGB-103C = RGB-103.
- The system operates without any standby compressors.

The results of the calculations are shown in Table 9.

Configuration B

Alternatively, the system can be modeled as a single integrated unit in which GB-113, and the three smaller compressors (GB-103A/B/C) operate in parallel as a unified subsystem. This configuration assumes no internal subdivision, and all compressors contribute simultaneously to the system's reliability and capacity, Fig. 5.

The overall system reliability can be expressed as follows:

$$RSystem = 1 - [(1 - R_{\mathrm{GB113}}) * (1 - R_{\mathrm{GB103A}}) * (1 - R_{\mathrm{GB103B}}) * (1 - R_{\mathrm{GB103C}})] \tag{7}$$

where:

- Dado que los compresores son idénticos, podemos suponer RGB-103A = RGB-103B = RGB-103C = RGB-103.
- The system operates without any standby compressors.

The results of the calculations are shown in Table 10.

Key Insights

- Redundancy strategy matters: Moving from 2-out-of-3 to 1-out-of-3 dramatically improves fault tolerance.
- GB-113 is critical: Its reliability dominates system performance; preventive maintenance here is essential.
- Trade-off between capacity and resilience: Configurations with backups (E01/E05) offer better operational continuity than full-load configurations (E12).

Table 9 Individual reliabilities and subsystem reliabilities in A (E12A)

E12 A	Subsystem reliability	Compressor	Compressor reliability
Subsystem 2	0.989949494	GB-103A	0.785
		GB-103B	0.785
		GB-103C	0.785
Subsystem 1	0.989949494	GB-113	0.989

Fig. 5 Configuration of subsystems S1 and S2 all in parallel and without backup

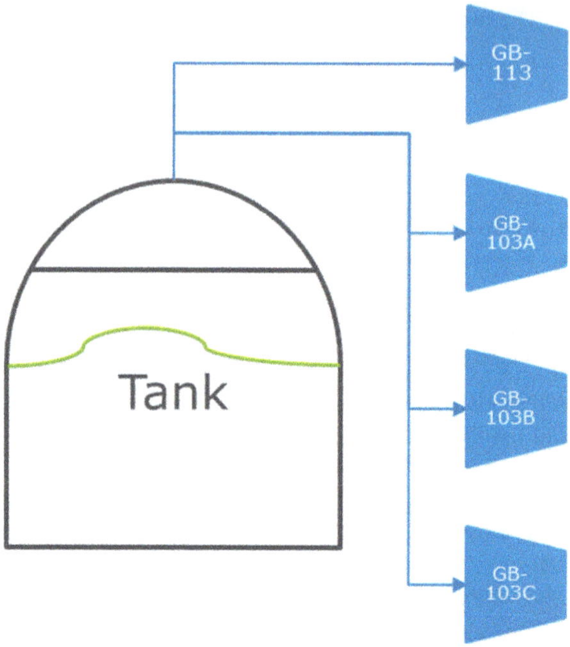

Table 10 Individual reliabilities and subsystem reliabilities in B (E12B)

E12 B	Subsystem reliability	Compressor	Compressor reliability
System	0.98	GB-103A	0.75
		GB-103B	0.75
		GB-103C	0.75
		GB-113	0.75

- Target reliability (98%) achieved: Through appropriate redundancy and subsystem design.

3.2 *The Impact of the Asset Health Index (AHI) on Reliability and Long-Term Projection*

Applying the AHI enables linking the technical condition of an asset to maintenance decisions and investment planning, within a structured asset management framework. This model researchers have adapted in the literature to industrial contexts by authors such as Crespo Márquez and De la Fuente (Crespo Márquez & De la Fuente, 2021), integrating AHI with probabilistic reliability models and operational risk assessment in critical systems.

Estimation of Failure Probability (PoF) from AHI

The next step in the causal chain is to transform the AHI value into an estimate of the asset's annual probability of failure (PoF), measured here as an annual failure rate. This relationship is modeled using a smoothed exponential function, based on a third-order Taylor series expansion, which avoids abrupt jumps in the risk curve:

$$PoF(AHI) = K * \left(1 + C * AHI + \frac{(1 + C * AHI)^2}{2} + \frac{(1 + C * AHI)^3}{6}\right) \quad (8)$$

where:

- K: Standard failure rate, calibrated to reflect the failure rate of a new asset.
- C: sensitivity coefficient to AHI. Must ensure the failure rate becomes worst known scenario (normally a multiple of the standard failure rate) when AHI reaches value 10.

The values of parameters K and C were selected for illustrative purposes to explore the model's behavior under realistic degradation scenarios. This model incorporates sensitivity to progressive asset deterioration. As noted by Achouch et al. (Achouch et al., 2022), the nonlinear growth of PoF is essential for anticipating intervention thresholds that ensure operational continuity and minimize unexpected failure events. From the threshold AHI $\approx$ 5.5—typically identified in practice as the zone of accelerated degradation—PoF begins to increase significantly.

Modeling the Impact of Health on System Reliability

The reliability R(t) of an asset is defined as the probability that it operates without failure over a time interval t, under specific conditions. Based on the annual PoF derived from AHI, individual reliability can be modeled using the negative exponential function:

$$R(t) = e^{-PoF*t} \quad (9)$$

This formulation aligns with an exponential distribution of time between failures, valid during the useful life phase where the failure rate is approximately constant. Its applicability is supported by studies in industrial maintenance (Crespo Márquez & De la Fuente, 2021).

When considering a system composed of multiple assets, overall reliability depends on its architecture:

$$\text{Series} : \mathrm{R}_{\text{series}} = \prod_i \mathrm{R}_\mathrm{i} \quad (10)$$

$$\text{Parallel} : \mathrm{R}_{\text{Parallel}} = 1 - \prod_i (1 - \mathrm{R}_\mathrm{i}) \quad (11)$$

$$\text{k-de-n} : R_{k-n} = \sum_{k}^{n} \binom{n}{i} R^i (1 - R)^{n-i} \tag{12}$$

System sensitivity to variations in individual AHI increases in series configurations or those with low redundancy. Therefore, AHI and its evolution directly influence aggregate reliability metrics and planning for shutdowns, spare parts, and resources.

Forecasting AHI Evolution Over Time

The evolution of AHI over time is modeled using a modified exponential function that integrates both the deterioration rate β2 and an aging reduction factor r:

$$AHIfuture(t) = AHI(t) * e^{(\beta_2 * t)/r} \tag{13}$$

where:

- AHI(t): current health index value.
- $\beta_2 = \frac{\ln\left(\frac{AHI(t)}{AHI_0}\right)}{Age}$: aging rate adjusted to the asset's actual condition.
- r: Ageing Reduction Factor, defined in CNAIM (2017) based on current AHI:
- r = 1.0 when AHI < 2
- r = 1.5 when AHI > 5.5
- Lineal interpolation when 2 ≤ AHI ≤ 5.5.

The result is bound below by 1 (undeteriorated asset) and above by 15 (asset with imminent failure). This model allows forecasting the trajectory of AHI under various operational and maintenance scenarios.

Applied Use Case: Compression System Divided into Two Subsystems

To illustrate the practical application of the Asset Health Index (AHI) methodology and its impact on system reliability, a representative use case has been modeled based on a liquefied natural gas (LNG) compressor installation divided into two functional subsystems:

- Subsystem S1: Composed solely of the high-capacity compressor GB-113. This compressor operates continuously and lacks redundancy, meaning its reliability directly determines the overall system reliability.
- Subsystem S2: Composed of three smaller compressors—GB-103A, GB-103B, and GB-103C—one of which serves as a backup. To ensure service continuity, it is sufficient for at least two of the three compressors in the subsystem to remain operational.

The minimum demand required is 14993 kg/h, while the total system capacity with all three compressors actively reaches 16,720 kg/h.

Initial AHI values for the four compressors are set as follows:

- 2.1 for GB-113,

- 2.5 for GB-103A,
- 4.5 for GB-103B, and
- 1.5 for GB-103C.

The temporal evolution of the AHI is projected over a 10-year horizon, applying a maintenance policy that schedules an intervention (e.g., overhaul) when the AHI reaches a value of 6. Restoration does not return the asset to its original condition (AHI = 1) but rather reduces it to slightly above 1.

From the AHI, the annual Probability of Failure (PoF) is calculated using a third-order Taylor-based function, followed by the estimation of the annual reliability of each compressor. Finally, the overall system reliability is computed considering the series configuration of S1 and the partial redundancy (2-out-of-3) configuration of S2.

$$R\text{system} = R\text{GB}113 * RS2 \tag{14}$$

where:

$$RS2 = P(\textit{at least } 2 \textit{ out of } 3 \textit{ compressors operational}) \tag{15}$$

Sensitivity Analysis of Parameter K

To evaluate how the standard failure rate (K) affects system performance, a sensitivity analysis was conducted by varying K in the calculation of the Probability of Failure (PoF). The range considered was 0,0001 < K < 0,5; however, to maintain an acceptable level of system reliability, the final analysis was restricted to cases where K ≤ 0,01.

Figure 6 illustrates the evolution of the Asset Health Index (AHI) across the four compressors over a 10-year period. A progressive degradation is observed, with restorative interventions triggered upon reaching an AHI value of 6, particularly evident in compressor GB-103A.

The timeframe is illustrative, as each compressor started with different initial conditions in wear and operating hours.

The following Fig. 7 presents the evolution of the Probability of Failure (PoF) for compressor GB-103A under different values of parameter K. A sustained increase is observed over time and with increasing values of K, confirming its key role in the model's sensitivity.

The next Fig. 8 shows the reliability of the complete system (S1 × S2) over a 10-year period for the selected values of K. It is evident that for K ≤ 0,01, system reliability remains above 85%, whereas higher values would lead to a premature decline in reliability.

As demonstrated in the sensitivity analysis, values of K greater than 0,01 rapidly degrade system reliability, underscoring the importance of carefully calibrating this parameter to keep the system within safe operational margins.

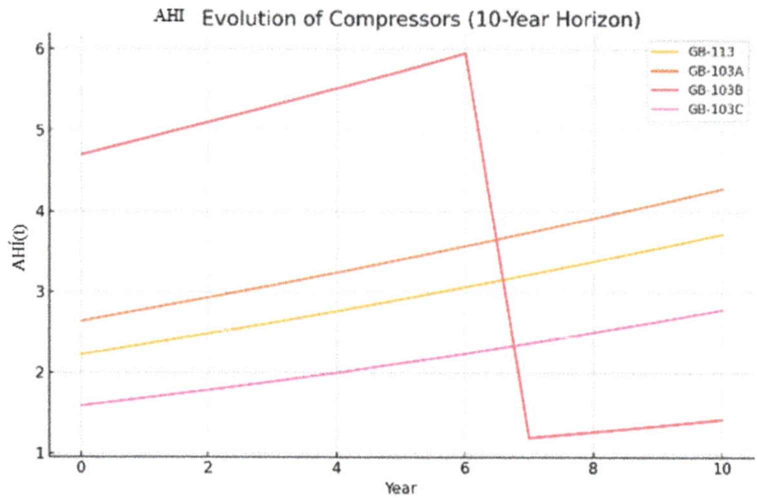

Fig. 6 Evolution of the AHI in the compressors over a 10-year period

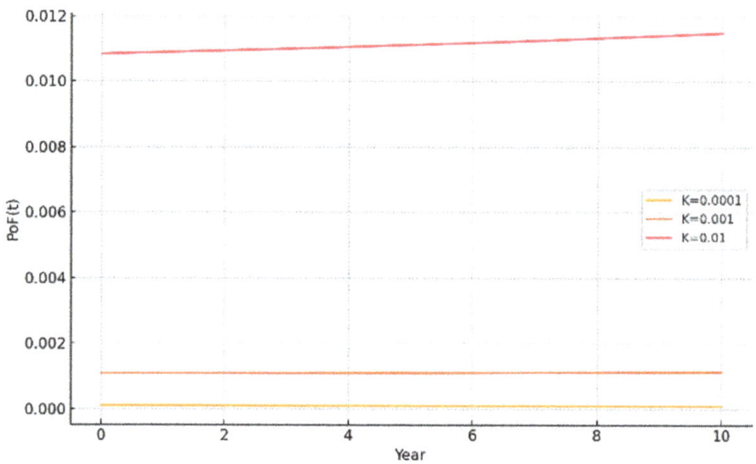

Fig. 7 Evolution of the PoF in GB-103A for different values of K

This use case confirms the usefulness of the AHI + PoF + R(t) model for evaluating maintenance scenarios and justifying investments (OPEX or CAPEX), providing a quantitative view of the impact of asset degradation on system performance.

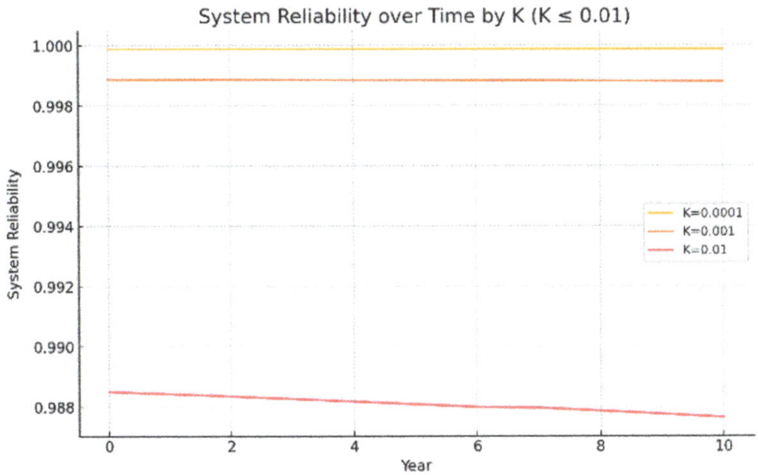

Fig. 8 Reliability of the complete S1 × S2 system for 10 years

4 Conclusions

The analysis demonstrates that system architecture and redundancy strategies are decisive factors for ensuring operational continuity in regasification facilities. Configurations such as 2-out-of-3 versus 1-out-of-3 reveal substantial differences in fault tolerance, reinforcing the need to design scenarios that balance capacity and resilience.

Moreover, the sensitivity of parameter **K** confirms that calibrating failure rates is critical to maintaining safe reliability margins. Values above 0.01 accelerate system degradation, highlighting the importance of defining clear technical thresholds during design and maintenance phases.

The projected degradation trends indicate that preventive interventions should be scheduled not only based on condition but also considering aging dynamics and subsystem interactions. This approach anticipates scenarios where the lack of redundancy in critical equipment (such as GB-113) could compromise overall operation.

Finally, the study shows that integrating probabilistic models with real operational data provides a robust foundation for technical and economic decision-making, particularly for assets nearing the end of their life cycle. Beyond the methodology, the real value lies in transforming data into objective criteria for defining maintenance and renewal policies that ensure service sustainability.

5 Implications for Future Research

This study assumes identical reliability across compressors and does not incorporate real-time sensor data or uncertainty in AHI estimation. These simplifications may limit the model's applicability in more dynamic or heterogeneous operational environments. Sensor inaccuracies or incomplete inspection data can introduce uncertainty in AHI values, potentially skewing PoF estimations. Incorporating confidence intervals or probabilistic bounds in future models could mitigate this risk and improve decision robustness.

Based on the results obtained, several development opportunities have been identified that could enrich and expand the applicability of the proposed model, both from methodological and operational perspectives:

1. **Extension of the AHI model to other critical assets**:
   The methodological approach based on the Asset Health Index (AHI) could be extended to other strategic equipment in regasification plants or energy infrastructures, such as cryogenic valves, heat exchangers, or pumping systems. This would allow for validation of its applicability and adjustment of the model's sensitivity parameters according to the type of asset. Recent studies report sensor error margins quantified through metrics such as MAE and RMSE and emphasize the need for confidence intervals in predictive models to mitigate these uncertainties (Belim et al., 2024; Okirie et al., 2024; Pakala et al., 2025; Ucar et al., 2024; Wiese, 2024). Incorporating confidence intervals or probabilistic bounds in future models could reduce this risk and improve decision robustness.
2. **Integration with digital twins and predictive maintenance**:
   The evolution of the AHI could be linked to digital twin platforms to simulate real-time degradation scenarios and optimize predictive maintenance strategies (Kerkeni et al., 2024; Martínez & Gómez, 2023; Wang et al., 2022). This research line would enable more accurate failure anticipation and reduced operational costs.
   To turn this line of inquiry into a research and implementation agenda, the following points are proposed:
   A well-designed digital twin should be based on a layered architecture.

- Physical layer: sensor data (temperature, vibration, pressure, operating hours).
- Data layer: continuous update of AHI values, enriched with environmental and operational data (Candón Fernández et al., 2025).
- Model layer: reliability models (Weibull, exponential, k-out-of-n) calibrated dynamically with incoming AHI updates (Duan et al., 2024).
- Decision layer: simulation of different maintenance or investment scenarios with predicted PoF trends (Mikołajewska et al., 2025).

This integration raises key questions: How does continuous AHI recalculation affect predictive accuracy compared to periodic updates? What benefits does scenario simulation offer in terms of cost optimization and risk reduction? Can a digital twin scale from a set of compressors to encompass critical assets such as valves, pumps, or heat exchangers without losing accuracy? These issues align with emerging trends in prescriptive maintenance, which seek to move from prediction to active recommendation of interventions (Orošnjak et al., 2025).

1. **Multi-criteria decision-making optimization**:
   Future research could incorporate multi-criteria decision-making (MCDM) techniques to balance reliability, cost, and risk in investment planning, integrating the AHI with decision models such as AHP, TOPSIS, or Bayesian analysis.
2. **Empirical validation with historical failure data**:
   It would be valuable to compare the predictions of the AHI + PoF model with actual failure and maintenance records, which would allow for calibration of model coefficients and enhancement of its predictive capability.
3. **Application in regulatory and normative contexts**:
   Given that the AHI is aligned with frameworks such as ISO 55001 and CNAIM, future studies could explore its use as a technical reporting tool for regulatory bodies, supporting investment justifications or asset renewal decisions.

These research directions open new opportunities for methodological refinement in asset management and contribute to advancing reliability-centered practices. They aim to enhance predictive accuracy, optimize maintenance strategies, and support the development of sustainable and efficient operational models within the energy sector.

References

Achouch, A., et al. (2022). Modelos de predicción de fallos en activos industriales críticos. *Journal of Asset Management, 23*(2), 145–162.

Belim, M., Meireles, T., Gonçalves, G., & Pinto, R. (2024). Forecasting models analysis for predictive maintenance. *Frontiers in Manufacturing Technology, 4*, 1475078. https://doi.org/10.3389/fmtec.2024.1475078

Candón Fernández, E., Crespo Márquez, A., Guillén López, A. J., & Hidalgo Fort, E. (2025). Framework for asset digitalization: IoT platforms and asset health index in maintenance applications. *Applied Sciences, 15*(3), 1524. https://doi.org/10.3390/app15031524

CNAIM (2017). *common network asset indices methodology*. Ofgem, Reino Unido.

Atlas Copco (s.f.). Catálogo técnico de compresores industriales. Recuperado de https://www.atlascopco.com

Crespo Márquez, A., & De la Fuente Carmona, A. (2021). *Gestión de activos industriales: Modelos de fiabilidad y riesgo aplicados al ciclo de vida*. Editorial Universidad de Sevilla.

Duan, C., Zhang, Z., Zhao, L., & Yu, Y. (2024). Reliability and risk assessment of digital twin system based on improved failure mode and effects analysis. *The International Journal of Advanced Manufacturing Technology, 133*, 3937–3955. https://doi.org/10.1007/s00170-024-13896-y

Fernández, R., et al. (2020). Condition-based maintenance strategy for LNG compressors using vibration analysis. *Reliability Engineering & System Safety, 193*, 106617.

ISO 14224 (2016). *Petroleum, petrochemical and natural gas industries—Collection and exchange of reliability and maintenance data for equipment*. International Organization for Standardization.

ISO 20815 (2008). *Production assurance and reliability management*. International Organization for Standardization.

ISO 55001 (2024). *Asset management—Management systems—Requirements*. International Organization for Standardization.

Kerkeni, R., Khlif, S., Mhalla, A., & Bouzrara, K. (2024). Digital twin applied to predictive maintenance for Industry 4.0. *ASME Journal of Nondestructive Evaluation, Diagnostics and Prognostics of Engineering Systems, 7*(4), 041008. https://doi.org/10.1115/1.4065875

Martínez, A., & Gómez, P. (2023). Integration of digital twins for reliability optimization in cryogenic compression. *Engineering Applications of Artificial Intelligence, 122*, 105678.

Mikołajewska, E., Mikołajewski, D., Mikołajczyk, T., & Paczkowski, T. (2025). Generative AI in AI-based digital twins for fault diagnosis for predictive maintenance in Industry 4.0/5.0. *Applied Sciences, 15*(6), 3166. https://doi.org/10.3390/app15063166

Musa, S. (2018). Reliability modeling of k-out-of-n systems in industrial applications. *Reliability Engineering & System Safety, 174*, 1–10.

Okirie, A. J., Barnabas, M., & Obinichi, N. (2024). Comparative study of sensor-generated operational data, equational calculation, and temporal data acquisition for optimal predictive maintenance decisions. *Global Journal of Engineering and Technology Advances, 20*(2), 61–73. https://doi.org/10.30574/gjeta.2024.20.2.0143

Orošnjak, M., Saretzky, F., & Kedziora, S. (2025). Prescriptive maintenance: A systematic literature review and exploratory meta-synthesis. *Applied Sciences, 15*(15), 8507. https://doi.org/10.3390/app15158507

Pakala, A., Shah, D., & Jha, S. (2025). Advancing predictive maintenance: A data-driven approach for accurate equipment failure prediction. In *Industry 4.0 and advanced manufacturing* (pp. 219–228). Springer. https://doi.org/10.1007/978-981-97-7150-9_19

Schultz, J., & Paulus, M. (2015). Cryogenic compressor design and maintenance. *Proceedings of the LNG Equipment Symposium, 12*(1), 45–58.

Ucar, A., Karakose, M., & Kırımça, N. (2024). Artificial intelligence for predictive maintenance applications: Key components, trustworthiness, and future trends. *Applied Sciences, 14*(2), 898. https://doi.org/10.3390/app14020898

Wang, H., et al. (2022). Digital twin framework for predictive diagnostics in LNG compressor systems. *Computers in Industry, 135*, 103567.

Wiese, T. L. (2024). Predictive maintenance using artificial intelligence in critical infrastructure: A decision-making framework. *International Journal of Engineering, Business and Management, 8*(4). https://doi.org/10.22161/ijebm.8.4.1

Zhou, Y., & Li, J. (2021). Predictive maintenance of cryogenic compressors using machine learning techniques. *Journal of Mechanical Systems and Signal Processing, 154*, 107538.

Artificial Intelligence and Machine Learning in Industrial Maintenance Optimization

Juan Francisco Gómez Fernández and Adolfo Crespo Márquez

Abstract Artificial intelligence (AI), machine learning (ML), and the Industrial Internet of Things (IIoT) are reshaping maintenance from failure reaction to decision-centric value creation. This chapter synthesizes the state of the art into a practitioner-oriented framework that connects sensing, analytics, and execution across strategic, tactical, and operational levels. We propose a task-driven taxonomy spanning diagnostics, prognostics (RUL with quantified uncertainty), prescriptive optimization, and multi-site orchestration, mapped to data modalities (tabular/events, time-series, images, text, and physics-informed digital twins) and governance constraints (explainability, latency, privacy, maturity). We consolidate enabling architectures—edge/cloud pipelines, data fabric and semantics, MLOps, drift management, XAI, and federated learning—and outline when to prefer classical models, deep learning, probabilistic/survival methods, hybrid physics-informed models, or reinforcement learning. Building on reported industrial impacts, we present a staged roadmap for first deployments with indicative effort, skills, and KPIs, emphasizing how to translate predictions into scheduling, inventory, and risk-based decisions. Finally, we discuss emerging agentic/LLM copilots and Industry 5.0 servitization, highlighting their implications for safety, resilience, and sustainability. The result is a concise guide to select models, design trustworthy pipelines, and scale maintenance optimization with measurable business outcomes.

Keywords AI-driven maintenance optimization · Predictive and prescriptive maintenance · Industrial internet of things · Digital twin-enabled decision support · MLOps for asset management

J. F. Gómez Fernández (✉) · A. Crespo Márquez
Department Industrial Management, University of Seville, Seville, Spain
e-mail: jfgomez@us.es

A. Crespo Márquez
e-mail: adolfo@us.es

A. Crespo Márquez et al. (eds.), *Digital Maintenance and Asset Digitalization*, Engineering Asset Management Review 5,
https://doi.org/10.1007/978-3-032-21502-4_6

1 Introduction

Over the past few years, the combined maturation of artificial intelligence (AI), machine learning (ML), and the industrial Internet of Things (IoT) has transformed maintenance practices from time-based and reactive routines into predictive—and increasingly prescriptive—decision-support systems operating in an integrated manner across the strategic, tactical, and operational layers. This proactive approach moves beyond the digitalization focus of Industry 4.0 toward the emerging Industry 5.0 paradigm, which emphasizes sustainability, resilience, and human-centric management. This chapter outlines key concepts (see Table 1 for the entire list of acronyms and abbreviations that will be used) and evidence for understanding the role of AI and ML in shaping the future of industrial maintenance.

Reviews in the manufacturing and industrial engineering domains converge on three main enablers of this shift (Carvalho et al., 2019; Dalzochio et al., 2020; Zonta et al., 2020):

- high-frequency IoT data streams
- scalable and explainable ML models for diagnostics, prognostics, and risk estimation
- process integration that closes the loop from analytics to work execution and value realization.

Importantly, these capabilities do more than compress costs and lead times; they reposition maintenance as a value-creating function that safeguards availability, stabilizes throughput, and supports safer, more sustainable operations.

- Strategic level—At the policy, portfolio, and value-management tier, digital decision frameworks connect asset condition and risk exposure to business objectives. Two streams of recent evidence are particularly salient. First, asset-health modelling integrated with simulation-based financial analysis enables boards to compare "repair/retrofit/replace" alternatives under uncertainty, translating degradation dynamics into life-cycle value and capital-allocation decisions (Crespo Márquez et al., 2021). Second, dynamic risk-assessment (DRA) methods formalize how monitoring events, predictive analytics, and inspection results update failure-risk levels over time and, in turn, guide maintenance policies within an asset-management governance aligned with ISO 31000 and ISO 55000. This establishes a traceable link between condition intelligence and risk-based planning at portfolio scale, reducing residual risk while preserving performance targets (Martínez-Galán Fernández et al., 2022). DRA's explicit treatment of evolving risk levels helps organizations move beyond static assessments and embed continuous risk control in strategic maintenance governance. For a cross-industry synthesis of AI-enabled digital twins linking asset condition, risk exposure, and value capture within enterprise governance, see Chen et al. (2025), which consolidates architectures and adoption patterns.

Table 1 List of acronyms and abbreviations

Acronym	Expansion	Acronym	Expansion
ABS	Agent-Based Simulation	AFT	Accelerated Failure Time
AHI	Asset Health Index	AI	Artificial Intelligence
AUC	Area Under the ROC Curve	CBM	Condition-Based Maintenance
CI	Confidence Interval	CI/CD	Continuous Integration/ Continuous Delivery
CMMS	Computerized Maintenance Management System	CP	Constraint Programming
CRPS	Continuous Ranked Probability Score	CNN	Convolutional Neural Network
Cox	Cox Proportional Hazards model	DES	Discrete-Event Simulation
DL	Deep Learning	DT	Digital Twin
DRA	Decision Risk Analysis	EAM	Enterprise Asset Management
FPR	False Positive Rate	FedAvg	Federated Averaging
FL	Federated Learning	GBM	Gradient Boosting Machine
IIoT	Industrial Internet of Things	IT	Information Technology
KG	Knowledge Graph	KS	Kolmogorov–Smirnov statistic
LIME	Local Interpretable Model-Agnostic Explanations	LLM	Large Language Model
LSTM	Long Short-Term Memory	MILP	Mixed-Integer Linear Programming
MLOps	Machine Learning Operations	MTBF	Mean Time Between Failures
MTTR	Mean Time To Repair	NHPP	Non-Homogeneous Poisson Process
PHM	Prognostics and Health Management	PINN	Physics-Informed Neural Network
PSI	Population Stability Index	RAG	Retrieval-Augmented Generation
RACI	Responsible, Accountable, Consulted, Informed	RF	Random Forest
RL	Reinforcement Learning	ROC	Receiver Operating Characteristic
RUL	Remaining Useful Life	SHAP	SHapley Additive exPlanations
SLA	Service-Level Agreement	SLO	Service-Level Objective
SOP	Standard Operating Procedure	SVM	Support Vector Machine
TPR	True Positive Rate	XAI	Explainable Artificial Intelligence

- Tactical level—Closer to the planning horizon, AI/ML converts predictions—such as remaining useful life (RUL) or component-level failure probabilities—into integrated maintenance programmes that coordinate work orders, spare-parts policies, and production windows. In safety–critical settings (e.g., aviation), discrete-event simulation frameworks that ingest prognostic outputs generate prescriptive schedules that reduce disruptions while balancing capacity constraints (Meissner et al., 2021). Reinforcement-learning formulations extend this logic to multi-constraint, combinatorial action spaces, recommending interventions that minimize penalty costs and improve service continuity (Goby et al., 2023). Evidence from digital-twin deployments further indicates that coupling ML forecasters/classifiers with optimization and decision-support engines reduces corrective downtime and stabilizes throughput (Deon et al., 2022). Taken together, these findings confirm that the tactical layer is where predictive insights are translated into resource-optimized plans—spanning staffing, spares, and outage windows—that protect value while respecting operational constraints.
- Operational level—At the plant or network edge, IoT connectivity and edge–cloud computing provide the data cadence necessary for robust diagnostics. Deep-learning models embedded in digital-twin loops improve early fault detection—especially when transfer learning and domain adaptation mitigate non-stationarity and label scarcity—shortening the detection-to-action cycle and enabling near-zero unplanned downtime aspirations (Xia et al., 2021). Edge-intelligence case studies have shown that pushing inference closer to machines reduces latency and bandwidth use without sacrificing accuracy—an essential requirement in tightly coupled production systems (Huang et al., 2021). Concept-drift detection and time-aware validation are critical for maintaining calibrated alerts and avoiding alarm fatigue in dynamic operating environments. Recent industrial studies emphasize drift monitoring as a first-order requirement for reliable predictive maintenance (Dalzochio et al., 2020; Zenisek et al., 2019). Finally, structured data-to-decision architectures—combining sensing, digital twins, analytics, and execution—are gaining traction as a pragmatic way to institutionalize operational learning (Friederich et al., 2022).

Integration across levels—Creating value depends chiefly on end-to-end integration—sensing, digital twin, analytics, and service execution—rather than on any isolated algorithm (Chen et al., 2025; Dalzochio et al., 2020; Zonta et al., 2020). Current best practice is defined not by a single modelling approach but by alignment across levels: strategic DRA and investment analysis set risk and value targets; tactical planning translates forecasts into coherent programmes of work and inventory; and operational analytics deliver timely, explainable signals that drive execution. This layered approach systematically optimizes resource consumption (spares, labour, and time) while reducing delays and variability, transforming maintenance from a cost centre into a value driver (Crespo Márquez et al., 2021; Zonta et al., 2020). In networked utilities and other asset-intensive sectors, the same principles support resilience: condition-aware policies and DRA reduce the likelihood and impact of service disruptions by prioritizing interventions where the risk-to-value trade-off is most favourable (Martínez-Galán Fernández et al., 2022). This is particularly critical in asset-intensive contexts, where maintenance decisions directly influence operational stability.

How to read this chapter: Sect. 2 gives a task-driven taxonomy and model/IoT patterns—when to use/avoid and data requirements. Section 3.1 summarizes advantages/limitations by organizational dimension (strategy, data, analytics, processes, people, value, cost, standards). Section 3.2 presents a staged roadmap with gates, KPIs, and cost signals to avoid pilot purgatory. Section 4 reframes Industry 5.0 and servitization toward outcome-based contracts.

2 State-of-the-Art AI/ML and IoT Technologies for Maintenance Optimization

Maintenance analytics has consolidated into a toolkit aligned with distinct business targets: diagnosis (identifying faults), prognosis (estimating time to failure), prescription (deciding what to do and when), and orchestration (executing at scale). Below, we synthesise the most widely used model families and enabling IoT patterns, highlight conditions under which they create value, and comment on their scalability across the enterprise.

Table 2 synthesizes this Sect. 2 into a structured decision aid. The recommended point of entry is to specify the primary analytical objective—detection, diagnosis, prognosis (RUL), prescription, or orchestration—followed by the prevailing data modality (tabular/events, raw time-series, imagery, textual records, or digital-twin/synthetic data) and any binding constraints (requirements for uncertainty quantification or explainability, edge-latency limitations, privacy conditions, organizational maturity, and labelling cost). The table then maps these factors to appropriate model families, provides a concise rationale, states minimum data prerequisites, indicates expected explainability/uncertainty artefacts, identifies typical deployment loci (edge versus cloud), and lists task-relevant evaluation metrics. This table is intended as an orienting framework rather than a prescriptive rule set; hybrid approaches are frequently justified (e.g., physics-informed deep learning; survival models coupled with deep architectures). Having identified a candidate row, readers are directed to the corresponding subsections (§2.1–§2.8) for methodological caveats and design patterns, and to §3.2 for scaling gates prior to CMMS/EAM integration.

2.1 Classical Supervised ML (Tree Ensembles, SVMs, and Linear Models)

These methods are primarily applied to fault detection, short-horizon remaining useful life (RUL) estimation, and alarm-quality improvement. For tabular sensor

Table 2 A model-selection "Rosetta Table"

§	Scope /Task	Typical data	Representative models	Use when	Avoid if	Deployment	Key metric
2.1	Diagnosis (fault/ anomaly) on tabular/events	Tabular, events, aggregated features	Tree ensembles (RF/ GBM), logistic/linear, SVM	Need speed and explainability with scarce labels	Only raw HF signals + strong non-stationarity with no feature refresh	Edge or cloud; drift monitors (PSI/KS)	F1/AUC
2.2	Early anomaly on raw signals/images	Raw time-series, vibration, imagery	Autoencoders, CNN/ LSTM/Transformers	Subtle patterns, multi-fault, image/ vision	Strict edge latency w/o accel; almost no labels and no pretraining	Cloud-train + edge-infer	TPR @fixed FPR
2.3	Prognosis/RUL with risk	Time-series + history; failure/ censoring	Survival (Cox/AFT), Bayesian reliability, hybrid DL + survival	Need calibrated intervals for planning/ spares/warranty	No failure/censoring info; org rejects uncertainty bands	Cloud	CRPS/Brier/ calibration
2.4	Physics-informed/ Digital Twin hybrid	Telemetry + twin inputs; synthetic	PINNs, grey-box ML, ML + simulation	Physics is clear; need scenario generation and sim-to-act	Twin cannot be validated or kept current	Layered (edge awareness)	Policy validity/ sim-to-real gap
2.5	Prescription (from predict → decide)	Health/RUL + constraints; twin/sim	Optimization (MILP/ CP), DES/ABS, RL	Need schedules/ policies under costs/ penalties	No simulator/twin; actions not enforceable	Cloud; shadow-mode before CMMS	Total cost/ penalties avoided
2.6	IoT/Edge and Federated (cross-cutting)	Multi-site streams; privacy/latency	Edge feature extractors; FL (FedAvg, etc.)	Latency/bandwidth or privacy matters; multi-site learning	No harmonized tags/ semantics/IDs	Edge preprocess + cloud analytics	ΔKPI per site/latency SLA
2.7	XAI, Drift and MLOps (cross-cutting)	All above	Model registry, CI/ CD, drift detectors, SHAP/LIME	Need trust, lineage, safe scaling	No governance bandwidth for lifecycle	Platform (cloud) + ops UIs	Uptime of pipeline/ retrain SLO
2.8	Agentic AI and LLM copilot (operator support)	SOPs, tickets, manuals, text	RAG + LLM, KG-grounded agents	Guided procedures; knowledge reuse	Uncurated sources; uncontrolled tool use	Cloud; audit logging	Task success/time saved

summaries and event histories, algorithms such as tree ensembles (Random Forest, Gradient Boosting/XGBoost), linear/logistic regression, and support vector machines (SVMs) remain robust baselines for fault classification and RUL regression. Evidence from manufacturing and utilities indicates that these models are data-efficient, relatively resilient to class imbalance (when combined with appropriate re-sampling), and straightforward to explain to planners—making them well suited to contexts where labels are scarce and governance demands transparency (Carvalho et al., 2019; Ferreira & Gonçalves, 2022). However, they are less effective with raw high-frequency signals and non-stationary regimes unless features are refreshed frequently or drift is actively monitored (Zenisek et al., 2019).

2.2 *Deep Learning (CNNs/RNNs, Autoencoders, and Transformers)*

These techniques excel in early anomaly detection, multi-fault diagnosis, and long-horizon RUL estimation. When raw time-series (e.g., vibration, current, traffic counters) or imagery is available, deep networks can directly learn discriminative features, capturing subtle degradation patterns. Benchmarks report strong performance gains from convolutional neural networks (CNNs) for time–frequency maps, long short-term memory (LSTM) or gated recurrent units (GRUs) for sequential trends, and autoencoders for anomaly detection. Transfer learning further improves accuracy when labels are limited (Ferreira & Gonçalves, 2022; Souza et al., 2021). Digital-twin-assisted deep transfer learning—pre-training models on synthetic or simulated conditions before adapting them to live machinery—has proven effective under domain shift, improving diagnostic accuracy (Xia et al., 2021). These gains, however, come with higher computational demands and increased effort for explainability.

2.3 *Probabilistic and Survival Models (Bayesian/RUL Reliability)*

To support consequence-aware RUL estimation, maintenance-interval optimisation, and decisions that integrate uncertainty—such as spares provisioning, warranty management, and risk–cost trade-offs—probabilistic RUL models and survival analysis remain indispensable. Recent studies highlight hybrid approaches that combine ML point predictions with uncertainty quantification (e.g., probabilistic regression, Bayesian updating) to align outputs with reliability KPIs and risk-based maintenance policies (Ferreira & Gonçalves, 2022).

2.4 Hybrid Physics-Informed Learning and Digital Twins

A major trend is hybrid modelling, which embeds physics-based constraints into ML or uses digital twins (DTs) to generate labelled scenarios for training and to close the loop between condition monitoring and decision support. DTs increasingly act as fusion points where simulations, real-time data, and ML co-evolve to support both diagnosis and prescription (Errandonea et al., 2020). Edge-enabled DTs reduce latency and bandwidth use while maintaining detection quality (Huang et al., 2021). Sector-specific studies (e.g., rail) demonstrate that DT-driven condition-based maintenance (CBM) applications can deliver measurable availability gains when paired with explainable analytics and integrated work management (Crespo Márquez et al., 2023). Industry-grounded reviews stress that DT + AI initiatives succeed when deployed via layered architectures (assets → connectivity → twin → analytics → services) and clear value-capture pathways.

2.5 Prescriptive Analytics and Reinforcement Learning (RL)

To integrate production and maintenance optimisation, it is essential to move from "predict" to "decide." Prescriptive models translate health estimates into action sequences that respect production schedules, safety constraints, and service-level penalties. Deep RL with combinatorial action spaces has been shown to improve maintenance scheduling under real-world constraints, reducing corrective interventions by jointly learning when and what to service (Goby et al., 2023). Where simulations or DTs are available, RL agents can be trained offline to mitigate operational risk.

2.6 IoT/edge Architectures, Data Governance, and Federated Learning

Enterprise-scale, sustainable solutions require robust architectures that combine edge-level preprocessing (e.g., feature extraction, compressive sampling) with cloud-based analytics, reducing both latency and network costs (Huang et al., 2021). In multi-site operations or partner ecosystems, federated learning and privacy-preserving analytics enable model training across sites without centralising sensitive data—supporting global learning while respecting local constraints. Synchronous acquisition networks for robots and complex lines have proven scalable and non-intrusive, facilitating standardised data collection even in brownfield environments (Izagirre et al., 2022).

2.7 Explainability (XAI), Drift Management, and MLOps at Scale

Two widely adopted post-hoc methods are:

- SHapley Additive exPlanations (SHAP): Based on cooperative game theory, SHAP assigns each feature a contribution value to the prediction, offering both global (model-wide) and local (instance-specific) interpretability. In maintenance, SHAP can reveal how vibration amplitude, temperature spikes, or load cycles influence failure predictions, enabling engineers to validate model reasoning (Mota et al., 2024).
- Local Interpretable Model-agnostic Explanations (LIME): LIME approximates the model locally with an interpretable surrogate (e.g., linear regression) to explain individual predictions. In spare-parts planning, LIME has shown which operational conditions triggered high replacement probabilities, helping planners justify procurement and avoid over- or under-stocking (Shah et al., 2024).

Continuous concept-drift detection in streaming data is equally critical to prevent silent model degradation; drift monitors tailored to PdM signals have been proposed (Zenisek et al., 2019). At enterprise scale, MLOps practices—standardised feature stores, CI/CD pipelines for models, lineage tracking, and automated retraining—make PdM solutions portable across sites and suppliers (Ferreira & Gonçalves, 2022; Giordano et al., 2022).

2.8 Agentic AI and LLM-Based Copilots (E.G., ChatGPT, Copilot, Gemini, DeepSeek) for Maintenance

"Agentic" AI couples large language models (LLMs) with planning, tool use, external search, and feedback loops, enabling multi-step task completion far beyond single-prompt Q&A. LLM-based agents are increasingly positioned as a natural evolution for smart manufacturing: they transform unstructured, siloed technical knowledge (manuals, work orders, alarms, standards) into task-level assistance and autonomous workflows that accelerate diagnosis, procedure authoring, and scheduling (Mustapha et al., 2025; Piccialli et al., 2025).

Across case reports, the most advanced pattern is retrieval-augmented generation (RAG) powered by curated repositories (EAM/CMMS tickets, OEM manuals, SOPs) and knowledge-graph context (Shi et al., 2025). These systems guide technicians through complex procedures, verifying each step against controlled vocabularies and facilitating enterprise-wide reuse of validated knowledge (Wan et al., 2024). For example, dialog-driven assistants grounded in RAG/KG can answer "Why is this alarm happening?", reference relevant symptoms and FMEA entries, cross-check with the latest bulletins, and propose validated step-by-step plans.

When integrated with optimisation and simulation services, agentic copilots can support capital-maintenance trade-offs, grounding recommendations in cost–risk–availability simulations rather than prose alone (Crespo Márquez et al., 2021).

3 Advantages, Limitations, and a First-Stage Roadmap for Organizational Adoption of AI/ML and IoT in Maintenance

This section distills the main advantages and limitations of the most-used technologies and global-scale considerations by organizational dimension, followed by the proposition of a pragmatic first-stage roadmap and the typical gaps to close that a company should follow to begin implementation while preparing for global scale-out.

3.1 Advantages and Limitations by Organizational Dimension

Summarizing from the previous mentioned references, we can introduce the following advantages and limitations for a company in projects of these technologies implementations:

- Strategy and governance (risk, value, policies)
  - Advantages. From a strategic perspective, AI, ML, and IoT strengthen the line of sight from asset condition to enterprise value. Even modest deployments improve the terminology, indicators, and accountability associated with risk, helping align maintenance with business objectives. As maturity increases, risk-aware governance enables policies to be fully traceable—linking health indicators and probabilities of failure to cost–availability–safety targets—and supports portfolio-level decisions (e.g., repair, retrofit, replace) based on comparable evidence. At the highest maturity tier, Dynamic Risk Assessment (DRA) formalises how monitoring events and predictive signals update risk levels and adjust maintenance plans, embedding continuous risk control in asset-management processes.
  - Limitations. Early governance frictions typically involve unclear ownership of indicators and thresholds. As initiatives scale, KPI misalignment between business units can weaken incentives. The most critical hazard is governance debt: without explicit approval gates and periodic policy reviews, models and plans can drift away from the firm's risk appetite, eroding trust.
- Data and integration (IoT/edge, data fabric, semantics)

- Advantages. At the data layer, edge-side preprocessing delivers rapid wins by reducing latency and bandwidth usage while sustaining analytics during network disruptions. Subsequently, synchronised acquisition architectures standardise data capture—even on brownfield lines—allowing pilots to be reproduced. At higher maturity levels, knowledge-graph (KG) layers harmonise codes and semantics (assets, parts, failure modes), enabling cross-site model reuse and accelerating replication worldwide (Wan et al., 2024).
- Limitations. Early challenges are primarily technical—protocol heterogeneity and connector engineering. As scope expands, robust security and identity management across OT/IT boundaries become essential. The most consequential risk is poor data quality and lineage (time synchronisation, missing data, provenance), which can undermine model reliability and auditability at scale.

- Analytics portfolio (classical ML, deep learning, reliability).
  - Advantages. Baseline models deliver rapid, explainable gains on tabular signals with modest labelling, ideal for initial deployments. With richer data streams, deep learning captures subtle degradation patterns; twin-assisted transfer learning enhances robustness under domain shift. At the highest value tier, reliability/survival formulations add calibrated uncertainty, supporting interval optimisation and spares planning aligned with KPIs.
  - Limitations. Early technical requirements—feature refreshes and drift monitoring—are manageable. With deep or hybrid models, however, data/compute demands and explainability burdens increase. The most significant hazard is deploying uncalibrated or opaque models in safety–critical contexts, which may slow adoption or cause systematic over- or under-maintenance.

- Process and operations (planning, scheduling, execution).
  - Advantages. Even simple what-if analyses de-risk plan changes by enabling offline scenario testing before work is scheduled. As maturity advances, prescriptive workflows—supported by discrete-event simulation—translate predictions into coherent schedules that respect production windows and resource constraints, reducing disruptions. At full maturity, integrating CBM analytics with a digital twin and work-management systems has demonstrated measurable availability gains in real deployments, showing that value is maximised when diagnosis and execution are tightly coupled.
  - Limitations. Initially, process changes introduce modest overhead (additional reviews, data entry). At scale, change-management requirements and planner workload may become bottlenecks. The most severe risk is simulator/twin fidelity mismatch: if the prescriptive engine diverges from operational reality, it can amplify errors and trigger inappropriate interventions.

- People and change (skills, adoption, explainability).
  - Advantages. Operator-grade explanations and case-based evidence make model outputs more actionable, improving acceptance and feedback quality.

With structured playbooks and on-the-job learning, sites converge on common practices; over time, capability building reduces dependence on a small expert core, enabling multi-site replication.
- Limitations. Training requirements are moderate at the outset, but a major risk is the skills gap in data engineering and MLOps. Without clearly defined roles and routines to maintain data pipelines and models, performance can degrade silently, eroding confidence. Additionally, new roles should combine sector-specific asset expertise with reliability engineering and ML skills; companies must design and reward career paths for this hybrid profile.

- Value realization (business case, scaling).
  - Advantages. Early deployments often deliver quick wins—fewer false alarms and improved work prioritisation. With prescriptive integration, firms report lower mean time to repair (MTTR), fewer unplanned stoppages, and better spares alignment. When data, model, and governance templates are codified, replication across sites compounds these benefits.
  - Limitations. The initial challenge is avoiding "pilot purgatory"—proof-of-concept projects without explicit value metrics or replication plans. The most damaging failure mode is neglecting to track value (ROI, avoided penalties, resilience metrics), without demonstrable benefits, expansion stalls despite technical success.

- Cost of the projects (budget structure, evolution, and scalability).
  - Advantages. Initial financial benefits—fewer emergency interventions and better prioritisation—appear quickly. As programmes mature, shared data/model assets (feature stores, reusable templates, twin components) reduce the marginal cost of replication. Cloud-native architectures allow capital expenditure (capex) to shift toward elastic operational expenditure (opex), enabling burst capacity for development (e.g., model training, simulation) and scaling down during steady-state inference. At the highest maturity level, disciplined value tracking—linking availability, MTTR, and inventory turns to avoided losses—creates a repeatable investment case that travels across the enterprise.
  - Limitations. Costs often rise before they fall. Early expenditures span integration and data engineering (connectors, time sync, quality assurance), domain-specific labelling (failure modes, ground truth), and OT/IT security compliance. Cloud costs can be volatile: data-egress fees, long-term storage, and GPU peaks during development add unpredictability; LLM-based copilots introduce inference costs tied to usage. The highest-impact risk is underestimating total cost of ownership (TCO)—particularly for data work and lifecycle MLOps—which can trap projects in pilot purgatory despite technical readiness.

- Standards and frameworks (coverage, gaps, and typical use).
  - Advantages. Standards and reference architectures provide a shared vocabulary across engineering, IT, and governance. In maintenance digitalisation, ISO

13372/13374 and related machine-condition standards define data processing and presentation; OSA-CBM (MIMOSA) specifies end-to-end flows from sensing to diagnostics/prognostics; ISO 55000 underpins asset-management governance; and ISA-95/IEC 62264 standardise enterprise–control integration. AI/ML implementations are supported by international standards such as ISO 14224 (reliability data collection) and IEC 81346 (reference designation). Frameworks like RAMI 4.0 and the Industrial Internet Reference Architecture (IIRA) ensure interoperability and lifecycle management. Organisations embedding these into their architectures report clearer roles, stronger traceability, and easier replication of solutions. In simulation and decision support, digital-twin frameworks from the smart-manufacturing literature formalise what-if analyses and shorten the loop to execution.

- Limitations. No single standard provides complete coverage for large-scale programmes. ISO 13374 and OSA-CBM cover condition monitoring and diagnostics but lack guidance on enterprise risk governance (addressed by ISO 31000/ISO 55000) or modern data/AI operations (feature stores, CI/CD pipelines, drift/XAI practices). RAMI 4.0 and IIRA define integration roles and data objects but leave analytics-lifecycle management and twin fidelity to individual project design. Firms must therefore assemble a "framework stack" (condition-monitoring standards + asset governance + integration + data/AI lifecycle) and align it via an internal style guide. Misalignment—duplicate codes, uneven data quality, or missing approval gates—is the most consequential failure mode at scale

Some of these presented advantages and limitations are organized in the Fig. 1 offering a strategic classification of AI/ML implementation outcomes across two temporal dimensions: short-term and long-term. This format provides a clear, decision-oriented overview of both immediate operational benefits and future systemic challenges, helping stakeholders anticipate trade-offs and prioritise interventions. By mapping advantages and limitations along a time axis, the chart adds analytical depth to the discussion—highlighting how early wins (e.g., latency reduction, KPI improvements) must be balanced against longer-term risks such as governance debt, hidden costs, and data visibility loss. This visual serves as a practical tool for framing expectations and guiding roadmap design in asset-intensive environments.

3.2 Roadmap for AI/ML Maintenance Projects

A successful AI/ML- and IoT-enabled maintenance programme should be conceived not as a standalone pilot, but as an integral component of the company's broader digitalisation ecosystem. This integration ensures alignment with data-governance policies and allows the programme to act as a lever for subsequent developments—supporting organisational transformation, strengthening data foundations,

Fig. 1 Strategic classification of AI/ML maintenance impacts: a short- versus long-term perspective

Short-Term Advantages	**Short-Term Limitations**
• Reduction of fault detection latency • Improvements in MTBF, OEE, and other KPIs • Maintenance of explainability in AI models	• Quality and availability of data • Alignment of KPIs with AI optimization functions • Additional workload for staff
Long-Term Advantages	**Long-Term Limitations**
• Risk-based maintenance planning • Multi-site replication of learning models	• Technical governancœ debt • Hidden costs and complexities associated with AI • Regulatory misalignment and data privacy

and evolving models-as-a-service to advance asset-management and risk-governance objectives.

In many asset-intensive companies, however, the "initial situation" presents a challenging baseline, with common conditions such as:

- Operations relying on individual goodwill rather than defined, repeatable, and formalised processes.
- Inconsistent documentation, no single authoritative inventory, and a high volume of engineering changes.
- Weak planning and coordination, reducing functional scalability.
- Minimal automation: many activities remain manual and repetitive.
- Loose process control, with limited end-to-end visibility.
- Unclear roles, accountabilities, and measurable objectives.
- A reactive organizational posture, shallow problem analysis, and limited root-cause investigation.
- Oversized, predominantly time-based preventive-maintenance regimes (e.g., blanket three-month intervals).
- Inadequate or ageing infrastructure.
- Fragmented monitoring across multiple platforms, generating excessive alarms.

- Strong dependence on external suppliers and partners.
- Fragile spare-parts management, with many items in critical status.

In such environments, launching AI/ML/IoT initiatives without first stabilising foundational processes is a poor bet. The risk of "pilot purgatory" is high. A minimum level of process control must be established before building models. Scaling requires a coherent framework and data model, with governance, data, infrastructure, and personnel prepared in parallel. Key preparatory steps include:

- Standardized processes with defined objectives and KPIs, supported by a RACI matrix for both operational processes and data governance.
- Consolidated master asset documentation (IDs, locations, criticality, configuration, bills of materials) and core failure-mode dictionaries. Version-control equipment changes and maintenance policies to avoid ambiguity under high engineering-change loads. ISO-aligned CBM data definitions and process views reduce misinterpretation between OT and IT teams.
- A single ingestion path for historian tags, alarms/events, CMMS orders, inspections, and contextual data (load, weather). Data contracts should specify SLAs, timestamps, and quality flags; harmonised terminology (assets, parts, symptoms, failure modes, variables) via a knowledge graph supports cross-site model reuse. Implement drift monitors (e.g., PSI/KS tests) to detect regime shifts that could degrade models.
- Edge-side preprocessing—feature extraction and data compression—to reduce latency and network utilisation, underpinned by elastic, cloud-based storage and compute for model training and batch inference. In parallel, adopt a Zero-Trust security posture, including strong device identity, micro-segmentation, and continuous verification, to mitigate early compromise risks.
- Alarm rationalisation (deduplication, suppression rules, evidence-based thresholds) and end-to-end telemetry (pipelines, feature store, models, decisions). Architect for portability (containerised services, open connectors) to avoid vendor lock-in and simplify multi-plant monitoring.
- Initial deployment of transparent baselines (tree ensembles; reliability/survival models) to validate signal value, advancing to deep/hybrid models where raw data streams warrant. MLOps-as-a-Service (feature store, CI/CD pipelines, model registry, automated validation, drift/health dashboards) should be institutionalised, with operator-grade explainability as a non-negotiable requirement.
- Simulation or lightweight digital-twin testing of recommendations before altering plant schedules; only then integrate with CMMS/EAM for automated execution. Evidence indicates that coupling health models with continuous/discrete-event simulation clarifies retrofit/replace/schedule trade-offs.
- Targeted model-literacy training for planners and runbooks for technicians; formalise feedback loops so that interventions generate labelled data for retraining. Adoption correlates more strongly with explanation quality and ownership routines than with raw model accuracy.

- Minimize over-dependence on vendors by mandating open interfaces and a documented standards stack (e.g., ISO 13372/13374 for condition-data definitions, ISO 55000 for asset governance, OSA-CBM/MIMOSA for functional interoperability).
- Link RUL/health estimates to critical-parts policies and supplier lead times; use uncertainty-aware intervals to avoid both stock-outs and over-stocking. Literature consistently highlights that reliability-aligned uncertainty quantification is essential for planning credibility.

3.3 Staged Roadmap for Implementation

Table 3 provides a concise, stage-by-stage overview of the roadmap used to translate predictive and prescriptive maintenance initiatives into deployable capabilities. For each stage it states the goal, the key activities required to achieve it, and an exit gate with sample KPIs that operationalize "definition of done." The table is intended as a practical checklist—rather than a prescriptive template—to help teams align value, data, models, and operations while avoiding "pilot purgatory." Detailed scope, artefacts, roles, and risk controls for each stage are described in the subsequent subsections.

Stage 1 Scope and Governance (4–8 weeks)

Establish business-value hypotheses (availability, service levels, risk reduction), a living asset inventory, and a minimum viable data architecture with security by design. Transition from goodwill-based operations to RACI-based ownership; form a joint Reliability–OT–IT steering group. Evidence shows that predictive- and prescriptive-maintenance programmes only scale when specifications encompass both data and decision integration (e.g., digital-twin touchpoints, CMMS/EAM connectors). Adopt a reference architecture explicitly linking sensing, twin, analytics, and work execution to reduce downstream rework (van Dinter et al., 2022, 2023).

Data to collect/interconnect: criticality-ranked asset list, failure modes, CMMS work orders, historian tags, condition signals (e.g., vibration, current, temperature), events/alarms, production context, spares and lead times. Standardise IDs and semantics (OPC UA tags, naming conventions) early; consolidate fragmented inventories; suppress alarm floods; define data retention and lineage. Define asset scope, value KPIs (availability, MTTR, penalty avoidance), and risk thresholds. Align failure-mode dictionaries and approvals to avoid ambiguity.

Example Azure baseline: Azure IoT Hub/Edge for ingestion; Azure Digital Twins for asset graphs; Azure Data Lake/Synapse for raw/curated data zones; Private Link/Virtual Network segregation; Entra ID + Key Vault for identity; Zero-Trust security.

Stage 2—Data Foundation and Quick-Win Baselines (8–16 weeks)

Table 3 Stage-by-stage overview of the roadmap

Stage	Goal	Key activities	Exit gate + sample KPIs
1. Scope and Governance	Align value, assets, and roles	Select assets/use cases; map failure modes; data inventory; define architecture; set RACI and data quality rules	**Gate**: RACI approved; asset and data register complete; success criteria fixed. **KPIs**: % assets with unique ID; % signals with SLA/ lineage
2. Data and Baselines	Stand up pipeline and first explainable models	Ingest/clean; feature store; baseline ML in shadow; drift and XAI dashboards; retrain procedure	**Gate**: Baselines reach targets in shadow; drift/XAI live; retrain SLO defined. **KPIs**: AUC/F1, latency, TPR@FPR
3. Prognostics and Integration	Deliver RUL with uncertainty and close the loop	Survival/Bayesian or hybrid DL; calibrated CIs; operator UI; CMMS/EAM connector	**Gate**: RUL calibrated; safe WO automation; operators trained. **KPIs**: Brier/CRPS, ↓MTTR, ↓unplanned downtime
4. Prescriptive (Decide)	Optimize schedules/ policies against cost and risk	Validate twin/ simulator; optimization or RL in shadow; guardrails and rationale logging	**Gate**: Policy beats baseline in shadow with guardrails. **KPIs**: Total cost vs. baseline; penalties avoided; schedule adherence
5. Scale and Operate	Make it robust and multi-site	Model registry and lineage; CI/CD; monitoring and audits; runbooks; federation where needed	**Gate**: Handover to ops; audits pass; KPIs sustained. **KPIs**: Pipeline uptime; retrain cadence; ΔKPI per site

Develop post-prognostic pipelines to convert predictions into schedule/spares decisions; design for drift detection and explainability; validate via digital twin or simulator before production integration. Reviews show that deep-learning pipelines (for anomaly/fault/RUL detection) create value when embedded in a reference architecture and paired with prescriptive logic—not as isolated models (Li et al., 2024; van Dinter et al., 2023).

Start with robust baselines (tree ensembles, survival models), advancing to deep learning where signals justify. Codify data contracts for features/labels; design A/B tests for policy changes. Establish MLOps early—feature stores, CI/CD for models, automated validation at edge and cloud—because industrial deployments face heterogeneous devices and retraining needs (Faubel et al., 2023).

Apply strong supervision to labelled datasets; augment with synthetic data from the digital twin. Where operating regimes evolve, implement concept-drift monitoring with scheduled recalibration. Edge preprocessing reduces latency and bandwidth load; numerous studies confirm its advantage in time-critical, control-proximate detection (Khan et al., 2019).

Stage 3—Installation on Plant IT/OT Platform and Commissioning (4–12 weeks)

Deploy secure ingestion and a minimal feature store for the pilot line. Implement classical ML baselines to validate signal utility; activate drift monitors (e.g., PSI/KS tests, residual analysis) from the outset. Integrate pipelines with SCADA/DCS, historians, and CMMS/EAM, while enforcing operational safety. Commissioning should include shadow-mode operation, rollback paths, and test fixtures replaying real event streams.

Design for interoperability and portability (containerised microservices, explicit data-egress protocols) (Eichelberger et al., 2024). Ensure pipelines can normalise diverse input formats (PDFs, CAD files, logs) to feed a RAG environment with proper governance (source-aware grounding, citation checks, version control). Multi-site scaling is accelerated by KGs harmonising terminology and codes, enabling a single assistant to support multiple plants via site-specific adapters (Wan et al., 2024).

Example Azure deployment: Azure Kubernetes Service for serving; Azure Machine Learning for registry/endpoints; Event Hub/Functions for orchestration; Logic Apps connectors to EAM/ERP; Defender for IoT and Sentinel for monitoring.

Stage 4—Supervision, Consulting, and Training (Ongoing)

Institutionalise the operating model by defining clear responsibilities: who monitors drift, who approves model promotions, how crews consume recommendations, and how benefits are verified. Training programmes should include model-literacy modules for planners and structured runbooks for technicians.

Operate model registries with lineage tracking; publish explanations and confidence intervals; and align model-review schedules with maintenance windows. Studies on MLOps in Industry 4.0 environments emphasise that the predominant challenges are organisational—such as heterogeneous devices and fragmented standards—rather than purely technical. Automated retraining and robust monitoring remain essential to sustaining performance (Faubel et al., 2023).

Stage 5—Usage Review and Periodic Updates (Quarterly)

Verify value capture, manage scope expansion, and harden governance. Reviews should include:

- Business KPIs (availability, MTTR/MTBF, service-penalty avoidance)
- Model portfolio health
- Security posture
- Backlog of new assets and additional signals to be integrated.

For capital-expenditure and maintenance decisions (e.g., retrofit vs. replace, spares sizing), combine asset-health models with discrete- or continuous-time simulations to make cost–risk–availability trade-offs explicit for decision-makers.

Scale-out patterns: Template-first approaches package validated models as microservices with embedded reliability-engineering workflows and risk registers. These models are lightweight to deploy alongside CMMS/ERP platforms. "Golden" pipelines and digital twins—validated per asset class—can be promoted as templates and rolled out to new sites with minimal adaptation (van Dinter et al., 2023). Where confidentiality is a concern, implement federated global models that avoid raw-data sharing (Boobalan et al., 2022). Publish reference architectures—including edge/data blueprints, model cards, promotion criteria, knowledge-graph taxonomies, and security/compliance frameworks. With such artefacts, onboarding a new site becomes largely a configuration task rather than a full re-engineering effort.

Recent industrial cases (Giordano et al., 2022; Meissner et al., 2021) suggest that budgets for a single site and one asset class over 6–9 months can range from €100 k to €1 M, with indicative allocations as follows:

- Edge and sensing: €40–120 k
- Cloud and data platform (storage, compute, observability): €25–60 k
- Model development and MLOps (2–3 FTEs): €150–300 k
- CMMS/EAM integration: €40–120 k
- Training and change management: €20–60 k
- Optional LLM copilot for RAG/documentation: €15–50 k.

These costs should be justified not only by earlier fault detection but—critically—by improvements in maintenance management, budgeting, asset management, and lifecycle decisions. In mature programmes, such mechanisms elevate maintenance to a value-generating function (Bokrantz et al., 2020; Ferreira & Gonçalves, 2022; Meissner et al., 2021):

- From a proactive stance, reducing unplanned downtime
- Right-sizing preventive work
- Aligning maintenance plans with production windows and resource constraints
- Minimizing schedule breaks and missed service commitments
- Aligning spares and capital expenditure with quantified risk and value.

When RUL and failure-time uncertainty are quantified, spares policies can be tuned to asset criticality and lead times—reducing both stock-outs and over-stocking. This highlights the budgeting advantage of calibrated uncertainty for service-part inventories and maintenance windows. Coupling asset-health models with continuous-time or discrete-event simulation further surfaces cost–risk–availability trade-offs for planners and controllers. As a result, day-to-day actions become traceable to risk and cost, spares sizing aligns with uncertainty, and capital decisions are validated against realistic digital surrogates.

The practical message: Benefits accrue when sensing, analytics, and planning are engineered as a single, standards-governed system sustained by MLOps—not when models are piloted in isolation. Reported Impacts from Literature are:

- Maintenance-task cost reductions up to 41.3%, avoidable delay minutes reduced by 89.5%, delay-cost reductions up to 99.2%, and CO_2 emissions reduced by 30.8%, with only a modest utilisation decrease of ~ 4.6 percentage points as a trade-off (Meissner et al., 2021).
- Maintenance cost reductions of ~ 25–30% and downtime reductions of ~ 35–45% when organisations adopt predictive approaches and use systematic PdM strategy-selection methods (Silveira et al., 2024).
- An AHI-based digital twin implementation in energy converters reduced unplanned failures by 43% and improved maintenance-planning accuracy by 30% (Gómez et al., 2025).
- An LSTM-based PdM model achieved > 99% prediction and forecasting accuracy with a false-alarm rate of ≈ 0.35–0.40%, demonstrating that high-fidelity signals combined with sequence models can materially reduce nuisance alarms and rework in asset-intensive fleets (De Simone et al., 2023).

4 Outlook of AI, ML, and IoT for Maintenance Optimization Under Industry 5.0 and Servitization

Servitization is the strategic shift from selling physical products to delivering integrated product–service systems (PSS) that emphasise outcomes rather than ownership. Over the next five years, AI- and IoT-enabled maintenance is expected to evolve from model-centric pilots into production-grade, auditable services embedded within contracts and value chains. This transition will hinge on explainability, safety, and measurable outcomes that align asset availability with energy efficiency, emissions reduction, and workforce well-being targets (Mahale et al., 2025).

In maintenance management, servitization replaces transactional "repair-when-broken" or "scheduled service" models with continuous, value-driven service delivery. Contracts will increasingly focus on guaranteed reliability, energy efficiency, and/or performance, transferring risk from the customer to the provider (Chaou et al., 2025). This incentive structure rewards providers for keeping assets healthy rather than profiting from additional repairs.

Digital Twins as Service Platforms extend these benefits by simulating asset behaviour under diverse conditions and virtually testing maintenance strategies before field application, thereby increasing transparency and trust through shared customer dashboards (Teguede Keleko et al., 2022). Federated machine learning further enables continuous improvement of predictive models across a provider's customer base without sharing raw data, steadily enhancing service quality.

The next stage is prescriptive maintenance orchestration—leveraging reinforcement-learning agents, collaborative robots (co-bots), augmented-reality headsets, and conversational copilots to make recommendations more explainable to technicians. Promptable workflows can accelerate root-cause analysis, generate context-aware work instructions, and guide complex repairs more quickly and safely across fleets, while balancing cost, risk, energy consumption, and contractual penalties.

OEMs, operators, and service partners will increasingly engage in cross-enterprise learning via federated analytics and shared ontologies, embedding tacit knowledge into digital twins. This will align maintenance practices with throughput, quality, and sustainability objectives (Kohtamäki et al., 2019), leading to auditable, economically robust service architectures that minimise downtime while maximising lifecycle value in servitized contexts.

For providers, these technologies represent a competitive advantage, fostering customer loyalty and enabling long-term partnerships. From the client's perspective, they provide access to advanced analytics without the capital investment, ensure predictable costs, and align operational outcomes with sustainability and resilience goals. Regulators, meanwhile, can use these advances to define standards for explainability, data governance, and performance metrics in AI-driven service contracts.

In summary, servitization reinforces the principles of Industry 5.0 by reframing maintenance around human-centricity, sustainability, and resilience. Maintenance becomes a co-created process between provider and client, where data, analytics, and human expertise are integrated to maximise asset value throughout its lifecycle. Providers who seamlessly combine predictive intelligence, real-time monitoring, and human collaboration into their service offerings will be best positioned to lead in the Industry 5.0 era (Fig. 2).

Fig. 2 Outlook of AI/ML/IoT for maintenance optimization under Industry 5.0 and servitization

5 Conclusions

This chapter has argued that maintenance analytics should be understood as an end-to-end capability that links sensing, digital twins, analytics, and execution. We introduced a task-driven taxonomy—diagnosis, prognosis (RUL), prescription, and orchestration—anchored in data modalities and governance constraints such as explainability, uncertainty, latency, privacy, and organizational maturity. The deployment patterns and the staged roadmap translate that conceptual view into operational steps with explicit gates and KPIs.

From a managerial perspective, value is realized only when model outputs systematically reshape plans, inventories, and risk postures. That requires disciplined governance—stable asset identities, lineage, and model registries—together with tight CMMS/EAM integration so insights become funded work. Calibrated uncertainty and operator-facing explanations are essential for accountability and adoption, and they justify sequencing efforts from explainable baselines toward more advanced capabilities.

Technically, hybridization is the norm rather than the exception. Deep learning is effective for raw signals and imagery, survival and Bayesian methods provide calibrated risk for planning, and physics-informed twins enable the step from predicting to deciding. Trust at scale depends on reproducible pipelines, continuous drift management, automated validation and retraining, and auditable XAI artefacts; multi-site roll-outs further benefit from federated learning when bandwidth or privacy constrain centralization.

These recommendations have scope conditions. Outcomes hinge on label quality, sensor reliability, and the availability and fidelity of simulators or digital twins for prescriptive steps. Reported impacts rarely transfer unchanged across assets or sites without local failure semantics, cost models, and structured change management; moreover, latency, safety, and regulatory constraints can narrow feasible model classes and heighten governance requirements.

Looking ahead, three directions appear most promising: agentic/LLM copilots grounded in curated knowledge graphs with strict tool-use guardrails; co-optimization of production, maintenance, energy, and emissions through coupled simulation; and standardized audit trails that support certification of models and policies. Practically, we recommend progressing through gated stages—baselines in shadow with XAI and drift monitoring, calibrated RUL feeding CMMS/EAM, and only then prescriptive policies validated against explicit cost and penalty models.

References

Bokrantz, J., Skoogh, A., Berlin, C., & Stahre, J. (2020). Smart Maintenance: An empirically grounded conceptualization. *International Journal of Production Economics, 223*, 107534. https://doi.org/10.1016/j.ijpe.2019.107534

Boobalan, P., Ramu, S. P., Pham, Q.-V., Dev, K., Pandya, S., Maddikunta, P. K. R., Gadekallu, T. R., & Huynh-The, T. (2022). Fusion of federated learning and Industrial Internet of Things: A survey. *Computer Networks, 212*, 109048. https://doi.org/10.1016/j.comnet.2022.109048

Carvalho, T. P., Soares, F. A. A. M. N., Vita, R., Francisco, R. P., Basto, J. P., & Alcalá, S. G. S. (2019). A systematic literature review of machine learning methods applied to predictive maintenance. *Computers & Industrial Engineering, 137*, 106024. https://doi.org/10.1016/j.cie.2019.106024

Chaou, F. E., Benmamoun, Z., & Benmamoun, M. (2025). Application of AI and IoT for predictive maintenance: A comparative study of algorithms and model performance. In *Progress in Intelligent Computing and Secure Communication Systems*. Springer. https://doi.org/10.1007/978-3-031-99997-0_41

Chen, S., Turanoglu Bekar, E., Bokrantz, J., & Skoogh, A. (2025). AI-enhanced digital twins in maintenance: Systematic review, industrial challenges, and bridging research–practice gaps. *Journal of Manufacturing Systems, 82*, 678–699. https://doi.org/10.1016/j.jmsy.2025.07.006

Crespo Márquez, A., Marcos Alberca, J. A., Guillén López, A. J., & de la Fuente Carmona, A. (2023). Digital twins in condition-based maintenance apps: A case study for train axle bearings. *Computers in Industry, 147*, 103980. https://doi.org/10.1016/j.compind.2023.103980

Crespo Márquez, A., Serra Parajes, J., de la Fuente Carmona, A., & Sola Rosique, A. (2021). Integrating complex asset-health modelling techniques with continuous-time simulation modelling: A practical tool for maintenance and capital investments analysis. *Computers in Industry, 133*, 103507. https://doi.org/10.1016/j.compind.2021.103507

Dalzochio, J., Kunst, R., Pignaton, E., Binotto, A., Sanyal, S., Favilla, J., & Barbosa, J. (2020). Machine learning and reasoning for predictive maintenance in Industry 4.0: Current status and challenges. *Computers in Industry, 123*, 103298. https://doi.org/10.1016/j.compind.2020.103298

De Simone, L., Caputo, E., Cinque, M., Galli, A., Moscato, V., Russo, S., Cesaro, G., Criscuolo, V., & Giannini, G. (2023). LSTM-based failure prediction for railway rolling stock equipment. *Expert Systems with Applications, 222*, 119767. https://doi.org/10.1016/j.eswa.2023.119767

de Souza, R. M., Nascimento, E. G. S., Miranda, U., Dantas da Silva, W. J., & Lepikson, H. A. (2021). Deep learning for diagnosis and classification of faults in industrial rotating machinery. *Computers & Industrial Engineering, 153*, 107060. https://doi.org/10.1016/j.cie.2020.107060

Deon, B., Cotta, K. P., Silva, R., Batista, C. B., Justino, G. T., Freitas, G. C., et al. (2022). Digital twin and machine learning for decision support in thermal power plant with combustion engines. *Knowledge-Based Systems, 253*, 109578. https://doi.org/10.1016/j.knosys.2022.109578

Eichelberger, H., Alamoush, A., & Schmid, K. (2024). Industry 4.0/IIoT Platforms for manufacturing systems—A systematic review contrasting the scientific and the industrial perspectives. *Information and Software Technology, 169*, 107650. https://doi.org/10.1016/j.infsof.2024.107650

Errandonea, I., Beltrán, S., & Arrizabalaga, S. (2020). Digital Twin for maintenance: A literature review. *Computers in Industry, 123*, 103316. https://doi.org/10.1016/j.compind.2020.103316

Faubel, L., Schmid, K., & Eichelberger, H. (2023). MLOps challenges in Industry 4.0. *SN Computer Science, 4*, 828. https://doi.org/10.1007/s42979-023-02282-2

Ferreira, C., & Gonçalves, G. (2022). Remaining useful life prediction and challenges: A literature review on the use of machine learning methods. *Journal of Manufacturing Systems, 63*, 550–562. https://doi.org/10.1016/j.jmsy.2022.05.010

Friederich, J., Francis, D. P., Lazarova-Molnar, S., & Mohamed, N. (2022). A framework for data-driven digital twins of smart manufacturing systems. *Computers in Industry, 136*, 103586. https://doi.org/10.1016/j.compind.2021.103586

Giordano, D., Giobergia, F., Pastor, E., La Macchia, A., Cerquitelli, T., Baralis, E., Mellia, M., & Tricarico, D. (2022). Data-driven strategies for predictive maintenance: Lessons learned from an automotive use case. *Computers in Industry, 134*, 103554. https://doi.org/10.1016/j.compind.2021.103554

Goby, N., Brandt, T., & Neumann, D. (2023). Deep reinforcement learning with combinatorial action spaces: An application to prescriptive maintenance. *Computers & Industrial Engineering, 179*, 109165. https://doi.org/10.1016/j.cie.2023.109165

Gómez, J.F., Candón, E., Crespo, A. (2025). Asset health index integration in energy converters. *Energies, 18*(3148). https://doi.org/10.3390/en18123148

Huang, H., Yang, L., Wang, Y., Xu, X., & Lu, Y. (2021). Digital twin-driven online anomaly detection for an automation system based on edge intelligence. *Journal of Manufacturing Systems, 59*, 138–150. https://doi.org/10.1016/j.jmsy.2020.12.005

Izagirre, U., Andonegui, I., Landa-Torres, I., & Zurutuza, U. (2022). A practical and synchronized data acquisition network architecture for industrial-robot predictive maintenance in manufacturing assembly lines. *Robotics and Computer-Integrated Manufacturing, 74*, 102287. https://doi.org/10.1016/j.rcim.2021.102287

Khan, W. Z., Ahmed, E., Hakak, S., Yaqoob, I., & Ahmed, A. (2019). Edge computing: A survey. *Future Generation Computer Systems, 97*, 219–235. https://doi.org/10.1016/j.future.2019.02.050

Kohtamäki, M., Parida, V., Oghazi, P., Gebauer, H., & Baines, T. (2019). Digital servitization business models in ecosystems: A theory of the firm. *Industrial Marketing Management, 84*, 45–57. https://doi.org/10.1016/j.jbusres.2019.06.027

Li, Z., He, Q., & Li, J. (2024). A survey of deep learning-driven architecture for predictive maintenance. *Engineering Applications of Artificial Intelligence, 133*, 108285. https://doi.org/10.1016/j.engappai.2024.108285

Mahale, Y., Kolhar, S., & More, A. S. (2025). A comprehensive review on artificial intelligence driven predictive maintenance in vehicles: Technologies, challenges and future research directions. *Discover Applied Sciences, 7*, 243. Springer. https://doi.org/10.1007/s42452-025-06681-3

Martínez-Galán Fernández, P., Guillén López, A. J., Crespo Márquez, A., Gómez Fernández, J. F., & Marcos, J. A. (2022). Dynamic risk assessment for CBM-based adaptation of maintenance planning. *Reliability Engineering & System Safety, 223*, 108359. https://doi.org/10.1016/j.ress.2022.108359

Meissner, R., Rahn, A., & Wicke, K. (2021). Developing prescriptive maintenance strategies in the aviation industry based on a discrete-event simulation framework for post-prognostics decision making. *Reliability Engineering & System Safety, 214*, 107812. https://doi.org/10.1016/j.ress.2021.107812

Mota, B., Faria, P., Corchado, J., & Ramos, C. (2024). Explainable artificial intelligence applied to predictive maintenance: Comparison of post-hoc explainability techniques. In *Explainable Artificial Intelligence* (pp. 353–364). Springer. https://doi.org/10.1007/978-3-031-63803-9_19

Mustapha, K. B., Adeniyi, O. D., & Alsheikh, M. A. (2025). A survey of emerging applications of large language models in engineering and manufacturing. *Advanced Engineering Informatics, 64*, 103066. https://doi.org/10.1016/j.aei.2024.103066

Piccialli, F., Esposito, C., & Cuomo, S. (2025). AgentAI: A comprehensive survey on autonomous agents in distributed AI for Industry 4.0. *Expert Systems with Applications, 291*, 128404. https://doi.org/10.1016/j.eswa.2025.128404

Shah, R., Pawar, A., & Kumar, M. (2024). Enhancing machine learning model using explainable AI. In *Advances in Data and Information Sciences* (pp. 287–297). Springer. https://doi.org/10.1007/978-981-99-6906-7_25

Shi, D., Chen, J., & Wu, Q. (2025). Enhancing retrieval-augmented generation for interoperable industrial knowledge representation and inference toward cognitive digital twins. *Computers in Industry, 155*, 104330. https://doi.org/10.1016/j.compind.2025.104330

Silveira, N. N. A., Meghoe, A. A., & Tinga, T. (2024). Quantifying the suitability and feasibility of predictive maintenance approaches. *Computers & Industrial Engineering, 194*, 110342. https://doi.org/10.1016/j.cie.2024.110342

Teguede Keleko, A., Kamsu-Foguem, B., Houe Ngouna, R., & Tongne, A. (2022). Artificial intelligence and real-time predictive maintenance in Industry 4.0: A bibliometric analysis. *AI and Ethics, 2*, 553–577. Springer. https://doi.org/10.1007/s43681-021-00132-6

van Dinter, R., Tekinerdogan, B., & Catal, C. (2022). Predictive maintenance using digital twins: A systematic literature review. *Information and Software Technology, 151*, 107008. https://doi.org/10.1016/j.infsof.2022.107008

van Dinter, R., Tekinerdogan, B., & Catal, C. (2023). Reference architecture for digital twin-based predictive maintenance systems. *Computers & Industrial Engineering, 177*, 109099. https://doi.org/10.1016/j.cie.2023.109099

Wan, Y., Liu, Y., Chen, Z., Chen, C., Li, X., Hu, F., & Packianather, M. (2024). Making knowledge graphs work for smart manufacturing: Research topics, applications and prospects. *Journal of Manufacturing Systems, 76*, 103–132. https://doi.org/10.1016/j.jmsy.2024.07.009

Xia, M., Shao, H., Williams, D., Lu, S., Shu, L., & de Silva, C. W. (2021). Intelligent fault diagnosis of machinery using digital-twin-assisted deep transfer learning. *Reliability Engineering & System Safety, 215*, 107938. https://doi.org/10.1016/j.ress.2021.107938

Zenisek, J., Holzinger, F., & Affenzeller, M. (2019). Machine-learning-based concept drift detection for predictive maintenance. *Computers & Industrial Engineering, 137*, 106031. https://doi.org/10.1016/j.cie.2019.106031

Zonta, T., da Costa, C. A., da Rosa Righi, R., de Lima, M. J., da Trindade, E. S., & Li, G. P. (2020). Predictive maintenance in Industry 4.0: A systematic literature review. *Computers & Industrial Engineering, 150*, 106889. https://doi.org/10.1016/j.cie.2020.106889

Digital Twins, Semantic Models, and Interoperable Architectures

Standards and Best Practices in Digital Maintenance and Asset Management

Adolfo Crespo Márquez and Juan Francisco Gómez Fernández

Abstract The digital transformation of maintenance and asset management requires a structured foundation of standards and best practices to ensure consistency, interoperability, and strategic alignment across systems and industries. This chapter explores the essential role of standards—such as ISO 55000, ISO 14224, IEC 81346, and frameworks like RAMI 4.0 and the Industrial Internet Reference Architecture (IIRA)—in guiding the evolution from traditional maintenance approaches to data-driven, digitally enabled practices. The chapter highlights how these standards support the integration of technologies like IoT, AI, and Digital Twins, and how they underpin advanced practices such as predictive maintenance, asset health indexing, and lifecycle optimization. Common implementation challenges are examined, including system integration, workforce readiness, and gaps in standard coverage. To support organizations in their transformation journey, the chapter introduces a maturity-based framework for aligning digital adoption with asset management objectives. By linking technical frameworks to practical decision-making models, the chapter offers a roadmap for sustainable, standards-compliant digital maintenance strategies that can evolve with the increasing complexity and demands of modern asset-intensive environments.

Keywords Standards-based digital maintenance · Asset management governance · Industrial reference architectures · Asset administration shell · Digital maturity models for asset management

A. Crespo Márquez (✉) · J. F. Gómez Fernández
Department Industrial Management, University of Seville, Seville, Spain
e-mail: adolfo@us.es

J. F. Gómez Fernández
e-mail: jfgomez@us.es

A. Crespo Márquez et al. (eds.), *Digital Maintenance and Asset Digitalization*, Engineering Asset Management Review 5,
https://doi.org/10.1007/978-3-032-21502-4_7

1 Introduction: Why Standards Matter

As industries accelerate the shift toward digital maintenance and intelligent asset management, the need for interoperability, consistency, and scalability becomes more critical than ever. Digital maintenance is not simply the adoption of new technologies—it represents a transformation in how assets are monitored, managed, and optimized throughout their lifecycle. This transformation introduces both complexity and opportunity. To manage this complexity effectively and realize the potential of digitalization, organizations must rely on a solid foundation of standards and best practices.

Traditionally, maintenance management has relied on fragmented systems, human expertise, and localized processes. While effective in stable environments, these approaches fall short in the face of today's connected, real-time, and data-driven operations. The integration of technologies such as the Internet of Things (IoT), Artificial Intelligence (AI), machine learning, and Digital Twins enables predictive and prescriptive capabilities, but also demands structured data, integrated systems, and consistent terminology (Crespo Márquez et al., 2022; GFMAM, 2024).

In this context, standards act as enablers. They define the technical and semantic rules needed to ensure that systems can communicate, data can be exchanged, and processes can be automated across multiple platforms. For instance, ISO 55000 provides a high-level management system framework for asset management, promoting alignment between asset-related decisions and organizational objectives (ISO, 2014). ISO 14224 (ISO, 2016) standardizes the collection and exchange of reliability and maintenance data, supporting performance benchmarking and decision-making. IEC 81346 (IEC, 2022a, 2022b) offers a methodology for classifying and structuring industrial systems, which is foundational for consistent digital asset modeling. In more advanced scenarios, frameworks like RAMI 4.0 and the Industrial Internet Reference Architecture (IIRA) provide layered models for integrating digital technologies within industrial ecosystems (Plattform Industrie 4.0, 2015; IIC, 2019).

Alongside formal standards, best practices provide pragmatic guidance based on real-world implementations. While standards outline what should be done and how, best practices illustrate how these principles are applied in operational contexts—often tailored to sector-specific needs. For example, the UIC digitalization framework for railways or BIM standards for the construction sector combine global standards with domain-specific adaptations to support structured digital transformation (ISO, 2019a, 2019b; UIC, 2023). These practices also evolve with technological maturity and often address challenges that standards alone cannot, such as organizational readiness, workforce capabilities, and change management.

The distinction between standards and best practices is therefore essential: standards ensure formal compliance, data integrity, and system interoperability; best practices ensure feasibility, value realization, and stakeholder engagement. When integrated, they support the effective deployment of digital maintenance strategies aligned with both operational excellence and long-term asset management goals.

This chapter explores how these standards and practices are being adopted and adapted in digital maintenance and asset management. Drawing on industry surveys (GFMAM, 2024), international frameworks, and case-based experiences, it offers a structured approach for leveraging standards as part of a maturity-aligned digitalization journey.

The selection of standards included in this chapter follows a criterion based on their direct contribution to digital maintenance and asset management processes. The focus has been placed on standards that explicitly support asset governance (ISO 55000), data structuring (ISO 14224, IEC 81346), lifecycle information models (ISO 10303, ISO 19650), and system integration frameworks (IEC 62264, RAMI 4.0, IIRA).

Complementary standards—such as OPC UA, DICOM/HL7, or communication-layer specifications—are acknowledged for their technological relevance but are not discussed in depth because their contribution is primarily operational or domain-specific rather than strategic for asset management. The chapter therefore prioritizes standards with cross-sector applicability, explicit asset lifecycle orientation, and a defined role in EAM, APM, or AIP system integration. This methodological choice ensures the necessary depth while maintaining coherence with the chapter's focus on maturity-aligned, standards-based digital transformation.

2 Reviewing International Standards Supporting Digital Maintenance

Digital maintenance relies not only on technological capabilities but on the integration of structured, interoperable information systems that ensure data integrity and traceability across the asset lifecycle. International standards provide the essential backbone for this integration, enabling organizations to align technological tools with strategic maintenance objectives. This section introduces the key foundational standards that support digital maintenance, followed by a review of relevant sector-specific standards that adapt these principles to industry-specific needs.

2.1 ISO 55000 Series—Asset Management Systems

The ISO 55000 series is a cornerstone for organizations seeking to align maintenance and asset management activities with business objectives. Comprising ISO 55000 (overview and principles), ISO 55001 (requirements), and ISO 55002 (guidelines for application), this standard defines the management system approach to asset management, focusing on value realization, risk management, and long-term planning (ISO, 2014).

From a digital perspective, ISO 55000 establishes the organizational and functional requirements that digital systems must support. This includes asset information management, performance monitoring, and decision-making structures—all of which are increasingly digitized through platforms such as Enterprise Asset Management (EAM), Asset Performance Management (APM), and Digital Twins. Digital maturity assessments are often benchmarked against ISO 55001 compliance, helping organizations identify where gaps exist in data governance, asset lifecycle coordination, and stakeholder alignment.

Importantly, the ISO 55000 series support integration with other standards, such as ISO 9001 (quality), ISO 31000 (risk), and ISO 14001 (environment), providing a coherent framework for managing digitalized maintenance in broader enterprise contexts.

2.2 *ISO 14224. Collect and Exchange Reliability and Maintenance Data*

ISO 14224 provides detailed guidance on the collection, exchange, and structure of reliability and maintenance (R&M) data. Originally designed for the oil and gas sector, its principles are broadly applicable to any asset-intensive industry requiring structured failure data, performance indicators, and lifecycle insights (ISO, 2016).

The standard classifies equipment, failure modes, and maintenance actions using a consistent taxonomy and data hierarchy. It enables organizations to build databases for asset reliability modeling, failure root cause analysis, risk-based maintenance, and AHI (Asset Health Index) development.

In digital maintenance systems, ISO 14224 supports the design of intelligent data layers: real-time asset monitoring systems (using IoT) can feed structured data into centralized repositories, enabling advanced analytics such as Mean Time Between Failures (MTBF), availability rates, and failure trend prediction. Combined with AI/ML, these datasets can evolve into predictive and prescriptive maintenance engines.

Integration with ISO 55000 is critical here—while ISO 55000 sets the management framework, ISO 14224 provides the operational data model that populates performance dashboards, risk matrices, and maintenance optimization models.

2.3 *ISO/IEC/IEEE 42010—Architecture Description*

Effective digital transformation requires a clear definition of system architecture. ISO/IEC/IEEE 42010 provides a comprehensive method for the description and modeling of system architectures, especially in complex, multi-stakeholder environments such as digital maintenance ecosystems (ISO/IEC/IEEE, 2022).

The standard introduces the concept of viewpoints, stakeholder concerns, and architecture frameworks, allowing organizations to represent their systems from multiple dimensions: operational, technological, organizational, and data-related. In maintenance contexts, this enables clarity in how Digital Twins, EAM systems, CMMS platforms, and IoT networks interact and exchange information.

For example, a railway operator implementing an IoT-based condition monitoring system would need to describe the architecture connecting field devices (sensors), edge processors, communication networks, cloud platforms, and decision-support applications. ISO 42010 helps align these elements with stakeholder goals, such as regulatory compliance, risk reduction, or maintenance optimization.

By using this standard in conjunction with digital frameworks like RAMI 4.0 or IIRA, organizations can avoid fragmented system design and ensure consistent evolution over time.

2.4 IEC 81346—Industrial Systems and Reference Designations

IEC 81346-1 and -2 provide principles for structuring complex industrial systems and defining reference designations for assets, systems, and components. The standard defines a multi-aspect classification model based on functional, product, and location views, offering a consistent language for identifying and organizing digital assets (IEC, 2022a, 2022b).

This structuring is fundamental to digital asset management. When deploying Digital Twins, for example, each asset must be uniquely identified, geolocated, and linked to its function and performance data. IEC 81346 ensures that this structure is scalable and compatible across platforms, enabling seamless data integration across EAM, GIS, IoT, and simulation environments.

The standard is particularly useful in infrastructure, energy, and manufacturing sectors where thousands of components must be tracked and maintained over decades. When integrated into the Asset Definition Model, IEC 81346 helps build digital asset registers that are interoperable and future-proof.

2.5 IEC 62264/ISA-95—Enterprise-Control System Integration

Digital maintenance thrives on integration—especially between enterprise-level planning systems and plant-floor automation systems. The IEC 62264/ISA-95 standard defines a hierarchical model and object-based interface architecture to support this integration (IEC, 2021; ISA, (2010).

The standard introduces the concept of "levels" of control—from field-level sensors (Level 0) to enterprise management (Level 4)—and defines how information should flow between them. In a digital maintenance context, this supports seamless communication between condition monitoring systems, computerized maintenance management systems (CMMS), and enterprise planning tools like ERP or AIP.

For example, when a predictive maintenance alert is triggered at the shop floor (Level 1–2), it must be translated into a work order in the CMMS (Level 3), and potentially into a revised investment plan (Level 4). IEC 62264 ensures these flows are standardized and traceable.

Its modularity and domain-agnostic nature make it applicable in manufacturing, energy, and transportation sectors, particularly when combined with digital twin orchestration and AI-enabled work order prioritization.

2.6 ISO 10303 (STEP)—Product Lifecycle Management

Known as STEP (Standard for the Exchange of Product model data), ISO 10303 enables the exchange of product lifecycle information between digital systems, including CAD, PLM, ERP, and APM platforms (ISO, 2022). It facilitates interoperability across the design, engineering, maintenance, and end-of-life stages of assets.

For digital maintenance, STEP allows organizations to integrate engineering data (such as 3D models, materials, tolerances) with operational data (like condition, maintenance history, or failure modes). This is essential when developing high-fidelity digital twins that combine static asset geometry with dynamic behavior.

STEP is especially useful in sectors such as aerospace, automotive, and heavy manufacturing, where design-for-maintenance and digital thread strategies are being deployed. When STEP-compliant models are aligned with AAS (Asset Administration Shell) structures, organizations gain a powerful platform for traceability, simulation, and lifecycle optimization.

2.7 Sector-Specific Standards Supporting Digital Maintenance

While foundational standards provide universal principles for structuring and managing digital assets, sector-specific standards ensure that these principles are effectively applied within the unique contexts of various industries. These standards reflect the regulatory requirements, operational constraints, and data conventions of specific sectors, providing a bridge between general asset management frameworks and practical implementation in the field. Let's review a good number of examples in the next Sections.

2.7.1 Building Information Modeling (BIM)—ISO 19650

In the construction and facilities management sectors, ISO 19650 establishes a global standard for Building Information Modeling (BIM), which defines processes for the organization and digitization of information about buildings and infrastructure throughout their lifecycle (ISO, 2019a, 2019b). BIM integrates 3D digital models with structured data, supporting planning, construction, operation, and maintenance.

In the context of digital maintenance, BIM enables asset tracking, spatial coordination, and lifecycle documentation. For example, HVAC systems, lighting, or structural components can be linked to their digital representations, inspection histories, and maintenance plans. The use of BIM allows maintenance professionals to simulate interventions, optimize workflows, and ensure that updated data is retained throughout refurbishment or renovation.

BIM's standardized data structure supports integration with CMMS, IoT-based monitoring platforms, and AI-driven diagnostics, enabling a more efficient and transparent approach to facilities maintenance. Combined with ISO 55000 principles, BIM enhances the alignment between built asset information and long-term asset management strategies.

2.7.2 Common Information Model (CIM)—IEC 61970

In the energy and utilities sector, the Common Information Model (CIM), defined in IEC 61970-301, provides a standardized schema for representing network components, configurations, and measurements in electric power systems (IEC, 2020). CIM is essential for ensuring interoperability among software tools used for grid planning, operation, and asset maintenance.

In digital maintenance, CIM enables the integration of real-time SCADA data, condition monitoring results, and maintenance histories into unified asset models. This supports not only predictive maintenance strategies but also long-term planning decisions, such as grid reinforcement or asset replacement.

For example, a transformer's operational data (voltage, temperature, load) can be harmonized with failure history and asset health index (AHI) calculations within a CIM-compliant platform. This data can be used to prioritize maintenance actions across the network and align them with energy availability and regulatory compliance.

CIM is increasingly linked to smart grid initiatives, where distributed generation, remote diagnostics, and cyber-physical systems are reshaping asset management practices. Combined with IEC 61850 for substation communication and IEC 62351 for cybersecurity, CIM is a core enabler of digital reliability-centered maintenance in the power sector.

2.7.3 UIC Digitalization Framework—Railway Sector

For railway infrastructure and rolling stock, the International Union of Railways (UIC) has developed a reference framework that guides digitalization in maintenance and asset management across the sector (UIC, 2023). While not a formal ISO standard, the UIC framework builds upon globally recognized asset management and safety principles (e.g., ISO 55000, EN 50126) and provides sector-specific models for implementation.

The UIC framework emphasizes:

- Use of condition monitoring technologies (axle counters, vibration sensors, smart bogies)
- Deployment of AHI-based prioritization and RCM strategies
- Integration of IoT, AI, and Digital Twins in both track and fleet management
- Importance of data harmonization and open platforms across national operators.

Infrastructure managers and train operators can move toward a predictive and risk-based maintenance regime, thanks to this framework adoption. For example, track geometry data and train vibration patterns can be fused to detect degradation trends and schedule targeted interventions.

The framework also emphasizes interoperability between existing legacy systems and new digital platforms, highlighting the importance of gradual transformation and system-wide maturity mapping. UIC's guidelines have been widely adopted in Europe, Asia, and Latin America, serving as a reference for harmonizing digital transformation in the rail sector.

2.7.4 Additional Sector-Specific References

Other sectors have also developed standards and frameworks tailored to their digital maintenance needs:

- ISO 20815 (Oil & Gas)—System reliability and cost management for upstream petroleum operations
- DICOM/HL7 (Healthcare)—For medical equipment maintenance and interoperability of health information
- ISO/TS 8000—Data quality standards critical in supply chains and enterprise maintenance databases
- SAE JA1011/JA1012 (Aerospace/Automotive)—Guidelines for Reliability-Centered Maintenance (RCM) processes in aviation and defense
- OECD AI Framework—Although not maintenance-specific, it provides guidance on responsible AI use, relevant for predictive maintenance tools.

These domain-specific standards help tailor digital maintenance strategies to sectoral challenges, whether in regulated environments, critical infrastructure, or consumer-facing industries.

3 Reviewing Reference Frameworks for Digitalization

The digital transformation of maintenance and asset management is not simply a matter of adopting new technologies—it requires a coherent architectural vision that aligns technological components, data flows, and operational processes throughout the asset lifecycle. To address this complexity, several reference frameworks have emerged, offering structured approaches to guide the integration of digital technologies across industries.

Among the most influential are the Reference Architecture Model for Industrie 4.0 (RAMI 4.0), the Industrial Internet Reference Architecture (IIRA), and the Asset Administration Shell (AAS). These frameworks are not mutually exclusive; rather, they provide complementary perspectives that help organizations design scalable, interoperable, and lifecycle-oriented digital ecosystems. This section presents these models and explores how they align with asset management standards and lifecycle stages.

3.1 RAMI 4.0—Reference Architecture Model for Industrie 4.0

RAMI 4.0 is a three-dimensional reference model developed by the German Plattform Industrie 4.0 initiative. It provides a structured framework to classify and organize the elements of Industry 4.0 environments across three axes: Hierarchy Levels, Lifecycle and Value Stream, and Layers (Platform Industrie 4.0, 2015).

- Hierarchy Levels (vertical axis): Derived from IEC 62264/ISA-95, this axis ranges from the physical asset level (e.g., field devices) up to the enterprise level (e.g., business processes), including elements like control systems, work centers, and connected world environments.
- Lifecycle & Value Stream (horizontal axis): Based on IEC 62890, this axis distinguishes between the type phase (design and development of the asset) and the instance phase (operation, maintenance, and disposal of the asset).
- Layers (depth axis): Represent the various architectural layers necessary to realize a digital system: Asset, Integration, Communication, Information, Functional, and Business.

RAMI 4.0 provides a complete reference for designing digital architectures that span from physical assets to business logic, integrating real-time data, analytics, and enterprise processes. In digital maintenance, RAMI 4.0 is used to:

- Map sensor data from the asset level to APM platforms at the enterprise level.
- Design digital twins that support both real-time monitoring and lifecycle simulation.
- Identify gaps in communication or integration layers that may hinder data interoperability.

RAMI 4.0 also establishes the conceptual foundation for the Asset Administration Shell (AAS), which serves as the digital interface of the physical asset within the framework.

3.2 IIRA—Industrial Internet Reference Architecture

The Industrial Internet Reference Architecture (IIRA) is developed by the Industrial Internet Consortium (IIC) to support digital transformation in industrial systems, particularly in IIoT (Industrial Internet of Things) contexts. While similar in intent to RAMI 4.0, IIRA takes a function-oriented approach, focusing on roles, viewpoints, and design patterns for building scalable and secure industrial solutions (IIC, 2019).

IIRA is structured around four key viewpoints:

- Business Viewpoint—Defines stakeholder objectives, business processes, and key performance indicators.
- Usage Viewpoint—Describes how the system is used in its operational context, including workflows, user interactions, and safety constraints.
- Functional Viewpoint—Outlines system capabilities, functions, and logical interactions between components (e.g., analytics, control, optimization).
- Implementation Viewpoint—Specifies the technical infrastructure and components used to realize the functional architecture.

In the context of digital maintenance, IIRA enables organizations to:

- Develop cross-functional digital strategies aligned with business goals.
- Identify use cases for predictive maintenance, such as vibration analytics or fault prediction.
- Ensure that systems are interoperable, modular, and secure, especially when integrating legacy equipment.

Unlike RAMI 4.0, which focuses more on structured classification, IIRA emphasizes design methodology and system behavior. The two models are complementary: RAMI provides the scaffolding for organizing digital elements; IIRA provides guidance on how to engineer and orchestrate them.

3.3 Asset Administration Shell (AAS)—Standardizing Digital Twins

At the heart of both RAMI 4.0 and the broader Industry 4.0 paradigm lies the Asset Administration Shell (AAS)—a standardized digital interface that serves as the "digital twin" of an asset. AAS encapsulates all relevant information about a physical or logical asset, including its structure, status, behavior, and interaction rules (Platform

Industrie 4.0, 2019). The AAS is composed of several sub models, each describing a specific aspect of the asset:

- Identification Sub model—Unique ID, manufacturer, versioning.
- Operational Data Sub model—Real-time parameters like temperature, pressure, cycles.
- Lifecycle Data Sub model—Maintenance history, performance trends.
- Simulation Sub model—Predictive models and what-if scenarios.
- Compliance Sub model—Standards, certifications, regulatory constraints.
- Communication Sub model—Supported interfaces and data formats.

The AAS allows assets to become self-descriptive, interoperable, and integrable within digital ecosystems. In digital maintenance, AAS enables:

- Plug-and-play onboarding of assets into CMMS/EAM platforms.
- Automated health assessment using Asset Health Index (AHI) submodels.
- Unified visualization of asset performance, condition, and maintenance needs.

Furthermore, the AAS supports vendor-neutral interoperability by defining common data exchange models, which is critical in environments with mixed OEM equipment and legacy systems.

When combined with ISO 81346 (structuring) and ISO 14224 (maintenance data), AAS provides a complete framework for developing robust, scalable digital twins.

3.4 Comparative Mapping Between Frameworks and Lifecycle Stages

Each of the above frameworks contributes differently across the asset lifecycle, from concept design to decommissioning. Table 1 summarizes how RAMI 4.0, IIRA, and AAS align with various lifecycle phases and standard categories.

This comparative view highlights that no single framework is sufficient on its own. Effective digital maintenance requires:

- The classification structure of RAMI 4.0
- The design logic and engineering principles of IIRA
- The interoperability and semantic modeling of AAS
- And the alignment with international standards for data quality, safety, and lifecycle management.

In order to consolidate the standards discussed in this section and clarify their respective roles within digital maintenance, Table 2 provides a summarized view of the main frameworks, their domains, lifecycle impact, and relevance to asset management practices.

Table 1 Frameworks and lifecycle phases

Lifecycle stage	RAMI 4.0	IIRA	AAS	Supporting standards
Concept and design	Type phase (IEC 62890)	Business and usage viewpoints	Identification/ functional models	ISO 10303 (STEP), ISO/IEC/ IEEE 42010
Engineering and integration	Integration layer, hierarchies	Functional viewpoint	Structural and operational sub models	IEC 81346,ISO 19650 (BIM)
Operation and monitoring	Instance phase, asset layer	Usage and implementation viewpoints	Real-time data, lifecycle models	ISO 14224, IEC 62264, CIM (IEC 61970)
Maintenance and optimization	Communication and information	Functional viewpoint	AHI, predictive and simulation sub models	ISO 55001, AAS, RAMS, RCM, SAE JA1011
End-of-life/ disposal	Lifecycle coordination	Business viewpoint	Lifecycle records, compliance sub model	ISO 55000, LCC Guidelines

Table 2 Summary of standards and their roles

Standard/ framework	Primary domain	Lifecycle impact	Relation to digital maintenance
ISO 55000	Asset governance	Full lifecycle	Aligns decision making and asset value
ISO 14224	Maintenance data	Operation	Enables RCM, AHI, predictive models
IEC 81346	Asset structuring	Design → Operation	Enables digital twins and asset registers
ISO 19650 (BIM)	Construction/ infrastructure	Design → O&M	Integrates 3D models with maintenance data
RAMI 4.0	Digital architecture	All layers	Guides data flow, integration, IIoT
IIRA	System engineering	Design → Integration	Supports IIoT design and use cases
AAS	Digital twin	Operation → Optimization	Standardizes digital asset interfaces
IEC 62264	Enterprise ↔ Control Integration	Operation	Ensures vertical integration CMMS ↔ MES

4 From Standards to Best Practices: Adoption Patterns

While standards provide a common language and structural backbone for digital maintenance and asset management, the journey from theory to practice is rarely straightforward. Organizations that successfully adopt digital strategies often go beyond compliance with formal standards and evolve toward best practices—pragmatic methods and configurations that balance technical feasibility, operational performance, and strategic goals.

This section examines how leading organizations implement key frameworks and standards in real-world contexts, with a focus on how these are integrated into digital systems such as Enterprise Asset Management (EAM), Asset Performance Management (APM), and Condition-Based Maintenance (CBM) platforms. Case-based insights from sectors such as rail transport, infrastructure, and manufacturing highlight the diversity of adoption patterns and the common principles behind them.

4.1 From Compliance to Optimization: Implementation Strategies

Adoption of digital standards typically follows a phased maturity pattern. In the initial phase, organizations often focus on establishing baseline compliance—applying standards like ISO 55000 for asset governance or ISO 14224 for maintenance data structuring. This is frequently accompanied by a data cleanup process and efforts to centralize asset registries within a CMMS or EAM platform.

In the intermediate phase, organizations move toward data integration and automation. Standards such as IEC 62264 or RAMI 4.0 help guide the vertical integration of data from sensors and automation systems to enterprise planning tools. Predictive models begin to emerge through pilot projects, often targeting critical assets with well-defined failure patterns.

In the advanced phase, organizations shift toward optimization and innovation. Digital twins and AI-based decision-support systems are deployed, often leveraging the Asset Administration Shell (AAS) as a digital interface for asset behavior. AHI models are implemented to support risk-based prioritization, and data flows are orchestrated across design, operation, and maintenance functions.

The transition between these phases is not purely technical—it requires a combination of change management, governance alignment, and capability building, including workforce training and supplier engagement.

4.2 Integration with EAM, APM, and AIP Systems

Digital maintenance relies on the orchestration of multiple software platforms that enable the collection, analysis, and utilization of asset-related information across the organization. The successful adoption of standards and best practices is determined not only by the availability of data, but by how well it is structured, interpreted, and actioned within enterprise systems. The most relevant platforms in this integration are:

- Enterprise Asset Management (EAM) systems, such as IBM Maximo, SAP EAM, or Infor, act as the backbone of maintenance operations. They manage asset registries, work orders, maintenance histories, and cost tracking. When configured in alignment with standards like ISO 55001 and IEC 81346, EAM systems ensure that asset hierarchies, failure modes, and maintenance activities are traceable and auditable across their lifecycle.
- Asset Performance Management (APM) platforms, such as GE APM, ABB Ability, or Siemens Navigator, extend the functionality of EAM by integrating real-time condition monitoring, reliability analytics, and Asset Health Index (AHI) models. Within APM systems, Condition-Based Maintenance (CBM) is no longer treated as a standalone process but as a core capability, supported by sensor integration, event processing, and predictive analytics. CBM strategies—enabled by ISO 14224-based failure data and IoT-driven observations—are now embedded in automated rule engines that trigger maintenance planning or re-prioritization.
- Asset Investment Planning (AIP) solutions, such as Copperleaf, DecisionPoint, or integrated modules within EAM/APM suites, support strategic maintenance and renewal decisions. These systems rely on standardized data models and health indices (e.g., from APM platforms) to forecast asset performance and degradation, simulate different intervention scenarios, and align capital planning with risk and service-level objectives. AIP tools increasingly integrate ISO 55000 principles with risk models and LCC (Life Cycle Cost) analysis, guiding asset managers in prioritizing interventions under constrained budgets.

A leading practice is to ensure that data flows seamlessly between these platforms. For example:

- Sensors and IIoT devices feed real-time condition data to the APM layer.
- APM algorithms compute health indices and failure probabilities.
- These outputs are passed to the EAM system to generate work orders or update maintenance plans.
- AIP tools receive updated forecasts and risk profiles to revise the investment roadmap.

This integrated ecosystem enables a transition from reactive to risk-informed and value-based maintenance planning, combining operational intelligence with long-term strategic alignment.

4.3 Cross-Industry Examples of Best Practice Adoption

4.3.1 Rail Sector: Predictive Maintenance and UIC Frameworks

Railway infrastructure and rolling stock operators have been early adopters of digital maintenance standards. Organizations such as DB Netz (Germany), SNCF (France), and ADIF (Spain) have developed digital strategies grounded in UIC guidelines, ISO 55000, and RAMS (EN 50126). Best practices include:

- Deployment of vibration, axle load, and temperature sensors for condition monitoring of both track and trains.
- Implementation of AHI models linked to maintenance planning tools.
- Integration of maintenance platforms with ERTMS/ETCS signaling systems, allowing maintenance actions to be aligned with traffic availability windows.

These organizations leverage structured asset definitions (IEC 81346), digital twins based on AAS, and risk models adapted from SAE JA1011 for prioritization. The result is a shift from time-based to condition-based interventions, increasing asset availability and reducing lifecycle costs.

4.3.2 Infrastructure and Bridges: BIM and Lifecycle Management

In civil infrastructure, especially bridges and tunnels, the combination of BIM (ISO 19650) and asset lifecycle standards (ISO 55000, ISO 15686) enables effective digital maintenance strategies.

Best practices include:

- Use of 3D BIM models enriched with inspection data and degradation histories.
- Integration of sensor-based monitoring (e.g., strain gauges, corrosion sensors) with digital dashboards.
- Application of lifecycle cost models to inform maintenance prioritization and capital planning.

Several European asset owners now maintain Digital Twins of bridges that consolidate design, as-built, and operational data in a single platform, facilitating predictive maintenance and long-term investment decisions.

4.3.3 Manufacturing: APM Integration and Smart Factories

In manufacturing, digital maintenance is a pillar of smart factory transformation. Companies like Bosch, Siemens, and Toyota have implemented fully integrated systems using RAMI 4.0 as an architectural guide.

Best practices include:

- Real-time condition monitoring of production assets linked to APM systems.

- Deployment of AI-based failure prediction algorithms that feed into EAM platforms.
- Use of IEC 62264 for harmonizing MES (Manufacturing Execution Systems) and ERP integration.

These organizations often create maintenance control rooms where data from multiple plants are aggregated and visualized, enabling remote diagnostics and centralized decision-making.

As a conclusion of this Section of Chap. 4, The successful implementation of digital maintenance standards depends on the ability to transform static frameworks into dynamic, embedded practices. Leading organizations across sectors demonstrate that standards must be actively interpreted and adapted to real-world workflows, supported by robust system integration, and embedded within organizational processes and cultures.

Best practices emerge not from blind adherence to standards but from strategic alignment, technological integration, and experimentation. By sharing these patterns, the digital maintenance community accelerates collective learning and increases the success rate of transformation initiatives.

5 Challenges in Standardization

The adoption of digital maintenance frameworks and standards has accelerated significantly in recent years, but their practical implementation continues to encounter major challenges. While international standards provide valuable guidance for structuring data, systems, and processes, gaps and inconsistencies persist, particularly in the context of interoperability, emerging technologies, and human factors.

This section outlines four key challenges that organizations frequently face when translating standards into operational reality: (1) data model inconsistencies, (2) lack of harmonization between overlapping standards, (3) insufficient coverage of AI and cybersecurity, and (4) workforce-related gaps in adoption and training.

5.1 Data Model Inconsistencies

One of the most common challenges is the inconsistency in how asset and maintenance data are structured and exchanged across systems. Even when organizations adopt standards such as ISO 14224 (for maintenance data) or IEC 81346 (for asset structuring), variability in interpretation and implementation leads to fragmented data landscapes. Examples include:

- Different departments or vendors using non-aligned taxonomies for asset hierarchies, resulting in duplicated or mismatched records.

- Legacy systems that were developed before standardization initiatives and cannot export data in a compliant format.
- CMMS, EAM, APM, and AIP platforms that support different data schemas or metadata structures, complicating integration.

Efforts like ISO/TS 8000 (Data Quality) and ISO 10303 (STEP for PLM) offer technical solutions, but widespread harmonization is still lacking. Even the Asset Administration Shell (AAS), designed to serve as a universal digital interface, depends on submodels that are often customized or vendor-specific, undermining cross-platform compatibility.

Several initiatives are emerging to address inconsistencies across data models and overlapping standards. The Digital Twin Consortium is advancing sector-agnostic ontologies to enable interoperable digital twins, while IDS and Gaia-X promote shared data spaces with strong data-sovereignty principles. The Open Industry 4.0 Alliance contributes harmonization maps linking RAMI 4.0, AAS, IEC 62264 and OPC UA models, and crosswalks are being developed between BIM (ISO 19650), CIM (IEC 61970), STEP (ISO 10303) and AAS submodels for infrastructure and energy applications. Together, these efforts show that future harmonization will depend increasingly on shared ontologies and machine-interpretable semantics rather than on structural standards alone.

5.2 *Lack of Harmonization Between Operational Standards*

Another major issue is the overlap and lack of harmonization between standards developed by different bodies (e.g., ISO, IEC, IEEE, ISA, UIC). While each standard provides value within its domain, organizations operating across sectors or regions often face:

- Redundant or conflicting requirements, e.g., between ISO 55000 and national infrastructure regulations.
- Gaps in coverage when trying to integrate horizontal and vertical standards (e.g., connecting ISO 19650 for BIM with IEC 62264 for system integration).
- Difficulty mapping high-level standards (e.g., RAMI 4.0, IIRA) into daily operational processes due to missing translational layers or implementation guides.

This misalignment affects procurement, compliance, and cross-organizational collaboration. For instance, infrastructure operators working with multiple contractors may receive digital models in different formats (BIM, CIM, AAS), forcing them to reconcile data manually.

To address this, initiatives like the Digital Twin Consortium, IEC Smart Manufacturing Standards Map, and Open Industry 4.0 Alliance are attempting to bridge gaps by providing reference mappings and shared ontologies. However, the pace of harmonization remains slower than the pace of technological innovation.

5.3 Gaps in AI and Cybersecurity Coverage

Traditional asset management and maintenance standards were not developed with AI, ML, or advanced analytics in mind. As a result, organizations face a growing regulatory vacuum when deploying intelligent systems for predictive or prescriptive maintenance. Key challenges include:

- Lack of standardized frameworks for explainability and model validation in maintenance AI tools.
- Limited guidance on data governance, model drift, or bias in predictive maintenance algorithms.
- Absence of sector-specific AI standards (outside generic frameworks like the OECD AI Principles or ISO/IEC 42001 on AI Management Systems).

Similarly, cybersecurity standards are lagging behind the complexity of interconnected maintenance ecosystems. While IEC 62443 provides a strong foundation for industrial control systems security, it is not always aligned with cloud-based APM or IoT platforms. Many AAS-based implementations lack formalized cybersecurity requirements, increasing exposure to supply chain attacks or unauthorized data manipulation.

Emerging frameworks are beginning to close these gaps. ISO/IEC 42001 introduces an AI Management System that covers explainability, data governance, and model validation, while the NIST AI RMF provides structured guidance for managing risks such as drift and bias. The OECD AI Principles remain a reference for responsible AI adoption, and recent extensions of IEC 62443 increasingly address cloud analytics, digital twins, and IoT device protection. These developments offer a path toward more coherent, secure, and accountable AI-enabled maintenance systems.

5.4 Workforce Alignment and Training

A less technical but equally critical challenge is the gap between standards and workforce capability. Digital transformation in maintenance requires staff who can:

- Understand and apply standards like ISO 55001 or IEC 62264.
- Interpret digital twin data and reliability models.
- Interact with integrated platforms (EAM/APM/AIP) and make informed decisions based on predictive insights.

However, many maintenance and operations teams lack this skillset. The complexity and volume of standards can be overwhelming, particularly when documentation is highly technical or abstract. Moreover, standards are often not written with practical usability in mind, making them difficult to translate into daily workflows.

Best practices observed in leading organizations include:

- Customized training programs that link standards to job roles.
- Digital maturity models that assess staff capabilities alongside system integration.
- Creation of cross-functional implementation teams that combine technical experts, reliability engineers, and IT professionals.

Workforce readiness can also be strengthened through targeted development programs aligned with digital maturity goals. These include role-based training paths, professional certifications (e.g., IAM, SMRP), vendor-neutral training on EAM/APM/AIP platforms, and change-management initiatives aligned with ISO 55002. Cross-functional collaboration between maintenance, IT/OT, and analytics teams further supports the adoption and sustained use of data-driven maintenance practices.

Ultimately, standardization will only succeed if accompanied by a parallel effort to upskill and engage the workforce, ensuring that technical frameworks are supported by organizational readiness.

As a conclusion of this part, the digitalization of maintenance and asset management cannot be achieved by standards alone. Despite their value in providing structure, consistency, and interoperability, several critical gaps persist—in data semantics, framework harmonization, emerging technology coverage, and human factors.

Addressing these challenges requires coordinated action from standards bodies, technology vendors, asset owners, and research institutions. It also demands a shift from passive compliance to active stewardship, where organizations invest in aligning systems, people, and practices with the evolving landscape of digital asset management.

Only through this multi-dimensional effort can standards fulfill their potential as enablers—not obstacles—of industrial innovation.

6 A Structured Approach: Aligning with Maturity Models

While standards and reference frameworks are essential to enable digital maintenance, their effective deployment across an organization requires a structured and adaptive approach. This is where maturity models play a pivotal role. Maturity models help organizations assess their current capabilities, identify gaps, and chart a roadmap for structured transformation over time.

This section proposes a dual-maturity framework that combines Asset Management (AM) Maturity with Digital Maturity and discusses how the adoption of standards and architectures (such as ISO 55000, RAMI 4.0, AAS) can be mapped across maturity levels. The aim is to support organizations in moving progressively from basic compliance toward optimization and innovation in digital maintenance.

6.1 The Dual Maturity Perspective: AM Maturity × Digital Maturity

Digital maintenance efforts often fail when pursued as technology-first initiatives without alignment to the organization's maturity in asset governance and management. Conversely, even mature asset management systems can become stagnant if they ignore the potential of digital innovation.

To address this, a two-dimensional maturity framework (Table 3) can be applied, based on experiences developed within the International Maintenance Association (IMA) and other international bodies (e.g., GFMAM):

In this view, best practices emerge in the upper-right quadrant, where digital capabilities and asset management maturity reinforce each other. A dual maturity model helps organizations:

- Avoid investing in digital platforms before process governance is established.
- Identify when it is appropriate to scale from pilots to enterprise-wide deployments.
- Prioritize enablers (training, standards, governance) according to both axes.

To illustrate the combined Asset Management × Digital Maturity perspective, consider a railway infrastructure operator implementing ISO 55000, ISO 14224, RAMI 4.0, and AAS across three maturity stages:

- Stage 1—Basic Compliance: The operator structures its asset hierarchy using IEC 81346 and standardizes failure data following ISO 14224. A central CMMS is deployed to unify maintenance histories and inspection records. Processes become auditable and aligned with ISO 55001 requirements, but analytics remain descriptive.
- Stage 2—Optimization: Condition monitoring systems are integrated into the EAM and APM platforms. RAMI 4.0 guides the vertical integration of data flows between field sensors, communication layers, and enterprise applications. AHI models are implemented for critical assets, enabling risk-based planning and optimized work scheduling.

Table 3 AM versus digital maturity

	Digital immature	Digital developing	Digitally mature
AM immature	Unstructured processes, limited data use	Ad hoc digital tools, no integration	High-tech fragmentation, no strategic AM alignment
AM developing	Isolated digital pilots supporting improved AM	EAM/APM integration aligned with ISO 55000	Risk-based AIP strategies, partially automated
AM mature	Manual but structured asset governance	Fully integrated digital systems, optimized CBM/APM	AI-supported lifecycle management, autonomous diagnostics

- Stage 3—Innovation: Full AAS submodels are developed to enable digital twins of track components, bridges, and energy systems. Predictive models autonomously generate maintenance recommendations, which are validated through simulation. AIP tools receive updated forecasts, ensuring coordinated operational and investment planning.

This step-by-step evolution demonstrates how organizations progress coherently by aligning standard adoption with organizational maturity and digital capabilities.

6.2 *Mapping Standards and Frameworks to Maturity Stages*

The adoption of standards such as ISO 55000, RAMI 4.0, or AAS does not occur all at once. Instead, organizations typically adopt frameworks progressively as their maturity evolves. Table 4 illustrates how this adoption might unfold across three maturity stages.

Each stage builds upon the previous one. For example:

- In Stage 1, structuring assets with IEC 81346 and ISO 14224 supports consistent maintenance histories.
- In Stage 2, the integration of APM tools with EAM platforms allows risk-based maintenance planning.
- In Stage 3, the adoption of full AAS and Digital Twins enables autonomous diagnostics and prescriptive interventions aligned with investment planning.

This structured mapping ensures that the implementation of digital tools is aligned with organizational readiness and standards adoption is not simply a box-checking exercise but a catalyst for improved performance.

Table 4 Standards and maturity stages

Maturity stage	Focus	Typical standards adopted	Capabilities enabled
Stage 1: Basic compliance	Governance, asset inventory	ISO 55001, ISO 14224, IEC 81346	Asset hierarchy structuring, data centralization
Stage 2: optimization	Integration and decision support	IEC 62264, BIM (ISO 19650), RAMI 4.0, basic AAS models	Condition monitoring, AHI, CBM, integration EAM/APM
Stage 3: innovation	Autonomous and predictive systems	AAS with full submodels, IIRA, AI governance (OECD, ISO/IEC 42001)	Digital twins, AI-based maintenance, dynamic AIP

6.3 A Progressive Roadmap: From Compliance to Innovation

A practical path for standard adoption and digital transformation can be framed as a three-step roadmap:

1. Basic Compliance. Organizations start by:
- Creating a central asset register.
- Structuring hierarchies (IEC 81346) and failure data (ISO 14224).
- Aligning governance processes with ISO 55001.
- Training staff to understand standards and system interfaces.

Success here is measured by data quality, asset visibility, and standard-compliant processes.

2. Optimization. Next comes:
- Integration of EAM and APM platforms.
- Implementation of condition monitoring (CBM) and health models (AHI).
- Application of RAMI 4.0 to structure data flows and system responsibilities.
- Gradual deployment of AAS-based digital representations.

Here, organizations shift from reactive or time-based maintenance to predictive and risk-informed approaches.

3. Innovation. At the highest level of maturity:
- AI/ML models support autonomous diagnostics and planning.
- Investment decisions are informed by integrated AIP systems.
- Digital twins evolve dynamically, simulating asset behavior.
- AI and cybersecurity governance standards (e.g., ISO/IEC 42001, IEC 62443) are embedded.

This stage allows for value-optimized and automated maintenance, with continuous feedback loops from operations into strategic decision-making.

As a conclusion to this part of the Chapter, the effective implementation of standards and digital tools in maintenance is not a binary state but a maturity journey. By combining asset management and digital maturity models, organizations can structure their transformation according to their current capabilities, resources, and goals.

Standards like ISO 55000 or RAMI 4.0 offer not just technical specifications but milestones within a broader developmental path. Recognizing where the organization stands—and what it needs to move forward—enables more targeted investments, better risk management, and higher returns from digital transformation.

Ultimately, aligning digital efforts with structured maturity models helps organizations move from compliance to strategic innovation, ensuring that technology enhances—not complicates—maintenance excellence.

7 Recommendations and Conclusions

The progressive digitalization of maintenance and asset management is reshaping how organizations operate, plan, and invest in their physical infrastructure. Throughout this chapter, we have reviewed the evolving role of standards and best practices as enablers of this transformation, and emphasized their importance in creating structured, interoperable, and future-ready systems. The experience across multiple sectors suggests that the successful adoption of digital frameworks depends not only on technological readiness but also on organizational alignment, maturity, and strategic planning.

One of the primary recommendations derived from this analysis is the necessity of embedding standardization efforts within a layered architectural model. Architectures such as RAMI 4.0 and the Industrial Internet Reference Architecture (IIRA) provide a valuable conceptual structure for aligning technical systems with asset lifecycle stages and business processes. These models help ensure that digital maintenance platforms are developed with clear roles for data acquisition, processing, decision-making, and value generation. Standards such as ISO 55001 and IEC 81346 should serve as foundational layers, ensuring consistent asset identification, structured hierarchies, and traceable governance mechanisms.

As organizations progress along their digital transformation journey, their adoption of standards must evolve accordingly. In early maturity stages, efforts should focus on building a unified asset inventory, centralizing maintenance data, and complying with basic governance structures. As maturity develops, integration between Enterprise Asset Management (EAM), Asset Performance Management (APM), and Asset Investment Planning (AIP) platforms becomes critical. In advanced stages, the adoption of digital twins structured around the Asset Administration Shell (AAS), combined with predictive analytics and AI-based optimization, marks a transition from optimization to innovation.

It is essential to view this trajectory not as a rigid path but as a flexible roadmap informed by dual maturity models—one assessing asset management capabilities, the other digital readiness. Such a dual approach, as previously explored in practical frameworks from the IMA and GFMAM, allows organizations to tailor their priorities and investments to their current context and strategic ambitions. Mapping standards and frameworks to defined maturity stages helps avoid technology overreach and supports more sustainable and effective deployments.

However, significant challenges persist. Inconsistencies in data modeling, limited harmonization between international and sector-specific standards, and gaps in standard coverage for emerging domains such as artificial intelligence and cybersecurity continue to hinder adoption. Moreover, workforce capacity remains a bottleneck, requiring targeted training and knowledge transfer to translate abstract standard documents into actionable procedures.

Looking forward, several trends will shape the next generation of standardization in digital maintenance. The development of semantic standards and ontologies will be critical to achieving machine-interpretable interoperability between platforms and vendors. Data sovereignty and trust frameworks, such as Gaia-X and IDS, will redefine the governance of asset-related data across organizational boundaries. Finally, as AI becomes increasingly embedded in maintenance decision-making, the emergence of AI governance standards, including those under ISO/IEC 42001, will play a central role in ensuring transparency, safety, and accountability.

In summary, standards and best practices should be seen not as static mandates but as dynamic instruments of strategic alignment and continuous improvement. Their role is not merely to ensure compliance but to enable learning, integration, and innovation across the full lifecycle of assets. As digitalization deepens, the organizations that approach standard adoption as a systemic, maturity-aligned, and future-conscious endeavor will be best positioned to realize the full benefits of intelligent maintenance.

References

Copperleaf Technologies. (2021). *Asset investment planning in practice: A guide for infrastructure managers.*

Copperleaf Technologies. (2022). *Asset investment planning and management: Enabling better decisions.* https://www.copperleaf.com (Visited on May 2025).

Crespo Márquez, A., et al. (2022). *Digitalization of assets, facilities and maintenance management.* IMA Research Committee.

Digital Twin Consortium. (2022a). *Ontology harmonization and semantic interoperability for digital twins.*

Digital Twin Consortium (2022b). *Taxonomy and definitions for digital twins.* https://www.digitaltwinconsortium.org

Gaia-X Association. (2022). *Policy rules and architecture—Gaia-X Framework 22.10.* https://www.gaia-x.eu (Visited on May 2025).

GE Digital. (2021). APM strategy: Asset performance management for predictive maintenance. *General Electric.* https://www.ge.com/digital

GFMAM. (2015). *The asset management landscape* (2nd edn). Global Forum on Maintenance and Asset Management. https://gfmam.org (Visited on May 2025).

GFMAM. (2021). *Digital readiness framework for asset management.* Global Forum on Maintenance and Asset Management.

GFMAM. (2024). *Digital transformation in maintenance and asset management—Survey report.* Global Forum on Maintenance and Asset Management.

Health Level Seven International (HL7). HL7 standards for the interoperability of health information. https://www.hl7.org

IBM. (2023). *IBM maximo application suite: Integrated EAM and APM platform.* https://www.ibm.com/products/maximo (Visited on May 2025).

IEC. (2020). *IEC 61970-301: Energy management system application program interface (EMS-API)—Part 301: Common information model (CIM) base.* International Electrotechnical Commission.

IEC. (2021). *IEC 62264-1: Enterprise-control system integration—Part 1: Models and terminology.* International Electrotechnical Commission.

IEC. (2022a). *IEC 62443: Industrial communication networks—Network and system security.* International Electrotechnical Commission.

IEC. (2022b). *IEC 81346-1: Industrial systems—Structuring principles and reference designations—Part 1: Basic rules.*

IIC. (2019). *The industrial internet reference architecture v1.9*. Industrial Internet Consortium.
Industrial Internet Consortium (IIC). (2019). *The Industrial Internet Reference Architecture (IIRA), Version 1.9*. https://www.iiconsortium.org/IIRA.htm (Visited on May 2025).
International Data Spaces Association (IDSA). (2021). *IDS reference architecture model, Version 3.0*. https://www.internationaldataspaces.org
International Maintenance Association (IMA). (2023). *Digital maturity in maintenance: Assessment framework for strategic transformation*. Internal Working Document. https://www.ima-world.org (Visited on May 2025).
International Society of Automation (ISA). (2010). ANSI/ISA-95.00.01-2010: *Enterprise-control system integration — Part 1: Models and terminology*. Research Triangle Park, NC: ISA.
ISO. (2006). ISO 20815: *Petroleum, petrochemical and natural gas industries—Production assurance and reliability management*. International Organization for Standardization.
ISO. (2009). *ISO/TS 8000-1: Data quality—Part 1: Overview*. International Organization for Standardization
ISO. (2011). *ISO/TS 8000-1: Data quality—Part 1: Overview*. International Organization for Standardization.
ISO. (2014). *ISO 55000: Asset management—overview, principles and terminology*.
ISO. (2016). ISO 14224: *Petroleum, petrochemical and natural gas industries—Collection and exchange of reliability and maintenance data for equipment*.
ISO. (2017). *ISO 15686-5: Buildings and constructed assets—Service life planning—Part 5: Life-cycle costing*. International Organization for Standardization.
ISO (2019a). *ISO 19650-1: Organization and digitization of information about buildings and civil engineering works, including building information modelling (BIM)—Information management using building information modelling—Part 1: Concepts and principles*. International Organization for Standardization.
ISO. (2019b). *ISO 19650: Organization and digitization of information about buildings and civil engineering works, including BIM*.
ISO/IEC/IEEE. (2022). *ISO/IEC/IEEE 42010:2022. Software, systems and enterprise — Architecture description*. Geneva: International Organization for Standardization.
ISO/IEC. (2023). *ISO/IEC 42001: Artificial intelligence management system*. International Organization for Standardization.
OECD. (2021). *Framework for the classification of AI systems*. Organisation for Economic Co-operation and Development. https://oecd.ai (Visited on May 2025).
Open Industry 4.0 Alliance. (2023). *Reference architecture and harmonization map*. https://openindustry4.com (Visited on May 2025).
Plattform Industrie 4.0. (2015). *RAMI 4.0—Reference architectural model Industrie 4.0*. Federal Ministry for Economic Affairs and Energy, Germany. https://www.plattform-i40.de
Plattform Industrie 4.0. (2019). *Details of the asset administration shell—Part 1: The exchange of information between partners in the value chain of Industrie 4.0 (Version 3.0)*. https://www.plattform-i40.de (Visited on May 2025).
SAE International. (2009a). *JA1011: Evaluation criteria for reliability-centered maintenance (RCM) processes*. Society of Automotive Engineers.
SAE International. (2009b). SAE JA1011: Evaluation criteria for RCM processes. Society of Automotive Engineers. (ya incluida antes, pero ahora aplicada como base para priorización de riesgos en ferrocarril).
SAP SE. (2023). *SAP EAM: Intelligent enterprise asset management overview*. https://www.sap.com
Siemens Energy. (2022). *Navigator: Asset performance suite for digital maintenance*. https://new.siemens.com (Visited on May 2025).
UIC. (2023). *Digital transformation framework for rail infrastructure managers*. International Union of Railways (UIC). https://uic.org. (Visited on May 2025).

Digital Servitization in Asset-Intensive Environments: Basic Requirements and Proposal for Service Validation

Vicente González Prida Díaz, Antonio J. Guillén López, Juan Francisco Gómez Fernández, and Antonio De la Fuente Carmona

Abstract This chapter presents a structured process to validate digital services within asset-intensive contexts, aligning with the principles of Industry 5.0 and digital servitization. The proposed methodology combines cost analysis, strategic fit, risk assessment, and user feedback to evaluate the feasibility and value contribution of digitally supported services. Special attention is given to the role of digital twins, prescriptive maintenance, and service-oriented architectures as enablers of scalable and human-centric service models. The proposal supports organisations in transitioning from product-based to service-oriented value propositions, leveraging digital capabilities to enhance operational resilience, customer experience, and decision-making. Use cases are mentioned in order to illustrate the application and adaptability of the methodology in real-world industrial settings.

Keywords Digital servitization in asset-intensive industries · Product-service systems · Digital service validation framework · Service-oriented architectures · Industry 5.0 human-centric services

V. González Prida Díaz (✉) · J. F. Gómez Fernández
University of Seville, Sevilla, Spain
e-mail: vgonzalezprida@us.es

J. F. Gómez Fernández
e-mail: jfgomez@us.es

A. J. Guillén López
ICEI and Department of Management, Complutense University of Madrid, Pozuelo de Alarcón, Madrid, Spain
e-mail: anguil02@ucm.es

A. De la Fuente Carmona
INGEMAN (Association for the Development of Maintenance Engineering), Sevilla, Spain
e-mail: adelafuente@ingeman.net

A. Crespo Márquez et al. (eds.), *Digital Maintenance and Asset Digitalization*, Engineering Asset Management Review 5,
https://doi.org/10.1007/978-3-032-21502-4_8

1 Introduction

Servitization is a strategic transformation in the business world that goes beyond the conventional sale of products and focuses on offering integrated solutions to meet emerging market needs. Product-Service Systems (PSS), broadly defined as integrated product–service offerings designed to meet customer needs, represent a foundational stage for digital servitization. Traditional PSS models rely on combining tangible and intangible components, whereas digital servitization builds upon them by embedding data-driven, connected, and smart capabilities that enable dynamic and adaptive service delivery (Kohtamäki et al., 2021).This approach implies a transformation towards service-centric business models, where products are integrated with a variety of services to generate added value and establish stronger relationships with customers (Pezzota et al., 2018). Through servitization, companies seek not only to provide tangible products, but also personalised experiences and solutions that promote customer loyalty. This paradigm goes beyond the simple addition of services; it represents a shift towards the formation of business ecosystems in which services play a central and distinctive role. It turns the relationship with customers into a continuous partnership, anticipating and adapting offerings to meet future demands. In parallel, emerging concepts such as Manufacturing-as-a-Service (MaaS) extend digital servitization principles by offering manufacturing capabilities as cloud-enabled, on-demand services. MaaS reinforces modularity, interoperability, and service scalability, complementing the evolution from traditional PSS towards digitally orchestrated service ecosystems (Srai & Kumar, 2020).

The role of innovation is fundamental, as it allows companies to stand out in the market and offer differentiating solutions (Sala et al., 2022). It builds lasting relationships with consumers and focuses on innovation and the creation of Product-Service Systems (PSS), integrating knowledge and expertise. Figure 1 shows Tukker's (2004) classical classification of Product-Service Systems (PSS), which distinguishes three major categories: product-oriented services, focused on improving product use; use-oriented services, in which the manufacturer retains ownership and commercializes the functionality; and result-oriented services, where the customer directly acquires an outcome or performance. This typology provides a conceptual foundation for understanding how servitization evolves from product-centric models toward fully service-oriented approaches.

Servitization has evolved from a traditional approach where services are offered in addition to products, to a deeper integration with digital technologies, representing a major shift in service offerings. Digital servitization is the convergence of servitization and digitalization, representing the adoption of digital technologies applied to servitization (Chirumalla et al., 2023). This concept refers to the stream of literature that examines how digital technologies influence servitization. As a strategy, digital servitization fundamentally involves manufacturing firms providing digital services integrated into physical products. Digital servitization is closely linked to industrial evolution, as it represents a profound paradigm shift in the manufacturing domain, particularly in the transition from Industry 4.0 to Industry 5.0 (Adel et al., 2024).

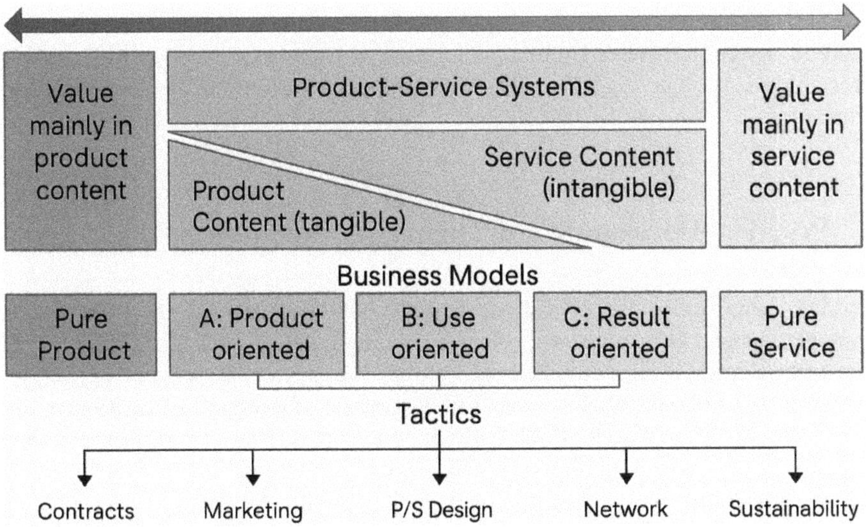

Fig. 1 Categories of the Product-Service System (Tukker, 2004)

Digital servitization is a modern approach that not only enhances the value proposition with additional services, but also uses connectivity, data analytics and artificial intelligence to deliver personalised and efficient experiences. Service delivery is redefined through digital servitization, leveraging such connectivity to improve the interaction between products, customers and internal systems, which facilitates real-time data capture and analysis (Martín-Peña et al., 2018). In this way, customer needs can be anticipated, and services can be proactively optimised. Artificial intelligence also enables advanced personalisation, as systems learn and adapt to user preferences, ensuring that services not only meet current expectations, but also adapt to future demands. In short, the digitalization of service radically transforms the way companies conceive and deliver services, putting technological innovation and customer satisfaction at the heart of their strategies.

Advanced digital technologies are becoming essential enablers of digital servitization. In particular, Artificial Intelligence and Digital Twins provide the analytical capabilities and high-fidelity environments needed to design, test, and support new service-oriented strategies. Their role becomes especially critical in asset-intensive environments, where Digital Twins enable coordinated, multi-level modelling of complex assets and operational conditions, offering a reliable ground for validating methods and anticipating service behavior under realistic constraints. Together, these technologies form a core foundation for Industry 5.0, allowing manufacturers to operationalize innovative service methodologies and deliver more adaptive, real-time digital services (Adel et al., 2024).

The contribution of this work lies in consolidating digital-twin-enabled service logic, service-oriented architectures, and structured validation metrics into a single, practical and methodological framework. Importantly, this contribution is rooted in real industrial needs: the proposed approach has been designed to be directly applicable in asset-intensive environments, offering companies a clear and operational procedure to validate digital services and support decision-making under realistic constraints.

2 Practical Development of Digital Servitization

Service digitalization involves a substantial transformation that transcends mere strategic change, becoming an evolution that integrates digital products, services and technologies in an ecosystem of constant innovation. Based on the Service Engineering Methodology for Smart Product Service Systems (SEEM-Smart), this process serves as an essential link between strategic vision and operational execution, laying the foundation for a complete and enduring transformation (Arioli et al., 2023). Embracing emerging technologies in the digitalization of services is critical, as they act as drivers of change towards a new business model. The integration of the Internet of Things (IoT) and the use of artificial intelligence are important examples of how each technology becomes a crucial element in redefining services. By tailoring service offerings to the specific needs of each customer, personalisation of these services is enhanced through detailed data analysis, improving customer satisfaction and opening avenues for loyalty and growth.

The digitalization of service is at the heart of generating enriched and adaptive customer experiences and goes beyond simply offering services to immerse the customer in an experiential narrative that transcends typical commercial transactions. Through intuitive user interfaces and personalisation of interactions, it prioritises the customer in an experience that transcends convention, strengthening ties with existing customers and attracting new seekers of unique experiences. It not only promotes continuous innovation but also enables companies to anticipate and shape future customer demands, acting as an impetus to move into the future. In this scenario, the digitalization of services becomes the core of business transformation, fostering a collaboration between products and services that meets the changing demands of increasingly discerning customers.

2.1 Industry 5.0 and Digitalisation. The Role of Human in Digital Servitization

A technological revolution driven by cutting-edge digital advances is at the core of the transformation towards Industry 4.0, marking not only an evolution but also a reinvention of business and innovation models within the business environment (Frank et al., 2019). The transformation is led by technologies such as the Internet of Things (IoT), cloud computing, Big Data and data analytics, the combination of which unleashes unprecedented transformative potential. This revolution has given rise to the concept of Industry 5.0, which extends beyond efficiency and automation to emphasise human-centricity, resilience, and sustainability. The European Commission (Breque et al., 2021) defines Industry 5.0 as a paradigm that complements the logic of Industry 4.0 by putting human well-being at the centre of technological transformation.

The Internet of Things (IoT) is the fundamental element that connects and brings to life the physical components of Industry 4.0, from advanced machinery to smart products. Linking these devices not only increases operational efficiency, but also enables the intelligent exchange and generation of data, creating a digital ecosystem that completely changes business operations and service delivery. The essential digital pillar underpinning the technological revolution is cloud services, as they provide ubiquitous access to computational resources and enable businesses to overcome physical barriers thanks to their scalability and flexibility characteristic of the digital era (Gaiardelli et al., 2021). In the cloud, this environment creates the right conditions for innovative ideas to emerge and allows solutions to be implemented in an agile and unprecedented way. In addition, Big Data and data analytics emerge as essential tools that extract valuable insights from the vast amount of data generated in the context of Industry 4.0. Analysing large datasets in real time not only improves operational efficiency, but also guides strategic decisions like a beacon. It is essential to turn raw data into meaningful information to understand market complexities, predict future trends and customise service offerings.

2.2 *Relationship Between Servitization and Digitalisation*

The rapid arrival of digital opportunities, driven by Industry 4.0, challenges the adaptability of firms and highlights the inevitable need for a symbiosis between servitization and digitalization (Gong and Ribieri, 2021). In this changing environment, digital technologies have not only altered competition, but also driven companies to use servitization as a key strategy to achieve competitive advantage. With the evolution towards. Industry 5.0, a new emphasis is placed on the central role of humans in the innovation and service delivery processes. In this emerging paradigm, services are not only technological interfaces but also social constructs that connect digital tools with human experiences. This connection makes servitization a privileged mechanism to align technological capabilities with human needs, both in service design and in its effective delivery, where the involvement of key personnel is often critical, as highlighted in recent literature.

Digitalisation becomes the key enabler of servitization by enabling deeper and more valuable analysis of data. It not only improves the understanding of customer behaviour, but also frees up human resources to focus on more intellectually valuable tasks this data processing. Internal processes are improved by detection and monitoring systems, allowing to anticipate failures and raise operational efficiency to unprecedented levels.

Servitization plays a crucial role in pushing digitalisation to new frontiers. The application of advanced technologies is achieved through the synergistic integration of products and services into Product-Service Solutions (PSS) (Sala et al., 2022). The relationship between companies and their customers is redefined through the realisation of services as manageable and monitorable entities, from the development of digital twins to the implementation of cloud computing. This broader concept of digital twin is already being successfully applied in condition-based maintenance for railway infrastructures. Guillén et al. (2023) describe a scalable digital twin architecture for track degradation monitoring using a laboratory setup based on Azure cloud services and RAMI 4.0. Their work demonstrates how digital models can support the diagnosis, prognosis, and risk assessment of asset failures, facilitating timely and effective maintenance decisions. In this regard, digital twins should not be limited to the replication of physical assets. A digital twin can integrate data, models, and service logic, and may represent an asset, a process, or even an entire service. This broader perspective highlights the strategic importance of service digitalisation, where services are conceived as customer-oriented processes capable of being simulated, monitored, and enhanced through digital means. In this complex digital intertwining, servitization and digitalization are not separate; rather, they are interdependent elements that drive business progress towards a horizon in which technology, innovation and excellence are strategically combined. Moreover, digital twins extend their utility beyond asset performance monitoring by enabling service providers to optimize associated logistics. This includes the coordination of spare parts, workforce allocation, and intervention timing based on predictive insights. As such, digital twins evolve into central tools for synchronising technical and logistical decision-making within service delivery chains.

3 Basic Requirements

3.1 Basic Requirements for Digital Servitization

Digital servitization transforms business models towards a service-centric approach, supporting and becoming key requirements for innovation and efficiency (Pezzota et al., 2018). In this work we present a digitalization of asset management and maintenance that includes a general approach to asset digitalization. Asset are the tools for generate value and in this view and in this area digital servitization should be based on an accurate and suitable asset digitalization.

The use of the term "requirement" in this context refers to the essential conditions, capabilities, or enablers that must be present in order to effectively implement digital servitization strategies. These requirements are not merely optional or context-dependent recommendations; rather, they represent structural prerequisites for ensuring that service-oriented digital transformation efforts are both technically feasible and strategically aligned. In the context of asset management, these requirements are particularly critical, as the complexity and criticality of physical assets demand robust digital foundations to support predictive, connected, and value-driven service models.

In this context some of the basic requirements for digital servitization are the following:

- Connectivity as a Technological Enabler for Scalable Digital Services:

The critical role of connectivity in servitization has been firmly supported by prior research, identifying real-time data exchange, remote diagnostics, and customer integration as structural enablers of digital service models (Lerch & Gotsch, 2015; Porter & Heppelmann, 2015). Connectivity therefore constitutes not only a technical condition but a core architectural requirement for scalable digital services.

- Integral Connectivity: Resetting the Boundaries of Digital Communication:

Prescriptive Maintenance Capabilities: From Data Insight to Service AssuranceEnd-to-end connectivity is essential, facilitating real-time data collection and analysis by enabling seamless communication between products, customers and systems. This dynamic and bidirectional exchange of information is not only necessary for improving data transmission and operational responsiveness, but also forms the core of advanced digital architectures such as the Digital Twin. In such models, connectivity ensures a constant link between the physical world and its digital representation, allowing the system to capture real conditions and respond through simulation, prediction or intervention. This live connection supports both monitoring and active decision-making, making connectivity a foundational requirement for intelligent service delivery.

- Predictive Analytics: Understanding the future in a clear way through da-ta analysis:

In the context of digital servitization, especially within asset-intensive environments, it is not sufficient to merely anticipate events—it is essential to act upon them intelligently. Prescriptive maintenance emerges as a critical requirement, integrating two key capabilities: (i) the use of predictive analytics to detect patterns, foresee failures, and anticipate needs; and (ii) decision-making mechanisms that translate those insights into actionable recommendations or automated interventions.

This dual capability is foundational for delivering advanced services that go beyond product functionality to ensure availability, performance, and lifecycle value—core promises of servitised business models. This interpretation aligns with prior studies highlighting how the convergence of servitization and digital technologies fosters proactive, value-oriented service models (Frank et al., 2019). Moreover, prescriptive maintenance enables providers to meet performance-based contracts (e.g., uptime guarantees), reduce unplanned downtime, and optimise resource allocation. By embedding intelligence into service operations, companies can move from reactive support to proactive, value-oriented partnerships, fulfilling the strategic objectives of digital servitization in asset management..

- Service-Oriented Architectures: A Foundational Requirement for Scalable and Intelligent Servitization:

The successful implementation of digital servitization in asset management requires more than isolated technologies—it demands a well-defined and adaptable system architecture. In this context, the adoption of service-oriented architectures (SOA) becomes a core requirement, as it provides the structural basis for integrating digital services, enabling data interoperability, and supporting continuous technological evolution.

Such architectures must allow for the interconnection of heterogeneous systems and technologies—including IoT, edge devices, legacy platforms, cloud services, and AI components—ensuring a cohesive, flexible ecosystem. This design approach is essential for achieving scalability, allowing service portfolios to expand and adapt dynamically to customer needs and operational contexts.

Furthermore, the emergence of advanced AI technologies, such as Large Language Models (LLMs) and Agentic AI, will require infrastructures capable of orchestrating intelligent agents, automating complex decisions, and embedding autonomy into service operations. Without a modular and open architecture, integrating these capabilities into service delivery would be infeasible.

Therefore, a service-oriented and future-ready architectural design is not merely a technical preference, but a strategic requirement to support the long-term evolution and resilience of digitally supported services.

These architectures must also ensure fluid interoperability between systems operating at different levels—from edge computing devices to cloud-based analytics—enabling cohesive asset management. In asset-intensive environments, this interoperability facilitates the integration of legacy systems with cutting-edge technologies such as LLMs or agent-based decision engines, forming a robust ecosystem capable of supporting prescriptive and autonomous interventions.

3.2 Basic Requirements for the Implementation of a Digital Servitization Project

Within any servitization project using digital tools, different solutions should be investigated and analysed to establish whether they are feasible and, if so, to implement them. Possible outcomes may include:

- Digitalization of the product:

Real-time digitalization and monitoring of the main operating variables of the product and of component status. Data collection from active equipment and modelling to estimate the health status of components may be considered. The product has alarms that indicate its performance and status, which facilitates proactive management of the product.

- Preventive maintenance:

  Improved preventive maintenance plans using the information gathered and models developed to reduce maintenance outages. Preventive maintenance planning can be adjusted according to predictive maintenance recommendations and product health condition. In that sense, it will be possible to propose better planning to carry out preventive maintenance and improve the scheduling of product fleets. Development of predictive and prescriptive maintenance for critical components.

- Asset life management:

  Component replacement analysis essential to prolonging the life of assets, including the study of a product health model, as well as life cycle cost analysis for effective management until asset decommissioning.

A complete procedure for the design and development of Product-Service Systems (PSS) can be based on the methodology proposed by the University of Bergamo (Italy) summarised in Fig. 2 (Arioli et al., 2023). The selection of this methodology is based on the proven support it has provided in manufacturing, integrating product and service components from the early stages of design to implementation.

The methodology is structured in a number of main phases: Examining the customer, developing the solution concept, elaborating the final solution and analysing the proposal. Through the implementation and use of specific tools such as the Product Service Concept Tree (PSCT), the procedure should simplify the creation and evaluation of PSS solutions, ensuring that they meet customer needs and business performance objectives.

To illustrate the practical applicability of the proposed methodology, consider a use case in a power converter (Gonzalez-Prida et al., 2024). A smart maintenance service is developed based on real-time monitoring of the asset degradation, predictive failure models, and service-oriented digital twins. This enables the dynamic scheduling of interventions, integration with asset management platforms, and decision-making supported by KPIs such as availability, lifecycle cost and failure rates. The implementation is scalable and aligns with Technology Readiness Levels (TRL) 6 to 8, ensuring maturity for deployment in operational contexts. The implementation of this procedure brings challenges in terms of cultural change and the development of new skills within companies, highlighting the relevance of an orderly transition from product to service.

4 Proposal for a Validation Procedure

According to the afore mentioned requirements and in order to validate the implementation of a given service, the company must follow a series of critical steps that will allow it to assess the feasibility of the service from different perspectives. Unlike classical validation approaches based on Service Blueprinting, Design

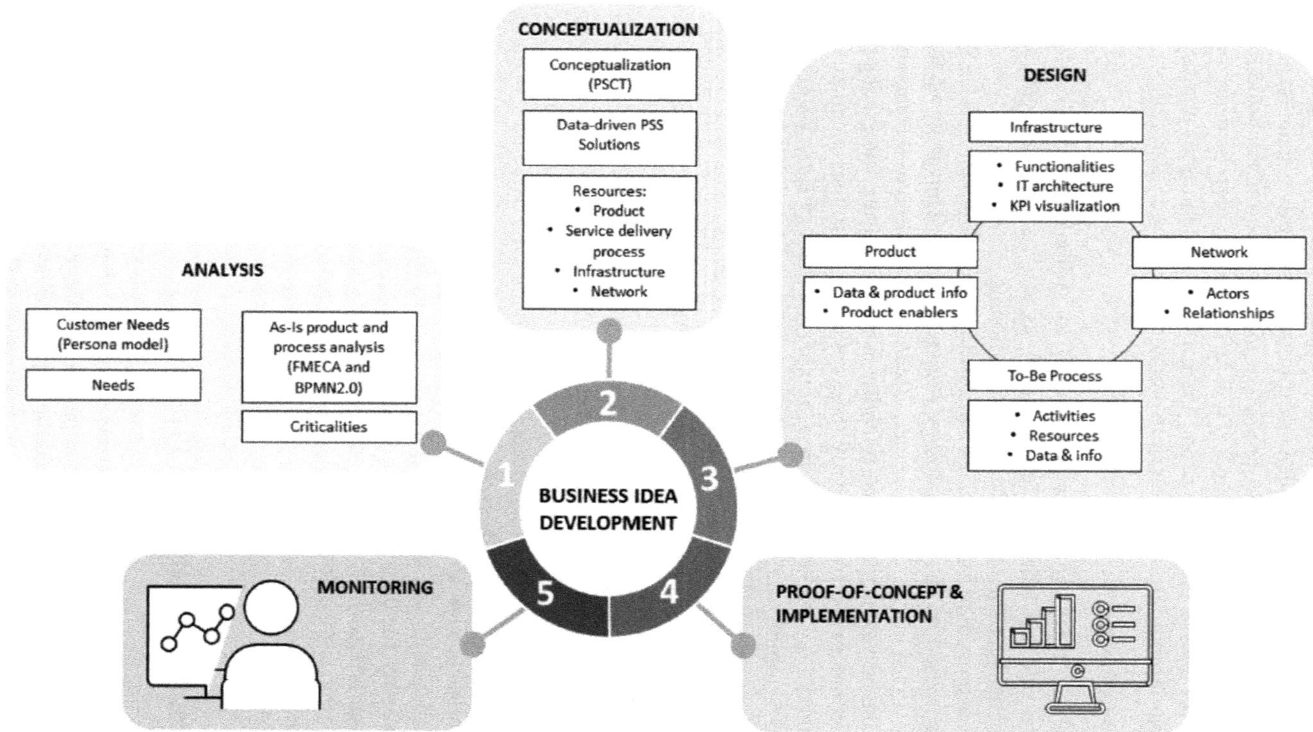

Fig. 2 Service engineering methodology for smart PSS (SEEM-Smart) (Arioli et al., 2023)

Thinking, or Systems Engineering V-models, the proposed framework explicitly integrates prescriptive maintenance logic, digital twin feedback, and asset-health-driven metrics, providing a novel alignment with Industry 5.0 requirements. The suggested steps are described below:

4.1 Step 1: Cost Analysis

Cost analysis is essential to determine the financial viability of the proposed service. This analysis should include:

- Human Resource Costs: Salaries and training required for staff involved in service delivery.
- Digital Platform and Technology Costs: Investments in technology infrastructure, software, and maintenance.
- Operational and Maintenance Costs: Costs associated with the ongoing operation and maintenance of the service.
- Marketing and Distribution Costs: Costs to promote and distribute the service.

The company should compare these costs with projected revenues to determine the profitability of the service. If costs exceed projected revenues, the company may consider redesigning the service or discarding its implementation.

4.2 Step 2: Qualitative Analysis of Implementation

This analysis involves assessing aspects such as:

- Alignment with Corporate Strategy: How the service aligns with the company's long-term objectives and strategies.
- Added Value for the Customer: Assess whether the service meets a real customer need and offers clear added value.
- Competitive Differentiation: Determine whether the service offers a sustainable competitive advantage.

The decision here may be to continue implementation, modify the focus of the service, or reconsider its launch if it does not align with the strategy or does not offer differential value.

4.3 Step 3: Risk Analysis

Identify and assess potential risks associated with the implementation of the service, including:

- Technical Risks: Failures in the technology or infrastructure necessary for the provision of the service.
- Market Risks: Market acceptance of the service, competition and changes in consumer demands.
- Financial Risks: Investments necessary for the development and launch of the service and their recovery over time.
- Operational Risks: The company's ability to maintain quality and continuity of service.
- Legal and Compliance Risks: Compliance with regulations and laws applicable to the new service.

The company should develop mitigation strategies for the identified risks. If the risks are manageable and the mitigation strategies are feasible, the implementation of the service can proceed (Manzini & Vezzoli, 2003). If not, the service plan should be reconsidered or adjusted.

4.4 Step 4: Validation of an Initial Version

Perform an initial release to validate the functionality and acceptance of the service. This includes:

- Development of a Prototype: Create an initial version of the service to test its operation in real conditions.
- Customer Validation: Obtain feedback from a selected group of customers to evaluate the usability, perceived value, and possible improvements of the service.
- Results Analysis: Evaluate the data collected during the validation of the initial version to determine whether the service meets the set objectives and customer expectations.

In this context, it becomes essential to evaluate not only technical attributes, but also the perceived quality of the service and its impact on the overall user experience. Services are often judged by responsiveness, clarity of communication, and emotional factors that extend beyond functional performance. To formalise this, Service Level Agreements (SLAs) can help define measurable commitments related to timeliness, reliability, and availability, reinforcing user trust and satisfaction.

To strengthen this assessment, measurable performance indicators should be defined, such as reductions in unscheduled downtime, improvements in Mean Time Between Failures (MTBF), or cost savings in Life Cycle Cost (LCC). Quantifying these impacts allows organisations to evaluate service viability in real operational terms and adjust the design accordingly. To reinforce objectivity, the validation process should incorporate quantitative KPIs such as uptime ratio, mean response time, mean cost-to-serve, and Net Promoter Score (NPS), ensuring measurable assessment of customer experience and operational performance. If the validation of the initial version is successful, the company can proceed with the full implementation of the service; if not, adjustments must be made based on the feedback received and possibly another round of validation with the customer.

Furthermore, service validation should account for the interoperability of the solution—both technical and functional—as a driver of seamless user experience. The ability to connect and interact with other digital services in real time enhances the perceived integration and value of the offering.

4.5 Step 5: User-Centric Validation Criteria: Enhancing Perceived Value Through Experience Metrics

In addition to technical performance indicators, it is crucial to incorporate user-centric criteria into the validation of digital services. These include metrics related to customer satisfaction, perceived service quality, and responsiveness, which directly affect the success and adoption of service-oriented models. The design and monitoring of Service Level Agreements (SLAs) that explicitly reflect user expectations, such as response times, uptime guarantees, or personalised support, can provide a more comprehensive view of service viability. Moreover, considering interoperability and seamless integration with other digital services reinforces the holistic experience of the end user, especially in multi-vendor or multi-system environments.

4.6 Step 5: Implementation

Once the service has been validated, proceed with its full implementation, which includes:

- Service Deployment: The full implementation of the service involves the operational deployment and integration of the service into the existing structure of the company. This includes the configuration of the technological infrastructure, the training of personnel and the implementation of the support processes necessary for the operation of the service. It is crucial to ensure that all components of the product-service system (PSS) function in an integrated and efficient manner.

4.7 Step 6: Monitoring and Evaluation

Once the service is implemented, it is essential to establish a monitoring and evaluation system to collect data on service performance and customer satisfaction. This includes:

Establishment of KPIs: Define key performance indicators to measure the effectiveness, efficiency and quality of the service.

- Collection of customer feedback: Implement mechanisms to collect customer opinions and feedback on the service. This may include surveys, interviews or analysis of service usage data.
- Data analysis: Evaluate data collected through KPIs and customer feedback to identify areas for improvement, adjust service as necessary and make informed strategic decisions.

4.8 Step 7: Continuous Improvement

Based on the analysis of the data collected, the company should enter into a cycle of continuous improvement, where optimisation opportunities are identified and changes are implemented to improve service. This may include: (i) adjustments to the service offering; (ii) improvements to the technological infrastructure; or (iii) changes to operational processes. Continuous improvement is critical to maintaining competitiveness and meeting changing customer needs (Neely, 2008).

5 Applicability of Use Cases in Digital Services

The steps proposed in the previous section highlight the importance of validating an initial version of the service. It is therefore appropriate to underline the applicability of use cases in digital services, for which certain elements must be considered and the purpose of the cases has to be defined.

5.1 Elements to Consider

In the development of digitally supported services, use cases can be applied to aspects that involve, for example:

End-to-End Connectivity, which facilitates real-time data collection and analysis enabling seamless communication between products, customers and systems. This connectivity not only improves data transmission, but also fosters dynamic interaction within the digital ecosystem, which is essential to effectively understand and meet user needs.

Predictive Analytics, which uses the data collected to predict trends, behaviours and possible failures, thus optimising decision-making and the personalisation of the services offered to customers.

Industry 4.0 and Digitalisation, where the technological revolution of Industry 4.0, fuelled by innovations such as the Internet of Things (IoT), cloud services, Big Data and Data Analytics, offers a vast application field for use cases. These technologies enable the transformation of business processes, improving operational efficiency and customer experience.

Digital Servitization, where properly, the integration of products and services into Product-Service Solutions (PSS) through digitalization enables the creation of new business models and the enhancement of the value proposition for customers. The use cases here can explore how digitalization facilitates the management and monitoring of services, redefining the relationship between businesses and customers.

These elements form the basis on which use cases can be developed and applied in the context of digitally supported services, opening up a range of possibilities for innovation and continuous improvement in service delivery. Although a full industrial case study is beyond this chapter's scope, related implementations such as the Azure-based digital twin for railway track degradation (Guillén et al., 2023) partially validate the feasibility of the proposed framework and illustrate its applicability in asset-intensive environments.

5.2 Purpose of the Use Cases

In the development of digitally supported services, use cases can be applied for several essential purposes:

1. Design of Particular Solutions: Use cases act as a fundamental support to design specific solutions adapted to the identified needs. They allow conceptualising and structuring how digital services can solve problems or improve processes within a given business scenario.
2. Requirements Definition and Project Design: These are essential for the identification of the different scenarios in which products and services can be framed. Through use cases, specific requirements and project design can be defined, ensuring that digital solutions are aligned with market expectations and needs.
3. Improving the Company's Value Proposition: Use cases allow the analysis of different business scenarios where the project results can be applied to improve the company's value proposition. This not only benefits the project in question but also provides a methodology to organise different types of scenarios and use cases, serving as a strategic tool for the company.
4. Implementation of Advanced Technologies: They facilitate the application of advanced technologies as part of digital servitization, integrating products and services into Product-Service Solutions (PSS). Use cases help redefine the relationship between companies and their customers, managing and monitoring services through the implementation of technologies such as digital twins and cloud computing.

In short, use cases provide a structure for designing specific solutions, defining requirements, enhancing the business value proposition and facilitating the implementation of advanced technologies.

Table 1 Types of services with respect to digitalization

Level of digitalization	Facilitation	Adaptative	Substitutive	Main goal
High	Facilitation services, integrated in factory	Adaptative services, integrated in factory	Substitutive services, integrated in factory	Improving value perceived by customer and company procedures
	Facilitation digital services	Adaptative digital services	Substitutive digital services	Improving value perceived by customer
Low	Facilitation manual services	Adaptative manual services	Substitutive manual services	

6 Conclusions

This article has dealt with the proposal and implementation of a validation procedure for digital services, in order to be incorporated into the service portfolio of a company. A series of steps have been defined, along which the company will be faced with critical decisions about the viability of the service. If at any stage it is identified that the service is not viable, whether for financial, technical, market or other reasons, the company must be prepared to make difficult decisions, which may include substantial modification of the service, postponement of its launch, or even cancellation of the project. It is crucial that these decisions are made based on sound data and thorough analysis to minimise risks and ensure that the company's resources are used efficiently. In addition, the company should consider the possibility of reusing the learnings, technologies or processes developed during the project in other business areas or in future servitization projects, thus maximising the value of the investments made and fostering a culture of innovation and adaptability. An important advantage of the proposed approach lies in its modular and scalable structure, which facilitates adaptation to various industrial domains. This proposal not only supports current needs in asset-intensive environments but also lays the groundwork for future research and industrial adoption of service-oriented digital twins under evolving paradigms such as Industry 5.0.

Acknowledgements This research was funded by MINISTERIO DE CIENCIA, INNOVACIÓN Y UNIVERSIDADES, grant number PID2022-137748OB-C32 funded by MCIN/AEI/ https://doi.org/10.13039/501100011033.

References

Arioli, V., Ruggeri, G., Sala, R., Pirola, F., & Pezzotta, G. (2023). A methodology for the design and engineering of smart product service systems: An application in the manufacturing sector. *Sustainability, 15*, 64. https://doi.org/10.3390/su15010064

Adel, A., Alani, N. H. S., & Jan, T. (2024). Factories of the future in industry 5.0—Softwarization, Servitization, and Industrialization. *Internet of Things, 28*, 101431. https://doi.org/10.1016/j.iot.2024.101431

Breque, M., De Nul, L., & Petridis, A. (2021). Industry 5.0: Towards a sustainable, human-centric and resilient European industry. Publications Office of the European Union. https://research-and-innovation.ec.europa.eu/knowledge-publications-tools-and-data/publications/all-publications/industry-50-towards-sustainable-human-centric-and-resilient-european-industry_en

Chirumalla, K., Leoni, L., & Oghazi, P. (2023). Moving from servitization to digital servitization: Identifying the required dynamic capabilities and related microfoundations to facilitate the transition. *Journal of Business Research, 158*, Article 113668. https://doi.org/10.1016/j.jbusres.2023.113668

Frank, A. G., Mendes, G. H. S., Ayala, N. F., & Ghezzi, A. (2019). Servitization and Industry 4.0 convergence in the digital transformation of product firms: A business model innovation perspective. *Technological Forecasting and Social Change, 141*, 341–351. https://doi.org/10.1016/j.techfore.2019.01.014

Gaiardelli, P., Pezzotta, G., Rondini, A., Romero, D., Jarrahi, F., Bertoni, M., Wiesner, S., Wuest, T., Larsson, T., Zaki, M., Jussen, P., Boucher, X., Ziaee Bigdeli, A., & Cavalieri, S. (2021). Product-service systems evolution in the era of Industry 4.0. *Service Business, 15*, 1–31. https://doi.org/10.1007/s11628-021-00438-9

Gong, C., & Ribiere, V. (2021). Developing a unified definition of digital transformation. *Technovation, 102*, Article 102217. https://doi.org/10.1016/j.technovation.2020.102217

González-Prida, V., de la Fuente Carmona, A., Guillén López, A. J., Gómez Fernández, J. F., & Crespo Márquez, A. (2024). Integrating digitalization and asset health index for strategic life cycle cost analysis of power converters. *Information, 15*(12), 749. https://doi.org/10.3390/info15120749

Guillén López, A. J., Gómez Fernández, J. F., Urda, P., Escalona, J. L., Crespo Márquez, A., & Olivencia Polo, F. (2023). Digital twin for condition-based maintenance within a railway infrastructure testing lab. In *4th Asia Pacific conference of the prognostics and health management*, Tokyo, Japan.

Kohtamäki, M., Parida, V., Patel, P. C., & Gebauer, H. (2021). The relationship between digital servitization and product-service systems: A research agenda. *Industrial Marketing Management, 93*, 332–345.

Lerch, C., & Gotsch, M. (2015). Digitalized product-service systems in manufacturing firms: A case study analysis. *Research-Technology Management, 58*(5), 45–52.

Manzini, E., & Vezzoli, C. (2003). A strategic design approach to develop sustainable product service systems: Examples taken from the environmentally friendly innovation Italian prize. *Journal of Cleaner Production, 11*(8), 851–857. https://doi.org/10.1016/S0959-6526(02)00153-1

Martín Peña, M. L., Díaz Garrido, E., & Sánchez López, J. M. (2018). The digitalization and servitization of manufacturing: A review on digital business models. *Strategic Change, 27*(2), 91–99. https://doi.org/10.1002/jsc.2184

Neely, A. (2008). Exploring the financial consequences of the servitization of manufacturing. *Operations Management Research, 1*(2), 103–118. https://doi.org/10.1007/s12063-009-0015-5

Pezzotta, G., Sassanelli, C., Pirola, F., Sala, R., Rossi, M., Fotia, S., Koutoupes, A., Terzi, S., & Mourtzis, D. (2018). The product service system lean design methodology (PSSLDM). *Journal of Manufacturing Technology Management, 29*, 1270–1295.

Porter, M. E., & Heppelmann, J. E. (2015). How smart, connected products are transforming companies. *Harvard Business Review, 93*(10), 96–114.

Sala, R., Pirola, F., Pezzotta, G., & Cavalieri, S. (2022). Data-driven decision making in maintenance service delivery process: A case study. *Applied Sciences, 12*, 7395. https://doi.org/10.3390/app12157395

Srai, J. S., & Kumar, M. (2020). Manufacturing-as-a-service: Understanding capabilities for digital servitization. *Journal of Manufacturing Technology Management, 31*(5), 1015–1036.

Tukker, A. (2004). Eight types of product service system: Eight ways to sustainability? Experiences from SusProNet. *Business Strategy and the Environment*, *13*(4). https://doi.org/10.1002/bse.414

Digital Twins for Asset Health Monitoring and Lifecycle Management: A Structured Approach Based on Basic Digital Twins

Antonio Sánchez Herguedas

Abstract This chapter presents a structured approach for developing and applying digital twins (DTs) in asset health monitoring and lifecycle management. The proposed methodology is based on the modular construction and integration of Basic Digital Twins (BDTs), which represent individual components, failure modes and inspection properties associated with physical assets. The chapter emphasises the importance of aligning the structure of the digital twin (DT) with the functional hierarchy of the asset, and its content with data models designed to support maintenance and investment decision-making processes. Special attention is given to the definition of health indicators such as the Asset Health Index (AHI) and the Remaining Useful Life (RUL), which enable the implementation of predictive maintenance strategies and scenario-based lifecycle management. The integration of artificial intelligence and machine learning techniques is also addressed in the context of an evolution from condition-based diagnosis towards prescriptive and risk-informed interventions. A case study on the lifecycle management of a Matisa B66 track tamping machine illustrates the practical application of the methodology. The chapter concludes with a discussion of implementation challenges and future research directions, highlighting the potential of DTs to become key tools within intelligent asset management systems.

Keywords Digitalisation · Digital twins · Basic digital twins · Asset health monitoring · Lifecycle management · Decision-making

---

A. Sánchez Herguedas (✉)
Department of Industrial Management, School of Engineering, University of Seville, Seville, Spain
e-mail: antoniosh@us.es

A. Crespo Márquez et al. (eds.), *Digital Maintenance and Asset Digitalization*, Engineering Asset Management Review 5,
https://doi.org/10.1007/978-3-032-21502-4_9

1 Introduction

Digital transformation has become a driver of change in the way organisations manage their physical, technical and infrastructure assets. This process has been built by incorporating digital technologies at all operational and strategic levels to increase efficiency and responsiveness in more complex and competitive environments, making organisations more sustainable and resilient.

Asset management has relied on corrective and preventive models, based on periodic inspections, historical records, mathematical models and accumulated operating experience, which require continuous calculations. Calculations to optimise policies have limited validity in terms of accuracy, agility and adaptability in the face of changing environmental dynamics or unforeseen conditions. Digitalisation reduces the limitations of these models by facilitating the acquisition, analysis, and interpretation of large volumes of data in real-time from sensors, IoT platforms, SCADA systems, or external sources (such as weather, geolocation, or market data).

In this context, technologies such as the Internet of Things (IoT), Artificial Intelligence (AI), Machine Learning (ML), Cloud Computing, and Predictive and Prescriptive Analytics enable the improvement of operational and strategic decision-making processes. This improvement is visible in the ability to anticipate failures, optimise resources, reduce unplanned costs, and enhance the availability and reliability of assets. Digitalisation allows for moving from a relatively static view of the asset to a dynamic understanding of its behaviour, state, and environment. This change enables the implementation of advanced management models, such as DTs, which represent a natural evolution in asset digitalisation.

The DT concept embodies the convergence between the physical and digital worlds, enabling a virtual representation of an asset that reflects its current state, its operating history and the possibility of predicting its future evolution under different scenarios. This capability enables the transformation of aspects related to the design, planning, operation, maintenance, and decommissioning of the asset. It opens up opportunities for more efficient lifecycle management, fostering data-driven decision-making, cross-functional collaboration, and continuous innovation. In this environment, DTs are positioned as an enabler to achieve a higher level of digital maturity and operational excellence. The concept has evolved from simple simulation models to intelligent, autonomous, and connected digital environments, known as autonomous DTs or cognitive DTs, which not only replicate but also learn and adapt to their environment. This progression reflects a path towards increasingly proactive asset management, based on accurate, contextualised and real-time information.

The main objective of this chapter is to analyse the role of DTs as a transformative tool in the field of asset health monitoring and lifecycle management. Specifically, the chapter aims to (i) examine the technological underpinnings of the DTs such as their architecture, key components, and associated technologies (IoT, AI and real-time data analytics), (ii) explore the applications in continuous asset health monitoring, (iii) analyse the impact on end-to-end asset lifecycle management, (iv) identify the technical, organisational and regulatory challenges that limit their use, (v) present real-world case studies that demonstrate the tangible benefits of their use, and (vi) propose a forward-looking vision for the future of DM. Khoshkenar and Nassereddine (2024) present a prioritised list of benefits and challenges of DTs that require investigation and implementation.

The contents of this section are presented in a thematic structure to address the article's central themes: conceptual and technological foundations, practical applications across different sectors, implementation challenges, and future projections. During the development of the chapter, a bibliographical review of aspects related to the specific objectives set out is presented.

2 Digital Twin Fundamentals

2.1 Key Components of a Digital Twin

A DT is a complex entity composed of a hierarchical structure that reflects the functional architecture of the physical asset and digital content representing its properties, behaviours, and states. In the field of maintenance and asset management, this representation is not limited to physical assets. Still, it encompasses people, tools, parts, and processes, all of which are interconnected through a network of data and functional relationships.

The five essential components of a DT in this context are: the hierarchical structural model, the BDTs, the data acquisition system, the analytical and simulation engine and the maintenance management tools. The hierarchical structural model reflects the functional decomposition of the asset, following its technical structure. This hierarchy comprises several levels of disaggregation, including subsystems, components, and subcomponents, which ultimately reach the level where failure modes can be identified. BDTs are the minimum units of digital representation associated with a specific failure mode of a component or process. Each basic digital twin (BDT) contains the properties that define the component and the failure (e.g., operating pressure, operating frequency, threshold temperature, mean time between failures). It includes the variables, derived from those properties, that enable the measurement, monitoring and instantiation of actual data from the physical asset. The BDT also contains the property/variable relationship, which structures how the data is collected, processed and managed. The data acquisition system captures the necessary variables through sensors or IoT/Edge platforms and instantiates the values in the DT in real time. The analytical and simulation engine enables the running of predictive, prescriptive, criticality, health index, or life cycle costing models to diagnose the health status of the asset and simulate the estimated life in future scenarios, supporting informed maintenance decision-making. Gómez Fernández et al. (2025)

provide a formal framework that connects physical attributes and measurable variables. Maintenance management tools are integrated with DTs to associate operational information, scheduled tasks, required spare parts and human resources linked to the asset life cycle. These five components enable the representation of the operational condition of the asset and its behaviour under different conditions, which is fundamental for health monitoring and lifecycle management.

2.2 *Typologies and Levels of Complexity*

The implementation of DTs in maintenance and asset management varies significantly depending on the level of detail, analysis capacity and scope of the twin. These levels are methodologically developed through the integration of BDTs in a modular and scalable structure.

In this context, we can classify DTs according to their complexity and purpose. The descriptive DT is limited to representing the current state of the asset from static or real-time updated data. It is helpful in the early stages of the lifecycle for visualisation and basic digital inventory (Asset Definition Model). The monitoring DT (monitoring twin) incorporates condition variables from IoT sensors, integrating with an Asset Monitoring Model (e.g. vibration, temperature or structural displacements). Here, the DT contains BDTs associated with specific failure modes, connected to real data. The predictive DT uses behavioural models to anticipate failures, estimate remaining useful life (RUL) and support predictive maintenance. It draws on BDTs enriched with degradation-defining properties and prognostic algorithms. The prescriptive DT simulates different scenarios and proposes optimal decisions. It integrates cost, risk, safety or sustainability models (IAMM, AHI, LCC, RUL) and relies on the interaction between multiple BDTs. The autonomous or cognitive DT is self-adjusting and makes decisions in real time with learning capabilities. It requires high integration of composite DTs, extreme modularity and management of multiple interdependent properties and variables.

Each type of DT is built through the progressive integration of BDTs, allowing for scaling from local representations (component, task, or failure mode) to systemic representations (complete asset, complex system, or critical infrastructure). This scalability is made possible by the hierarchical design of the DT structure, which respects the functional architecture of the physical asset. On the other hand, modularity enables the inclusion of component DTs that are repeated within a hierarchically superior element. For this, the coding of each of the variables is essential, so that, for example, the DT of an axle can distinguish between the right and left wheel. Starting from the components at a lower level (level 1) that exhibit failure modes, the BDTs of their failure modes are developed to compose the DT of the component. To develop higher-level DTs (level 2), the DTs of the lower-level components and the higher-level BDTs are modularly aggregated. These BDTs correspond to higher-level failure modes that are not captured at the lower level. In the next step, the level

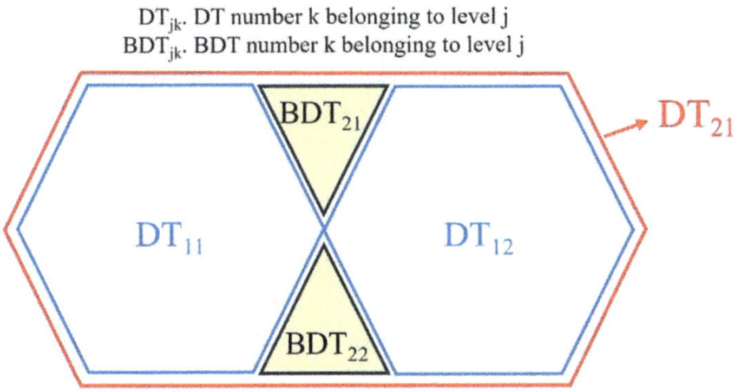

Fig. 1 Composition of higher-level DTs from their BDTs and lower-level DTs

3 DT is developed. It is modularly constructed from the level 2 DTs, and the level 3 BDTs will be added to it. Figure 1 represents this process.

2.3 *Technological Architecture (IoT, Sensors, Edge/cloud Computing, AI)*

The functional development of a DT (Fig. 2) requires a distributed and modular technological architecture that supports dynamic representation, variable instantiation and decision-making in real operating environments. This architecture is articulated on several levels or layers:

The data acquisition layer (Edge/IoT) utilises distributed IoT sensors that capture values of critical variables associated with BDT properties (e.g., bearing temperature, structural deformation, load cycles, humidity). These variables feed the BDTs, giving digital life to the failure modes and the processes in which they intervene. To transmit this information, low-consumption protocols and NB-IoT, LoRa or 5G networks are used to ensure connectivity in complex infrastructures (such as trains, facilities or bridges).

The intermediate integration layer (Fog computing) is responsible for pre-processing, cleansing and fusion of data at the local level. It performs ETL (Extract, Transform, Load) tasks associated with the DT data models and supports information consistency and reduced latency (edge computing) for systems requiring real-time decisions.

The processing and storage layer (Cloud computing) hosts the DT as a composite object and enables its scalability. It integrates structured storage platforms (asset databases) and calculation engines for simulations and prediction. It is also the place where predictive analytics and computational models (AHI, LCC) are run, based on historical and real-time data.

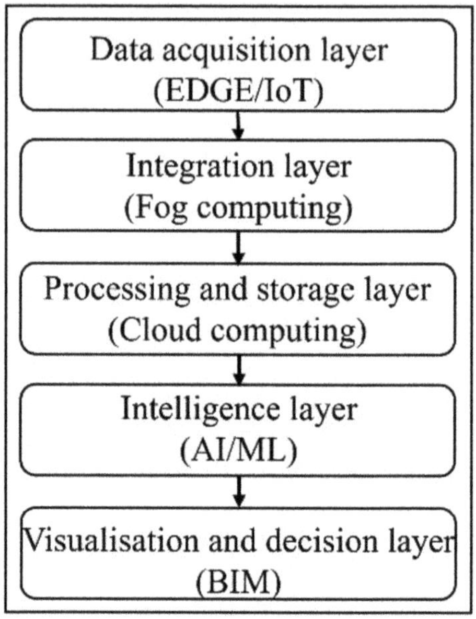

Fig. 2 Functional development of a digital twin

The intelligence layer (AI/ML) runs algorithms for fault diagnosis and classification, probability inference and evaluation of maintenance alternatives. These models are fed with data from the BDTs (temperature, pressure, cycles, etc.) and return results such as deterioration curves, the probability of failure, criticality, or the need for intervention.

The visualisation and decision layer provides interactive visual interfaces for technical staff and managers. It also allows consulting the asset health status (AHI), visualising life cycle projections, and simulating scenarios. This entire architecture is designed under the principles of modularity and scalability, allowing for the progressive integration of new BDTs or DTs of components, along with their respective properties y variables.

2.4 *Differences with Other Digital Technologies (Simulation, BIM, Etc.)*

DTs share certain fundamentals with technologies such as simulators, CAD or BIM, but present key differences that make them unique and superior for integrated lifecycle management and maintenance due to their dynamic nature, their bidirectional connectivity, their focus on maintenance throughout the asset lifecycle, their high scalability and interactivity and their capacity for data instantiation. Amin et al. (2025) support this technological evolution of DTs in the energy sector.

3 Asset Health Monitoring with Digital Twins

Asset Health Monitoring is one of the most strategic and mature applications of DTs within intelligent maintenance. Its main objective is to detect, anticipate, and understand changes in the behaviour of physical assets, allowing the prevention of failures, optimising resources, and aligning operational decisions with availability, reliability, safety, and cost objectives. In this context, DT is an integrating tool that transforms data into useful information, adapted to each failure mode during the entire asset lifecycle.

3.1 The Role of the Digital Twin in Monitoring the Health Status of Physical Assets

To monitor the health of the asset, the DT needs to incorporate and represent all its failure modes. This representation is not static and is based on the integration of BDTs, each one associated with a specific component, failure mode and operational context. The hierarchical structure of the DT allows the use of sensors and information gatherers to represent complex systems. Each failure mode is defined by a set of properties (e.g., threshold temperature, vibration range, cycle limit), the variables associated with these properties, their real-time instantiations, and the functional relationships or rules linking the component to its process, tool, or location. This structure allows the DT to reflect the current state of the asset. It also allows diagnosing deviations, detecting anomalies, calculating its current health and inferring its evolution. Abdullahi et al. (2024) propose structures that efficiently use data and software to implement asset management solutions, involving condition monitoring and predictive maintenance to detect anomalies.

The information generated by each BDT is fed in real time from the sensor network (IoT system) and data capture systems. The asset health models integrate the information coming from the BDTs and compress and simplify it into health indices. Their application by the DTs is conditional on the characteristics of the designed health model.

3.2 Sensor Integration and Real-Time Data Collection

The ability of the DT to accurately reflect the operational condition depends on its continuous connection to the physical asset. This process is structured on several technological levels. The first level consists of localised IoT sensors. These are devices installed on the asset that capture critical physical quantities (such as temperature, vibration, strain, and humidity) associated with the properties of the BDT. Fog/edge computing nodes form a second level. These nodes locally process signals, filter noise, and run pre-diagnostics before sending the data to the central system. Secure communication networks form a third level. These are responsible for maintaining connectivity based on NB-IoT, LoRaWAN, 5G, or industrial protocols (such as MQTT and OPC-UA). The last level is ETL systems and cloud storage. At this level, data transformation and structuring processes are carried out for use by the DT and, in particular, analytical models. This data flow enables the DT to remain synchronised with the real state of the asset, continuously instantiating the variables of the BDTs. This instantiation allows for both the calculation of health indices (such as the AHI) and the activation of alarms in the event of relevant deviations.

3.3 Fault Detection and Predictive Analysis

One of the key functions of DT in maintenance is to anticipate failures before they occur. To do this, the DT integrates anomaly detection techniques to identify anomalous patterns in time series of key variables; Fault Classification techniques to determine the probability of failure based on multiple possibilities (wear, fatigue, corrosion, etc.); and Remaining Useful Life (RUL) estimation techniques based on actual degradation detected and projections using Weibull models, Machine Learning (ML) or statistical analysis.

These functions are configured within the DT by executing algorithms that process the structured data coming from the BDTs. For example, a railway axle bearing BDT can detect anomalous thermal cycles, diagnose a fatigue failure mode, and project its RUL considering its operating environment, kilometres travelled and historical temperature. This predictive intelligence enhances the operational availability of the asset and informs strategic decisions throughout its life cycle, including scheduled replacements, redesigns, criticality changes, and reinvestment strategies.

3.4 Applications in Key Industries (Energy, Manufacturing, Transport, Etc.)

TD-based monitoring has cross-cutting applications in multiple sectors, adapting to the criticality, operational context and functional structure of each asset. It is currently being applied in rail transport to thermal control of bearings, detection of structural fatigue in bridges, and vibration monitoring in braking systems. In civil infrastructure, it is used for real-time structural condition monitoring of bridges, tunnels and dams, including alerts for displacement, moisture or corrosion. Hagen and Andersen (2024) present a real case of DTs applied to structural monitoring of bridges. In the energy sector, it is applied to predicting failures in wind turbines or generators through the integration of sensors and digital simulations. In manufacturing, supervision of production lines is achieved using DTs that detect deviations in quality or performance by component or process. In all these cases, the DT enables transitioning from a reactive or preventive maintenance strategy to a proactive management approach, based on condition and risk, aligned with the lifecycle objectives of the asset.

4 Asset Life Cycle Management

The life cycle management of an asset encompasses all phases from its conception and design to its retirement or renewal. In each of these phases, critical decisions are made that affect not only the technical performance, but also the economic, environmental and operational sustainability of the system. DTs are a transformative tool in this context, providing an integrated and evolving digital representation of the asset that enables the continuous management of information, condition, and context over time.

DTs, based on the integration of BDTs, act as a backbone between design, operation, maintenance, and reinvestment activities. This allows for monitoring the status of all failure modes and forecasting into the future, thereby becoming a living and functional model for strategic decision-making.

4.1 Phases of an Asset's Life Cycle: Planning, Operation, Maintenance, Dismantling

Each phase of the life cycle benefits from the use of DG. In the design and planning phase, BDTs enable the modelling of components, processes, and expected failure modes, helping to define technical and maintenance requirements from a reliability, availability, maintainability, and safety (RAMS) perspective. Table 1 provides a structured overview of the key functions that the Digital Twin fulfils throughout each phase of the asset lifecycle.

For example, simulating failure modes in a pump during design allows vulnerabilities to be identified before they occur and new pumps to be redesigned before they are manufactured. During the construction and installation phase, the hierarchical structure of the BDT is integrated with BIM and PLM systems to accurately reflect the physical assembly and ensure consistency between design and execution. After commissioning, in the operation and maintenance phase, BDTs are instantiated with real-time data. This instantiation allows continuous monitoring, diagnosis and prediction of failures. In this phase, the DTs are integrated with EAM and CMMS to support daily operational decisions. The historical data stored in these systems (failure history, interventions, and operational conditions) enable intelligent maintenance planning, aligned with the criticality level of the assets, as calculated from criticality analysis models (CAM). Before the dismantling phase, a remaining useful

Table 1 Functions of the digital twin across the asset lifecycle

Lifecycle phase	Functions of the digital twin
Design and planning	• Models' components, processes, and expected failure modes using BDTs • Supports RAMS-driven definition of technical, reliability and maintenance requirements • Enables early identification of vulnerabilities by simulating behaviour and degradation
Construction and installation	• Ensures consistency between design and physical assembly through integration with BIM and PLM systems • Maintains hierarchical alignment between the physical asset structure and the DT architecture • Supports verification and traceability of component installation
Operation	• Instantiates BDTs with real-time and historical data from IoT, sensors and inspections • Provides continuous condition monitoring of all failure modes • Detects anomalies and deviations using embedded analytical models
Maintenance	• Performs diagnosis of failure modes and identification of deterioration trends • Generates predictive outputs (RUL, AHI) and integrates with EAM/CMMS systems • Supports preventive, predictive and prescriptive maintenance decisions
Renewal, refurbishment and decommissioning	• Produces lifecycle cost (LCC) analyses and RUL projections to guide end-of-life decisions • Simulates alternative intervention scenarios (partial renewal, full replacement, upgrades) • Assesses the technical and economic impact of reinvestment actions

life (RUL) projection and life cycle cost (LCC) analysis help determine whether to maintain, refurbish, or decommission an asset. DT allows simulating replacement or upgrade scenarios and assessing their economic and technical impact. Iranshahi et al. (2025) provide an overview of the different services that DTs can offer at each stage of the product lifecycle, in collaboration with other digital technologies.

4.2 *How Digital Twins Support Decision Making Throughout the Lifecycle*

The DT becomes a decision support system by containing, in a structured way, all relevant asset information, the physical, functional and regulatory properties of the asset, failure modes associated with components and processes, instantiated operational and historical data, results of predictive models (RUL, AHI) and indicators of cost, criticality, environmental impact and availability. Through the integration of these data and models, the DT allows for answering key management questions, such as: When and how to intervene in a critical asset? Is it more cost-effective to repair, redesign or replace? How does a failure mode affect the rest of the system? What investment maximises the residual value of the asset? The integration of BDTs with APM (Asset Performance Management) and AIP (Asset Investment Planning) models enables the creation of twins that connect technical condition with financial CAPEX and OPEX decisions. Abdessadak et al. (2025) analyse the use of DT application in CAPEX/OPEX and sustainability decisions in the energy sector.

4.3 *Cost Reduction and Sustainability Improvement*

The use of TD in the life cycle management generates measurable impacts, savings in OPEX, thanks to predictive maintenance management, reduction of unexpected failures and optimisation of the use of spare parts; a reduction in avoided CAPEX, by being able to postpone investment in renewal through condition-based maintenance; an increase in sustainability, by extending service life, reducing energy consumption and minimising waste. In this sense, DT contributes to the objectives of the circular economy and energy efficiency. On the other hand, the ability to simulate and anticipate future behaviour allows DT to prepare strategies for critical failures or extreme events, thereby increasing its resilience.

4.4 *Representative Use Cases*

There are several representative cases in the literature that illustrate the use of DTs in life cycle management, for example, long-span bridges, where DT enables simulating structural ageing, estimating future interventions, planning inspections, and financially justifying reinvestments based on the structural health index (AHI). In railway components, such as bearings, DT enables the management of the complete maintenance cycle, from installation to RUL prediction and replacement decision optimisation, based on criticality and cost. In discrete manufacturing production lines, DT assists in redesigning configurations in response to bottlenecks or inefficiencies detected during their operation.

5 Integration of Artificial Intelligence and Machine Learning

The combination of DTs with AI and ML techniques is radically transforming the way asset health is monitored and managed. AI transforms the DT into an intelligent system capable not only of representing and simulating, but also of analysing, learning, and anticipating the behaviour of assets in various operational and lifecycle scenarios. This analytical capability becomes indispensable for improving real-time decision-making, reducing risks, and optimising costs throughout the asset lifecycle. In the methodological framework based on BDTs, AI and ML algorithms operate on sets of instantiated properties, variables and histories, transforming DTs into predictive, prescriptive or even cognitive twins, depending on the level of integration and autonomy achieved.

5.1 Historical and Real-Time Data Analysis

The first level of integration between IA and DT occurs in the processing and analysis of large volumes of historical and operational data. Descriptive and diagnostic analysis enable the understanding of behavioural patterns, relationships between variables, failure modes, and critical operational conditions. This analysis is applied to structured data in BDTs, and may include supervised failure classification, correlation analysis or clustering of operating profiles. Regression and classification models utilise algorithms such as Random Forest, Support Vector Machine (SVM), or neural networks to estimate the mean time between failures (MTBF), classify symptoms into specific failure modes, or determine asset criticality. Thanks to edge/cloud platforms and microservice-oriented architecture, sensor data is analysed online (streaming), triggering alerts or reconfigurations of the DT when significant deviations are detected. BDTs act as contextualised knowledge containers. Their modular growth through scaling allows these twins to be applied at different levels (component, subsystem, system) and reused in new assets.

Operational and historical data collected and instantiated by BDTs can feed algorithms that analyse trends, diagnose failures and predict future conditions. This information can be visualised in real time or processed to adjust the maintenance strategy. In the case documented by Crespo Márquez et al. (2020), a DT developed to manage railway axle bearings integrated a Deep Learning model for failure mode classification from thermal cycles. Temperature data and kilometres travelled were combined to identify, with more than 95% accuracy, fatigue and lubricant degradation failures. The DT integrated BDTs containing these key variables, which allowed the model to be instantiated and automated preventive maintenance tasks to be triggered.

5.2 Asset Performance Prediction Models

One of the most advanced applications of ML in DTs is the prediction of future asset and system behaviour. This function is essential for both predictive maintenance and life cycle management (AIP, LCC, AHI). Prova et al. (2025) integrate IoT sensor networks with advanced ML models and expose the benefits of their application, achieving longer lifetime for equipment and execution of more economical maintenance techniques.

The most common techniques applied in TDs are time series models (ARIMA, Prophet, LSTM), to predict the evolution of variables such as temperature, load cycles, energy consumption or structural displacements, and also RUL (Remaining Useful Life) models to estimate the RUL of a component, feeding on operational and historical data instantiated in the BDTs. They can combine statistical (Weibull, Kaplan–Meier) and AI approaches. It is also interesting to comment on the use of (historical) twins to initiate new DTs, calibrating them by ML using previous data from similar twins, accelerating the implementation of predictive strategies (transfer learning). The use of predictive models makes it possible to anticipate failures and project asset behaviour under different load, environment or usage scenarios. These models are trained with data instantiated in BDTs and are modularly scaled to simulate the future state of more complex systems. For example, in the energy sector, Siemens Gamesa has integrated wind turbine DTs with supervised Machine Learning algorithms to predict the RUL of blades and gearboxes. The system utilises vibration, wind, temperature, and torque history to feed nonlinear regression models and neural networks, integrated within the DG. From this, remaining life is projected with error margins of less than 10%, allowing maintenance to be planned months in advance. Rolls-Royce uses DTs with AI algorithms to simulate in real time the behaviour of each aircraft engine during flight. Millions of data points (pressure, vibration, fuel consumption, altitude) are analysed using predictive models based on Random Forest and Gradient Boosting, updating the BDT variables for each engine failure mode. AI has reduced unexpected incidents by 25% and increased fleet availability.

5.3 Autonomous Digital Twins and Self-learning

At the most advanced levels of integration, DTs evolve towards cognitive systems, capable of adapting to operational changes, learning from their environment and making automated decisions. This evolution is achieved through continuous re-training of models based on new data (incremental learning); prescriptive optimisation when proposing or executing the optimal action (e.g. reconfiguring a process, adjusting a parameter or reordering a maintenance task); the use of AI-based recommendation systems that help the operator or engineer decide between different maintenance or investment alternatives; and integration with management systems to automatically execute work orders, spare parts requests or schedule changes. In this phase, the DTs can function as 'federated digital twins', (Kim et al., 2025), integrating multiple DTs of interconnected assets that collectively learn from their operation (e.g. a fleet of trains or a network of wind turbines).

For example, in advanced manufacturing environments (such as Bosch or Schneider Electric plants), AGVs integrate DTs with reinforcement learning models that optimise routes, load cycles, and maintenance based on actual wear and tear. Each vehicle has more basic DTs of its engines, batteries and wheels, and the data is used to locally retrain models that are shared in a federated twin for the entire fleet. The federation has improved logistical efficiency and reduced failures by 30% over the past year. In critical infrastructure projects such as bridges (e.g. in Germany and Switzerland), DTs have been developed that integrate structural simulation models with AI-powered deterioration forecasting algorithms. These DTs update their knowledge by receiving new sensor data (deformations, moisture, corrosion) and automatically adjust the frequency of inspections. The AI identifies anomalous patterns of degradation caused by specific environmental conditions and proposes interventions even before degradation is visually apparent. These cases demonstrate how the integration of AI and ML becomes the core that transforms DT into a proactive management system, capable of evolving with the asset and dynamically adapting to new operational, regulatory or environmental challenges by detecting asset health and modifying lifecycle management. (Alhadi et al., 2025) discuss the capability of DTs for continuous permitting and compliance verification in the construction industry.

6 Challenges and Limitations

Despite their enormous transformative potential, the effective implementation of TDs in asset health monitoring and lifecycle management presents significant technical, organisational and methodological challenges. These challenges must be recognised and carefully managed to ensure that DTs are technically feasible, sustainable, scalable and applicable in real-world operation and maintenance contexts. The modular and hierarchical nature of DTs built from BDTs adds complexity to the process of DT development, integration and evolution as it extends through the lifecycle of diverse assets. Sharma et al. (2022) seek to identify the current limitations and reasons for the delay in the widespread implementation and adoption of DTs.

6.1 Interoperability and Standardisation

One of the main obstacles is the lack of common standards and interoperable models that allow DTs to integrate effectively with other management systems (CMMS, EAM, APM) and technology platforms (IoT, SCADA, PLM, BIM). This lack includes health, degradation and lifetime models. Differences in data formats, ontologies and hierarchical structures impede the reuse and scalability of DTs across different manufacturers or sectors. Nor do these organisations often have a standard asset definition model aligned with frameworks such as ISO 14224 (failure, damage, and maintenance in the petroleum industry), ISO 81346 (functional asset structure), or ISO 42010 (architecture). On the other hand, the current platforms where DTs are hosted present closed or proprietary environments that hinder the cross-integration of DTs developed in different ecosystems, as well as migration between them. These problems lead to the progressive adoption of open models, such as the Asset Administration Shell (AAS), the use of architectures based on RAMI 4.0 or IIRA, and the development of standardised BDTs with semantic layers, allowing them to be reused in federations of twins.

6.2 Cybersecurity and Data Privacy

The continuous acquisition and exchange of real-time operational data make TDs potential targets for cyberattacks. The connection between physical assets and the digital environment creates a distributed attack surface, spanning from sensors to the cloud. DTs handle sensitive information such as health indices (AHI), remaining useful life (RUL) estimates, failure models or structural integrity parameters. This information is critical for operation and strategic decision-making. Its improper manipulation can compromise asset safety or financial planning. In addition, there are legal risks associated with the management of personal data, in cases where the DTs also represent operators, technicians or human tasks. Cybersecurity specialists recommend implementing multi-level security architectures (zero-trust), segmenting OT/IT networks, utilising two-factor authentication mechanisms, and tracking access to DTs using blockchain or secure logs. Above all, the isolation of personal data.

6.3 Scalability and Implementation Costs

The development of large-scale DTs is a resource-intensive process, mainly when distributed, critical or structurally complex assets need to be represented. This consumption of resources is evidenced by the need to design customised BDTs for each failure mode and component, which can lead to high initial modelling costs. Later, the progressive integration of BDTs in real-world environments requires a robust data and service architecture, with edge and cloud capabilities to handle large volumes of heterogeneous information. The evolution of the DT over time requires sustained effort to maintain and update models and data. These problems can be minimised by establishing a development methodology based on modularity and reusability of BDTs, prioritising assets according to their criticality and expected return. It would be advisable to apply progressive scalability according to an organisation's digital maturity and the use of automation tools for ETL and data validation from the physical asset and its environment.

6.4 Organisational and Cultural Barriers

Beyond technological challenges, one of the most significant barriers to adopting TDs is cultural transformation. This transformation from traditional maintenance models to digitalised, predictive and data-driven strategies. In many organisations, formal asset health models that integrate structural, functional, environmental and maintenance indicators do not exist. In addition, there is resistance to change from operational teams, and a notable lack of professional profiles specialised in BDT design, property modelling, variable development, and data governance. This challenge requires strategic alignment in organisational structures between engineering, information technology, and maintenance, as well as investment in training and retraining of technical profiles (digital upskilling). It also involves promoting the role of the Digital Twin Architect and data stewards, and creating multidisciplinary teams with a vision for the complete asset lifecycle.

6.5 Specific Problems of Design, Development and Data Capture

In addition to the above problems, the development of a DT for monitoring the health of an asset and managing its life cycle involves solving three different but interrelated issues: (i) designing the properties for each failure mode. This development requires the selection of properties that define the behaviour, failure and environment of the component. (ii) definition of variables, associating with each property the technical variables that can be captured and analysed. (iii) data capture and instantiation, transformation and exploitation by the DG.

7 Case Study

A track tamping machine is a railway maintenance machine whose primary function is to compact the ballast under the sleepers, thereby correcting the track geometry. The Matisa B66-U is a representative example of these machines, characterised by its structural, mechanical, and hydraulic complexity. To circulate on the Railway Network, the tamping machine must pass periodic safety inspections, according to three levels of development: IS1 (annual), IS2 (biannual) and IM (decennial), aimed at obtaining and maintaining the Certificate of Aptitude for Service (CAS) that enables its transit through the Railway Network. During these inspections, 13 systems are analysed to ensure safe and efficient movement: running gear system, crash/traction system, suspension, pneumatic brake system, parking brake system, engine, hydraulic system, safety devices, signalling, mirrors and whistles, clearance, exterior system, and instrumentation. Each system is broken down into components and sub-components (such as bogie, axle, wheel, axlebox, bearing, etc.), each with its inspection operations, critical parameters, measurement tools, and acceptance criteria.

From the technical documentation of the tamping machine, the failure data recorded in the CMMS and the Railway Network regulations, all specific failure modes associated with each system are identified. These failure modes are defined at the maintenance operation level on the inspected component (intervention level). For example, in the running-in system, the following issues are identified: wear of the flange height, decrease in flange thickness, loss of flange slope, decrease in outer rim thickness, and appearance of planes or deposits on the tread. For each of these five failure modes, we identify properties that enable monitoring or measurement. Also, the variables to be controlled and instantiated, along with their relationships, are used to organise the information. The control of these variables enables the detection of when the data exceeds the threshold values established in the variable relationships. For example, the wheel presents the properties: flange height, thickness, slope, rim thickness, and flatness. For each property, a variable is defined that is instantiated with the data collected in each of the inspections. Each property and variable has a defined relationship that determines whether its state is admissible. This is equivalent to determining whether the component is faulty or not, due to this failure mode. For example, flange height less than 36 mm, thickness greater than 25 mm, slope less than 6.5 mm.

For each failure mode, a BDT is defined that will acquire the properties, variables and relationships of the failure mode it represents. In its definition, the method by which the data that instantiates the variables is acquired must be included. In our case, this is achieved through a technical inspection; however, the data could also be collected, for example, by sensors when the tamping machine passes through a rolling system evaluation portal. For other types of failure modes, the acquisition could be online by using sensors such as temperature sensors on the wheel axle bearings. The BDT must also have an algorithm or rule that discriminates between the states of the component. In this case, the value instantiated in the flange height variable must be compared with the proposed threshold (36 mm). The result of this comparison constitutes an output of the BDT, establishing its fitness for service or, conversely, the need for an intervention to restore its fitness for service.

Following this procedure, the BDTs for each failure mode affecting a component, in this case, the wheel, are defined. By composing the five BDTs of the wheel, the DT of the wheel is constructed. This wheel DT will contain the five properties and variables that define the five BDTs. This procedure describes how the DTs are scaled. Similarly, the failure modes of other components of the rolling system are analysed. For the axles, the distance between the inner faces of the wheels and the presence of cracks are considered. These two failure modes give rise to two BDTs, whose properties are the distance between inner faces and the existence of cracks. For these properties, their variables will be defined and instantiated with data also coming from the measurements made during the inspection and from the ultrasonic analysis. The defined relationships will establish their fitness or unfit-for-service status. Combining the axle's two BDTs with the DTs of both wheels allows the construction of an initial axle DT. In this way, the scaling of the axle BDTs occurs, enhanced by the modularity provided by the wheel DTs. To this initial DT of the shaft, other DTs from components associated with the shaft, such as the DTs of the axle boxes or the DTs of the bearings, are modularly added, obtaining the DT of the shaft (See Fig. 3). A subsequent step would be to scale the DTs of the shafts to build the bogie's DT modularly. To do this, we would complement the axle DTs with the spring DTs. In this case, the bogie does not include BDTs, as it does not include new failure modes. To build the DT of the running gear system, you would have to integrate the DTs of the two bogies. To obtain the DT of the machine propulsion, you would have to compose the DTs of the thirteen systems. The DT of the machine would be composed of all properties/variables/relationships of all failure modes related to the propulsion of the machine.

The life cycle of the tamping machine is modelled considering the functional deterioration of its thirteen systems. In this case, the design and manufacturing phase of the tamping machine will not be considered. During the operational phase, variables are instantiated based on actual measurements obtained during inspections (such as lengths, pressures, flexibility, temperature, etc.), and the BDTs are fed with field data (including GOOD/BAD classifications, numerical values, and technical protocols). The accumulation of these instantiated values over time allows us to know the past and current state of each component. To achieve this, the machine's DT must contain functionalities (models/microservices) associated with the DTs of the

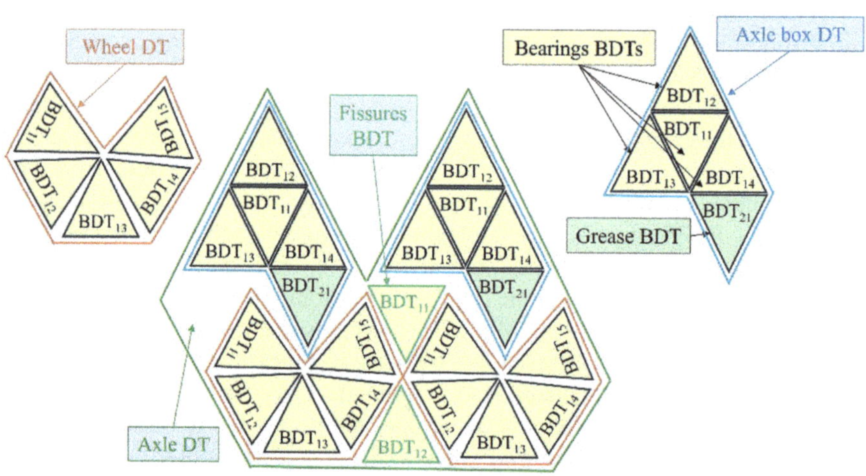

Fig. 3 Construction of the DT of the axle based on the wheel and grease box DTs, and their BDTs for fissures and separation between the back rim faces of the wheels

components (such as wheels and axles) that display this information. The functionality incorporation involves incorporating the properties, variables, and relationships that functionalities use into these BDTs. The same happens with future projections of the component state. They are necessary to predict the evolution of each variable and its relationship with its failure threshold, utilising statistical and forecasting models. Similarly, the machine's DT must contain functionalities associated with the DTs of the components that display this evolution. During the use of the tamping machine, its DT may be able to evaluate the accumulated deterioration of each BDT and its evolution.

The incorporation of the functionality that generates an Asset Health Index (AHI) will be carried out at the tamping machine. Still, it must collect the deterioration of the BDTs to determine the Index. This recompilation requires a dedicated calculation model that consolidates the deterioration contributions of each BDT, incorporating preventive and corrective updates from the CMMS and EAM. The inputs to this AHI model are the outputs of past and current degradations for each BDT. The model's output will be the desired Index. The DT of the tamping machine must visualise the output of this model.

Similarly, another functionality must be incorporated that calculates the Life Cycle Cost (LCC) and the Remaining Useful Life (RUL) for each component and the tamping machine. As in the AHI model, the LCC and RUL models are based on the degradation information generated by each BDT and combine it to calculate the LCC and RUL of each component DT and the tamping machine DT.

In parallel with the AHÍ, LCC and RUL models, models should be developed that allow simulated scenarios to be constructed (partial renewal, total replacement, modernisation). These models will be created at the component DT level and will enable the exploration of other possible scenarios, beyond the evolution of the physical asset. These scenario simulation models will provide new input data (not generated in the physical asset) for use in the AHI, LCC and RUL models.

8 Future Trends and Research Perspectives

As the digital transformation in asset management advances to more complex levels, the concept of DT is evolving beyond its representational function towards a predictive, adaptive, and autonomous system that serves as the operational core of smart maintenance and lifecycle management strategies. New emerging technologies, advances in data modelling and the maturation of distributed architectures are redefining the potential of DTs to address complex asset health and sustainable investment issues.

This section focuses on two key areas: the technological trends that will affect the design and operation of DTs applied to health and lifecycle management, and the research perspectives needed to mature their effective implementation. Ai and Ziehl (2024) provide a comprehensive literature review on the application of DTs.

This review explores the various applications, challenges, and prospects of DTs in the aerospace, manufacturing, construction, and energy industries.

8.1 Technological Trends for the Design and Operation of Digital Twins

Technological trends are advancing in three areas. On the one hand, besides building individual DTs for each asset, the trend will be to connect multiple DTs through federated structures, where the DTs of components, processes, people, and environments collaborate in real time. This connection is essential for monitoring distributed assets (fleets, networks, complex systems) and understanding how failure modes interact between subsystems and how asset health indices change. On the other hand, life cycle management will enable the projection of renewal, reconditioning, or reinvestment scenarios with a systemic perspective. For example, a federated DT of railway infrastructure that synchronises the DTs of bearings, bogies, track sections and bridges, sharing health information to prioritise investments based on cross-impact. Another line would lead to the design of DTs that promote self-explanatory models, which justify their recommendations on health, failures, or life cycle decisions. At the same time, hybrid models that combine physics and data (grey-box) will be consolidated, integrating AI modules to calculate RUL, classify failure modes, or infer health indicators (AHI), with simulated models to validate behaviour under future conditions. This process will enable more reliable calibration of decisions regarding asset renewal, redesign, or relocation. A third line would lead to DTs being integrated directly into maintenance platforms (EAM with APM and AIP models) and workflows. In this way, each DT will include physical properties, functional, contractual, regulatory, and economic properties to guide intervention decisions. In addition, condition monitoring will be integrated with tasks, costs, resources and risks, enabling prescriptive maintenance connected to lifecycle value.

8.2 Research Prospects in DTs for Health and Life Cycle

The second axis focuses on research prospects in DTs, specifically about the health and life cycle of assets. At both the academic and industrial levels, there are significant research opportunities to develop further the fundamentals, methodologies, and tools necessary for the maturation of DTs. In this context, lines of research can be strengthened by developing unified and sectorally validated methodologies for designing BDTs that represent failure modes, relevant properties, and measurable variables. Current and future standards can help to achieve this. A second line would include an integrated and dynamic health assessment. Research on asset health models needs to advance by integrating structural, operational, environmental, and maintenance data in the design of adaptive models that update health based on contextual changes and health indicators geared towards strategic life cycle decisions (e.g., replacement, redesign, redistribution, sale). A third line of development for DTs is as support for risk-based investment. The use of DTs to manage the life cycle requires integration models with risk analysis, LCC, RAMS, and sustainability tools. A field is emerging to study how DTs can support methodologies such as RCM, AIP models, or multi-criteria models, considering criticality, financial impact, and ESG (Environmental, Social, Governance) objectives. Metrics would also need to be developed to assess the impact of decisions made based on DT on the longevity, cost and value of the asset. A fourth line of research would focus on achieving adaptive and resilient DTs. This line requires investigating how DTs can dynamically adjust to changes in asset configuration, the emergence of new failure modes, the retraining of health models without human intervention (continuous learning), and the replanning of the life cycle in the face of crises or regulatory changes.

Together, these trends and lines of research described above constitute a new paradigm in physical asset management: one where DTs not only inform the present but also simulate, project, justify, and recommend decisions based on health, context, and future value. The consolidation of this approach will enable more proactive, efficient and sustainable lifecycle management, guided by the intelligence embedded in each DT, structured to provide continuous support for the health of the asset in its operational reality.

9 Conclusions

The development and implementation of DTs in the field of physical asset management is substantially transforming maintenance, operation, and decision-making strategies throughout the asset lifecycle. This chapter proposes a structured approach to designing and integrating DTs for health monitoring and lifecycle management, based on the modular construction of BDTs and their functional hierarchical integration.

Throughout the text, it has been demonstrated that a DT should not be understood solely as a visual replica of the asset, but rather as a dynamic, operable representation model, based on instantiated data, aimed at supporting specific maintenance and renewal decisions. The decomposition of the asset to the failure mode level and the formalisation of the relationships between properties and variables, ensuring the DT's ability to evolve and adapt to new operating contexts.

The integration of artificial intelligence and machine learning techniques allows DT capabilities to be extended from condition-based diagnostics to forecasting and recommending optimal actions, raising its value from operational to strategic. Likewise, the need to overcome barriers related to interoperability, semantic standardisation, cybersecurity, and organisational maturity has been identified to achieve sustainable and fully functional models.

The case study of the Matisa B66 track ballast tamping machine has demonstrated how a complex technical asset can be represented in a structured way through a DT built from BDTs. This representation allows the capture and monitoring of variables associated with the failure modes and also the continuous evolution of the asset health model, through the indicators such as the AHI or RUL. Likewise, integrating this model into lifecycle management enables the simulation and comparison of various maintenance, renewal, or withdrawal scenarios, considering their impact on operational availability, accumulated costs, and regulatory compliance. This approach transforms the DT into a key tool for strategic decision-making, combining technical diagnosis, operational forecasting, and economic evaluation within a single, federated, and modular digital environment.

References

Abdessadak, A. et al. (2025). Digital twin technology and artificial intelligence in energy transition: A comprehensive systematic review of applications. *Energy Reports*, *13*(May), 5196–5218. Available at: https://doi.org/10.1016/j.egyr.2025.04.060

Abdullahi, I., Longo, S., & Samie, M. (2024). Towards a distributed digital twin framework for predictive maintenance in industrial Internet of Things (IIoT). *Sensors*, *24*(8). Available at: https://doi.org/10.3390/s24082663

Ai, L., & Ziehl, P. (2024). Advances in digital twin technology in industry: A review of applications, challenges, and standardization. *Journal of Intelligent Construction*, *3*(2), 1–19. Available at: https://doi.org/10.26599/jic.2025.9180083

Alhadi, A., Tom, B., & Yacine, R. (2025). Enhancing asset management: Integrating digital twins for continuous permitting and compliance—A systematic literature review. *Journal of Building Engineering*, *99*(December 2024), 111515. Available at: https://doi.org/10.1016/j.jobe.2024.111515

Amin, U., et al. (2025). Digital twins for smart asset management in the energy industry: State-of-the-art. *Expert Systems with Applications*, *289*(May), 128358. Available at: https://doi.org/10.1016/j.eswa.2025.128358

Crespo Márquez, A., et al. (2020). Designing CBM plans, based on predictive analytics and big data tools, for train wheel bearings. *Computers in Industry*, *122*. Available at: https://doi.org/10.1016/j.compind.2020.103292

Gómez Fernández, J. F., Candón Fernández, E., & Márquez, A. C. (2025). A structured data model for asset health index integration in digital twins of energy converters. *Energies*, *18*(12), 1–22. Available at: https://doi.org/10.3390/en18123148

Hagen, A., & Andersen, T. M. (2024). Asset management, condition monitoring and digital twins: Damage detection and virtual inspection on a reinforced concrete bridge. *Structure and Infrastructure Engineering*, *20*(7–8), 1242–1273. Available at: https://doi.org/10.1080/15732479.2024.2311911

Iranshahi, K., et al. (2025). Digital twins: Recent advances and future directions in engineering fields. *Intelligent Systems with Applications*, *26*(January), 200516. Available at: https://doi.org/10.1016/j.iswa.2025.200516

Khoshkenar, A., & Nassereddine, H. (2024). Digital twin benefits and challenges in asset management during the O&M phase: A systematic review. In *Proceedings of the creative construction conference*. Budapest. Available at: https://doi.org/10.3311/ccc2024-029

Kim, Y. J., et al. (2025). Federated digital twins: A scheduling approach based on temporal graph neural network and deep reinforcement learning. *IEEE Access*, *13*(December 2024), 20763–20777. Available at: https://doi.org/10.1109/ACCESS.2025.3530558

Prova, N. N. I., et al. (2025). Advancing predictive maintenance and asset management through digital twin technology: A step towards Industry 4.0. In *1st international conference on advances in computer science, electrical, electronics, and communication technologies, CE2CT 2025* (pp. 1179–1185). Available at: https://doi.org/10.1109/CE2CT64011.2025.10939840

Sharma, A., et al. (2022). Digital twins: State of the art theory and practice, challenges, and open research questions. *Journal of Industrial Information Integration*, *30*(November 2020), 100383. Available at: https://doi.org/10.1016/j.jii.2022.100383

Industrial and Sectorial Applications of Digital Maintenance

Digitalisation of Maintenance in Rolling Stock Assets

Alfonso Carballo Menayo, Antonio Sánchez Herguedas, and Adolfo Crespo Márquez

Abstract This chapter presents a practical framework for guiding the digitalisation of maintenance processes. It introduces a structured, step-by-step methodology covering the main phases of digital transformation. The guide includes assessing current practices, defining goals, selecting technologies, and building data infrastructure. Its purpose is to support maintenance professionals in transitioning from manual to digital systems. The approach emphasises the use of structured data models and scalable digital tools. A real-world case study is included to demonstrate the methodology in action. The case focuses on the digitalisation of the Certificate of Aptitude for Service (CAS) process in the railway sector.

Keywords Rolling stock maintenance digitalization · Methodology for the digitisation of maintenance · Digital twin architecture · Asset data modelling and ontologies · Lakehouse data architecture for maintenance

1 Introduction

This chapter serves as a practical guide for maintenance engineers seeking to digitalise maintenance processes in an operational and structured manner. The framework outlined here can be adapted to various maintenance contexts, offering step-by-step guidance for transitioning from traditional, paper-based workflows to advanced digital solutions supported by data modelling, IoT integration, and digital twins (DTs).

A. Carballo Menayo (✉) · A. Sánchez Herguedas · A. Crespo Márquez
Department of Industrial Management, School of Engineering, University of Seville, Seville, Spain
e-mail: acarballo@us.es

A. Sánchez Herguedas
e-mail: antoniosh@us.es

A. Crespo Márquez
e-mail: adolfo@us.es

A. Crespo Márquez et al. (eds.), *Digital Maintenance and Asset Digitalization*, Engineering Asset Management Review 5,
https://doi.org/10.1007/978-3-032-21502-4_10

To illustrate this approach, the chapter presents a real-world example: the digitalisation of the process used to obtain the CAS for locomotives in the railway network. This certification process is critical for ensuring that each unit in the machinery fleet meets the necessary safety, reliability, and compliance standards before being authorised for service. In the example presented, a digital transformation roadmap was implemented to transition from a state of low digital maturity, where inspections were manually recorded on paper, to a data-driven process that leverages structured asset models, real-time monitoring, and digital tools. The goal was not only to streamline the CAS process but also to lay the foundation for broader digitalisation of maintenance management.

By following this guide, maintenance professionals can adopt a replicable model that enhances traceability, operational efficiency, and data-driven decision-making, while meeting industry standards and preparing for future scalability.

2 Methodology for Digitalising Maintenance Processes

This guide outlines a practical roadmap for digitalising maintenance processes, supported by structured data models, digital tools, and scalable platforms. The goal is to help maintenance engineers track progress through key milestones while building a long-term vision for sustainable digital transformation. Ma et al. (2024) provides a requirement-based roadmap to support standardized predictive maintenance automation using DT technologies. Our guide contains seven steps.

Step 1: Assess the Current State of Maintenance Management

The digitalisation process begins with a clear understanding of the current maintenance environment. This effort involves evaluating strategies, tools, and operational practices to establish a baseline for future improvement. The key actions in this step are three: conducting a comprehensive audit of existing maintenance approaches (e.g., reactive, preventive, predictive); identifying gaps in current technologies, data systems, and staff competencies; and evaluating organisational readiness for digital transformation, including cultural and structural factors.

The outcome will be a diagnostic report that highlights the current maturity level, existing strengths, and specific areas for improvement. This result forms the foundation for a targeted transformation strategy.

Step 2: Define Digitalisation Goals and Objectives

Once the current state is understood, it's essential to establish clear and measurable objectives for digitalisation that align with the broader organisational goals. There are two key actions in this step: engaging stakeholders to define strategic priorities (e.g., improved reliability, reduced downtime, and cost optimisation); and identifying and prioritising critical assets and maintenance processes for early digitalisation.

The outcome will be a well-defined digitalisation roadmap with clear objectives and prioritised targets, aligned with both operational needs and long-term strategic ambitions.

Step 3: Select and Implement Digital Technologies

Selecting the right technologies is crucial for building an effective and scalable digital ecosystem. This step focuses on deploying the foundational tools required to support digital maintenance practices. The three key actions in this step are: select technologies that match organisational needs, such as IoT sensors, predictive analytics, AI/ML models, and digital twins (Jiao et al., 2023) give an example for building infrastructures; integrate new tools with existing systems like Enterprise Asset Management (EAM) and Computerised Maintenance Management Systems (CMMS); and design and implement robust data pipelines using ETL (Extract, Transform, Load) processes to enable consistent and reliable data flow.

The outcome will be the deployment of interoperable digital systems capable of real-time monitoring, advanced analytics, and decision support. Karkaria et al. (2024) show an example of these techniques applied to DTs. Early integration of data models ensures a standardised and scalable framework.

Step 4: Build the Data Infrastructure

The success of any digitalisation initiative depends on the quality, organisation, and accessibility of data. This step involves creating a data infrastructure that supports efficient storage, analysis, and decision-making. There are three key actions in this step: set up data platforms—such as cloud-based environments, fog computing, or data warehouses—to store and manage maintenance-related data; implement Business Intelligence (BI) tools to enable advanced data visualisation and reporting, providing actionable insights for engineers, planners, and decision-makers; and apply strong data governance practices to guarantee data quality, consistency, timeliness, and security. Well-structured data models support these practices by defining clear relationships and standards across data sources, which also aids in maintaining data lineage and integrity. Ben Amor et al., (2024) provide a comprehensive analysis of the current state of DT for additive manufacturing, examining their applications, benefits, challenges, and future directions.

The outcome will be a scalable, secure, and well-structured data platform that provides the foundation for ongoing digitalisation, analytics, and optimisation of maintenance practices.

Step 5: Train and Upskill the Workforce

Successful digital transformation depends not only on technology but also on people. Training and upskilling are essential to ensure that staff can effectively use the new digital tools and systems. The key actions in this step are deliver practical training on IoT platforms, data visualisation tools, and other new technologies; enhance employee capabilities in areas such as predictive maintenance, data analysis, and AI-based decision-making; and promote a culture of innovation and continuous improvement.

The outcome will be a capable and confident workforce, empowered to operate and maintain advanced digital systems.

Step 6: Pilot and Test Digital Solutions

Before full implementation, it's essential to validate the digital tools and processes in a controlled setting to ensure functionality and relevance. There are three key actions in this step: launch a pilot program on a high-impact asset or process, use KPIs (e.g., uptime, failure rates, cost savings) to assess effectiveness, and collect feedback to refine the system accordingly.

The outcome will be proven digital solutions, validated in real-world conditions and ready for broader application.

Step 7: Scale and Optimize Digital Maintenance

After successfully validating digital solutions, the final step is to scale these technologies across the organisation and refine them through continuous improvement. This phase ensures that digital maintenance becomes a sustained and integrated part of operational strategy. The key actions in this step are: roll out digital tools and practices to additional assets, workshops, or regions; apply predictive analytics and AI to fine-tune maintenance strategies and improve asset performance over time; ensure seamless integration between all systems, including GIS, mobile platforms, and asset management tools, to support unified operations.

The outcome will be a fully deployed, organisation-wide digital maintenance system that drives efficiency, improves decision-making, and supports long-term sustainability.

While the complete digitalisation roadmap encompasses seven key steps, this chapter primarily focuses on the first four steps, which are essential for designing a digital maintenance strategy. These initial phases—assessing the current state, defining objectives, selecting technologies, and building the data infrastructure—form the core foundation of any successful digital transformation. Steps 5 to 7, which involve training personnel, piloting the solution, and scaling it organisation-wide, represent the operational deployment of the strategy. Though summarised here, these steps fall outside the main scope of this chapter. They are addressed more briefly, as the emphasis is on equipping readers with a detailed methodology for planning and designing a digital maintenance system.

3 Assess the Current State of Maintenance Management

Before beginning the digitalisation process, an evaluation was conducted on the existing maintenance strategies and tools related to obtaining the CAS. The company's machinery operated under structured maintenance plans, which included a predefined set of tasks intended to preserve the vehicle's operational condition and ensure compliance with safety, reliability, technical compatibility, health, environmental protection, and, where applicable, interoperability standards—aligned with national technical specifications for certification and approval.

These maintenance plans were primarily focused on ensuring the locomotive's operational readiness and circulation capability, with particular emphasis on obtaining the CAS. However, maintenance execution was largely manual. Data collection relied on operator-performed measurements and handwritten reports, which were then archived on paper. This approach limited traceability, data reuse, and analytical insights.

To objectively assess the organisation's readiness for digital transformation, a maturity evaluation was carried out using a dual-axis matrix that measures both Maintenance Management Maturity and Digital Integration Level. This custom matrix classifies organisational maturity across six levels—from Level 0 (unstructured, manual processes) to Level 5 (fully integrated, AI-supported digital ecosystems). It encompasses key dimensions, including data utilisation, technology integration, process standardisation and strategic alignment.

Based on the maturity assessment, the organisation was positioned at Level 2 in Maintenance Management Maturity and the lowest level in Digital Integration. On the maintenance side, formal plans and procedures were in place; however, they were rigid, bureaucratic, and offered little flexibility or strategic coordination. These processes focused more on compliance than performance optimisation. In terms of digitalisation, the organisation operated with minimal technological support. Documentation was paper-based, and digital tools—if present—were isolated and not integrated into operational workflows. There was no real-time data acquisition, no use of analytics, and no structured data models. See Table 1.

4 Define Digitalisation Goals and Objectives

Once the initial state of the maintenance process has been assessed, the next step is to define clear and measurable objectives for digitalisation. In this case, the primary goal is to fully digitise the process of obtaining the CAS for railway machinery. This process, which was previously manual and paper-based, will be transformed into a structured, digital workflow integrated into a larger digital twin system.

The digitalisation of the CAS process addresses the following objectives. First, it will significantly reduce human error by replacing handwritten measurements and paper reports with digital data captured through specialised software. Second, it will optimise maintenance operations by improving traceability, enabling automated validations, and streamlining inspections. Third, it will enhance the quality and organisation of maintenance mapping files by standardising how data is recorded, stored, and retrieved.

To support the implementation of a digital twin (DT), it is essential to define a well-structured data model that includes all the variables and entities involved in the CAS process—from asset components and technical locations to measurement

Table 1 Maintenance maturity versus digitalisation maturity matrix

Maintenance Maturity Level	Low digitalisation	Initial digitalisation	Partial digitalisation and IoT adoption	Advanced digitalisation and analytics	Full digital twin integration	Innovation leadership
Level 0—Unaware	Manual work, no structured process	Minimal recognition of digital tools	No integration or strategy	Fragmented systems with unclear value	No digital twin or analytics	No digital vision
Level 1—Reactive	Maintenance based on urgent repairs	Use of spreadsheets and reports	Basic CMMS or EAM implemented	Data not linked to operations	Occasional dashboards	Innovation team initiated
Level 2—Administrative	Formal maintenance plans	Basic digital records in place	Isolated IoT pilots	Initial data models without real use	No analytics used in decision-making	Siloed experiments
Level 3—Structured	Maintenance with internal standards	CMMS connected to assets	Predictive tools	Data used for planning	Pilot digital twin cases	Projects without scaling
Level 4—Optimized	Data-driven preventive maintenance	Broad use of analytics tools	Real-time monitoring on key assets	Dashboards support decisions	Digital twins in core areas	Early AI-assisted decisions
Level 5—Proactive	Maintenance with business strategy	Advanced analytics and BI platforms	IoT, AI, and digital twins	Predictive models guide decisions	Digital twins used across lifecycle	AI enabled optimization and innovation

parameters and responsible personnel. This model must be scalable, interoperable, and designed to enable real-time data access and visualisation. Additionally, one of the key objectives is to ensure the localisation of both assets and measurement devices, enabling geospatial integration within the DT. This will enable maintenance teams to visualise the position and condition of each machine and component on a virtual map, making planning and monitoring more efficient. Ultimately, the objective is to evolve from a fragmented and manual system to a robust, data-driven process. Werbińska-Wojciechowska et al. (2024) give examples of DTs applications in the transport sector. The digitised CAS process will serve as a pilot and foundation for broader digitalisation across the organisation's maintenance operations.

In terms of maturity progression, the organisation began this initiative at Level 2 in maintenance management maturity, characterised by formal but bureaucratic processes with limited adaptability and low strategic alignment. At the same time, the digitalisation level was at its lowest point, relying on paper-based documentation and disconnected tools. The objective of this digitalisation effort is to advance toward Level 4 in maintenance maturity, a stage defined by data-driven decision-making, optimised workflows, and proactive management practices. See Fig. 1. On the digital axis, the goal is to achieve an advanced stage of digitalisation, where real-time data collection, integrated systems, and DTs enable predictive maintenance, enhanced traceability, and intelligent process control. This shift represents a transformation from administrative maintenance to a fully optimised, technology-supported operational model.

To get this level of digitalisation, the following three objectives have been defined as essential for the digitalisation of the CAS process:

1. Identify and implement the technological components necessary to support the integration of the CAS process within a DT architecture. van Dinter et al. (2023) develop and evaluate a reference Architecture designed using renowned software architecture methods. The identification includes sensors, IoT devices, data acquisition systems, and connectivity tools that enable real-time monitoring and interaction with the DT.
2. Define detailed data models that accurately represent all relevant entities, including assets, subcomponents, facilities, measuring instruments, and human resources. These models must include hierarchical structures and relational links to allow their integration and traceability within the DT environment.
3. Create a structured data infrastructure that ensures reliable data flow, storage, and analysis. This includes selecting suitable platforms for data ingestion (ETL/ELT pipelines), storage (e.g., lakehouse architecture), and visualisation (BI tools).

5 Selection and Implementation of Digital Technology

The digitalisation of the CAS process requires careful selection and integration of technologies that enable structured data collection, automated processes, and seamless connectivity with a DT environment. From a technological standpoint, the

Maturity Level	Low Digitalization	Initial Digitalization	Partial Digitalization & IoT Adoption	Advanced Digitalization and Analytics	Full Digital Twin Integration	Innovation Leadership
Level 0 - Unaware	Manual work, no structured process.	Minimal recognition of digital tools.	No integration or strategy.	Fragmented systems with unclear value.	No digital twin or analytics.	No digital vision.
Level 1 - Reactive	Maintenance based on urgent repairs.	Use of spreadsheets and reports.	Basic CMMS or EAM implemented.	Data not linked to operations.	Occasional dashboards.	Siloed experiments
Level 2 - Administrative	Formal maintenance plans.	Basic digital records in place.	Isolated IoT pilots.	Initial data models without real use.	No analytics used in decision-making.	Projects without scaling.
Level 3 - Structured	Maintenance with internal standards.	CMMS connected to assets.	Predictive tools.	Data used for planning.	Pilot digital twin cases.	Innovation team initiated.
Level 4 - Optimized	Data-driven preventive maintenance.	Broad use of analytics tools.	Real-time monitoring on key assets.	Dashboards support decisions.	Digital twins in core areas.	Early AI-assisted decisions.
Level 5 - Proactive	Maintenance with business strategy.	Advanced analytics and BI platforms.	IoT, AI, and digital twins.	Predictive models guide decisions.	Digital twins used across lifecycle.	AI enabled optimization and innovation.

Fig. 1 Digitalisation goal in maturity matrix

primary objective is to develop a system that supports real-time data flow, improves operational traceability, and lays the foundation for predictive and condition-based maintenance in the future. While the broader digital transformation plan considers the implementation of advanced tools, such as Enterprise Asset Management (EAM) and Asset Performance Management (APM) systems, the specific focus of this case study is on predetermined maintenance, which does not require the full complexity of AI-based predictive models at this stage. Davari et al., (2021) discuss the main approaches for the railway application within a taxonomy defined by the type of task, employed methods, metrics of evaluation, the specific equipment or process, and datasets.

IoT connection plays a crucial role in the broader digitalisation of rail transport. The IoT ecosystem facilitates the physical connection of the DT, enabling the tools necessary for digitising workshop processes. Once deployed, the DT automates inspection processes by recognising machines, equipment, technicians, and assigned resources. It manages permits and certificates, informs technicians of tasks, and guides them through a mobile interface. This structured data entry system generates alerts based on measurements, tracks task execution times, and ensures that all inspections are traceable and verifiable, thereby guaranteeing process quality.

The IoT connection will facilitate obtaining the CAS through the recognition of machines, tools, and technicians via RFID or NFC identification. This recognition

Fig. 2 Sensor, geolocation device with solar panel, RFID-NFC reader, NFC watch and processing unit

will enable the management of work permits, inspection tasks, and digital certification through mobile interfaces. Additionally, it will guide operators step by step, log time and actions, and issue alerts when measurements exceed predefined thresholds, ensuring full traceability and quality control of the maintenance and certification process. A central component in enabling this transition is the development of an Asset Identification Model, which will provide a unified structure for organising digital records of machinery, workshop tools, personnel, and certification reports. These models will ensure consistency and allow for scalable integration within the DT.

Figure 2 illustrates the core physical components that form the foundation of this infrastructure. These include various devices, such as IoT sensors, geolocation modules powered by solar panels, RFID/NFC readers, wearable identification systems (e.g., NFC-enabled wristbands), and mobile processing units. Together, these tools support real-time data capture, automated identification, and seamless communication between physical assets and digital systems.

Building on these physical components, the proposed IoT solution is structured around five key functional layers: data capture, data processing and analysis, data distribution and visualisation, data storage, and policy-based data management.

Data Capture uses IoT Sensor Nodes and Automatic Identification Devices. The first are Data collector devices equipped with a variety of sensors to collect operational and environmental status data from trains and their surroundings. Essential for real-time monitoring. Geolocation devices with solar panels will provide precise train location data and temperature information, aiding fleet management and coordination. The second ones are applying technologies using RFID and NFC for fast and accurate identification of railway components and personnel, facilitating inventory tracking. NFC Watches Worn by maintenance personnel will identify individuals during measurement tasks and ensure precise tracking of intervention steps.

Data Processing and Analysis is configured using three different types of elements: processing units, IoT communication gateways network, and data distribution and visualisation. The processing units are components that preprocess sensor data, filtering and condensing it before transmitting to the central analysis platform, optimising data transmission. The IoT Communication Gateways Network is a dedicated network for transmitting data collected by sensor nodes to a centralised system. Operates across wide geographical ranges, ensuring uninterrupted and secure data coverage. The data analytics cloud platform is a central system for processing and analysing large volumes of data using advanced cloud solutions, AI, and ML algorithms. Provides predictive maintenance alerts and optimised recommendations.

The data distribution and visualisation is an intuitive application and dashboard for maintenance technicians and operators to access relevant information, customised maintenance plans, and tools for data-driven decision-making. The data storage system contains scalable and secure storage solutions designed to handle the exponential growth of data generated by the IoT system. The policy-based data management regulates the lifecycle of data, from capture to archiving or disposal, ensuring compliance with privacy and data protection regulations.

6 Construction of the Data Infrastructure

The construction of a robust data infrastructure is a fundamental pillar in the digitalisation of the CAS process. This section outlines the elements necessary to support a DT environment that ensures data traceability, process automation, and real-time monitoring. The development of this infrastructure is addressed in two interconnected parts, each essential to enabling a scalable, intelligent, and efficient maintenance system.

First, we define the data models required to represent machinery, tools, workshop resources, and inspection processes in a structured and digital format. These models serve as the foundation for consistently and hierarchically organising information across all assets and operations. Second, we present the data structure, explaining how information is stored, validated, and made accessible for analysis. This explanation includes the definition of data layers, ontologies between entities, and the logic that supports both historical and real-time data use.

6.1 Data Model for Obtain the CAS

The development of structured, scalable, and interoperable data models is a critical pillar in the digitalisation of the CAS process. Without a consistent and detailed representation of the key entities and their relationships, it would be impossible to support traceability, automate processes, or integrate data into a DT environment. Data modelling serves not only to standardise the information used in maintenance workflows but also to enable its reuse, analysis, and validation in a digital system.

To understand the need for comprehensive data models, it is necessary to describe the CAS process briefly. In the railway sector, each machine must pass a series of inspections—performed annually, biennially, and once every ten years—to maintain its certification for safe and legal operation. These inspections are organised into maintenance plans that define a series of interventions, which in turn are composed of tasks, each made up of multiple operations. During each operation, measurements

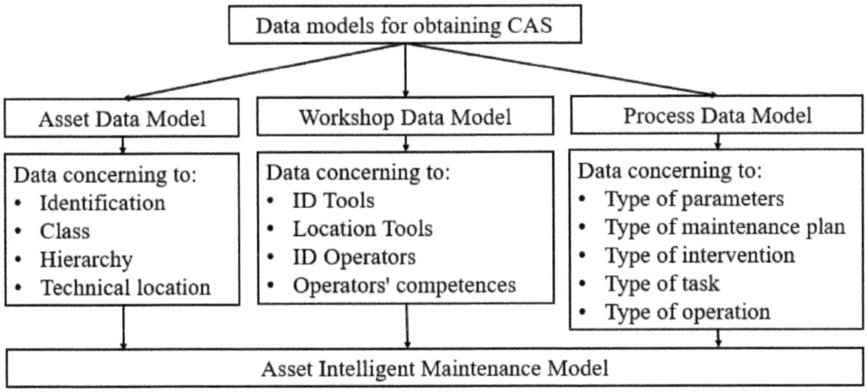

Fig. 3 Data model for obtaining the CAS

are performed by operators using specific tools. These results are documented and stored in official inspection reports.

To digitalise this process, we must model and integrate all relevant components. The data modelling effort is divided into several interconnected models, each addressing a specific domain of the CAS process. These include the Asset Data Model, Workshop Data Model, Process Data Model, and Intelligent Asset Management Model. The Asset Data Model represents railway machinery, including its systems, subsystems, and components, each of which is identified and coded hierarchically. The Workshop Data Model encompasses tools, measurement devices, and personnel, along with their functional locations. The Human Resources Model identifies and tracks qualified personnel assigned to specific tasks. The Process Data Model defines maintenance plans, interventions, tasks, operations, and measurement parameters. The Intelligent Asset Management Model records real maintenance activities, measurement outcomes, and links all other models together into a cohesive system. See Fig. 3.

In addition to defining these models individually, it is essential to develop the ontologies, that is, the relationships and dependencies between them (Louadah et al., 2024). For example, a task is performed as part of a specific intervention, which is part of a maintenance plan applied to a machine. Each operation within a task is executed by a technician using a tool and generates a measurement linked to a specific component.

The remainder of this section provides a detailed explanation of each data model, supported by examples and tabular representations of the key variables involved. These models form the backbone of the digital CAS process, ensuring that every asset, action, and measurement is accurately tracked, structured, and ready for integration within a DT.

Asset Data Model

To support the digitalisation of the CAS process, it is essential to develop a detailed and structured Asset Data Model that accurately represents each machine and its components. This model enables traceability, consistent identification, and integration of asset-related information across different systems. In the context of DTs, such modelling becomes even more crucial, as it provides the semantic foundation upon which all further operations—monitoring, diagnostics, and decision-making—are built.

The complete asset modelling framework comprises four complementary sub-models, each with a distinct function in the asset lifecycle. The Asset Definition Model (ADM) describes the static characteristics of assets, including their identity, structure, classification, and physical configuration. The Asset Criticality Model (ACM) evaluates and prioritises assets based on risk, safety, operational impact, and maintenance cost, supporting resource allocation and reliability centered maintenance strategies. The Asset Monitoring Model (AMM) focuses on real-time condition tracking, enabling continuous monitoring through the use of IoT sensors and cloud-based systems, which provide data for predictive maintenance and performance optimisation. And the Intelligent Asset Management Model (IAMM) connects structured asset data with analytics and decision-making tools. It supports the execution of digital maintenance strategies by incorporating insights from historical data, condition monitoring, and criticality assessments.

In the context of the CAS process, the most relevant sub-model is the Asset Definition Model, as it serves as the foundation for all data structuring efforts. The CAS process requires detailed knowledge of each machine and its components, including which systems are inspected, which elements are measured, and how results are linked to specific parts. The ADM provides the necessary coding system and hierarchical breakdown to manage this complexity.

To achieve this, a multi-level structure is used to represent each asset, starting from the machine and progressing down to its systems, subsystems, and components. Each element is assigned a unique alphanumeric code, allowing for precise identification and consistent referencing throughout its lifecycle. This coding enables the digital platform to link inspection data, maintenance records, and measurement results directly to the physical asset elements involved.

Figure 4 illustrates the format of the identification code used in this case study. This code is divided into five sections, each representing a specific level in the asset hierarchy:

1. Type of Machinery (01): The first block identifies the general category or type of machinery, such as tamping machines, locomotives, or inspection vehicles.
2. Specific Machinery (01): This section distinguishes between different individual machines within the same category. For instance, two tamping machines of the same type would each have a unique identifier here.
3. System of the Machinery (040): This segment identifies a primary system within the machine, such as the hydraulic system, electrical system, or braking system.

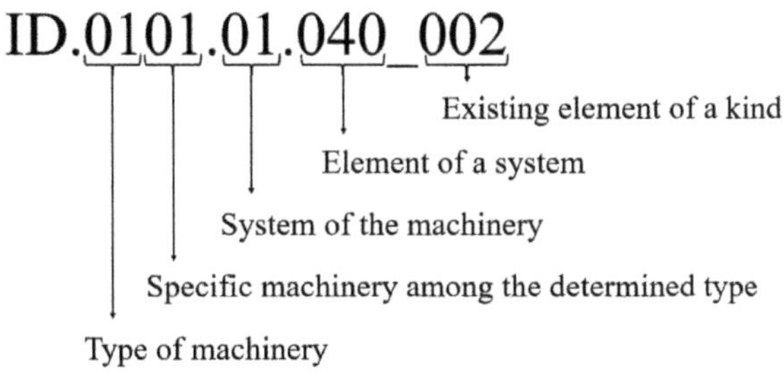

Fig. 4 Identification code

4. Element of a System (002): This portion refers to a specific component within the defined system, such as a pressure sensor, pump, or control unit.
5. Existing Element of a Kind (_002): This final section differentiates between multiple instances of the same component type, such as two identical sensors mounted in different positions.

Through this codification, any physical or functional element of a machine can be uniquely and consistently referenced across the entire platform, facilitating data integration, inspection traceability, and digital maintenance planning. The same code structure is used throughout the Asset Definition Model to link inspection data, tasks, and measurement records to their corresponding components.

In the context of obtaining the CAS, one of the foundations for digitalisation is the precise requirements and modelling of the machinery involved. The CAS process requires linking inspection activities, maintenance tasks, and measurement results to the exact physical components of a machine. To make this possible within a digital platform, it is necessary to build a robust and structured data model that reflects the full composition of the asset. This process involves two key steps that are essential for constructing the Asset Definition Model.

The first step involves establishing the hierarchical structure of the asset. This entails decomposing the machine into its main systems (e.g., propulsion, rolling, electrical) and further into its constituent components (e.g., axles, wheels, sensors). The hierarchy must reflect both the physical and functional relationships between the components, allowing for intuitive navigation and accurate traceability. The structure also supports the definition of dependencies, which is crucial for understanding how specific elements contribute to overall machine performance and for organising inspection tasks logically.

The second step is to identify and catalogue each asset element within the hierarchy. For each machine, every system and component must be assigned a unique alphanumeric code, based on the coding structure introduced earlier. This process ensures that no component is duplicated and that every measurement, inspection result, or maintenance task can be associated with the exact asset to which it pertains. Along with the code, each item is also assigned a brief textual description, which aids in interpretation and usability by operators and technicians. Additionally, it is necessary to specify the technical location of each component, indicating its physical position within the machine. This spatial reference is particularly important in maintenance planning and reporting, as it defines the exact location where an intervention occurs.

To illustrate the application of the Asset Definition Model, the following example focuses on the running gear system of a tamping machine. This system comprises multiple components, including bogies, axles, and wheels, which must be identified and associated with their technical location within the machine. Figure 5 shows the structure of the running gear system:

Table 2 presents the data model used to define the technical location of a wheel within the running gear system. This location is linked to the unique identifier of the component and includes references to the parent element and the machine to which it belongs. This structured information must be recorded for each component of the tamping machine.

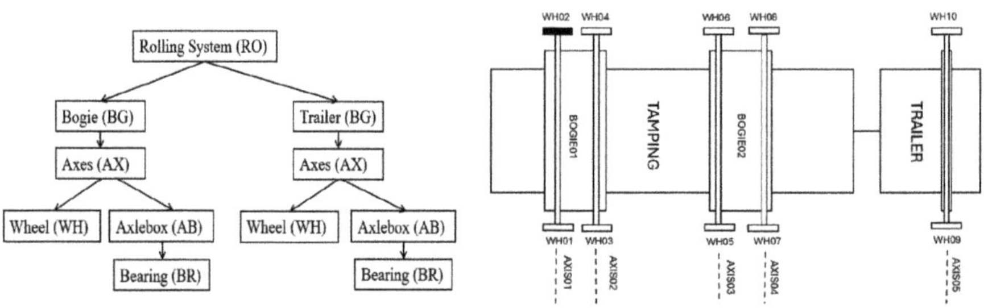

Fig. 5 Running gear system schematic

Table 2 Data model for technical location

Property	Description	Example
ID-TECHLOCMAC	Technical location of the component	FU.0101.01.050_0002
I-TECHLOCMAC-BE	Reference to the technical location of the item at the top level	FU.0101.01.040_0001
ID-MACHINERY	Machinery identification	01
ID-SYSTEM	System identification	ID.0101.01.010_0001
ID-COMPONENT	Component identification	ID.0101.01.050_0002
T-NAME	The name of the technical location	WHEEL02
N-ORDER	Order of the technical locations of the same type of component	0002
T-DESCRIPTION	Description of the technical location	Left wheel of axis 01 of bogie 01

Workshop Data Model

Once the data model for the machinery has been defined, the next essential step is to construct the Workshop Data Model. This model serves to represent the physical and operational environment in which CAS inspections are carried out. It must include all tools and equipment used during the certification process, each with its corresponding technical location to ensure precise identification and traceability within the facility.

In addition, the model must incorporate the human resources assigned to workshop activities. This incorporation includes the identification of operators and technicians, enabling the system to track who performs each task, link actions to specific personnel and process validation. By structuring the workshop model in this way, the digital platform can manage the complete set of resources involved in the CAS process, including both material and human resources. Table 3 provides an example of how a measuring device, such as a calliper for rolling parameter inspection, is represented in the data model.

Process Data Model

The Process Data Model defines the structure of activities carried out during the CAS certification process. It organises the complete set of inspection actions in a hierarchical and standardised manner, enabling traceability, consistency, and integration with the DT.

Each element in this model (maintenance plans, interventions, tasks, operations, and parameters) is assigned a unique code and accompanied by a description that defines its purpose, structure, and scope. The code ensures that all CAS-related procedures are documented, digitised, and traceable within the system. The model is structured as follows:

1. Maintenance Plan: To digitalise maintenance plans, a code and a description of the plan are defined for each. Maintenance plans typically include several interventions.
2. Intervention: They are digitized using a code and description. Interventions are made up of different tasks.
3. Task: Tasks are identified and defined. They consist of several operations.
4. Operation: Each operation is defined by a unique code and a description that explains what the operator must do, what tool they must use, or the measurement they must take.
5. Parameters: Parameters are associated with operations and are defined by code and a description that provides information about the measure. For example, if

Table 3 Workshop data model

Property	Description	Example
ID-MEASDEV	Device identification	ID.HER.0101.006_0001
T-NAME	Description	Caliber rolling parameter
ID-TECHLOCMEASDEV	Technical location	FU.HER.0101.006_0001

the wheel of a tamping machine needs to be measured, the operation specifies how to perform the measurement and which instrument to use. However, the parameter establishes the measurement limit; that is, if it falls below a specific value, the workshop must replace the wheel.

The Intelligent Asset Management Model

Following the definition of the asset, workshop, and process data models, the final piece in the digitalisation of the CAS process is the implementation of the Intelligent Asset Management Model (IAMM). This model integrates and records all interventions (both past and ongoing) while ensuring that all activities comply with predefined parameters and that only authorised, qualified operators carry out the tasks. It serves as the dynamic layer of the system, where execution, monitoring, and traceability converge in real-time.

Operators interact with the model through digital devices, which guide them throughout the inspection process. Upon initiating a session, the operator selects the relevant maintenance plan, identifies themselves securely, and proceeds to perform the assigned tasks. As operations are executed, measurements are recorded directly into the system, ensuring immediate validation and alignment with required thresholds. The IAMM not only verifies compliance but also preserves this data for future audits, certification validation, performance analysis, or pre-failure anomaly detection (Rojas et al., 2025).

Moreover, the model continuously tracks the progress of ongoing interventions, reflecting the current state of each plan. It records which tasks have been completed and which remain pending, while also logging the actual start and end dates of every intervention. Each measurement captured is linked to its corresponding operation, parameter, and component, allowing for complete reconstruction of the process if needed. In this way, the IAMM provides a live and historical view of maintenance activity, reinforcing transparency, operational control, and regulatory compliance within the DT framework.

Table 4 presents the data model used to capture individual measurement records. Each entry uniquely identifies the measurement and associates it with the relevant operational context, including the asset, component, parameter type, responsible user and measurement device. Additionally, it stores the measured value and its final status, allowing the platform to register not only what was measured, but also the result's validity within the expected range.

Figure 6 provides an integrated view of data architecture supporting the digitalisation of the CAS process. It visually represents the different types of data models—each associated with a specific domain (machine, process, workshop, or intelligent asset management)—and shows how these models are logically connected to one another. The diagram is colour-coded to distinguish between the four main categories:

- Machine Data Model, which defines the structure and identity of the physical asset, including machinery and its components.
- Workshop Data Model, which includes measurement devices and human resources (users).

Table 4 Data model of measurement

Property	Description	Example
ID-MEASUREMENT	Measurement identification	MM.0001.001.0101.01.01
ID-OPERATION	Operation identification	MM.0001.001.0101.01.00
ID-TYPEPAR	Type parameter identification	416
ID-MACHINERY	Machinery identification	ID.0101.00.000_0001
ID-COMPONENT	Component identification	ID.0101.01.050_0003
ID-USER	User identification	ID.RHH.0000.001_0001
ID-MEASDEV	Device identification	ID.HER.0101.006_0001
T-VALUE	Value of the measure	29,5
B-RESULT	Status of the measure	Successful

Asset management model

- Process Data Model, which establishes the procedural hierarchy of the CAS system, including maintenance plans, interventions, tasks, operations, and parameters.
- Intelligent Asset Management Model, which manages live operational data, including the actual interventions, performed tasks, and measured results.

6.2 *The Necessary Architecture for the CAS Process Digital Twin*

Although the main objective of this initiative is to digitalise the process of obtaining the CAS, doing so in isolation would limit the system's future scalability and interoperability. Because the CAS process will ultimately operate within a broader DT environment, it is essential to define the architecture of the entire DT platform from the outset. This definition ensures that the CAS process is integrated using a consistent data structure, shared models, and common technological standards. By embedding CAS digitalisation into a well-designed architectural framework, the solution not only meets immediate needs but also lays the groundwork for incorporating additional maintenance processes in the future, avoiding redundancies, ensuring data integrity, and supporting long-term system evolution.

The development of data architecture for DTs has been carried out with specialised companies. Salierno et al. (2024) approach for creating a DT model in the railway domain, emphasising the critical role of big data in supporting decision-making. Their expertise has contributed significantly to ensuring the robustness, scalability, and functionality of the solution. Below is the solution that the company should adopt to define the architecture of the digital platform for a DT. The data infrastructure is divided into layers, each serving distinct functions.

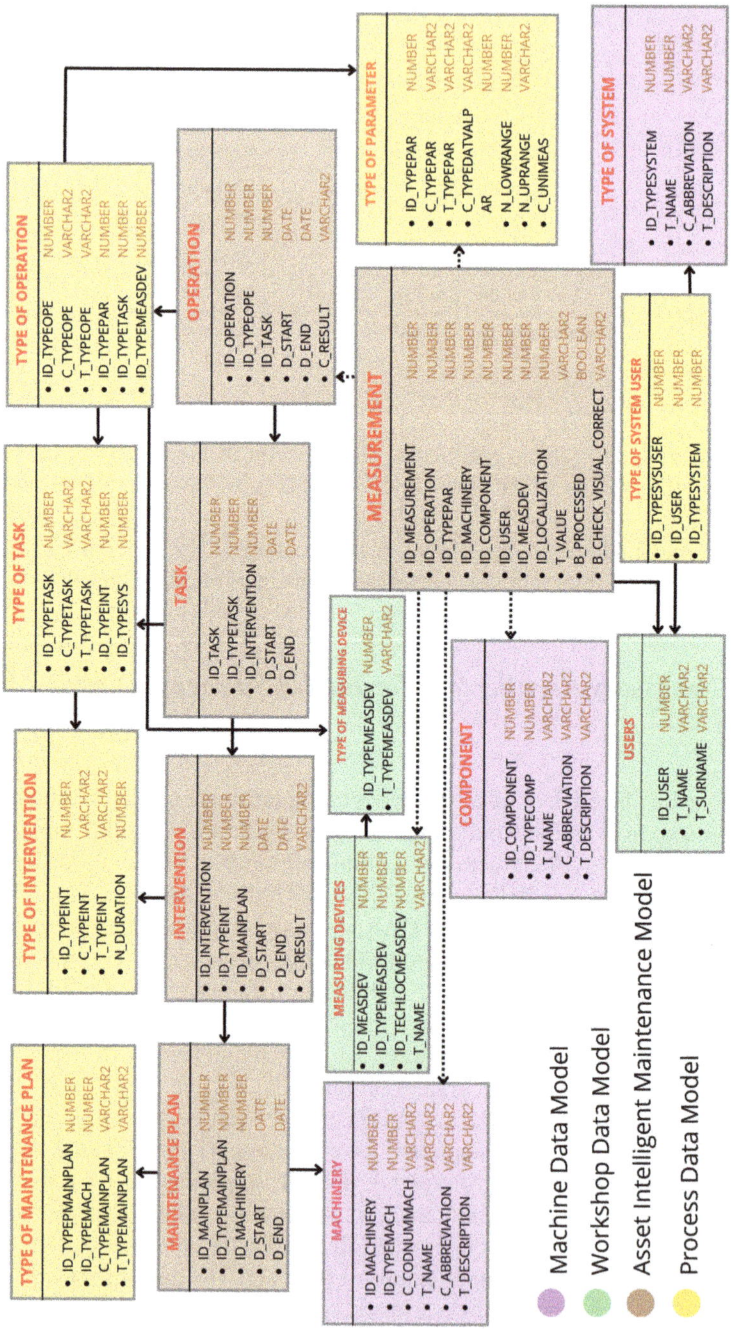

Fig. 6 Ontologies connecting data models

The goal is to create a solid, modern, modular, extensible, and scalable architecture that meets the current and future requirements of DTs. The criteria used for selecting the various components are as follows:

- Compliance with standards.
- Use of consolidated components that are widely used in the market, primarily based on Apache Software Foundation projects.
- Adoption of open-source projects with no associated licensing costs.
- Ease of integration of new components/technologies.
- Ease of maintenance and sustainability of the complete solution.
- 100% on-premises deployment: the chosen solution must allow deployment and management entirely within proprietary hardware infrastructure.

The proposed architecture comprises several functional layers, each with a specific role in the flow, processing, and utilisation of maintenance and operational data. See Fig. 7.

Data Sources Layer

The Data Sources Layer, although not always considered a formal architectural layer, plays a critical role by representing all the potential sources from which data is obtained. These include IoT sensors, CMMS applications, cloud-based services,

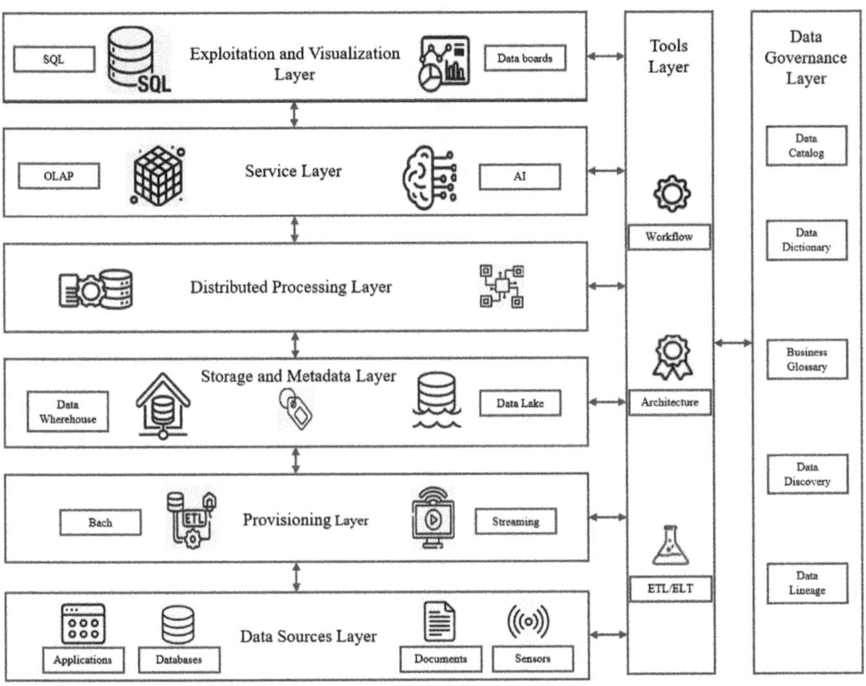

Fig. 7 Conceptual schematic of the architecture of the DT

internal databases, user devices, and web applications. The data arriving from these sources is highly heterogeneous, ranging from structured records to semi-structured logs and completely unstructured content such as images or free-text reports.

Provisioning Layer

The Provisioning Layer is responsible for establishing connections with the identified data sources and managing the processes of data extraction and ingestion. This layer enables both batch and real-time (streaming) data flows, facilitating continuous data intake for historical analysis and live monitoring. Its primary function is to feed the storage layer with clean, traceable, and accessible data. Designing appropriate ingestion mechanisms is essential to ensure that all data, regardless of its origin or format, can be efficiently imported into the digital platform.

To manage the ingestion of data into the platform, the Provisioning Layer is built upon the Lambda Architecture, a hybrid model that supports both batch and real-time data processing. This architecture is composed of three interconnected layers: a batch layer for high-latency processing, a service layer for querying processed data, and a speed layer that ensures low-latency access to data that the batch system has not yet processed. This configuration ensures that all incoming data is quickly accessible for querying, while also enabling in-depth analysis once batch processing is complete.

In addition to traditional ETL (Extract, Transform, Load) processes, this architecture adopts a modern ELT (Extract, Load, Transform) model, more suitable for Data Lake and Lakehouse environments. In the ELT approach, raw data is first extracted from source systems and then directly loaded into a centralised storage environment (e.g., Amazon S3, Azure Blob Storage, or Google Cloud Storage) without preliminary transformation. Data is transformed into demand within the storage system itself, using available computational resources as analytical tasks arise. This shift reduces initial processing overhead, increases flexibility in how data is reused, and enables organisations to postpone transformation logic until it is specifically needed. As a result, the platform is better equipped to handle large volumes of diverse data types, support multiple analytical use cases, and enable exploratory data science workflows.

This provisioning layer ensures a continuous, resilient, and scalable data pipeline, serving as the bridge between raw data sources and the analytical core of the DT system.

Storage and Metadata Layer

The Storage and Metadata Layer serves as the core repository for all information within the platform. This layer is responsible for hosting and systematically organising the ingested data, ensuring it is accessible, traceable, and secure. Designed for horizontal scalability, it uses distributed storage technologies that operate transparently across the infrastructure. A key feature of this layer is its ability to support semantic organisation using metadata, capturing details such as data origin, structure, relationships, and usage patterns.

This layer is structured under the Lakehouse architecture model, which combines the flexibility of a Data Lake with the robustness of a Data Warehouse. This approach enables the system to manage structured, semi-structured, and unstructured data, as is typical in a Data Lake, while also providing the data quality, performance, security, and governance expected from a traditional Data Warehouse. This hybrid model enables efficient data storage and access while maintaining the reliability and integrity required for advanced analytics, regulatory compliance, and DT integration.

This architecture is organised into three logical layers: Bronze, Silver, and Gold, each corresponding to a different stage in the data refinement process. Data moves progressively through these layers, gaining structure, quality, and analytical value at each stage. This layered approach enables better data governance, reusability, and performance optimisation for both operational use and analytics.

The Bronze Layer is the foundation of architecture and is responsible for storing raw data exactly as it is ingested from the various source systems. This includes structured, semi-structured, and unstructured data, captured without any initial transformation. The table structure in this layer mirrors the original format of the source systems, but with added metadata fields such as upload timestamp, source file name, and unique identifiers. This metadata is crucial for building a robust catalogue that enables efficient indexing, querying, and traceability. The Bronze Layer also functions as a cold storage repository, maintaining a complete historical archive of raw data. This procedure ensures auditability, supports data lineage tracking, and allows for complete reprocessing if future use cases require it.

The Silver Layer represents the intermediate stage of the Lakehouse architecture, where the data stored in the Bronze Layer undergoes filtering, cleaning, validation, and transformation. At this stage, quality control rules are applied to standardise formats, correct inconsistencies, and remove duplicates or irrelevant entries. The goal is to convert raw data into a more refined, structured form suitable for operational use and analysis. This layer supports the generation of ad hoc reports, the development of machine learning models, and other advanced analytical tasks. Moreover, it serves as a central integration point, bringing together data from multiple sources under a unified schema. By enhancing data consistency and interpretability, the Silver Layer ensures that downstream users and systems can work with reliable, high-quality datasets.

The Gold Layer is the final and most refined level of Lakehouse data architecture. It contains fully processed, curated, and enriched datasets that are ready for use in strategic analysis, business intelligence, and DT simulations. In this layer, business rules and quality policies are applied to ensure that the data is not only accurate but also aligned with the organisation's decision-making frameworks. Gold Layer data is optimised for performance, typically involving fewer joins and lighter, denormalised models that offer faster querying and easier access. It serves as the authoritative source for reporting, visualisation, and predictive modelling, supporting real-time insights and operational efficiency across the platform. See Fig. 8.

Processing Layer

The Processing Layer is responsible for performing operations that transform raw data into actionable information. This includes data cleansing, transformation, aggregation, and the training of machine learning models. Like the storage layer, it is

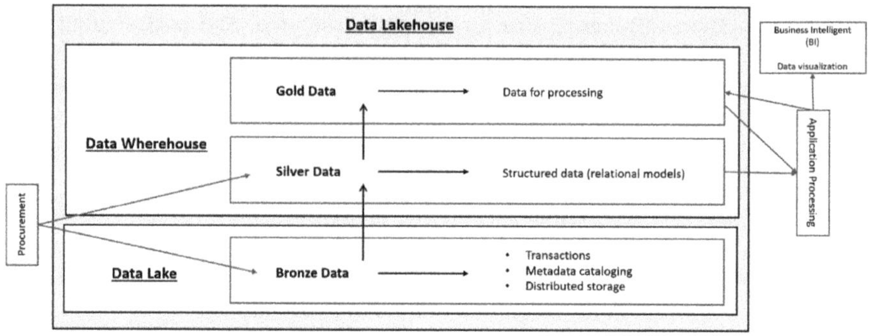

Fig. 8 Schematic of Lakehouse storage

built to support horizontal scalability, allowing workloads to be distributed across multiple nodes to ensure optimal performance. This layer enables efficient processing of large volumes of distributed data, making it suitable for both real-time analytics and complex predictive maintenance tasks.

Services Layer

The Services Layer provides advanced, value-added functionalities that build upon the data processed and stored in previous layers. It enables key capabilities, such as access to the distributed storage environment using familiar database services (e.g., SQL queries); support for multidimensional OLAP models, facilitating descriptive and comparative analytics; and integration of advanced analytics frameworks, including artificial intelligence and machine learning engines.

This layer plays a strategic role by unlocking the analytical potential of the infrastructure, maximising the platform's computational power, and enabling intelligent, automated decision-making.

Data Exploitation, Visualization, and Publication Layer

The Data Exploitation, Visualisation, and Publication Layer is responsible for making data understandable and usable for end-users. This includes designing and deploying dashboards, reports, and visual interfaces that allow users—from technicians to managers—to interact with and interpret data in real-time. It ensures that the large volumes of structured data available within the system are presented clearly, securely, and in formats that support operational decision-making.

Data Governance Layer

The Data Governance Layer establishes the framework for managing data across the entire platform. It defines the practices, policies, roles, and responsibilities that ensure data is accurate, secure, and used appropriately. This layer plays a central role in maintaining data integrity and regulatory compliance by controlling who can access what data, under what conditions, and for what purposes. Jahangir et al. (2024)

identify forty barriers that impede the adoption of DT in the building development process.

Tool Layer

The Tool Layer provides users with a comprehensive toolbox for interacting with and managing the data environment effectively. This layer supports a wide range of tasks and user profiles, including data engineers, analysts, and developers. Among its key features the data transformation utilities aligned with the Medallion Architecture, allowing for structured progression from raw to enriched data (e.g., bronze, silver, gold layers); and notebook environments for the creation, testing, and experimentation of machine learning models, which can then be deployed through the Services Layer for operational use.

7 Lessons Learned and Practical Impacts

The digitalisation of the CAS process has provided valuable lessons applicable to broader maintenance transformation efforts. One of the main lessons learned is the importance of defining consistent and interoperable data models from the outset. Without a structured information backbone, integrating tools, processes, and analytics becomes fragmented and challenging to scale.

Another key insight was the need to align technological solutions with existing workflows and user capabilities. Instead of deploying overly complex predictive models prematurely, the project focused on digitising high-impact manual processes, building confidence and acceptance among technicians.

The practical impacts of this approach include a significant reduction in manual reporting errors, improved traceability of inspections, and enhanced standardisation across maintenance records. Furthermore, the groundwork laid by the CAS DT has expedited the onboarding of additional maintenance processes into the digital ecosystem, thereby reducing implementation times and eliminating duplication of effort. In their review, Lam et al., (2023) highlight how DT brings traceability and efficiency to the supply chain.

8 Conclusions

The digitalisation of maintenance processes in the railway sector, as illustrated through the transformation of the CAS process, demonstrates the potential of structured methodologies and data-driven architectures to modernise traditional workflows. The case study presented in this chapter highlights how organisations can progress from paper-based procedures to integrated digital ecosystems by following a phased roadmap grounded in maturity assessment, goal setting, technology adoption, and data infrastructure design.

Key outcomes of this approach include the development of a robust asset data model, the integration of IoT and identification technologies for real-time monitoring, and the implementation of a modular, scalable data architecture. These elements form the foundation of a DT environment capable of supporting traceable, standardised, and intelligent maintenance operations.

By embedding the CAS process within a DT framework, the organisation has laid the groundwork for wider digital transformation across the maintenance function. The structured ontologies linking asset, process, workshop, and operational data ensure consistency and interoperability, enabling predictive maintenance, automated validation, and improved decision-making. Moreover, the layered architecture, based on Lakehouse principles and ELT pipelines—ensures scalability, governance, and adaptability to future requirements.

This initiative demonstrates that even highly regulated and manual processes, such as CAS certification, can be successfully digitalised when approached with a coherent methodology and supported by the right technological and data foundations. As organisations in the railway sector and beyond pursue their digital transformation journeys, the principles and models presented in this chapter offer a practical and replicable pathway to achieving operational excellence, regulatory compliance, and long-term sustainability in maintenance management.

Competing Interests The author(s) has no competing interests to declare that are relevant to the content of this manuscript.

References

Ben Amor, S., et al. (2024). Digital twin implementation in additive manufacturing: a comprehensive review. *Processes, 12*(6), 1–15. https://doi.org/10.3390/pr12061062

Davari, N., et al. (2021). A survey on data-driven predictive maintenance for the railway industry. *Sensors, 21*(17), 5739. https://doi.org/10.3390/s21175739

Jahangir, M. F., Schultz, C. P. L., & Kamari, A. (2024). A review of drivers and barriers of digital twin adoption in building project development processes. *Journal of Information Technology in Construction.* https://doi.org/10.36680/j.itcon.2024.008

Jiao, Z., et al. (2023). Sustainable operation and maintenance modeling and application of building infrastructures combined with digital twin framework. *Sensors.* https://doi.org/10.3390/s23094182

Karkaria, V., Chen, J., Luey, C., Siuta, C., Lim, D., Radulescu, R., & Chen, W. (2024). A digital twin framework utilizing machine learning for robust predictive maintenance: Enhancing tire health monitoring. *IEEE Transactions on Industrial Informatics.*

Lam, W. S., Lam, W. H., & Lee, P. F. (2023). A bibliometric analysis of digital twin in the supply chain. *Mathematics, 11*(15). https://doi.org/10.3390/math11153350

Louadah, H., et al. (2024). Supporting the management of rolling stock maintenance with an ontology-based virtual depot. *Applied Sciences (Switzerland), 14*(3). https://doi.org/10.3390/app14031220

Ma, S., Flanigan, K. A., & Bergés, M. (2024). State-of-the-art review and synthesis: a requirement-based roadmap for standardized predictive maintenance automation using digital twin technologies. *Advanced Engineering Informatics, 62*(PC), 102800. https://doi.org/10.1016/j.aei.2024.102800

Rojas, L., Peña, Á., & Garcia, J. (2025). AI-driven predictive maintenance in mining: A systematic literature review on fault detection, digital twins, and intelligent asset management. *Applied Sciences (Switzerland), 15*(6). https://doi.org/10.3390/app15063337

Salierno, G., Leonardi, L., & Cabri, G. (2024). A big data architecture for digital twin creation of railway signals based on synthetic data. *IEEE Open Journal of Intelligent Transportation Systems, 5*, 342–359. https://doi.org/10.1109/OJITS.2024.3412820

van Dinter, R., Tekinerdogan, B., & Catal, C. (2023). Reference architecture for digital twin-based predictive maintenance systems. *Computers and Industrial Engineering, 177*, 109099. https://doi.org/10.1016/j.cie.2023.109099

Werbińska-Wojciechowska, S., Giel, R., & Winiarska, K. (2024). Digital twin approach for operation and maintenance of transportation system—systematic review. *Sensors, 24*(18). https://doi.org/10.3390/s24186069

A Probabilistic Physics-Aware Battery Health Management Approach for Inspection Drone Operations

Jokin Alcibar, Aitor Aguirre Ortuzar, and Jose I. Aizpurua

Abstract The increasing deployment of inspection drones for monitoring remote and critical infrastructure presents new opportunities and challenges in asset management. These drones operate in demanding environments, where ensuring operational reliability is essential. Among the various subsystems, battery health plays a central role in determining mission success and safety. This chapter presents a physics-aware probabilistic approach for battery health management, integrating data-driven techniques with physics-based models to improve the predictability of battery performance. At the core of this methodology lies a probabilistic machine learning model that provides uncertainty quantification, enabling more informed and robust decision-making. By incorporating this uncertainty-aware perspective into battery discharge forecasting, the approach supports advanced digital maintenance strategies. The methodology is demonstrated to drone-based inspections of offshore wind energy infrastructure, highlighting its contribution to enhancing asset reliability and enabling condition-aware maintenance strategies.

Keywords Probabilistic battery health management · Physics-aware machine learning · Uncertainty quantification · End-of-discharge voltage prediction · Drone-based infrastructure inspection

J. Alcibar (✉) · A. Aguirre Ortuzar
Electronics, Computer Science Department, Mondragon University, Mondragón, Spain
e-mail: jalcibar@mondragon.edu

A. Aguirre Ortuzar
e-mail: aaguirre@mondragon.edu

J. I. Aizpurua
Computer Science and Artificial Intelligence Department, University of the Basque Country (UPV/EHU), Donostia, Spain
e-mail: joxe.aizpurua@ehu.eus

A. Crespo Márquez et al. (eds.), *Digital Maintenance and Asset Digitalization*, Engineering Asset Management Review 5,
https://doi.org/10.1007/978-3-032-21502-4_11

1 Introduction

Unmanned Aerial Vehicles (UAVs) are widely used in civilian operations including surveillance and inspection through their vertical take-off capabilities and precision in remote environments rations (Valavanis & Vachtsevanos, 2015). They significantly enhance safety and data collection efficiency in hazardous conditions (Eleftheroglou et al., 2019). However, UAV reliability remains challenged by battery limitations, payload constraints, and weather conditions that can cause mission failures (Gatti et al., 2015).

Digital maintenance strategies highlight the critical role of Battery Management Systems (BMS) in real-time diagnostics and intelligent decision support (Sierra et al., 2019). These systems enable proactive fault detection and dynamic path replanning to ensure mission continuity. However, accurate end-of-discharge (EOD) voltage prediction faces challenges from environmental uncertainties and measurement errors (Sierra et al., 2018). In addition, reliable estimation of State of Health (SOH) and Remaining Useful Life (RUL) are necessary to quantify battery degradation and anticipate end-of-service conditions during operation. Integrating uncertainty modeling into battery degradation analysis is essential for developing robust predictive maintenance methodologies supporting autonomous UAV operations (Zhang et al., 2022).

Battery health management methods are categorized as physics-based, data-driven, or hybrid (Demirci et al., 2024; Vanem et al., 2021). Physics-based methods use physical models, often updated with algorithms like Particle Filtering (PF) (Djuric et al., 2003) or Unscented Kalman Filter (UKF) (Bai et al., 2023) to estimate battery health. Data-driven approaches instead rely on degradation data to model capacity fade (Mitici et al., 2023). Finally, hybrid methods integrate both strategies, leveraging the accuracy of physical modeling and the adaptability of data-driven techniques (Guo et al., 2015).

Physics-Based Approaches

Physics-based approaches to battery degradation have been explored in various studies. Daigle and Kulkarni (2013) proposed a prognostics method grounded in electrochemical modeling, where the system state is updated using the UKF. This approach yielded precise EOD predictions with quantified uncertainty, though it demands the estimation of numerous parameters, complicating optimization. In another contribution, Pola et al. (2015) developed an empirical state-space model for estimating state of charge (SOC) and EOD using a PF. Their model accurately forecasted battery discharge duration and offered confidence intervals. However, it lacked adaptability for multi-cell batteries due to a static open-circuit voltage curve. In this direction, Sierra et al. (2019) designed a prognostics framework for Li-Po batteries that integrates a simplified battery model with evolutionary strategies for parameter estimation. Their method includes a feedback mechanism to correct process noise variance, reducing estimation bias. Nonetheless, such physics-based methods often require intensive computation, limiting real-time deployment.

Data-Driven Approaches

Several data-driven methods have been proposed to overcome the limitations of physics-based models (Ng et al., 2020). Data-driven methods, such as Artificial Neural Networks (ANNs), Gaussian Processes, and Support-Vector Machines, have addressed EOD prediction and degradation inference (Ochella et al., 2022). Deep learning techniques, including Convolutional Neural Networks (CNNs) (Couture & Lin, 2022; Mitici et al., 2023), Recurrent Neural Networks (RNNs) (Guo et al., 2024; Zhao et al., 2023), and hybrid models (Mazzi et al., 2024), excel in extracting temporal features and mapping nonlinear relationships. However, purely data-driven approaches face limitations in robustness for unseen data and uncertainty quantification (Aizpurua et al., 2023; Arias Chao et al., 2022).

To improve uncertainty estimation, advanced methods like encoder-decoder architectures with Monte Carlo (MC) dropout (Biggio et al., 2023), Bayesian techniques (Zhang et al., 2022), and Probabilistic Neural Networks (Che et al., 2024) have been developed. While these enhance prediction accuracy and uncertainty quantification, data-driven models remain largely interpretability-limited, often seen as black-box solutions.

Hybrid Approaches

Hybrid modeling approaches that combine physical principles with data-driven techniques have gained attention for enhancing interpretability in predictions (Fink et al., 2020). For instance, Yeregui et al. (2023) developed a model integrating a Reduced Order Model (ROM) with a Long Short-Term Memory (LSTM) network to estimate the SOC in lithium-ion batteries. Nevertheless, this work did not analyze uncertainty. Similarly, Fernández et al. (2023) introduced a Bayesian neural network guided by physical knowledge to improve predictions in lateral-load test scenarios. Their model uses Approximate Bayesian Computation instead of conventional loss functions, leading to better performance in prediction and uncertainty quantification (UQ).

A related methodology involves Physics-Informed Neural Networks (PINNs), which incorporate governing physical laws into the training process by embedding them in the loss function. PINNs have shown strong results across engineering fields, such as computational mechanics (Li et al., 2021), fluid dynamics (Raissi et al., 2020), material engineering (Zhang & Gu, 2021), and fault diagnosis (Feng et al., 2023; Ni et al., 2023). More recently, Sun et al. (2023) proposed a physically informed LSTM model for battery prognostics, though without addressing uncertainty. Nascimento et al. (2023) used a physics-guided RNN framework with ROMs and neural networks to model voltage discharge and represent model uncertainty.

Table 1 summarizes recent advancements in battery health-state estimation and emphasizes the key contributions of this research. As shown in the table, only a few works have focused on analyzing drone battery data collected under real-world operating conditions (Sierra et al., 2018, 2019). Most existing research relies on battery data obtained from controlled laboratory discharge processes. Additionally, many analytical approaches fail to explicitly quantify or differentiate between data uncertainty and model uncertainty. Addressing these gaps, this study introduces a physics-aware probabilistic model that leverages real-world operational battery data to quantify uncertainty.

This paper presents a novel hybrid probabilistic approach for predicting EOD voltage in Li-Po batteries. The method combines MC dropout for epistemic uncertainty and Negative Log Likelihood (NLL) loss for aleatoric uncertainty within a residual architecture. The approach integrates a physics-based discharge model with a probabilistic error-correction component, reducing computational costs and data requirements. The physics-based model extracts battery behaviour features without complex electrochemical details, enhancing efficiency and scalability for complex scenarios. This strategy offers a robust, efficient, and data-aware solution for battery voltage prediction under uncertainty.

Subsequently, probabilistic error correction is implemented by explicitly integrating uncertainty via CNN and MC dropout. A benchmarking analysis is conducted to assess the accuracy and uncertainty of various probabilistic models.

The proposed approach effectively addresses various battery parameter errors, such as calibration issues, enabling accurate EOD voltage prediction across diverse drones. Its effectiveness is demonstrated using an industrial dataset from real drone inspections involving varied manoeuvres and loading conditions, offering practical value to drone fleet operators.

Table 1 Summary of recent battery health-state estimation methods

References	Dataset	Model	Output	UQ
Sierra et al. (2019)	Operational	Physics based	*EOD_t, SOC	Yes
Sierra et al. (2018)	Operational	Physics based	*EOD_t, SOC	None
Bai et al. (2023)	Laboratory	Physics based	RUL	Yes
Hong et al. (2020)	Laboratory	Data-Driven	RUL	Yes
Hsu et al. (2022)	Laboratory	Data-Driven	**EOD_V, EOL	None
Zhao et al. (2023)	Laboratory	Data-Driven	SOH	None
Han et al. (2022)	Laboratory	Data-Driven	SOH, RUL	None
Meng et al. (2023)	Laboratory	Data-Driven	SOH	None
Biggio et al. (2023)	Laboratory	Data-Driven	**EOD_V	Partial
Zhang et al. (2022)	Laboratory	Data-Driven	RUL	Yes
Yeregui et al. (2023)	Laboratory	Hybrid	SOC	None
Sun et al. (2023)	Laboratory	Hybrid	SOH	None
Nascimento et al. (2023)	Laboratory	Hybrid	SOC	Yes
Proposed Approach	Operational	Hybrid	**EOD_V	Yes

Legend: * EOD_t: EOD time. ** EOD_V: EOD voltage

2 Understanding Predictive Uncertainty

Battery EOD voltage predictions can be evaluated based on both accuracy and uncertainty. Uncertainty reflects the model's confidence in its output (Heo et al., 2018), but low uncertainty values alone do not guarantee reliability. This reliability depends on calibration, meaning that the predicted uncertainty must align with the true likelihood of error (Rathnakumar et al., 2023).

To build robust predictive models, it is essential to understand and represent the sources of uncertainty present in the modeling process. In general, uncertainty in machine learning is categorized into two main types: **aleatoric** and **epistemic** uncertainty (Der Kiureghian & Ditlevsen, 2009). Capturing these uncertainties often involves moving beyond deterministic point estimates and instead inferring full probability density function (PDF) over predicted outcomes (Hüllermeier & Waegeman, 2021).

Aleatoric uncertainty arises from inherent randomness in the data-generating process. This form of uncertainty is considered irreducible, as it stems from factors such as measurement noise or environmental variability (Kendall & Gal, 2017). It reflects the stochastic nature of the world, and even with perfect knowledge of the system, such variability cannot be eliminated. In predictive modeling, quantifying aleatoric uncertainty requires characterizing the conditional distribution of the output given the input, rather than just its mean (Tagasovska & Lopez-Paz, 2019).

$$Var(\epsilon|X) = \frac{1}{T}\sum_{t=1}^{T}\hat{\sigma}_t^2(X) \tag{1}$$

here $\sigma^2(X)$ indicates that the variance of residuals is dependent on X.

In contrast, **epistemic uncertainty** reflects the model's ignorance or lack of knowledge. Unlike aleatoric uncertainty, epistemic uncertainty is reducible: it can be decreased by collecting more data, particularly in regions of the input space that were underrepresented during training (Tagasovska & Lopez-Paz, 2019). This type of uncertainty is especially relevant evaluating model robustness. One common way to capture epistemic uncertainty is to examine the variability of predictions across multiple models trained under different assumptions or initializations (Lakshminarayanan et al., 2017). Such ensemble-based approaches reveal the uncertainty due to limited information, such as ambiguity in model parameters or architecture choices (Hüllermeier & Waegeman, 2021). Epistemic uncertainty is represented as (Kendall & Gal, 2017):

$$Var(y) = \frac{1}{T}\sum_{t=1}^{T} f(x, \theta_t)^2 - \left(\frac{1}{T}\sum_{t=1}^{T} f(x, \theta_t)\right)^2 \tag{2}$$

where $f(x, \theta_t)$ denotes the output of the model for the t th sample, x signifies the sample in question and θ represents the parameters of the model.

The **total uncertainty** (TU), which integrates both epistemic uncertainty (EU) and aleatoric uncertainty (AU), can be expressed as follows (Abdar et al., 2021):

$$TU = EU + AU \tag{3}$$

This formulation ensures consistent units among the uncertainty terms and adheres to the law of total variance, which governs uncertainty propagation in Bayesian predictive models.

3 Uncertainty-Aware Battery Health Management Approach

Figure 1 illustrates the proposed uncertainty-aware battery health management approach, which consists of three main stages: (i) EOD voltage prediction, (ii) post-processing UQ and (iii) health state diagnosis.

3.1 EOD Voltage Prediction

This section details Step 1 of Fig. 1. The EOD voltage prediction combines a physics-based model with a data-driven model in an error-correction configuration. Before these steps, a preprocessing stage is performed to clean the monitored data by removing empty variables, duplicate records, and erroneous sensor readings. Missing values are imputed using average values to maintain data consistency.

The physics-based model captures the discharge behaviour of the battery. Given the load at instant t, denoted as $i_{d(t)}$, it estimates the terminal voltage $v'_{d(t)}$. This estimate is then passed to the probabilistic data-driven model, which predicts the error. Finally, the last stage applies dynamic error correction to estimate the discharge voltage $v_{d(t)}$.

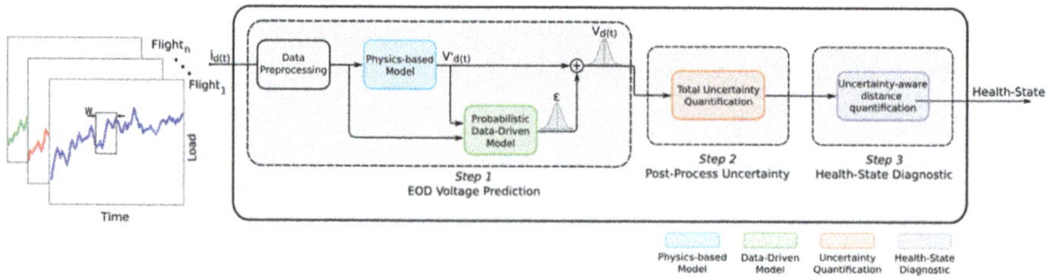

Fig. 1 Uncertainty-aware battery health management approach

Physics-Based Discharge Model

The physics-based discharge model is electrochemistry-based battery discharge model is inspired from Daigle and Kulkarni (2013) and implemented through the Prognostics Model Library (Teubert et al., 2023) from NASA Ames Research Center. This model operates using a set of ordinary differential equations to determine the total battery voltage, *V(t)*, which is defined as the difference in potential between the positive and negative current collectors, accounting for the resistance losses come across these current collectors. The state-space of the battery model, $x(t)$, input vector, $u(t)$, and output vector, $y(t)$ are defined by the next equations (Salinas-Camus et al., 2023):

$$x(t) = \left[q_{s,p}, q_{b,p}, q_{s,n}, q_{b,n}, V', V'_{n,p}, V'_{n,n}\right]^T \tag{4}$$

$$u(t) = \left[i_{app}\right] \tag{5}$$

$$y(t) = [V] \tag{6}$$

The state-space includes q and V', corresponding to the charge on the electrodes and the voltage differentials, respectively. The notations p and n indicate the positive and negative electrodes, which are divided into two volumes representing the surface layer (s) and the bulk layer (b). The input vector, indicates the electric current applied to the battery and the output vector denotes the discharge voltage of the battery.

Probabilistic Data-Driven

A probabilistic CNN was developed for the error-correction stage, leveraging its strengths in feature extraction and uncertainty estimation. In drone operations, identifying uncertainty is critical. Aleatoric uncertainty arises from inherent system randomness, such as wind or sensor noise, while epistemic uncertainty results from gaps in knowledge, including modeling errors. Distinguishing between these types of uncertainties enables better decision-making and mitigate risks associated with uncertain information.

CNNs are deep learning models designed to exploit local spatial or temporal patterns, allowing them to capture meaningful structured features in high-dimensional data (Xu et al., 2022). Applying Monte Carlo dropout during both training and testing enhances their robustness and provides a more comprehensive probabilistic interpretation (Choubineh et al., 2023; Mitici et al., 2023). Figure 2 shows the structure of the proposed CNN-based error-correction model, with each layer described below.

- *Input Data*: The input to the CNN is organized as a tensor. Each row represents a data sample obtained through windowing. Each column corresponds to a sensor measurement from the inspection drone, such as the current load or the estimated voltage computed using a physics-based model.

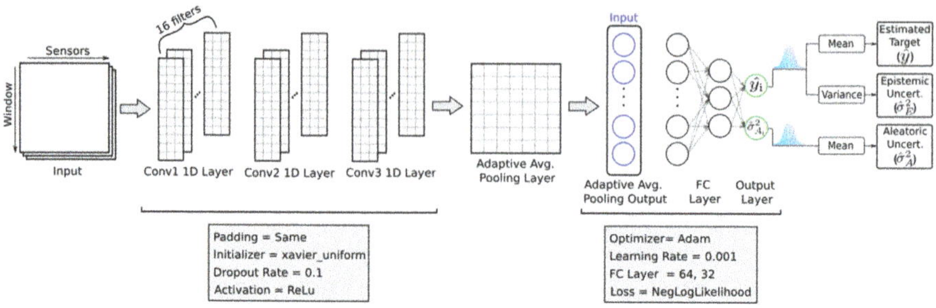

Fig. 2 Structure of the proposed uncertainty-aware CNN architecture

- *Convolutional Layers* (Conv1 to Conv3 in Fig. 2): These layers consist of Conv1D layers, which apply a series of convolutional filters to extract features from the input data. The filters scan the input sequence to identify distinctive patterns related to the target prediction variable. In the context of battery behavior, these filters specifically detect temporal patterns such as voltage-current discharge characteristics, capacity degradation trends across cycles, and variations in discharge profiles that indicate early-stage degradation signatures. Each convolutional layer uses 16 filters to generate the feature maps.
- *Adaptive Average Pooling Layer*: In this layer, the average of all activations is computed for each feature map, producing a single scalar value per map. This operation reduces the spatial dimensions and provides a compact summary of each feature map. This layer provides a fixed-size representation independent of the input sequence length and offers a smoother, more stable summary than max-pooling, which is advantageous given the noisy nature of battery signals.
- *Fully Connected (FC) Layers*: These layers transform the extracted features into predictions using activation functions. Two fully connected (FC) layers are used, allowing the model to learn complex relationships and patterns from the features. This enables accurate predictions based on the input data.
- *Output Layer*: This layer generates the final output based on the inputs and the learned weights from the previous layers. It includes two neurons, one representing the mean and the other the variance, to capture both the expected value and its associated uncertainty. To ensure the variance remains positive, an exponential activation function is applied to that neuron.

Dropout layers are strategically placed between the fully connected layers during training to prevent overfitting by randomly deactivating neurons in the network. At inference time, the MC dropout technique is applied to approximate a predictive distribution in a computationally efficient manner (Gal & Ghahramani, 2016). As shown in Fig. 3, during training, each distinct dropout mask effectively simulates a different draw from the approximate posterior distribution over the model's parameters. This stochastic sampling enables the estimation of epistemic uncertainty by computing the variance (${\sigma_E}^2$ in Fig. 2) across multiple forward passes improving the model's robustness and predictive accuracy.

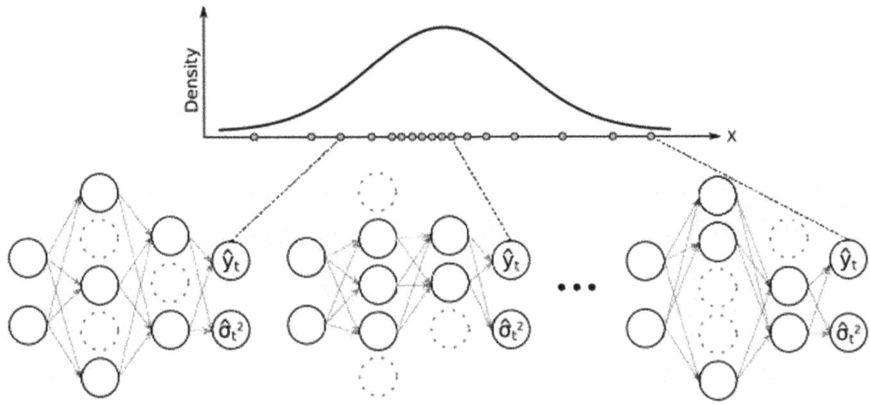

Fig. 3 Use of dropout at test stage with MC sampling

Finally, to capture aleatoric uncertainty, assuming it follows a Gaussian distribution $N(\mu, \sigma^2)$, the CNN architecture is modified to include an additional output for the variance σ^2, as shown in Fig. 2. Combined with a negative log-likelihood (NLL) loss function, this allows the model to learn uncertainty directly from the data (Kendall & Gal, 2017).

$$\mathcal{L}_{NN}\left(y_{true}|\mu, \sigma^2\right) = \frac{1}{N}\sum_{i=1}^{N}\frac{(y_i - \mu(x_i))^2}{2\sigma(x_i)^2} + \frac{1}{2}\log\sigma(x_i)^2 \quad (7)$$

where y_i is the true value for the i th element in the batch, $\mu(x_i)$ is the predicted mean, and $\sigma(x_i)^2$ represents the variance of the distribution.

When the CNN predicts the target variable accurately, the estimated variance is low, minimizing the MSE loss in Eq. 7. In high data uncertainty scenarios, the CNN increases the variance to reflect the noise. Thus, the variance (i) quantifies prediction uncertainty and (ii) balances capturing data variability with avoiding overly uncertain predictions.

This approach improves the ability of the CNN to provide accurate predictions while capturing data uncertainty, making it a valuable asset for decision-making in inspection drones.

3.2 *Post-Process Uncertainty*

This section describes Step 2 of Fig. 1, which corresponds to the post-processing stage. This stage aims to infer the total uncertainty to enhance decision-making under uncertain conditions.

Total Uncertainty Quantification

Integrating aleatoric and epistemic uncertainty is essential for capturing and interpreting the total uncertainty within a system, process, or model. To address this, Algorithm 1 outlines the complete procedure for quantifying total uncertainty.

Algorithm 1 Total Uncertainty Inference

```
Input: data X_test, prediction model h(·), number of iterations N
Output: total uncertainty σ_TU
for each i ∈ N do
    [y_i, σ²_{A_i}] = h(X_{test_i})              ▹ cf.Figure 2
    y⃗[i] = y_i                                   ▹ Store mean results
    σ⃗²_A[i] = σ²_{A_i}                           ▹ Store variance results
end for
ŷ = mean(y⃗)                                     ▹ Infer mean pred. values
σ²_E = var(y⃗)                                   ▹ Infer Ep. Uncertainty
σ²_A = mean(σ⃗²_A)                               ▹ Infer Al. Uncertainty
σ_TU = σ²_E + σ²_A
return σ_TU
```

Summing the squares of individual uncertainties emphasizes the contribution of larger ones, as they have a greater influence on the overall measure. This approach ensures that significant sources of uncertainty are not underestimated. Finally, taking the square root of the sum restores the total uncertainty to the original scale, providing a interpretable measure of overall uncertainty.

3.3 Battery Health-State Diagnostics

This section describes Step 3 of Fig. 1. Drone health-management decisions are made based on available data, observations, and evidence. In this context, UQ plays a key role by accounting for model and data-related uncertainty, supporting decision-making under uncertain conditions.

In the proposed methodology, uncertainty analysis is used to estimate the battery's health state. A prediction interval, learned from healthy battery data, is defined based on total uncertainty. When new flight data from the inspection drone is available, (i) EOD voltage predictions are made considering this uncertainty, and (ii) the result is assessed to determine whether the observed voltage falls within the predicted range.

The Prediction Interval Coverage Probability (PICP) metric quantifies the proportion of true values that fall within the predicted interval defined by total uncertainty (González-Sopeña et al., 2021). Figure 4 illustrates how PICP is used to infer battery health. The green line shows cases where most true values fall within the confidence intervals, indicating a healthy battery (Batt. OK). In contrast, the red line highlights cases where most values lie outside the intervals, suggesting poor battery health (Batt. NOK).

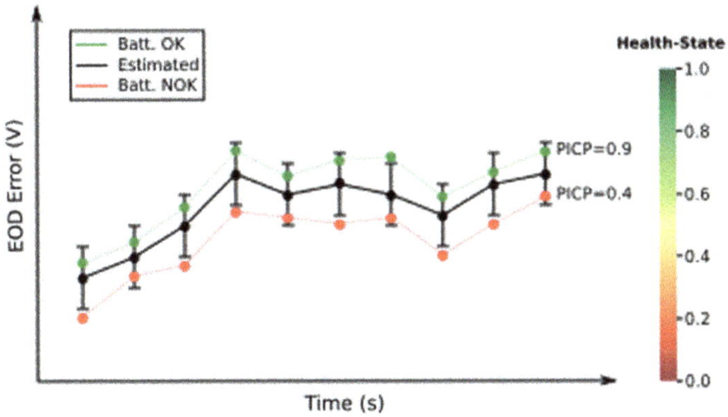

Fig. 4 Health-state inference example based on prediction interval quantification

Based on PICP results, a health-state diagnosis is computed for each flight. This metric is essential for evaluating predictive performance and serves as a key indicator in the battery health diagnostic system.

4 Case Study

The proposed approach is evaluated using data from multiple flights conducted with inspection drones. These drones are used for the inspection of defects in offshore wind turbines, e.g. cracks, which are processed through on-boarding processing software. All drones are equipped with Li-Po batteries. In this study, a single cell extracted from a 6S Li-Po battery pack is analysed, where 6S denotes six cells connected in series. The full battery pack has a nominal capacity of 30,000 mAh.

During each flight, several parameters are recorded, including load and discharge voltage. Current is measured via an ACS758 Hall effect sensor placed on the main positive wire to reduce the risk of short circuits. Voltage is monitored using a filtered voltage divider circuit, helping to prevent false return-to-launch events, especially under strong winds that cause sudden motor speed increases. While external factors such as ambient temperature and pressure also influence battery discharge, their effects are manifested through changes in current consumption. Accordingly, it is assumed that the current variable implicitly captures the environmental variability, and the estimation therefore relies on it to accurately predict the EOD voltage.

Although ambient temperature and pressure can influence battery discharge, their effects are largely manifested through changes in current consumption. Because our model directly incorporates the load current, we assume that this variable implicitly captures most of the environmental variability. For this reason, temperature and pressure were excluded from the analysis. We note this as a limitation and identify the explicit integration of these factors as future work.

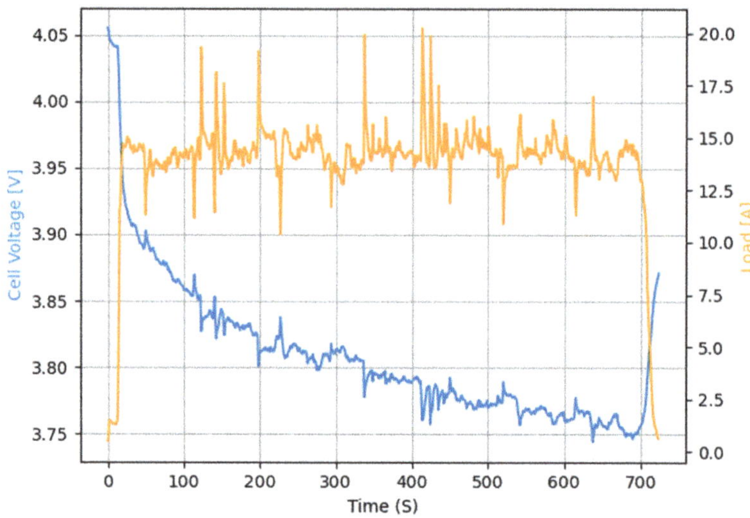

Fig. 5 Available datasets for the flight #73

Figure 5 presents a sample of the variables collected per flight in this study. The dataset comprises 26,156 samples gathered from 33 separate flight sessions. The number of samples used for validation varies depending on the duration of each flight. To process this large volume of data, a laptop with an Intel® Core™ i5-10210U processor (1.60 GHz) and 16 GB of RAM was used, leveraging the PyTorch framework for deep learning analysis.

Table 3 shows the distribution of how flight data has been split into training and testing subsets over a three-year period. It also presents the total number of recorded flights for each year.

The CNN hyperparameters shown in Table 2 were tuned based on the training dataset. Optimal performance was achieved using the Adam optimizer with a learning rate of 0.001, applying 16 filters, and configuring the two fully connected layers with 64 and 32 neurons, respectively.

5 Results

The validation of the proposed method is carried out in two stages. The first phase involves benchmarking the accuracy and robustness of EOD voltage prediction models to identify the most effective approach. The second phase addresses battery health diagnostics, where flight data from different batteries is analyzed to estimate uncertainty and evaluate their health status.

Table 2 Architectural and optimization hyperparameters of CNN

Category	Hyperparameter	Value
Architecture	Window-size	10
	Convolutional layers	3
	Number of filters	16
	Kernel size	3
	Padding	Same
	Initializer	Xavier Uniform
	Activation	Rectified Linear Unit
	Number of fully connected layers	2
	Number of nodes in fully connected layers	64,32
Optimization	Loss function	NLL
	Optimizer	Adam
	Learning rate	0.001
	Number of epochs	130
	Monte Carlo dropout rate	0.1
	Number of Monte Carlo inferences	100

Table 3 Train-test split on the flights within the dataset

	2021	2022	2023	Total
Train	18	3	3	24 (72.72%)
Test	7	1	1	9 (27.27%)
Total	25	4	4	33 (100%)

5.1 EOD Voltage Prediction

The predictive accuracy of the proposed CNN model has been compared with other probabilistic models. Namely, Quantile Linear Regression (QLR) (Chung et al., 2021), Quantile Regression Forest (QRF) (Meinshausen, 2006), and Quantile Gradient Boosting (QGB) (Friedman, 2001) have been selected as these probabilistic models exhibit high performance in analogous scenarios, demonstrating robustness and accurate predictions across varied applications (Bracale et al., 2023; Jiang & Meng, 2023; Song et al., 2022).

Table 4 shows the Continuous Ranked Probability Score (CRPS) metric to evaluate the accuracy and calibration of the probabilistic forecasts (Zamo & Naveau, 2018), along with the corresponding standard deviations (Std.) tested on real flight data (Table 3).

CRPS metric is computed for each test sample within every flight, resulting in a collection of CRPS values per flight. This collection is then modeled using a Gaussian probability distribution, defined by its mean and standard deviation. A smaller

Table 4 CRPS (Std.) of different probabilistic models tested across real flights

Flight (#)	Sample (%)	QLR	QRF	QGB	CNN MC dropout
11	14.14	0.023 (0.007)	0.028 (0.021)	0.024 (0.019)	**0.022 (0.003)**
30	15.92	0.037 (0.013)	0.037 (0.024)	0.039 (0.033)	**0.023 (0.003)**
39	15.51	0.017 (0.005)	0.027 (0.023)	0.021 (0.027)	**0.016 (0.006)**
44	3.99	0.031 (0.009)	0.036 (0.021)	0.033 (0.019)	**0.026 (0.003)**
69	13.83	0.029 (0.011)	0.034 (0.022)	0.035 (0.031)	**0.023 (0.002)**
73	14.71	0.031 (0.009)	0.036 (0.024)	0.038 (0.034)	**0.023 (0.003)**
85	13.41	0.045 (0.014)	0.066 (0.037)	0.049 (0.056)	**0.034 (0.008)**
88	8.49	0.027 (0.007)	0.032 (0.019)	0.035 (0.031)	**0.022 (0.002)**
Total	100	0.027 (0.009)	0.037 (0.023)	0.034 (0.031)	**0.023 (0.003)**

standard deviation indicates higher consistency between the predicted distribution and the actual outcomes. It is important to clarify that this standard deviation refers to the variability of the CRPS values across samples, not the dispersion of the predictive distribution itself.

Results indicate that the CNN MC dropout achieves superior performance compared to the other probabilistic approaches. It yields both the lowest prediction error and the smallest standard deviation, suggesting that its forecasts are not only more accurate but also more stable and reliable.

Figure 6 provides an overview of error prediction for a single flight using various data-driven error-correction methods. The results show that (i) all physics-aware models effectively capture voltage discharge error dynamics, and (ii) each approach incorporates different sources of uncertainty through probabilistic error estimates.

The performance results in Table 4 are consistent with the flight results in Fig. 6. Specifically, the CNN with MC dropout achieves superior probabilistic accuracy and reliability regarding voltage estimation errors and prediction consistency compared to other evaluated models [see Fig. 6(a)]. This is further supported by the low standard deviation of 0.009 V in Table 4. In contrast, Fig. 6c, d show the largest prediction errors and highest variance, which aligns with the data for flight #73 (QRF, QGB) in Table 4. Based on these errors, Fig. 7 illustrates the overall voltage drop of a single-cell battery alongside its uncertainty.

Evaluating the PDF is essential for quantifying uncertainty. To this end, calibration and sharpness are evaluated. Calibration reflects the statistical consistency between predicted distributions and actual observations, representing a joint property of forecasts and empirical data (Jung et al., 2022). Sharpness indicates how concentrated the predictive distributions are, indicating how tightly confidence intervals focus around a single value (Kuleshov et al., 2018).

Figure 8 shows the calibration plots of the developed models, where the X-axis represents predicted probabilities and the Y-axis shows observed outcomes. Ideally, a well-calibrated model aligns along the diagonal, indicating close agreement between predictions and actual results. Calibration quality, illustrated by solid blue lines, is

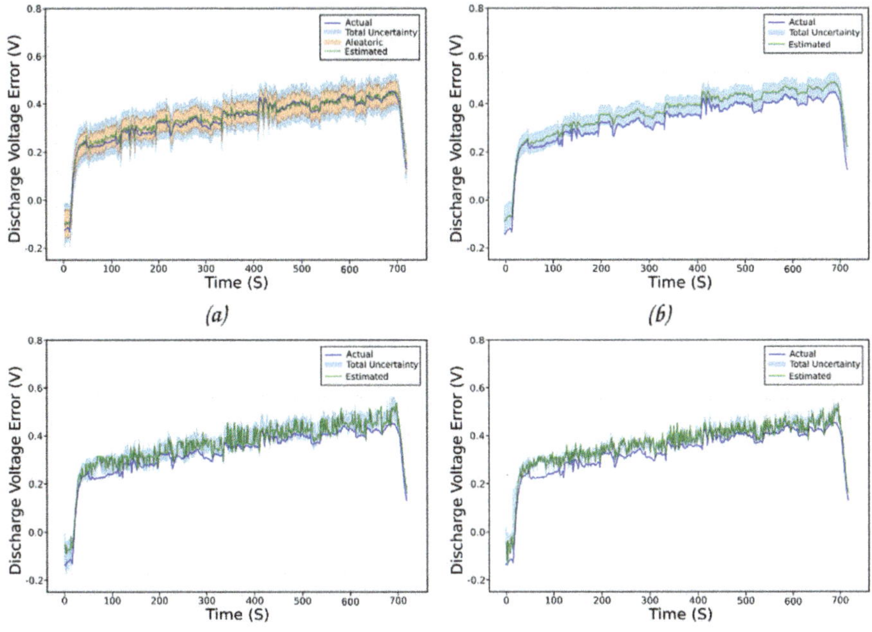

(a) (b) (c) (d)

Fig. 6 Error correction performance across different models for flight #73: **a** Error correction with CNN dropout, **b** error correction with QLR, **c** error correction with QRF and **d** error correction with QGB

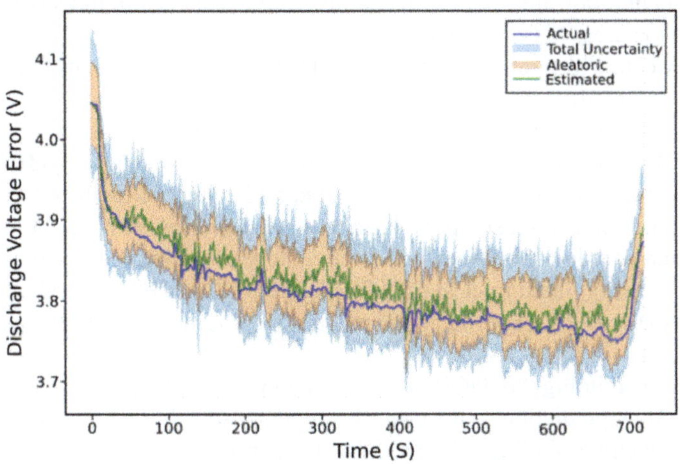

Fig. 7 EOD Voltage estimation of a battery cell in flight #73 using CNN MC dropout

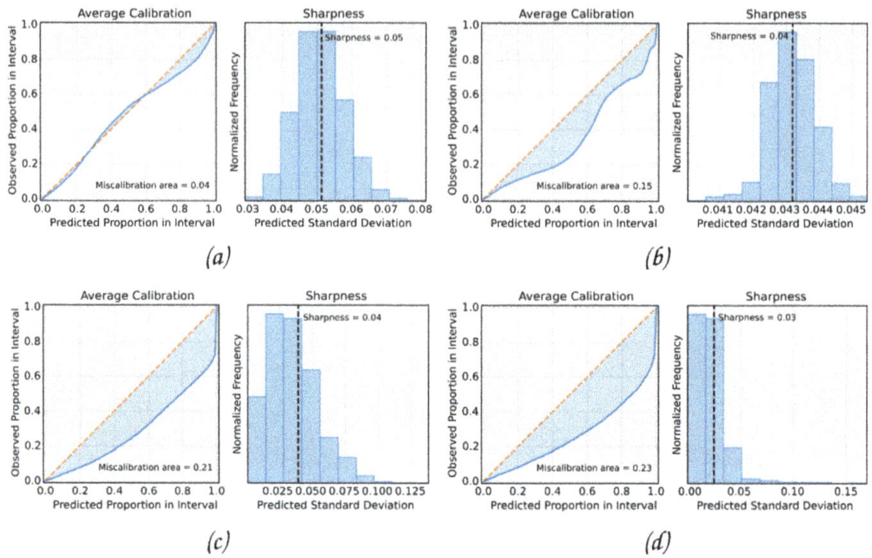

Fig. 8 Calibration and sharpness metrics for all UQ methods used in this study. **a** CNN MC dropout model, **b** QLR model, **c** QRF model and **d** QGB model

assessed by the area between the calibration curve and the diagonal, referred to as the miscalibration area, represented in blue shaded area. Smaller areas imply better calibration (Tran et al., 2020). The CNN MC dropout model [Fig. 8a] displays the lowest miscalibration area of 0.04. In contrast, the QRF and QGB models have higher miscalibration areas of 0.21 and 0.23, indicating poorer calibration. The QLR model falls in between, with a miscalibration area of 0.15, showing acceptable performance compared to the other quantile models.

At the same time, sharpness is assessed as a measure of how concentrated the predictive distributions are (Tran et al., 2020). Since the model outputs are Gaussian distributions, sharpness is typically quantified using the predicted variance. A lower variance indicates a sharper distribution. However, it is important to note that there is often a trade-off between how well a model is calibrated and the sharpness of its predictions (Gneiting et al., 2007). Figure 8 illustrates the predictive uncertainty distributions for all probabilistic models, with vertical lines representing their corresponding sharpness levels.

As illustrated in Fig. 8d, QGB presents the lowest sharpness, indicating minimal variability in its predictions. However, this model also exhibits inferior calibration, aligning with earlier findings. This highlights the necessity of balancing calibration and sharpness. Within this framework, QLR stands out by achieving an effective compromise between these two aspects, with a sharpness value of 0.04 V, as shown in Fig. 8b.

On the other hand, although the CNN MC dropout model exhibits the highest sharpness, the difference compared with the other models is minimal [Fig. 8a]. It achieves a sharpness of 0.05 V, only 0.01 V higher than that of QLR. This small margin suggests that the increased sharpness of the CNN MC dropout model does not significantly compromise its calibration.

The results demonstrate that the proposed probabilistic physics-aware model outperforms alternatives in terms of CRPS, calibration, and sharpness. This superior performance validates the contribution of the methodology and highlights its effectiveness in predicting EOD voltage.

5.2 *Health-State Diagnostic*

Table 5 presents the estimated health-states derived from eight different drone flights, each fitted with distinct distinct Li-Po batteries sharing identical capacity specifications. Specifically, each drone flight in the testing dataset employs unique batteries with matching capacity characteristics. Battery degradation was qualitatively evaluated by experts, who classified battery health into categories of good, medium, and bad based on their operational history and usage conditions. Nevertheless, this qualitative classification does not offer precise quantitative metrics. To achieve quantitative degradation measurement, total predictive uncertainty is employed, represented numerically as illustrated in Fig. 4, where 0 corresponds to degraded battery health and 1 signifies optimal battery condition.

A detailed analysis of the results presented in Table 4 indicates that the UQ modeling based on the QGB method is less accurate in determining the true health-state of the batteries across different flights. In comparison, the QRF method achieves superior performance, with significantly better results in identifying the batteries corresponding to flights #11, #39, #44, and #88.

On the other hand, the QLR method demonstrates robust health-state index modeling for most batteries, except for flights #30 and #85. In these particular cases,

Table 5 Health-state estimation of different models for different real flights equipped with batteries in different health conditions

Flight (#)	QLR	QRF	QGB	CNN MC dropout	Ground Truth
11	0.956	0.806	0.601	**0.998**	Good
30	0.602	0.471	0.191	**0.993**	Good
39	**1.0**	0.841	0.605	0.997	Good
44	0.938	0.903	0.541	**1.0**	Good
69	0.834	0.659	0.306	**1.0**	Good
73	0.763	0.506	0.157	**1.0**	Good
85	0.283	0.184	0.068	**0.948**	Good
88	0.961	0.727	0.241	**1.0**	Good

a substantial number of observations fall outside the uncertainty interval, pointing to a suboptimal battery health condition.

Finally, the CNN MC dropout demonstrates the most effective uncertainty modeling, successfully estimating health-states across various batteries, as validated by domain experts. By integrating both aleatoric and epistemic uncertainties, the model offers detailed and accurate insights, allowing the probabilistic CNN to produce a well-calibrated, uncertainty-aware health indicator (Abdar et al., 2021). This method of uncertainty quantification supports the final contribution of the work, showing that jointly addressing aleatoric and epistemic uncertainty enhances the overall quality of decision-making.

6 Discussion

This research presents a robust probabilistic physics-aware battery health management approach for inspection drones. However, before reaching conclusions, it is important to discuss key aspects of the developed methodology in more detail.

6.1 *Uncertainty Decomposition*

The proposed CNN MC dropout method demonstrates enhanced performance in both accuracy and uncertainty quantification (cf. Section 5.1). Notably, this approach quantifies aleatoric and epistemic uncertainty. As shown in Fig. 9, the blue region indicates data-related uncertainty, typically caused by sensor noise (aleatoric), while the purple-shaded region reflects model uncertainty (epistemic).

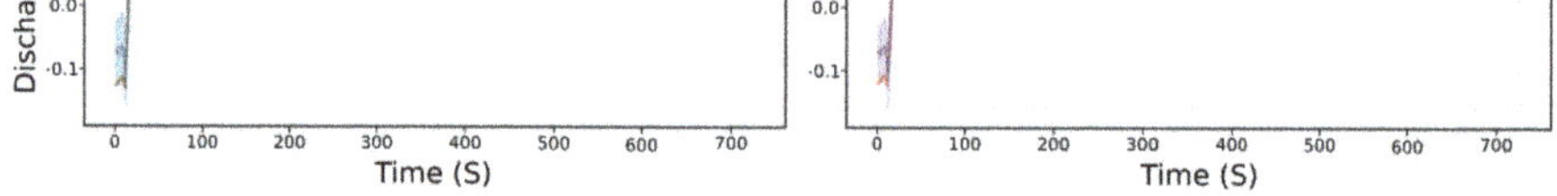

Fig. 9 Estimation of EOD voltage correction in flight #73 using CNN MC dropout for the discrimination of aleatoric and epistemic uncertainty

Table 6 Sensitivity analysis of dropout rate for the flight #73

Dropout Rate	Calibration	Sharpness	CRPS
0.01	0.06	0.05	0.0178
0.05	0.09	0.09	0.0267
0.1	0.24	0.18	0.0482
0.15	0.28	0.21	0.0503
0.2	0.29	0.23	0.0561

The analysis shows epistemic uncertainty is greater than aleatoric uncertainty, indicating that methods to reduce epistemic uncertainty like improving model calibration or expanding training data could address the primary uncertainty source. Distinguishing between uncertainty types is a crucial benefit of this method. The proposed UQ approach offers important insights that enhance our understanding of uncertainty compared to alternative probabilistic approaches (cf. Section 5).

6.2 *Sensitivity Analysis of Dropout Rate*

To assess how the dropout rate affects the outcomes, this section examines its impact on various performance measures. Using flight #73 as a benchmark, the analysis evaluates how changes in the dropout rate influence calibration, sharpness, and CRPS metrics. The resulting findings are presented in Table 6.

The results show that the dropout rate has a significant impact on calibration, sharpness, and CRPS. In particular, increasing the dropout rate from 0.01 to 0.2 leads to a deterioration in these metrics. Calibration shifts from 0.06 to 0.29, sharpness increases from 0.05 to 0.23, and CRPS rises from 0.0178 to 0.0561. Therefore, the choice of a dropout rate of $\rho = 0.1$ in the experiments represents a balanced trade-off between overfitting and high model uncertainty.

6.3 *Limitations*

Despite its contributions, this research faces several limitations. First, implementing real-time processing on drones is challenging due to the computational cost of CNNs and MC dropout. Second, the dataset may not fully capture the diversity of operating scenarios, potentially excluding irregular or extreme environmental conditions. It also exhibits a temporal imbalance, with most data concentrated in a single year, which may hinder generalization. Third, the ground-truth health labels rely on expert assessments and may introduce subjective bias. Fourth, all cells originate from a single battery manufacturer, limiting the applicability of the findings to other chemistries or designs. Finally, the test set is relatively small and cross-validation was not performed, reducing statistical confidence.

7 Conclusion

This research introduced a physics-aware drone battery health assessment approach combining physics-based models with probabilistic data-driven error prediction. The methodology demonstrated robust uncertainty performance in predicting battery discharge voltage while effectively quantifying data and model related uncertainties.

Empirical evaluation on EOD voltage data from real offshore wind turbine inspection missions showed that the probabilistic CNN achieved 14.8% better accuracy than QLR, with 37.8% and 32.3% improvements over QRF and QGB respectively. The framework maintained high prediction performance even when applying a Li-Ion physics-based model to Li-Po batteries, suggesting potential for cross-chemistry transfer, pending validation on other battery chemistries.

Future work will focus on computational efficiency using techniques such as quantization (Cheng et al., 2018), tensor factorization (Kim et al., 2016), and low-rank approximation (Tai et al., 2016). The integration of PINNs will also be explored to incorporate physical constraints directly into the learning process, and benchmarked against the current physics-aware approach. Alternatively, expanding the dataset to include diverse operational scenarios, enriched with environmental sensor data and controlled charge/discharge cycles, will improve model robustness.

Moreover, prediction accuracy could potentially be improved by applying calibration techniques, such as isotonic regression (Kuleshov et al., 2018), and by comparing performance with models like Bayesian Neural Networks to combine the strengths of different UQ methods (Alcibar et al., 2024). Finally, while the framework provides decision support, it does not implement a complete maintenance strategy or formal operational decision-making process.

Competing Interests The author(s) has no competing interests to declare that are relevant to the content of this manuscript.

Glossary

End-of-discharge (EOD) Voltaje de fin de descarga
Particle Filtering (PF) Filtrado de Partículas
Unscented Kalman Filter (UKF) Filtro de Kalman Sin Aroma
Reduced Order Model (ROM) Modelo de orden reducido
Long Short-Term Memory (LSTM) Termino de Memoria a Medio (largo-corto) Plazo (LSTM)

References

Abdar, M., Pourpanah, F., Hussain, S., Rezazadegan, D., Liu, L., Ghavamzadeh, M., Fieguth, P., et al. (2021). A review of uncertainty quantification in deep learning: Techniques, applications and challenges. *Information Fusion, 76*, 243–297. https://doi.org/10.1016/j.inffus.2021.05.008

Aizpurua, J. I., Ramirez, I., Lasa, I., del Rio, L., Ortiz, A., & Stewart, B. G. (2023). Hybrid transformer prognostics framework for enhanced probabilistic predictions in renewable energy applications. *IEEE Transactions on Power Delivery, 38*(1), 599–609. https://doi.org/10.1109/TPWRD.2022.3203873

Alcibar, J., Aizpurua, J. I., & Zugasti, E. (2024). Towards a probabilistic fusion approach for robust battery prognostics. In *PHM society European conference* (Vol. 8, p. 13). https://doi.org/10.36001/phme.2024.v8i1.3981

Chao, A., Manuel, C. K., Goebel, K., & Fink, O. (2022). Fusing physics-based and deep learning models for prognostics. *Reliability Engineering & System Safety, 217*, Article 107961. https://doi.org/10.1016/j.ress.2021.107961

Bai, G., Su, Y., Rahman, M. M., & Wang, Z. (2023). Prognostics of lithium-ion batteries using knowledge-constrained machine learning and Kalman filtering. *Reliability Engineering & System Safety, 231*, Article 108944. https://doi.org/10.1016/j.ress.2022.108944

Biggio, L., Bendinelli, T., Kulkarni, C., & Fink, O. (2023). Ageing-aware battery discharge prediction with deep learning. *Applied Energy, 346*, Article 121229. https://doi.org/10.1016/j.apenergy.2023.121229

Bracale, A., De Falco, P., Noia, L. P. D., & Rizzo, R. (2023). Probabilistic state of health and remaining useful life prediction for Li-ion batteries. *IEEE Transactions on Industry Applications, 59*(1), 578–590. https://doi.org/10.1109/TIA.2022.3210081

Che, Y., Zheng, Y., Forest, F. E., Sui, X., Xiaosong, H., & Teodorescu, R. (2024). Predictive health assessment for lithium-ion batteries with probabilistic degradation prediction and accelerating aging detection. *Reliability Engineering & System Safety, 241*, Article 109603. https://doi.org/10.1016/j.ress.2023.109603

Cheng, J., Jiaxiang, W., Leng, C., Wang, Y., & Qinghao, H. (2018). Quantized CNN: A unified approach to accelerate and compress convolutional networks. *IEEE Transactions on Neural Networks and Learning Systems, 29*(10), 4730–4743. https://doi.org/10.1109/TNNLS.2017.2774288

Choubineh, A., Chen, J., Coenen, F., & Ma, F. (2023). Applying Monte Carlo dropout to quantify the uncertainty of skip connection-based convolutional neural networks optimized by big data. *Electronics, 12*(6), 1453. https://doi.org/10.3390/electronics12061453

Chung, Y., Neiswanger, W., Char, I., & Schneider, J. (2021). Beyond Pinball loss: Quantile methods for calibrated uncertainty quantification. *Advances in Neural Information Processing Systems, 34*, 10971–10984.

Couture, J., & Lin, X. (2022). Image- and health indicator-based transfer learning hybridization for battery RUL prediction. *Engineering Applications of Artificial Intelligence, 114*, Article 105120. https://doi.org/10.1016/j.engappai.2022.105120

Daigle, M., & Kulkarni, C. S. (2013). Electrochemistry-based battery modeling for prognostics. In *Annual conference of the PHM society* (Vol. 5, p. 13).

Demirci, O., Taskin, S., Schaltz, E., & Demirci, B. A. (2024). Review of battery state estimation methods for electric vehicles—Part I: SOC estimation. *Journal of Energy Storage, 87*, Article 111435. https://doi.org/10.1016/j.est.2024.111435

Kiureghian, A. D., & Ditlevsen, O. (2009). Aleatory or epistemic? Does it matter? *Structural Safety, 31*(2), 105–112. https://doi.org/10.1016/j.strusafe.2008.06.020

Djuric, P. M., Kotecha, J. H., Zhang, J., Huang, Y., Ghirmai, T., Bugallo, M. F., & Miguez, J. (2003). Particle filtering. *IEEE Signal Processing Magazine, 20*(5), 19–38. https://doi.org/10.1109/MSP.2003.1236770

Eleftheroglou, N., Mansouri, S. S., Loutas, T., Karvelis, P., Georgoulas, G., Nikolakopoulos, G., & Zarouchas, D. (2019). Intelligent data-driven prognostic methodologies for the real-time remaining useful life until the end-of-discharge estimation of the lithium-polymer batteries of unmanned aerial vehicles with uncertainty quantification. *Applied Energy, 254*, Article 113677. https://doi.org/10.1016/j.apenergy.2019.113677

Feng, K., Xu, Y., Wang, Y., Li, S., Jiang, Q., Sun, B., Zheng, J., & Ni, Q. (2023). Digital twin enabled domain adversarial graph networks for bearing fault diagnosis. *IEEE Transactions on Industrial Cyber-Physical Systems, 1*, 113–122. https://doi.org/10.1109/TICPS.2023.3298879

Fernández, J., Chiachío, J., Chiachío, M., Barros, J., & Corbetta, M. (2023). Physics-guided Bayesian neural networks by ABC-SS: Application to reinforced concrete columns. *Engineering Applications of Artificial Intelligence, 119*, Article 105790. https://doi.org/10.1016/j.engappai.2022.105790

Fink, O., Wang, Q., Svensén, M., Dersin, P., Lee, W.-J., & Ducoffe, M. (2020). Potential, challenges and future directions for deep learning in prognostics and health management applications. *Engineering Applications of Artificial Intelligence, 92*, Article 103678. https://doi.org/10.1016/j.engappai.2020.103678

Friedman, J. H. (2001). Greedy function approximation: A gradient boosting machine. *Annals of Statistics*, 1189–1232.

Gal, Y., & Ghahramani, Z. (2016). Dropout as a Bayesian approximation: Representing model uncertainty in deep learning. In *International conference on machine learning* (pp. 1050–1059). PMLR.

Gatti, M., Giulietti, F., & Turci, M. (2015). Maximum endurance for battery-powered rotary-wing aircraft. *Aerospace Science and Technology, 45*, 174–179. https://doi.org/10.1016/j.ast.2015.05.009

Gneiting, T., Balabdaoui, F., & Raftery, A. E. (2007). Probabilistic forecasts, calibration and sharpness. *Journal of the Royal Statistical Society Series B: Statistical Methodology, 69*(2), 243–268. https://doi.org/10.1111/j.1467-9868.2007.00587.x

González-Sopeña, J. M., Pakrashi, V., & Ghosh, B. (2021). An overview of performance evaluation metrics for short-term statistical wind power forecasting. *Renewable and Sustainable Energy Reviews, 138*, Article 110515. https://doi.org/10.1016/j.rser.2020.110515

Guo, J., Li, Z., & Pecht, M. (2015). A Bayesian approach for Li-ion battery capacity fade modeling and cycles to failure prognostics. *Journal of Power Sources, 281*(May), 173–184. https://doi.org/10.1016/j.jpowsour.2015.01.164

Guo, L., He, H., Ren, Y., Li, R., Jiang, B., & Gong, J. (2024). Prognostics of lithium-ion batteries health state based on adaptive mode decomposition and long short-term memory neural network. *Engineering Applications of Artificial Intelligence, 127*, Article 107317. https://doi.org/10.1016/j.engappai.2023.107317

Han, T., Wang, Z., & Meng, H. (2022). End-to-end capacity estimation of lithium-ion batteries with an enhanced long short-term memory network considering domain adaptation. *Journal of Power Sources, 520*, Article 230823. https://doi.org/10.1016/j.jpowsour.2021.230823

Heo, J., Lee, H. B., Kim, S., Lee, J., Kim, K. W., Yang, E., & Hwang, S. J. (2018). Uncertainty-aware attention for reliable interpretation and prediction. In S. Bengio, H. Wallach, H. Larochelle, K. Grauman, N. Cesa-Bianchi, & R. Garnett (Eds.), *Advances in neural information processing systems* (Vol. 31, pp. 1–10). Curran Associates, Inc.

Hong, J., Lee, D., Jeong, E.-R., & Yi, Y. (2020). Towards the Swift prediction of the remaining useful life of lithium-ion batteries with end-to-end deep learning. *Applied Energy, 278*, Article 115646. https://doi.org/10.1016/j.apenergy.2020.115646

Hsu, C.-W., Xiong, R., Chen, N.-Y., Li, J., & Tsou, N.-T. (2022). Deep neural network battery life and voltage prediction by using data of one cycle only. *Applied Energy, 306*, 118134. https://doi.org/10.1016/j.apenergy.2021.118134

Hüllermeier, E., & Waegeman, W. (2021). Aleatoric and epistemic uncertainty in machine learning: An introduction to concepts and methods. *Machine Learning, 110*(3), 457–506. https://doi.org/10.1007/s10994-021-05946-3

Jiang, Y., & Meng, X. (2023). A battery capacity estimation method based on the equivalent circuit model and quantile regression using vehicle real-world operation data. *Energy, 284*, Article 129126. https://doi.org/10.1016/j.energy.2023.129126

Jung, Y., Jo, H., Choo, J., & Lee, I. (2022). Statistical model calibration and design optimization under aleatory and epistemic uncertainty. *Reliability Engineering & System Safety, 222*, Article 108428. https://doi.org/10.1016/j.ress.2022.108428

Kendall, A., & Gal, Y. (2017). What uncertainties do we need in Bayesian deep learning for computer vision? In I. Guyon, U. Von Luxburg, S. Bengio, H. Wallach, R. Fergus, S. Vishwanathan, & R. Garnett (Eds.), *Advances in neural information processing systems* (Vol. 30, p. 11). Curran Associates, Inc.

Kim, D., Park, C., Oh, J., Lee, S., & Yu, H. (2016). Convolutional matrix factorization for document context-aware recommendation. In *Proceedings of the 10th ACM conference on recommender systems (RecSys '16)* (pp. 233–240). Association for Computing Machinery. https://doi.org/10.1145/2959100.2959165

Kuleshov, V., Fenner, N., & Ermon, S. (2018). Accurate uncertainties for deep learning using calibrated regression. In J. Dy & A. Krause (Eds.), *Proceedings of the 35th International conference on machine learning* (Vol. 80, pp. 2796–2804). PMLR.

Lakshminarayanan, B., Pritzel, A., & Blundell, C. (2017) Simple and scalable predictive uncertainty estimation using deep ensembles. In I. Guyon, U. Von Luxburg, S. Bengio, H. Wallach, R. Fergus, S. Vishwanathan, & R. Garnett (Eds.), *Advances in neural information processing systems* (Vol. 30, p. 12). Curran Associates, Inc.

Li, W., Bazant, M. Z., & Zhu, J. (2021). A physics-guided neural network framework for elastic plates: Comparison of governing equations-based and energy-based approaches. *Computer Methods in Applied Mechanics and Engineering, 383*, Article 113933. https://doi.org/10.1016/j.cma.2021.113933

Mazzi, Y., Sassi, H. B., & Errahimi, F. (2024). Lithium-ion battery state of health estimation using a hybrid model based on a convolutional neural network and bidirectional gated recurrent unit. *Engineering Applications of Artificial Intelligence, 127*, Article 107199. https://doi.org/10.1016/j.engappai.2023.107199

Meinshausen, N. (2006). Quantile regression forests. *Journal of Machine Learning Research, 7*(35), 983–999.

Meng, H., Geng, M., & Han, T. (2023). Long short-term memory network with Bayesian optimization for health prognostics of lithium-ion batteries based on partial incremental capacity analysis. *Reliability Engineering & System Safety, 236*, Article 109288. https://doi.org/10.1016/j.ress.2023.109288

Mitici, M., De Pater, I., Barros, A., & Zeng, Z. (2023). Dynamic predictive maintenance for multiple components using data-driven probabilistic RUL prognostics: The case of Turbofan engines. *Reliability Engineering & System Safety, 234*, Article 109199. https://doi.org/10.1016/j.ress.2023.109199

Nascimento, R. G., Viana, F. A. C., Corbetta, M., & Kulkarni, C. S. (2023). A framework for Li-ion battery prognosis based on hybrid Bayesian physics-informed neural networks. *Scientific Reports, 13*(1), 13856. https://doi.org/10.1038/s41598-023-33018-0

Ng, M.-F., Zhao, J., Yan, Q., Conduit, G. J., & Seh, Z. W. (2020). Predicting the state of charge and health of batteries using data-driven machine learning. *Nature Machine Intelligence, 2*(3), 161–170. https://doi.org/10.1038/s42256-020-0156-7

Ni, Q., Ji, J. C., Halkon, B., Feng, K., & Nandi, A. K. (2023). Physics-informed residual network (PIResNet) for rolling element bearing fault diagnostics. *Mechanical Systems and Signal Processing, 200*, Article 110544. https://doi.org/10.1016/j.ymssp.2023.110544

Ochella, S., Shafiee, M., & Dinmohammadi, F. (2022). Artificial intelligence in prognostics and health management of engineering systems. *Engineering Applications of Artificial Intelligence, 108*, Article 104552. https://doi.org/10.1016/j.engappai.2021.104552

Pola, D. A., Navarrete, H. F., Orchard, M. E., Rabié, R. S., Cerda, M. A., Olivares, B. E., Silva, J. F., Espinoza, P. A., & Pérez, A. (2015). Particle-filtering-based discharge time prognosis for lithium-ion batteries with a statistical characterization of use profiles. *IEEE Transactions on Reliability, 64*(2), 710–720. https://doi.org/10.1109/TR.2014.2385069

Raissi, M., Yazdani, A., & Karniadakis, G. E. (2020). Hidden fluid mechanics: Learning velocity and pressure fields from flow visualizations. *Science, 367*(6481), 1026–1030. https://doi.org/10.1126/science.aaw4741

Rathnakumar, R., Pang, Y., & Liu, Y. (2023). Epistemic and aleatoric uncertainty quantification for crack detection using a Bayesian boundary aware convolutional network. *Reliability Engineering & System Safety, 240*, Article 109547. https://doi.org/10.1016/j.ress.2023.109547

Salinas-Camus, M., Kulkarni, C., & Orchard, M. (2023). Battery state-of-health aware path planning for a mars rover. In *Annual conference of the PHM society* (Vol. 15, No. 1). https://doi.org/10.36001/phmconf.2023.v15i1.3511

Sierra, G., Orchard, M., Kulkarni, C., & Goebel, K. (2018). A hybrid battery model for prognostics in small-size electric UAVs. In *Annual conference of the prognostics and health management society 2018* (p. 11).

Sierra, G., Orchard, M., Goebel, K., & Kulkarni, C. (2019). Battery health management for small-size rotary-wing electric unmanned aerial vehicles: An efficient approach for constrained computing platforms. *Reliability Engineering & System Safety, 182*, 166–178. https://doi.org/10.1016/j.ress.2018.04.030

Song, B., Zhang, Z., Qin, Y., Liu, X., & Hao, H. (2022). Quantitative analysis of freight train derailment severity with structured and unstructured data. *Reliability Engineering & System Safety, 224*, Article 108563. https://doi.org/10.1016/j.ress.2022.108563

Sun, B., Pan, J., Zeyu, W., Xia, Q., Wang, Z., Ren, Y., Yang, D., Guo, X., & Feng, Q. (2023). Adaptive evolution enhanced physics-informed neural networks for time-variant health prognosis of lithium-ion batteries. *Journal of Power Sources, 556*, Article 232432. https://doi.org/10.1016/j.jpowsour.2022.232432

Tagasovska, N., & Lopez-Paz, D. (2019). Single-model uncertainties for deep learning. In H. Wallach, H. Larochelle, A. Beygelzimer, F. dAlché-Buc, E. Fox, & R. Garnett (Eds.), *Advances in neural information processing systems* (Vol. 32, p. 12). Curran Associates, Inc.

Tai, C., Xiao, T., Zhang, Y., Wang, X., & Weinan, E. (2016). *Convolutional neural networks with low-rank regularization*. https://arxiv.org/abs/1511.06067

Teubert, C., Griffith, K. J., Corbetta, M., Kulkarni, C., Banerjee, P., & Daigle, M. (2023). *ProgPy python prognostics packages*. https://doi.org/10.5281/ZENODO.8097013

Tran, K., Neiswanger, W., Yoon, J., Zhang, Q., Xing, E., & Ulissi, Z. W. (2020). Methods for comparing uncertainty quantifications for material property predictions. *Machine Learning: Science and Technology, 1*(2), Article 025006. https://doi.org/10.1088/2632-2153/ab7e1a

Valavanis, K. P., & Vachtsevanos, G. J. (2015). *Handbook of unmanned aerial vehicles* (Vol. 1). Springer.

Vanem, E., Salucci, C. B., Bakdi, A., & Sheim Alnes, Ø. Å. (2021). Data-driven state of health modelling review of state of the art and reflections on applications for maritime battery systems. *Journal of Energy Storage, 43*, 103158. https://doi.org/10.1016/j.est.2021.103158

Xu, Y., Yan, X., Sun, B., & Liu, Z. (2022). Global contextual residual convolutional neural networks for motor fault diagnosis under variable-speed conditions. *Reliability Engineering & System Safety, 225*, Article 108618. https://doi.org/10.1016/j.ress.2022.108618

Yeregui, J., Oca, L., Lopetegi, I., Garayalde, E., Aizpurua, M., & Iraola, U. (2023). State of charge estimation combining physics-based and artificial intelligence models for lithium-ion batteries. *Journal of Energy Storage, 73*, Article 108883. https://doi.org/10.1016/j.est.2023.108883

Zamo, M., & Naveau, P. (2018). Estimation of the continuous ranked probability score with limited information and applications to ensemble weather forecasts. *Mathematical Geosciences, 50*(2), 209–234. https://doi.org/10.1007/s11004-017-9709-7

Zhang, S., Liu, Z., & Hongye, S. (2022). A Bayesian mixture neural network for remaining useful life prediction of lithium-ion batteries. *IEEE Transactions on Transportation Electrification, 8*(4), 4708–4721. https://doi.org/10.1109/TTE.2022.3161140

Zhang, Z., & Gu, G. X. (2021). Physics-informed deep learning for digital materials. *Theoretical and Applied Mechanics Letters, 11*(1), Article 100220. https://doi.org/10.1016/j.taml.2021.100220
Zhao, H., Chen, Z., Shu, X., Shen, J., Lei, Z., & Zhang, Y. (2023). State of health estimation for lithium-ion batteries based on hybrid attention and deep learning. *Reliability Engineering & System Safety, 232*, Article 109066. https://doi.org/10.1016/j.ress.2022.109066

Digitalization for Enhanced Management of Perishable Assets: A Case Study on Vaccine Cold-Chain Logistics

Amir Farmanesh and Joaquín Ordieres Meré

Abstract This paper explores the transformative impact of digitalization on the management of perishable assets, focusing specifically on vaccine cold-chain logistics. Efficiently maintaining the integrity of vaccines from manufacturer to patient is paramount, and traditional logistics systems often face challenges in ensuring consistent temperature control, traceability, and timely delivery. We present a case study approach to investigate how digital technologies—such as IoT sensors, blockchain, cloud computing, and data analytics—can enhance visibility, accountability, and decision-making within the vaccine supply chain. The study identifies key benefits, including reduced spoilage, improved regulatory compliance, and optimized resource allocation. Furthermore, it discusses implementation challenges and proposes a framework for integrating digital solutions to create a more resilient and responsive cold-chain. The findings underscore the potential of digitalization to significantly improve public health outcomes by ensuring the safe and effective distribution of vaccines.

Keywords Digital cold chain management · IoT-enabled vaccine logistics · Distributed ledger technology for supply chains · LoRaWAN-based monitoring systems · Perishable asset lifecycle management

1 Introduction

The global imperative for effective vaccine distribution, highlighted by recent pandemics, underscores the critical need for robust cold-chain logistics. Perishable assets like vaccines demand stringent temperature control and meticulous tracking throughout their journey. This section introduces the challenges inherent in traditional

A. Farmanesh · J. Ordieres Meré (✉)
Industrial Engineering School, Universidad Politécnica de Madrid, Madrid, Spain
e-mail: j.ordieres@upm.es

A. Farmanesh
e-mail: amir.farmanesh@upm.es

A. Crespo Márquez et al. (eds.), *Digital Maintenance and Asset Digitalization*, Engineering Asset Management Review 5,
https://doi.org/10.1007/978-3-032-21502-4_12

vaccine supply chains and sets the stage for exploring how digitalization offers potent solutions.

Vaccines are highly sensitive biological products that must be maintained within a strict temperature range (typically between + 2 °C and + 8 °C) throughout their journey from production to patient (Liu et al., 2021). As highlighted by Kristensen et al. (2016), any failure to preserve this cold-chain can significantly compromise vaccine efficacy, thereby endangering population health. The World Health Organization (WHO) estimates that up to 50% of vaccines are wasted globally each year due to cold-chain disruptions and logistical shortcomings (WHO, 2020). This alarming rate of wastage underscores the urgent need to strengthen cold-chain logistics. Furthermore, as emphasized by Ergetie et al. (2023) and Talbot et al. (2025), deficiencies in cold-chain infrastructure disproportionately affect low-resource countries, where access to vaccines remains unreliable due to inadequate distribution networks. Guaranteeing an unbroken cold-chain is therefore not only essential for operational efficiency but also a critical matter of global health equity. In recent years, vaccine researchers have expanded efforts to develop thermostable formulations capable of withstanding elevated temperatures and reducing reliance on continuous refrigeration (Acharya & Phuyal, 2025; Garcia-Valtanen et al., 2025; Raut et al., 2025). These approaches aim to simplify logistics in regions with limited cold-chain infrastructure, but they remain confined to a few experimental vaccines and are not yet applicable to most routine immunizations (Hosangadi et al., 2021; Kristensen et al., 2016). Despite these advances, most licensed human vaccines still require strict cold-chain conditions, and large-scale deployment of thermostable alternatives remains limited. As a result, enhancing the transparency, resilience, and real-time monitoring of existing cold-chain systems continues to be a practical and critical strategy for safeguarding vaccine efficacy worldwide.

As shown in Fig. 1 which show the stages of the vaccine cold-chain, the vaccine cold-chain involves a series of refrigerated storage and transport stages (cold rooms, freezer trucks, vaccine refrigerators, cold boxes, etc.) that move vaccines from manufacturers through national and regional warehouses down to local clinics (Jiang & Song, 2023). Maintaining the required temperature at each node throughout the cold chain remains a significant challenge in immunization programs which demands temperature monitoring throughout the supply chain for ensuring vaccine quality and integrity (Kartoglu & Ames, 2022). Historically, this has been achieved through manual checks and data loggers, but such approaches provide limited real-time visibility and are prone to human error or delayed response, particularly at district storage levels and during transportation (Kitamura et al., 2018; Yauba et al., 2017). In recent years, digitalization of supply chains has emerged as a solution to these limitations and offer opportunities to improve cold chain management (Crnjac Milić et al., 2023; Ren et al., 2021).

The advent of inexpensive sensors, widespread connectivity, and advanced data systems allows continuous monitoring and instant data sharing across the logistics chain (Kumar et al., 2018; Ullo et al., 2018). In many industries, digital technologies have improved supply chain performance by increasing visibility, agility, and control. For example, in pharmaceutical and healthcare supply chains, Internet of

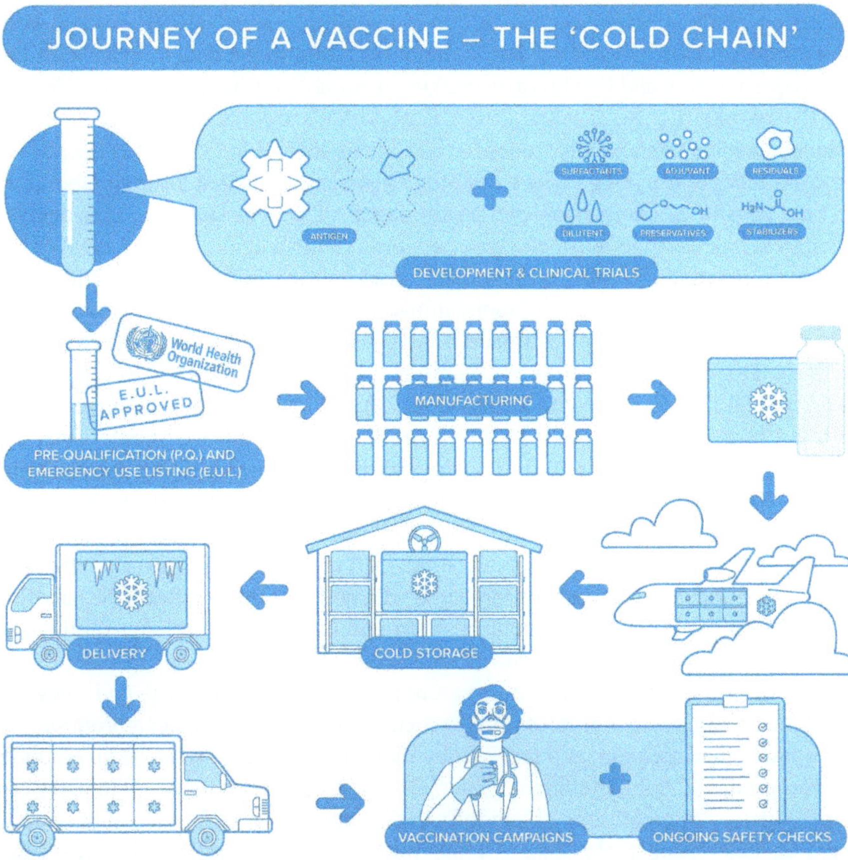

Fig. 1 Vaccine cold-chain stages (PAHO/WHO 2021)

Things (IoT) devices enable real-time data acquisition on conditions such as temperature, humidity, and location tracking, which helps optimize routes, reduce spoilage, and ensure timely deliveries (Balfaqih et al., 2023). The role of IoT is particularly critical in vaccine cold-chain management, where real-time data is essential for maintaining proper temperature and condition control (Jiang et al., 2024; Verma Pargaien et al., 2021). IoT-based systems can continuously monitor storage conditions, thereby reducing human errors and minimizing vaccine wastage (Jiang et al., 2024; Shashi, 2022). These systems rely on a combination of technologies, including RFID, Wi-Fi, Bluetooth, and GPS, to ensure the safe storage and transportation of vaccines (Mohsin & Yellampalli, 2017; Verma Pargaien et al., 2021). To support such real-time, energy-efficient monitoring across wide geographic areas, appropriate wireless communication technologies are essential.

Long Range Wide Area Network (LoRaWAN), a low-power wide-area network (LPWAN) protocol, has emerged as a promising solution for IoT applications, addressing challenges of long-range communication, energy efficiency, and scalability (de Carvalho Silva et al., 2017). It enables long-range data transfer with low power consumption and low bit rates, making it suitable for battery-powered devices in IoT networks (Lavric & Popa, 2017). LoRaWAN's architecture and protocol are designed to solve connectivity issues for billions of devices in the coming decade (de Carvalho Silva et al., 2017). The technology has been evaluated through laboratory and field tests to assess its link-level performance, as well as simulations to analyze system level capacity in multi gateway networks (Feltrin et al., 2022). LoRaWAN's characteristics make it a strong candidate for addressing IoT challenges and obstacles, supporting a wide range of applications (Ibrahim, 2019). As IoT continues to grow rapidly, LoRaWAN is positioned to play a significant role in its development.

As the IoT ecosystem continues its rapid expansion, LoRaWAN is expected to play a pivotal role in its evolution. However, simply increasing the volume of data collected related to the asset does not inherently resolve all logistical issues. As noted by Balfaqih et al. (2023), significant challenges persist regarding data security, immutability, trustworthiness, and information sharing within multi-party vaccine distribution networks. In this context, it is essential that asset stakeholders, including manufacturers, shippers, healthcare facilities and regulators can trust that environmental condition data has not been tampered with and accurately reflects the handling history of each shipment, particularly when determining liability for spoilage or verifying vaccine potency (Balfaqih et al., 2023).

To address the issues of data transparency, security, immutability, and integrity, Distributed Ledger Technologies (DLTs) such as blockchain have been proposed for supply chain management, as suggested by Zichichi et al. (2020). By storing records in a decentralized, tamper-evident ledger, DLTs can ensure that no single party can alter the history of conditions or handoffs in the supply chain (Zichichi et al., 2020). In the vaccine context, this means temperature readings and custody events can be recorded immutably, providing an audit trail for regulators and enabling rapid root cause analysis of any excursion. Blockchain pilots in food and pharmaceutical supply chains, like using Hyperledger or Ethereum-based solutions, have demonstrated improved traceability and recall efficiency (Dash et al., 2024; Gaynor et al., 2024). However, traditional blockchains often come with drawbacks such as transaction fees, limited scalability, and confirmation latency, which may be problematic when handling the high frequency of IoT sensor data (Makhdoom et al., 2018; Song et al., 2018). An alternative DLT particularly suited for IoT applications is IOTA and its Tangle architecture (Rhee & Lee, 2024; Zichichi et al., 2020). IOTA's Tangle is a directed acyclic graph (DAG) ledger that permits feeless transactions validated in a decentralized manner, achieving high scalability and low power usage (Quintero, 2019; Shabandri & Maheshwari, 2019). Rather than requiring miners and incurring fees, each device that submits an IOTA transaction also helps validate others, making it attractive for the massive data volumes that billions of IoT devices can generate, as described by Pullo et al. (2024). By leveraging IOTA, an IoT-based cold-chain monitoring system can continuously write sensor data to a tamper proof ledger without the cost overhead of fees or the throughput bottlenecks of a typical blockchain (Shabandri & Maheshwari, 2019).

This research explores an integrated approach to improve perishable asset management by digitalizing cold-chain logistics, with a focus on vaccine logistics, through the combination of IoT sensing, LoRaWAN communication technology, and the IOTA distributed ledger. While existing solutions proposed in the literature aim to digitalize perishable asset management, many of them face critical limitations, such as high costs, lack of accessibility and scalability, and technical barriers which hinder widespread implementation. Our proposed solution addresses these gaps by employing wireless environmental sensors, low-power long-range communication (LoRaWAN), and IOTA's Tangle to create a real time, trustworthy, and cost effective monitoring system. The aim is to enhance the cold-chain by enabling affordable real-time monitoring of temperature and conditions for quick response to excursions, ensuring end-to-end traceability with immutable data recording, and improving stakeholder trust and regulatory compliance through automated logging and reporting. By addressing both data visibility and security while overcoming the limitations of current solutions, our approach seeks to reduce vaccine spoilage, improve accountability, and ultimately bolster confidence in immunization programs.

2 Literature Review

The digitalization of cold chain management is becoming increasingly necessary due to the complex challenges in maintaining precise temperature control for perishable goods, particularly in the pharmaceutical industry (Shashi, 2022). Cold Chain 4.0 integrates digital and sustainable technologies to address these challenges, improving supply chain efficiency and sustainability. The implementation of IoT, DTLs, Cloud computing and robotic process automation (RPA) in cold-chain logistics can significantly reduce data processing time, enhance shipment tracking, and provide immediate notifications for abnormal situations (Lam & Tang, 2023).

2.1 Digitalization in Supply Chain Management

Digitalization in supply chain management (SCM) refers to the integration of digital technologies such as the IoT, cloud computing, big data analytics, blockchain, artificial intelligence (AI), and advanced robotic into every stage of the supply chain, from procurement and production through distribution to the end customer. Rather than simply automating individual tasks, digitalization transforms supply chains into interconnected, data driven networks that enable real-time visibility, enhanced collaboration among trading partners, and rapid, informed decision making (Bigliardi et al., 2022; Büyüközkan & Göçer, 2018).

One of the earliest frameworks for a Digital Supply Chain (DSC) highlights key enablers including IoT sensors for real-time asset tracking, cloud platforms for scalable data storage and sharing, and analytics engines to extract actionable insights from high volume, heterogeneous data streams (Büyüközkan & Göçer, 2018). By deploying IoT devices such as RFID tags and environmental sensors, companies can continuously monitor inventory levels, location, and condition data like temperature and humidity throughout transit and storage, reducing losses and ensuring product integrity, especially for perishables and pharmaceuticals (Taghipour et al., 2022; Oliveira, 2024). Moreover, cloud computing provides the infrastructure to aggregate and process these data streams, enabling dashboards and alert systems that light up deviations from pre-set thresholds and trigger automated remediation workflows (Agrawal & Narain, 2018).

Blockchain and DTL technologies address the long-standing challenge of trust in multi-party supply chains by creating an immutable, shared record of transactions and handoffs. In a DSC context, each IoT-captured event like temperature reading or custody transfer, can be anchored as a transaction on a permissioned ledger, ensuring that no single party can tamper with recorded data without detection (Taghipour et al., 2022). Smart contracts which are a self-executing code deployed on the ledger, can further automate conditional workflows, reducing administrative overhead and disputes (Taghipour et al., 2022).

Big data analytics and AI bring the predictive and prescriptive layers to a digital supply chain. By applying machine learning algorithms to historical and real-time data, organizations can forecast demand more accurately, optimize inventory placements, and simulate what-if scenarios to identify optimal routing or production plans under different constraints (Bigliardi et al., 2022; Oliveira, 2024).

Together, these technologies create a seamless digital supply chain system. They give businesses full transparency at every step, strengthen reliability, boost responsiveness, and streamline operations. This is especially critical for cold-chain logistics where temperature control is vital. Early adopters are already seeing measurable results including less product waste, fewer inventory gaps, quicker order fulfillment, and improved customer experiences. These outcomes make it clear that digital transformation has moved from being optional to essential in today's supply chain landscape (Büyüközkan & Göçer, 2018; Oliveira, 2024; Łukasiewicz, 2019).

2.2 *Vaccine Cold-Chain Management and Its Challenges*

Effective vaccine cold-chain management is critical to ensuring the potency, efficacy, and safety of vaccines from production to administration. The vaccine cold chain encompasses a coordinated system of storage, transportation, and handling processes, designed to maintain vaccines within specific temperature ranges, commonly between 2 °C and 8 °C, though certain vaccines require ultra-low temperatures (Hanson et al., 2017; Kitamura et al., 2018). Despite significant advances, maintaining vaccine integrity throughout this chain remains complex, particularly in resource-limited countries.

Temperature excursions, both freezing and overheating, present the most significant challenges within vaccine cold-chain management. Exposure to freezing temperatures is particularly harmful, causing irreversible damage to sensitive vaccines such as those containing aluminum adjuvants, hepatitis B, and diphtheria-tetanus-pertussis (DTP) vaccines (Kartoglu & Milstien, 2014; Pajić et al., 2024). Hanson et al. demonstrated through extensive literature review that freezing incidents persist as a significant issue, affecting between 14 and 35% of vaccines at different points in the supply chain, predominantly due to improper packing of ice packs and mismanagement in refrigeration (Hanson et al., 2017). Similarly, Kitamura et al.'s assessment in Lao PDR highlighted temperature excursions outside recommended ranges occurring at provincial and district levels, demonstrating systemic weaknesses particularly pronounced at the periphery of distribution networks (Kitamura et al., 2018).

The suitability and functionality of cold chain equipment also pose critical barriers. Inadequate infrastructure, such as often outdated or improperly maintained refrigeration units, has been documented as a recurring challenge across various global contexts. For example, Ashok et al. reported that many refrigeration units in resource-limited areas frequently failed under extreme environmental conditions, these problems exacerbated by unreliable electricity supplies, poor maintenance culture, and difficulty accessing spare parts (Ashok et al., 2017). Pambudi et al. emphasized that reliability of the energy supply directly affects the quality of vaccine storage, thus advocating the integration of solar-powered refrigeration systems in remote and energy-insecure locations to mitigate these risks (Pambudi et al., 2022).

Proper temperature monitoring throughout the vaccine cold chain is essential but is often inadequately performed. Kartoglu and Milstien discussed traditional manual temperature monitoring methods as insufficient and error-prone, leading to undetected temperature deviations and subsequent vaccine spoilage (Kartoglu & Mistein, 2014). The introduction of vaccine vial monitors (VVM) significantly improved heat-exposure monitoring by providing a visible cumulative heat-exposure indicator directly in vaccine vials (Kartoglu & Mistein, 2014; Kartoglu & Ames, 2022). However, despite their utility, VVMs do not address freezing issues, which requires additional monitoring tools such as freeze indicators or electronic continuous temperature monitoring devices (Kartoglu & Ames, 2022; Kumru et al., 2014). Kartoglu and Ames reinforced the need for comprehensive temperature monitoring strategies, highlighting the critical role of electronic data loggers in detecting temperature excursions promptly and allowing corrective actions to preserve the integrity of the vaccine (Kumru et al., 2014).

Human factors and operational practices further compound vaccine cold chain challenges. The cross-sectional study by Erassa et al. in Ethiopia underscored that inadequate training and knowledge among healthcare personnel significantly increased the likelihood of cold chain mismanagement, including improper use of cooling equipment and inadequate recording and analysis of temperature logs (Erassa et al., 2023). This study found that only 61% of the facilities maintained adequate cold chain practices, directly correlated with the experience and training of healthcare workers (Erassa et al., 2023).

Transportation logistics, particularly the last mile delivery, poses substantial risks to the integrity of the vaccine due to variable and often challenging environmental and infrastructure conditions. Hasanat et al. developed an IoT-based real-time monitoring system to mitigate these issues by continuously tracking the temperature, humidity and GPS location of vaccine shipments, providing alerts upon detection of deviations. The study highlighted the potential of IoT to dramatically improve oversight and responsiveness in cold chain logistics (Hasanat et al., 2020). However, the broad implementation of such advanced monitoring solutions faces significant challenges, including limited connectivity, higher initial costs, and infrastructure demands, particularly in low-resource settings (Hasanat et al., 2020).

Future demands on the cold chain of vaccines are expected to increase with the growing complexity of vaccine formulations, including those that require ultra-cold chain conditions such as COVID-19 mRNA vaccines, further intensifying existing challenges (Ashok et al., 2017; Hanson et al., 2017). To address these increasing requirements comprehensively, a multidimensional approach is crucial integrating technological innovations, infrastructure improvements, workforce capacity building, and robust monitoring practices.

2.3 *IoT in Logistics and Cold-Chain Applications*

The integration of IoT technologies within logistics, particularly in cold chain management, has emerged as a transformative approach to ensuring the integrity, quality and traceability of perishable goods, notably vaccines and pharmaceuticals. IoT applications in logistics encompass sensor-based monitoring, real-time data analytics, and intelligent control systems designed to mitigate risks associated with temperature-sensitive supply chains (Katoch, 2022; Mohsin & Yellampalli, 2017; Salunkhe & Nerkar, 2016).

At its core, IoT enhances logistics by enabling the collection, processing and sharing of extensive data from various points within the supply chain. This real-time data-driven approach significantly improves operational transparency and enables a rapid response to anomalies (Mohsin & Yellampalli, 2017; Sarkar et al., 2022). For example, Mohsin and Yellampalli (2017) demonstrate the effectiveness of IoT in monitoring critical parameters such as temperature and humidity in pharmaceutical logistics, thus preventing spoilage and ensuring regulatory compliance through immediate anomaly detection and automated alerts (Mohsin & Yellampalli, 2017).

In vaccine logistics, IoT is increasingly critical given the stringent requirements for temperature management. Recent literature underscores the potential of the Internet of Things to drastically reduce vaccine wastage due to temperature deviations. Verma Pargaien et al. (2021) present a data-centric monitoring system using IoT technologies that include RFID, Wi-Fi, Bluetooth, and GPS to maintain vaccine integrity during transit. Their study emphasizes that IoT can significantly improve the traceability and responsiveness in real time of vaccine distribution, which is essential in pandemic conditions such as COVID-19 (Verma Pargaien et al., 2021).

Halim et al. (2021) propose an integrated IoT and blockchain architecture to manage vaccine logistics, emphasizing improved transparency, accountability, and trust across the supply chain. This integration enables secure, tamper-proof records of temperature conditions, significantly improving reliability and efficiency during critical vaccine distributions, especially in remote or resource-limited regions (Halim et al., 2021).

The COVID-19 pandemic has further underscored the importance of IoT in managing cold chains due to the unprecedented logistical challenges it presented. Kumar et al. (2024) examined the implementation of IoT in vaccine supply chains in India, highlighting that IoT improved supply chain performance by addressing issues related to demand forecasting, real-time monitoring, and inventory management. Their findings indicate that adoption of IoT positively impacts both operational efficiency and compliance with public health guidelines.

In addition, the role of the Internet of Things extends beyond the simple monitoring of temperature to encompass comprehensive environmental monitoring systems, including humidity, gas emissions, and even lighting conditions, all critical for sensitive products. Sarkar et al. (2022) developed an IoT-enabled monitoring system capable of detecting methane emissions from perishable spoiled goods and alerting users in real time, significantly improving the overall environmental and operational safety of the cold supply chain.

Elngar et al. (2023) emphasize IoT's contribution to enhancing vaccine cold chains specifically within educational institutions. They deployed IoT sensors and smart controllers to monitor temperature conditions within vaccine containers, with real-time alerts and cloud-based data visualization tools enabling proactive management. Their system achieved remarkable accuracy, underscoring IoT's potential for broad-scale adoption to safeguard public health.

Furthermore, the integration of IoT with Artificial Intelligence (AI) has led to the development of responsive and sustainable vaccine supply chains. Goodarzian et al. (2023) introduced an innovative IoT-AI hybrid model, incorporating responsive, green practices for COVID-19 vaccine distribution. This comprehensive approach simultaneously addresses environmental sustainability, waste management, and demand coverage, providing a robust framework for future logistics operations.

LoRaWAN has emerged as an effective communication protocol to support IoT applications in logistics, particularly cold-chain management. LoRaWAN technology stands out due to its extensive range, low power consumption, scalability, and cost-effectiveness, making it particularly suitable for tracking and monitoring logistics operations across geographically dispersed or resource-constrained environments. Bonilla et al. (2023) highlight that LoRaWAN sensors are highly adaptable and widely used in logistics and environmental monitoring due to their flexibility and low implementation cost.

Recent studies illustrate LoRaWAN's practical applications within cold-chain logistics. Redondo and Coutinho (2024) presented a LoRa-based monitoring solution specifically tailored to cold-chain transportation, demonstrating how real-time data transmission through LoRaWAN significantly improved monitoring accuracy and response times to temperature deviations, thereby reducing product spoilage and enhancing logistic efficiency. Similarly, Prayudi et al. (2024) integrated LoRaWAN with blockchain technology to develop a secure, transparent, and immutable monitoring system for refrigerated transport, further emphasizing LoRaWAN's capability to enhance data security and integrity within cold-chain logistics.

Overall, the adoption of IoT technologies, complemented by LoRaWAN communication protocols, represents a significant advancement toward sustainable asset management and operational resilience. This integration facilitates enhanced data visibility, rapid responsiveness, reduced wastage, improved regulatory compliance, and ultimately ensures greater assurance of product integrity throughout the supply chain.

2.4 Blockchain and IOTA Technologies in Supply Chains and Vaccine Cold-Chains

Blockchain technology has significantly reshaped the landscape of supply chain management by providing enhanced transparency, traceability, and security. It functions through distributed ledger technology (DLT), enabling secure and tamper-resistant recording of transactions across a network. By decentralizing data storage and verification processes, blockchain offers significant advantages over traditional, centralized supply chain systems, including reduced fraud, increased efficiency, and improved trust among stakeholders (Rejeb et al., 2019; Singh et al., 2020).

Rejeb et al. (2019) highlighted that blockchain, when combined with IoT technologies, significantly enhances supply chain transparency, allowing for accurate tracking and tracing of products throughout the supply chain. This capability is critical in sectors where product authenticity and integrity are paramount, such as pharmaceuticals and food supply chains. Singh et al. (2020) further reinforced this point, proposing a blockchain integrated IoT model specifically aimed at addressing temperature control and counterfeit drug prevention, essential for pharmaceutical supply chains.

Vaccine supply chains pose unique challenges, notably related to temperature sensitivity, counterfeit vaccines, and distribution inefficiencies. Recent literature underscores blockchain's role in addressing these issues. Yong et al. (2020) introduced an intelligent blockchain-based system tailored for vaccine supply chains, which included features such as vaccine traceability, smart contracts for transaction automation, and machine learning for predictive analytics. These elements together improve vaccine safety, reducing the risk of expiration and fraud in the vaccine distribution process.

Similarly, Hu et al. (2023) presented an integrated intelligent system utilizing blockchain, IoT, and machine learning specifically to manage vaccine supply chains during the COVID-19 pandemic. The authors found that blockchain technology notably enhanced transparency among stakeholders, allowing for secure, immutable, and real-time monitoring of vaccines. The integration of machine learning provided capabilities for accurate demand forecasting and sentiment analysis, significantly improving operational efficiency and trust in vaccine management.

Blockchain has also been pivotal in improving vaccine efficacy tracking and reducing vaccine wastage. Sharmila et al. (2022) emphasized blockchain's potential to provide immutable vaccine records, significantly reducing the risks associated with counterfeit vaccines. The blockchain-powered system allows stakeholders to verify vaccine authenticity and efficacy securely and transparently, reducing vaccine wastage and improving overall distribution effectiveness.

Integrating blockchain technology with IoT presents a robust solution to vaccine cold chain management. Vargis et al. (2022) conducted a scoping analysis demonstrating the benefits of blockchain and IoT integration for real-time temperature and moisture monitoring within vaccine cold chains. This integrated approach ensures vaccine efficacy throughout transit by leveraging IoT sensors and secure blockchain transactions, providing transparent, verifiable, and real-time data to stakeholders.

While blockchain addresses many supply chain management concerns, scalability remains a key challenge, especially for high-volume applications involving numerous IoT devices. IOTA, a novel distributed ledger technology designed specifically for IoT applications, offers a promising solution to these scalability issues. Unlike traditional blockchains, IOTA uses a structure known as Tangle, a Directed Acyclic Graph (DAG) allowing fee-free transactions, enhanced scalability, and efficient data handling for IoT environments (Silvano & Marcelino, 2020; Al-shaikhli et al. 2022).

Alshaikhli et al. (2022) described IOTA as a next generation blockchain alternative tailored explicitly for IoT environments, significantly overcoming traditional blockchain limitations such as high transaction fees and scalability constraints. Its unique design facilitates unlimited scalability, essential for supporting extensive IoT networks in complex supply chains, such as vaccine distribution systems, without compromising performance or security.

Silvano and Marcelino (2020) reinforced the potential of IOTA Tangle technology, highlighting its suitability for IoT-based supply chains. The absence of transaction fees and the capability for high scalability position IOTA as particularly advantageous for managing extensive IoT deployments in cold chain logistics, providing efficient, cost-effective and secure transaction processing. Compared with traditional blockchain frameworks such as Ethereum and Hyperledger, which have demonstrated strong performance in auditability and traceability, IOTA provides a more lightweight and cost-efficient architecture for continuous IoT telemetry. Conventional blockchains rely on sequential block validation and often incur transaction fees, consensus delays, and substantial energy costs that make them unsuitable for high-frequency sensor data. In contrast, IOTA's Directed Acyclic Graph (Tangle) allows parallel validation and feeless transactions, enabling real-time data anchoring from large numbers of IoT devices without congestion or additional cost (Haque et al., 2024; Villafranca et al., 2025). This makes IOTA particularly suited for scenarios such as vaccine cold-chain monitoring, where numerous low-power sensors transmit frequent updates requiring both scalability and immutability.

From all the literature related to blockchain and IOTA technology clearly we can find that integrating blockchain and IOTA technologies offers substantial advancements for managing complex and sensitive supply chains, particularly vaccine cold chains. Their combined strengths address critical challenges such as transparency, scalability, security, and trust, significantly improving the management of perishable and sensitive assets within global supply chains. Recent research has further expanded these technological foundations into integrated "Digital Supply Chain 4.0" frameworks that combine IoT, artificial intelligence, and distributed-ledger technologies to build resilient, data-driven logistics networks (Alfaqiyah et al., 2025). The COVID-19 pandemic served as a catalyst for adopting IoT-enabled visibility in vaccine distribution, underscoring the need for real-time tracking and condition management (Ali & Khan, 2023). In parallel, work on IoT-enabled cold-chain frameworks for vaccines has matured, showing how sensor networks and connectivity solutions can enhance monitoring, traceability, and performance in low-resource settings (Jiang et al., 2024). Together, these advances show a clear evolution toward more intelligent, adaptive supply chains. Our study situates its IOTA–LoRaWAN-based architecture within this emerging context, offering a practical and interoperable solution for vaccine-cold-chain transparency and scalability.

2.5 Gap in Current Systems and Literature

The existing body of literature extensively explores IoT and blockchain applications in supply chain and cold-chain logistics, offering solutions to improve traceability, transparency, and security (Hu et al., 2023; Kartoglu & Ames, 2022; Mohsin & Yellampalli, 2017; Verma Pargaien et al., 2021). While IoT driven systems effectively enable real-time monitoring and data collection from various points within supply chains, a substantial number of these solutions rely on centralized databases or internal servers for data storage (Erassa et al., 2023; Kitamura et al., 2018). This centralized approach introduces risks related to data security, vulnerability to tampering, and a lack of immutable records, potentially leading to mistrust among stakeholders (Rejeb et al., 2019; Singh et al., 2020).

Recent studies incorporating blockchain technology significantly mitigate some of these issues by providing immutable and secure transaction records. However, traditional blockchain solutions present inherent limitations, including high transaction fees, mining dependency, scalability constraints, and delayed transaction confirmations, which can hinder practical implementation in high-throughput IoT environments (Alshaikhli et al., 2022; Silvano & Marcelino, 2020). In addition, conventional blockchain platforms often incur substantial operational and maintenance costs, particularly problematic for applications that require extensive device integration and continuous data collection (Yong et al., 2020).

In addressing these gaps, our proposed system leverages Directed Acyclic Graph (DAG) technology, specifically IOTA's Tangle, instead of traditional blockchain. IOTA offers a distinct advantage, characterized by free transactions, no dependency on miners, enhanced scalability, and rapid transaction confirmations, making it highly suitable for IoT-intensive applications such as vaccine cold-chain logistics (Hu et al., 2023; Sharmila et al., 2022).

Furthermore, many current IoT logistics solutions rely heavily on LTE or Wi-Fi connectivity, which is often unavailable or unreliable in remote or mobile vaccine distribution scenarios (Bonilla et al., 2023). To overcome this critical communication challenge, our system incorporates LoRaWAN technology. LoRaWAN provides low power consumption, extensive range coverage, and robust connectivity even in areas without traditional network infrastructure, thereby ensuring uninterrupted real-time data transmission and monitoring (Prayudi et al., 2024; Redondo & Coutinho, 2024).

Finally, existing IoT blockchain systems are often associated with considerable initial setup and operational costs, limiting their widespread adoption, particularly in regions with limited resources (Vargis et al., 2022). In contrast, our proposed integrated approach significantly reduces these costs, making it feasible and sustainable for broad implementation in diverse logistical contexts.

A notable gap in the existing literature is the absence of integrated frameworks that simultaneously combine IoT sensing, LoRaWAN long-range communication, and a feeless DAG-based ledger such as IOTA within a single cold-chain monitoring solution. While prior studies have explored IoT–blockchain architectures or IoT–LoRaWAN systems independently, few have brought all three technologies together to address visibility, connectivity, and data integrity in one coherent framework. The synergy of these components enables continuous environmental monitoring, transmission over long distances with minimal power consumption, and tamper-proof anchoring of data on a decentralized ledger. This combination directly targets several persistent weaknesses in vaccine logistics, limited connectivity in remote areas, reliance on manual logs, and susceptibility to data manipulation, yet remains under-explored in contemporary research. Our work addresses this gap by proposing and validating a unified architecture that operationalizes all three layers in a practical cold chain use case.

3 Methodology and System Architecture

This research adopts a Design Science Research (DSR) approach, following structured guidelines such as those described by Venable et al. (2017), to design, build, and evaluate an IoT-based solution for vaccine cold-chain monitoring. The objective is to achieve continuous environmental sensing, long-range and energy-efficient communication, and tamper-proof data logging to increase transparency and operational reliability. The system is organized using a layered architecture inspired by the semantic modeling principles discussed in Ordieres-Mere and Ortega-Mier (2024), which emphasize consistent data conceptualization across complex industrial processes (Fig. 2).

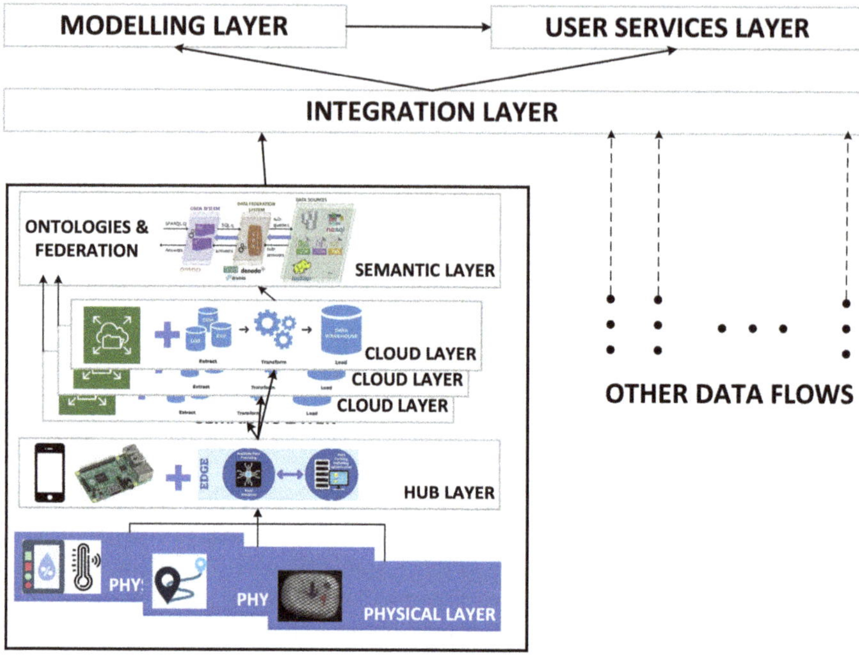

Fig. 2 Adopted framework

The architecture spans from physical devices at the bottom to user-facing applications and analytics at the top. Each layer has a distinct role but interacts seamlessly with its neighboring components. The key layers include:

Physical Layer. This layer consists of the sensors and hardware that directly measure environmental parameters. In our prototype, temperature, humidity, and atmospheric pressure sensors are placed with vaccine payloads and generate readings at regular intervals.

Hub Layer. Intermediary microcontrollers collect sensor readings and perform lightweight preprocessing. For instance, the hub may apply basic filtering, compute simple aggregates (such as minimum or maximum temperature), or format data prior to transmission. Our implementation uses an ESP32-based device with WiFi, Bluetooth, and LoRaWAN capabilities, which also buffers data when connectivity is temporarily unavailable.

Network/Communication Layer. This layer is responsible for long-range, energy-efficient transmission of data from the hub to the cloud. LoRaWAN was selected because it provides multi-kilometer range, low energy consumption, and reliable performance in both urban and remote settings. Although LoRaWAN supports only low data rates, the compact nature of environmental telemetry makes it well suited for this application. Uplink frames are encrypted using LoRaWAN's AES-128 keys, which protects the payload against eavesdropping and prevents unauthorised devices from injecting bogus messages into the network. Sensor packets are transmitted through public networks (e.g., The Things Network) or private gateways deployed by health authorities.

Cloud Layer. Once data reach the Internet, they are processed by cloud-based services. An event-driven server subscribes to the LoRaWAN MQTT feed and receives packets in real time over secure MQTT/TLS channels. The server decodes each payload, extracts the raw telemetry, and associates it with the device identifier provided by the LoRaWAN network (*DevEUI*). The semantic transformation is delegated to the dedicated Semantic Layer described below, ensuring a modular design.

Each device's DevEUI is mapped during registration to a Decentralized Identifier (DID) linked to an IOTA wallet containing its public–private key pair. When a new reading is processed, the JSON-LD payload is signed with the device's private key (Fig. 3). Any stakeholder can verify authenticity using the DID document and the corresponding public key. The signed payload is then recorded to the IOTA Tangle, creating an immutable, tamper-resistant history of measurements (Fig. 4). A parallel copy is written to a time-series database to support dashboards and alerting (Fig. 5). Only environmental variables (e.g., temperature, humidity, pressure), time stamps, and device identifiers are stored on the public ledger; no personal or patient-level information is transmitted or anchored, which reduces privacy risks even though the ledger is globally accessible.

Because IOTA validates transactions in parallel and operates without fees, the system can ingest rapid telemetry updates from many devices without increased latency or operational cost.

Semantic Layer. The Semantic Layer attaches contextual meaning to the raw sensor measurements before they are permanently stored on the ledger. This is the layer that transforms numeric readings into structured information that external systems can reliably interpret.

Using standardized vocabularies such as SOSA/SSN for observations and QUDT for units, the layer annotates each reading with machine-understandable descriptors. These may include the observed property (e.g., temperature), unit of measurement, time of observation, the sensor that produced it, and, when applicable, its relation to logistic context such as shipment ID, location, or whether the asset is "in transit" or "in storage." This transforms the data from isolated measurements into meaningful, query available information elements.

An example of a semantically enriched JSON-LD record is shown below:

```
{
"@context": {
```

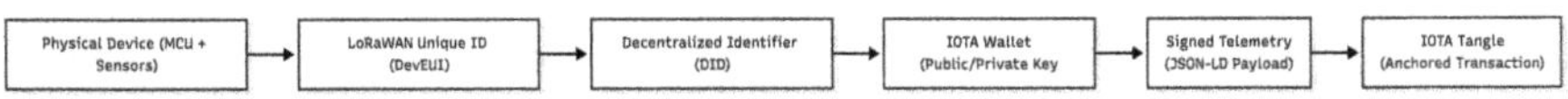

Fig. 3 Identity chain flow

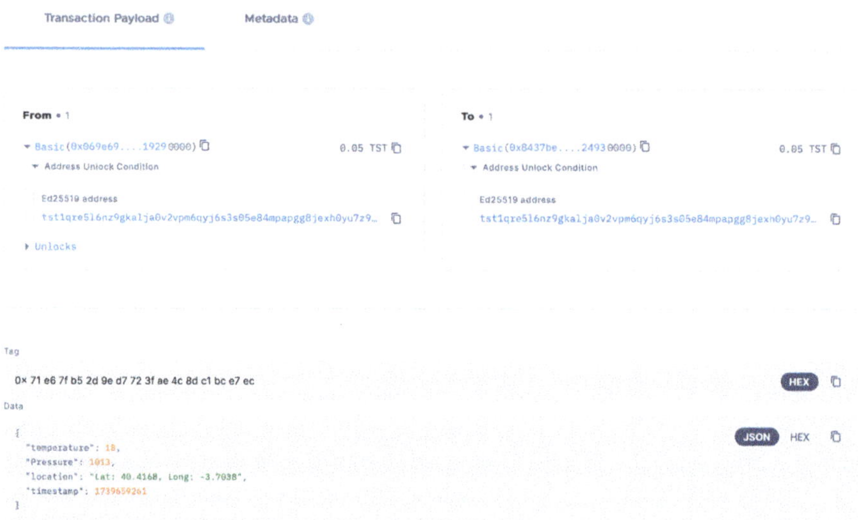

Fig. 4 IOTA explorer

```
"sosa": "http://www.w3.org/ns/sosa/",
"qudt": "http://qudt.org/schema/qudt/",
"unit": "http://qudt.org/vocab/unit/",
"geo": "http://www.w3.org/2003/01/geo/wgs84_pos#"
},
"sosa:madeBySensor": "did:iota:tst1qre516n2gk...",
"sosa:observedProperty": "sosa:Temperature",
"sosa:resultTime": "2025-11-11T14:31:01Z",
"sosa:hasResult": {
"sosa:hasSimpleResult": 18,
"qudt:unit": "unit:DEG_C"
},
"geo:lat": 40.4168,
"geo:long": -3.7038
}
```

In deployments where a single microcontroller aggregates multiple sensors, one DID can represent the entire device. Individual sensor readings are distinguished using semantic descriptors such as `sosa:observedProperty` or custom tags (e.g., sensor channel or position).

Because this structure complies with widely recognized semantic standards, any external information system capable of reading JSON-LD can immediately interpret and integrate it without custom adapters or translation layers. In our prototype, these semantic annotations were implemented in a lightweight manner: each reading was linked to the device's DID, a simple batch identifier used during the tests, and its operational state ("in transit" or "in storage"). While minimal, this structure already improves data organization and traceability. The same mechanism can be extended

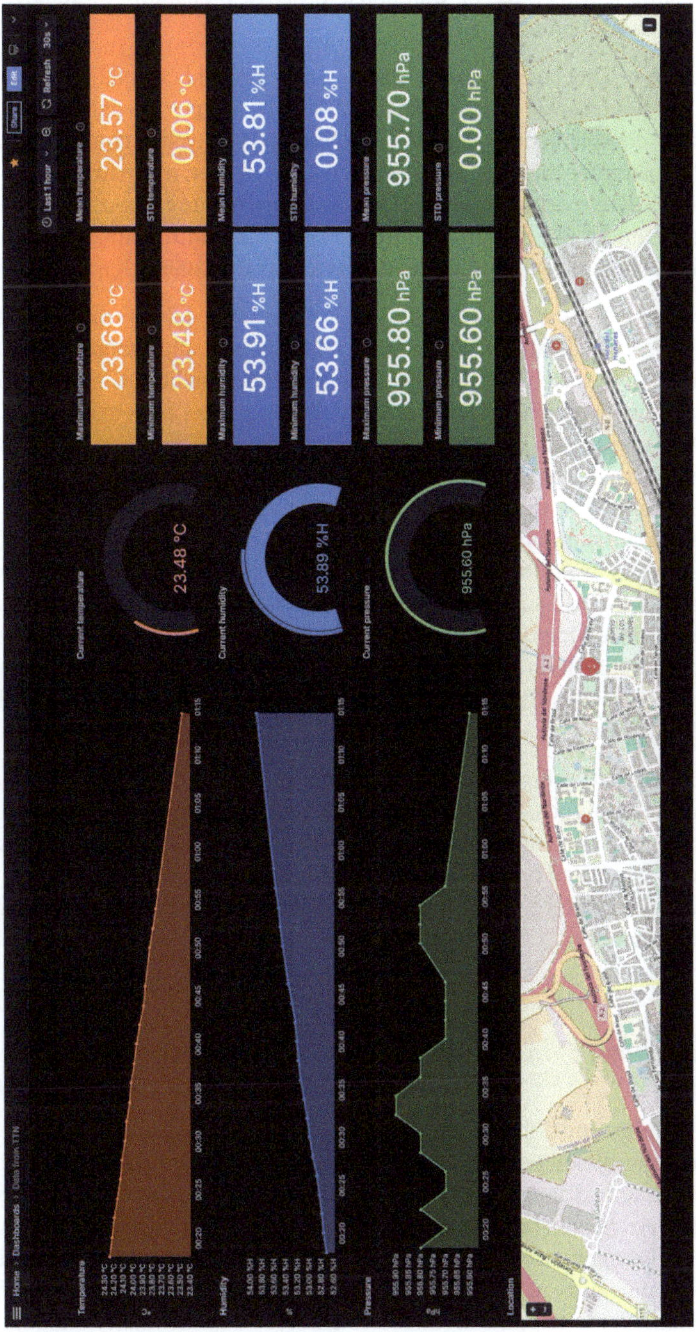

Fig. 5 Data visualization console

in real deployments using richer ontologies to connect measurements with inventory systems, shipment records, or warehouse processes, enabling more advanced analytics and cross-system integration.

Integration Layer. This layer manages data aggregation and correlation with additional contextual information from external or auxiliary sources. It enables the future incorporation of complementary datasets, such as local weather conditions, route data, or traffic patterns, that can be fused with the sensor telemetry to enhance analytics and predictive capabilities. By consolidating heterogeneous data streams within a unified model, the integration layer ensures that information is coherent, quality-checked, and ready for higher-level services and visualization.

User Services Layer. At the top of the architecture, this layer delivers the information to both human users and external systems. It includes web and mobile dashboards (see Fig. 5) that allow stakeholders to visualize real-time conditions, monitor alerts, and verify the authenticity of each measurement through direct links to its transaction identifier (TXID) on the IOTA ledger (see Fig. 4). Because the data stored on the ledger follow a semantically defined JSON-LD structure, interoperability is achieved natively, thus external platforms, such as national vaccine management systems, regulatory dashboards, or supply-chain applications, can consume these standardized datasets directly from the IOTA Tangle through public APIs. Thus, all parties access the same verifiable and machine-understandable information without the need for bespoke data conversions or centralized intermediaries. This layer therefore represents the practical realization of transparency and interoperability, allowing both end users and partner systems to trust, interpret, and integrate the same decentralized data stream in real time.

Modelling Layer. Operating parallel to user-facing services, the Modeling Layer supports advanced analytics. Although outside the main scope of our prototype, this layer can host prediction models, anomaly detection, or optimization algorithms that learn from the accumulated historical data. Over time, these models can support route planning, equipment failure prediction, and risk assessment to further strengthen supply-chain resilience.

3.1 Architectural Consideration

This layered architecture follows modern IoT design principles: sensors are kept simple and energy-efficient; communication is optimized for long-range low-power operation; semantic and integration processes are centralized for consistency; and user-facing services remain flexible and system-agnostic. The modularity also makes it easy to replace components as technology evolves, for instance, integrating satellite IoT or 5G communication in the future without redesigning the entire system. From a data-protection perspective, the architecture enforces confidentiality and integrity at several points along the path. LoRaWAN encryption protects radio transmissions, MQTT/TLS secures the connection between the network server and the cloud backend, and digital signatures on JSON-LD payloads ensure that any modification of records anchored to the IOTA Tangle is detectable. Because the system records only environmental telemetry and device-level identifiers on the public ledger, it is compatible with strict privacy regulations; any future integration with patient or clinic information can be handled through separate, access-controlled systems that query the telemetry rather than exposing sensitive data directly.

4 Proposed IoT-IOTA Monitoring System

Based on the layered architecture described in Sect. 3, we developed a tangible prototype to validate the feasibility, functionality, and end-to-end integration of the proposed approach. Whereas Sect. 3 outlined the conceptual and methodological design of the system, this section presents its practical realization through hardware components, sensing firmware, communication modules, and cloud-side processing. The following subsections demonstrate how each architectural layer, physical sensing, hub processing, LoRaWAN communication, semantic enrichment, and IOTA anchoring, was instantiated in a working prototype, forming the case study used for evaluation.

We implemented this prototype using a hardware setup consisting of the following key components (see Fig. 6 for a labelled photograph of the device):

4.1 System Components and Hardware

Wireless Sensor. We employed a high accuracy RuuviTag sensor, which is a small Bluetooth low energy device (BLE) capable of measuring temperature, relative humidity, air pressure, and motion. It operates reliably between − 20 and + 70 °C and comes in an IP67-rated enclosure. RuuviTag was chosen for its precision and long battery life (approximately 12–24 months in a coin cell), which is vital for continuous monitoring during vaccine distribution. In a deployment, one or more RuuviTags would be placed inside each vaccine container or shipping box to capture the ambient conditions around the vaccines (see Fig. 6(1)).

Microcontroller and Hub (ESP32 board). To collect data from the BLE sensor and forward them via LoRaWAN, we used a Heltec WiFi LoRa 32 development board. This board is built around an ESP32 microcontroller that provides WiFi and BLE connectivity and an onboard LoRa transceiver (Semtech SX1276). The board also includes an OLED display for local status information and ample memory (520 KB SRAM, 8 MB flash) for our application code. As illustrated in Fig. 7, the ESP32 acts as a bridge, periodically scanning for RuuviTag's BLE broadcasts to

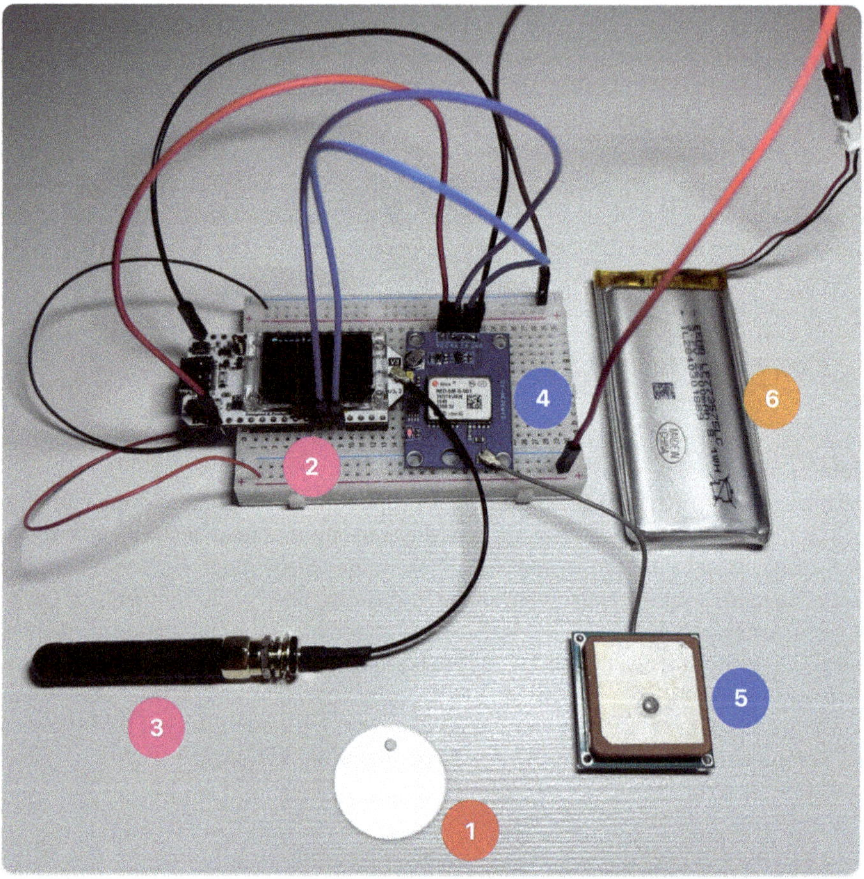

Fig. 6 Prototype IoT monitoring device for vaccine cold-chain monitoring. Labels: (1) RuuviTag BLE environmental sensor, (2) Heltec ESP32 LoRa hub, (3) LoRaWAN antenna, (4) NEO-6 M GPS module, (5) GPS antenna, (6) Li-Po battery pack

retrieve environmental sensor data (e.g. temperature, humidity) while simultaneously acquiring GPS coordinates from the NE06MV2 receiver. Processes these data by calculating metrics such as maximum, minimum or standard deviation (std), filtering GPS outliers, and then packages the refined data set with a timestamp and device ID (DID) into a LoRaWAN message for transmission. The low-power features of the ESP32 are utilized to conserve battery when not actively transmitting or scanning. Notably, the Heltec board can also use Wi-Fi if available, but in our scenario, we prioritize LoRaWAN because of its independence from local infrastructure. This entire sensing and transmission workflow is implemented using custom MicroPython firmware developed by our team and made publicly available on GitHub Jordieres (2024) (see Fig. 6(2)).

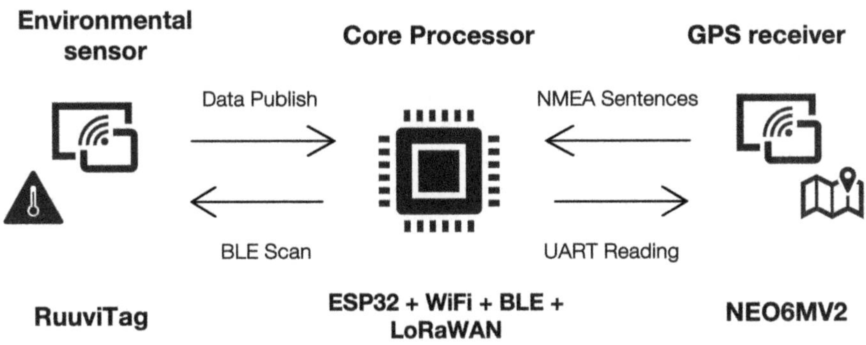

Fig. 7 Data collection workflow executed on the ESP32 hub, including BLE scanning of the RuuviTag, GPS acquisition, local preprocessing (filtering and aggregation), payload encoding, and LoRaWAN transmission

LoRa Module + Antenna. The device takes advantage of the Semtech SX1276 LoRa module, integrated onboard the Heltec ESP32 microcontroller, paired with an external antenna to ensure long-range communication. This combination (module + antenna) significantly extends transmission reach, enabling data delivery to gateways several kilometres away which is a critical capability for tracking moving vaccine shipments in rural areas. The antenna was tuned for region specific frequency bands, and in our tests, the 868 MHz band was used (Europe), though other regions may employ 915 MHz or similar bands as needed (see Fig. 6(2 and 3)).

GPS Module + Antena. To log the geographic location of vaccines, which is important for traceability and to analyse if certain routes or locations are problematic, a GPS receiver module is integrated. We used the NEO-6 M GPS module from u-blox, which can track up to 22 satellites and provides location updates. The GPS antenna is attached to ensure good reception of the satellite signal. The ESP32 reads data from the GPS module through the serial interface concurrently with sensor data; thus, each dataset includes not only environmental parameters but also latitude/longitude coordinates. The NEO-6 M is energy-intensive if run continuously, so our code uses it intelligently, for example, turning it on at set intervals or when movement is detected, to get a location fix, then potentially powering it down to save battery (see Fig. 6(4 and 5)).

Power Source. The entire assembly is powered by a rechargeable lithium-polymer battery (Li-Po) (3.7 V, 2200 mAh). This battery capacity was chosen to allow multiple days of operation without recharging, assuming a transmission interval on the order of minutes and the use of low power modes. In our design, this battery could be recharged via USB or possibly through a solar panel or vehicle power when available. Power management circuitry ensures stable voltage to the ESP32 and GPS module, and we included battery monitoring so that the device can report its own battery level. This is important information for maintenance and to know when to swap or recharge units (see Fig. 6(6)).

Enclosure. It is worth mentioning that the above parts are assembled on a breadboard for prototyping, but in a real deployment they would be integrated into a compact enclosure. The enclosure should be durable, waterproof, shock resistant and capable of maintaining a signal made of plastic or another RF-transparent material. It might also include insulation if it needs to be inside a very cold environment for long periods, also for ultra-cold chain, one might keep electronics outside the freezer but cabled to inside sensors, given many electronics cannot operate at − 70 °C. For the typical 2–8° C vaccine cold chain, our components function within that range.

4.2 Data Flow

As can be seen in Figs. 7 and 8, the operation of the system follows a cyclical workflow. Initially, the ESP32 hub wakes up from sleep at predefined intervals. Our open-source ESP32-based MicroPython firmware (Jordieres, 2024) reads the latest sensor measurements from the RuuviTag via BLE. ESP32 simultaneously polls the GPS module to get the current location coordinates. The microcontroller processes these data by calculating some metrics and filtering GPS outliers, then integrates these pieces of information by creating a data record. This record is then encoded into a compact format suitable for LoRaWAN transmission which often is just a few bytes after applying scaling and offsets to numerical values to minimize payload size. The device then transmits this payload over the LoRa radio.

On the network side, any LoRaWAN gateway in range will receive the radio packet. The gateway forwards it through the LoRaWAN network server infrastructure. In our implementation, we used The Things Network (TTN), a community/public LoRaWAN server, to handle device communications. The device was registered with TTN (using its unique DevEUI and AppKey), so TTN would authenticate the packet, decrypt it, and then make the data available to our application via MQTT. We set up an MQTT broker client on our cloud server to subscribe to the TTN data feed for our application. Based on our event-driven architecture, as soon as the data arrive, the server triggers a processing function that decodes the payload back into human-readable values, attaches additional metadata, and then performs two crucial actions in parallel.

First, the data are forwarded to our IoT platform (ThingsBoard). This involves calling an API to send the data to the platform's device entry. The platform stores the new data point in its database and updates any relevant real-time dashboards or triggers alerts. For example, if the temperature exceeds a threshold, the platform rule engine could immediately send an SMS or email to administrators.

Simultaneously, the data is formatted as a JSON message and sent to an IOTA node for inclusion in the Tangle. Each device in our system has its own decentralized identifier (DID), which is cryptographically linked to a dedicated digital wallet address on the IOTA network. When sensor data are ready for transmission, they are packaged as a transaction and sent directly to the device's wallet address.

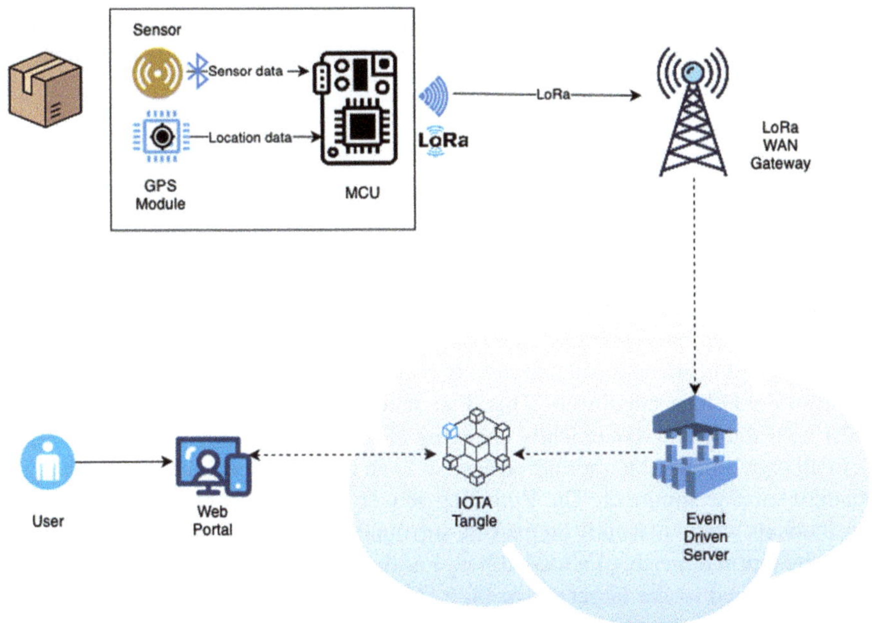

Fig. 8 System-level data flow model showing how sensor readings are collected by the ESP32 hub, transmitted via LoRaWAN, processed in the cloud, semantically annotated, and anchored to the IOTA Tangle

Thanks to the fast and feeless confirmation transactions of IOTA, each data point is recorded as a transaction in the device's wallet history. For example, a temperature reading from a sensor is submitted as a transaction to the wallet of that device, where it becomes permanently and immutably stored in the Tangle (see Fig. 4). This allows any user to review the complete transaction history of the device wallet, effectively providing an auditable trail of all recorded environmental data, such as temperature fluctuations during vaccine transport.

In our prototype, we used a public IOTA Testnet node, with each transaction tagged for easy filtering. Before submission, the server cryptographically signs the data using the device's DID, ensuring authenticity. Since each DID is tied to a specific wallet, the transaction not only proves that the data originated from a trusted device but also automatically organizes them in the immutable ledger of that device.

At this point, the data from one cycle are fully processed and visualized for users and secured in a ledger. The ESP32 then goes back to sleep to conserve power until the next cycle. The cycle time can be adjusted depending on the use case, and our system often used a 5-min interval as a balance.

An important aspect of the methodology was the evaluation under realistic conditions. We tested the system in both controlled environments and semi-controlled real-world scenarios to observe performance. The metrics evaluated included data reliability (packet loss rates), communication range and latency, power consumption/

battery life, and the throughput/latency of writing to the IOTA ledger. The results of these tests are discussed in the next section in context of Results and discussion.

5 Results

To evaluate the performance of the proposed IoT–LoRaWAN–IOTA monitoring system, we conducted three independent 24-h experimental test cycles using two prototype devices. The first device was placed inside a controlled cold room (4–6 °C) to simulate stationary vaccine storage conditions, while the second device was embedded inside an insulated mobile cooler during a delivery route to simulate in-transit cold-chain conditions. This dual-setup allowed us to assess performance under both stable and dynamically changing environments.

In all experiments, the monitored asset was an insulated container representing a standard vaccine shipment. The RuuviTag sensor was placed at the position where vaccine vials would normally be packed, surrounded by foam cushioning to approximate the thermal inertia of a loaded box. For the cold-room scenario, the container was conditioned to the target range (4–6 °C) and then stored on a shelf to reproduce routine vaccine storage. For the mobile scenario, the same container was placed inside a transport cooler and subjected to a typical urban delivery sequence, including loading, vehicle movement, short stops, and handover at the destination. This procedure effectively implements a miniature vaccine cold chain, conditioning, stationary storage, transport, and delivery, providing a realistic context for interpreting the performance metrics reported below.

Each test cycle followed the same operational pattern: the ESP32 hub executed a 5-min sensing and transmission interval, collecting sensor data from the RuuviTag, obtaining GPS coordinates when available, and sending LoRaWAN uplink packets to the gateway. Throughout the experiments, we evaluated packet delivery rate (PDR), communication latency, battery consumption, and LoRaWAN link stability. To validate data integrity, we performed random audits by cross-checking the raw sensor logs from the ESP32's local buffer with the corresponding signed JSON-LD entries stored on the IOTA Tangle. These audits confirmed that the measurements recorded on the ledger matched the original unprocessed sensor values without any discrepancies. The results presented below aggregate the outcomes from all three test cycles and represent both stationary and mobile operating conditions.

The tests mainly focused on data reliability, communication latency, power consumption, and system scalability, all of which are crucial metrics in IoT and logistics applications.

Across all test cycles, LoRaWAN-based communication maintained an average packet delivery rate (PDR) above 95%, despite intermittent signal attenuation in dense urban areas. This performance aligns with previous findings that LoRaWAN can maintain robust long-range connectivity for IoT implementations. Furthermore, each data record was associated with a Decentralized Identifier (DID) before being published on the IOTA Tangle, ensuring tamper evidence and traceability. Random

Table 1 Latency breakdown by processing stage

Stage	Avg (ms)	Contribution (%)
LoRa uplink	1200	40
MQTT forward	~ 800	15
DID + tangle total	< 2000	45
Total	< 6000	100

integrity audits were performed by comparing locally stored raw sensor logs with the corresponding IOTA Tangle entries. In all sampled cases, the signed payloads recorded on the ledger exactly matched the raw readings, confirming that no modification occurred during transmission or storage and validating the tamper-proof properties of the system.

In terms of communication latency as can be seen in Table 1, the interval from sensor data capture to its appearance on the Tangle remained under 6 s for most transmissions. The primary contributors to this latency were the LoRaWAN uplink (1.2–2.5 s) and MQTT-based forwarding (0.8 s), followed by DID attachment and Tangle publication (under 2 s).

These timings meet real-time monitoring needs for various logistics scenarios, particularly those requiring frequent updates on environmental conditions. Regarding battery consumption, nodes powered by 3.7 V, 2200 mAh Li-Po battery consistently operated for roughly 90 days at a 60-min sensing interval, in line with reported low-power capabilities of LoRaWAN, emphasizing the importance of duty cycle and sleep mode strategies in optimizing battery longevity. This power profile is especially relevant for extended logistics operations, where on-site maintenance opportunities may be limited.

In our tests, even with several nodes on the move and transmitting data, the increase in latency was negligible and did not significantly impact the system performance, confirming that the scalability of our system is not adversely affected by the number of nodes. This ensures that the system is fully scalable and can accommodate a large-scale deployment without critical data transmission bottlenecks. The combination of such systems with an IoT platform, such as Thingsboard or a similar one, provides a good combination to deal with the robustness and scalability aspects (Shvaika et al., 2024).

Finally, user feedback collected from a pilot group of logistics managers highlighted the perceived benefits of real-time dashboards, which displayed key indicators such as temperature, humidity, and pressure readings alongside verifiable IOTA transaction hashes. Participants emphasized the audit ability and trustworthiness of the data, particularly crucial for sensitive goods that demand stringent handling conditions. In general, the results of the experiments confirm that the proposed architecture effectively addresses transparency, integrity, and operational efficiency for modern logistics use cases.

6 Discussion

The experimental results show that an IoT-based monitoring system combining LoRaWAN communication with the IOTA Tangle for data anchoring can greatly enhance the transparency, reliability, and security of logistics operations. By linking IoT devices to IOTA's feeless and immutable ledger, stakeholders gain continuous, end-to-end visibility into environmental conditions and shipment status, along with cryptographic assurance that no data have been altered. The network maintained stable data throughput, confirming that LoRaWAN is a suitable low-power and robust technology for mobile cold-chain monitoring.

A key element of the system is the use of decentralized identifiers (DIDs) to associate each sensor reading with its original device before it is published to the Tangle. This process ensures that every data point is verifiably tied to its source and cannot be modified afterward. During randomized verification tests, no evidence of tampering was found, validating the Tangle's resistance to manipulation and reinforcing confidence in the integrity of the stored information, an essential quality for multi-party logistics chains where accountability and custody tracking are critical.

In terms of performance, the system achieved an average end-to-end latency below six seconds per transmission (see Table 1), comfortably meeting real-time monitoring requirements for vaccines and other temperature-sensitive goods. While certain use cases such as ultra-cold logistics or sub-second event tracking might need further latency optimization or alternative communication paths (e.g., cellular or satellite), the observed results are more than sufficient for proactive decision-making in standard cold-chain scenarios. LoRaWAN's low energy consumption also extends battery life significantly, minimizing maintenance needs and improving the system's sustainability for long-distance routes.

The integration of decentralized identifiers with the IOTA Tangle proved particularly effective in maintaining data integrity at scale. Each message was digitally signed with the device's private key, allowing its authenticity to be verified by any stakeholder through the corresponding public key and DID record. The Tangle's parallel validation and feeless operation supported high-frequency data publishing without adding noticeable delay, demonstrating that secure, real-time anchoring of telemetry is achievable even for large IoT deployments.

Overall, the proposed architecture addresses key logistical needs by creating immutable, device-bound records that foster trust, ensure full visibility, and reduce both spoilage and manual record keeping. To support broader adoption, it will be necessary to establish standardized frameworks and industry guidelines that promote interoperability between distributed ledgers and existing supply-chain management systems. Well-defined data schemas and open APIs will be especially important to prevent fragmented implementations and to enable seamless, end-to-end integration.

A meaningful point of comparison emerges when contrasting our decentralized IoT–DLT architecture with traditional centralized cold-chain monitoring systems. Conventional approaches, such as standalone USB data loggers, siloed warehouse databases, or proprietary IoT dashboards, typically provide only delayed visibility, since temperature records are often retrieved manually at the end of a shipment or synchronized intermittently. These systems also rely on internal servers or individual administrators, creating single points of failure and increasing the risk that undetected modifications, accidental overwrites, or inconsistent data reconciliation may occur across multiple actors in the supply chain. As a result, stakeholders often operate with fragmented or outdated information, which slows incident detection and complicates root-cause analysis. By contrast, the decentralized design presented in this study provides a real-time, tamper-evident "single source of truth" that is simultaneously accessible to all authorized stakeholders. Each measurement is cryptographically signed and immutably anchored to the IOTA Tangle, ensuring end-to-end provenance without requiring trust in a centralized operator. This reduces manual processes, eliminates cross-database inconsistencies, and allows regulatory agencies, logistics providers, and healthcare facilities to verify the same data stream in parallel. Although our decentralized architecture introduces additional technical complexity compared with simpler centralized deployments, the gains in transparency, trust, and responsiveness are particularly valuable in high-stakes contexts such as vaccine distribution, where deviations must be detected and acted upon immediately. In this sense, the improved accountability and real-time visibility justify the added implementation effort.

6.1 Limitations

While the proposed architecture demonstrates clear advantages in transparency, scalability, and long-range monitoring, several practical limitations must be acknowledged. First, the system depends on the availability of LoRaWAN coverage; although gateways can be deployed locally, connectivity gaps in remote areas may still result in delayed transmissions. LoRaWAN's low data rate also constrains the size and frequency of messages, requiring careful duty-cycle management to avoid network congestion. Second, the architecture relies on an active internet connection at the cloud ingestion layer to submit signed telemetry to the IOTA Tangle, introducing a potential point of delay during connectivity outages. Third, although IOTA offers feeless and parallelized validation, the network continues to evolve, and its long-term stability and tooling maturity are still developing compared to more established blockchain platforms. Finally, integrating IoT sensing hardware, LoRaWAN communication, semantic annotation, and decentralized ledger components adds system complexity and requires technical expertise for deployment and maintenance. These limitations do not diminish the value of the architecture but highlight areas where continued refinement and infrastructure investment will be necessary for large-scale adoption.

6.2 Business and Managerial Implications

The system's real-time visibility helps managers detect temperature excursions early, prevent spoilage, and avoid the financial impact of reshipments, rejected batches, and insurance claims. Because every reading is automatically logged and cryptographically sealed, the evidence needed for audits and regulatory checks is generated without extra effort. This reduces administrative workload, improves the reliability of documentation, and eliminates the typical inconsistencies that arise from manual record keeping.

Beyond operational efficiency, the ability to provide verifiable cold-chain data strengthens an organisation's credibility with health authorities, suppliers, and logistics partners. Demonstrating a consistently well-monitored cold chain becomes a competitive advantage when bidding for contracts or managing large-scale vaccine programs. Since the system operates on low-power, long-range communication, it also scales easily without increasing maintenance costs, allowing organisations to expand monitoring coverage while keeping day-to-day operations simple and predictable.

6.3 Academic Implications

From a scholarly perspective, this case study contributes to the emerging literature on "Cold Chain 4.0" by illustrating how low-power wide-area networks (LPWANs) and Directed Acyclic Graph (DAG) ledgers can be combined to address persistent traceability and trust challenges. Our empirical findings with over 95% packet delivery in urban tests, under six second end-to-end latency, and zero detected ledger tampering, provide quantitative evidence supporting the feasibility of fee-less, high-throughput DLTs in IoT-intensive applications. Future research can build on this work by exploring cross industry use cases like, applying the same architecture to food supply chains, cold storage of biologics or chemical reagents, or any scenario where environmental integrity is mission-critical. Additionally, the semantic layering we adopted suggests avenues for interdisciplinary collaboration between supply chain management, information systems ontology, and human–computer interaction scholars, particularly in devising intuitive interfaces that translate complex data streams into actionable insights.

6.4 Technical Implications

On the technical front, our prototype demonstrates a modular and layered architecture that combines physical sensing, hub processing, LoRaWAN communication, cloud ingestion, IOTA anchoring, and MicroPython-based sensing firmware. The design can be easily adapted or extended in other contexts without disrupting the core structure. The complete MicroPython firmware and integration scripts are available in our public GitHub repository (Jordieres, 2024), where practitioners can review and adapt the code that links sensor readings to decentralized identifiers (DIDs) and publishes them as transactions on the IOTA Tangle.

By releasing the system under an open-source license, the project aims to foster a collaborative ecosystem for digital cold-chain innovation. Community participation can drive the evolution of the platform by incorporating alternative LPWAN technologies such as NB-IoT, LTE-M, or satellite IoT, and by developing enhanced visualization dashboards and mobile applications for real-time analytics. Open collaboration not only accelerates technical progress but also ensures that the architecture remains adaptable to new contexts, regulatory standards, and emerging hardware over time. In this way, the framework can evolve beyond a single research prototype into a living, community-driven infrastructure for resilient and transparent cold-chain monitoring.

The use of a Directed Acyclic Graph (DAG) ledger such as IOTA eliminates transaction fees and scalability bottlenecks typical of conventional blockchains while maintaining high-frequency data logging and immutability. Developers can build on this blueprint to integrate additional analytics modules, such as AI-based anomaly detection or predictive maintenance, without redesigning the telemetry pipeline. The proposed architecture addresses key logistical needs by providing immutable, device-bound records that enhance visibility, reduce manual record keeping, and improve operational efficiency.

To enable broader adoption, the establishment of standardized frameworks or consortium-level agreements will be essential to ensure interoperability across different distributed ledger technologies and existing supply-chain platforms. Although the current prototype focused on the integration of IoT and IOTA components, the architecture already includes a semantic interoperability mechanism that defines how ontology-based data models, including SOSA/SSN and QUDT, can structure and expose sensor data in JSON-LD format. This approach supports future cross-platform understanding and automatic data integration. Harmonized data schemas and open APIs will be critical to prevent fragmented deployments and enable smooth, end-to-end interoperability.

6.5 *Future Research*

Future research should concentrate on scaling strategies that integrate heterogeneous information flows into more comprehensive, AI-enhanced management dashboards. By superimposing semantic abstractions that incorporate factors such as weather forecasts, traffic conditions, and inventory levels on top of raw sensor data, it will become possible to develop predictive analytics and automated optimization routines. Achieving these higher levels of integration will require well-defined ontologies and semantic frameworks capable of harmonizing data from IoT devices, distributed ledgers, enterprise resource planning systems, and other sources. Recent studies emphasize that combining IoT-driven monitoring with artificial intelligence and semantic modelling can significantly improve decision-making, predictive capabilities, and operational efficiency across cold-chain and logistics environments (Habazin et al., 2025; Onyeaka et al., 2025). Advancements in this direction are central to the broader vision of Cold Chain 4.0, where digital platforms evolve from simple data visualization tools into adaptive, data-driven ecosystems capable of anticipating disruptions and autonomously optimizing storage and transport conditions. Such progress promises to shift vaccine and asset logistics from reactive monitoring toward anticipatory orchestration, thereby strengthening global supply-chain resilience against spoilage, theft, and operational disruptions.

7 Conclusion

The integrity of the vaccine cold chain underpins the success of immunization programs worldwide and improve management of this valuable and vital asset. In this research, we have shown that digitizing this process through the deployment of IoT sensors for real time monitoring and the anchoring of data to an immutable distributed ledger, can overcome many of the limitations inherent in traditional systems. Our prototype, which combines LoRaWAN communications with the IOTA Tangle, demonstrated reliable long range data transmission, low end-to-end latency, and tamper proof logging of every sensor reading. These capabilities not only prevent undetected thermal excursions that compromise vaccine efficacy but also furnish stakeholders with a single, verifiable source of truth for accountability and rapid decision making.

The practical performance of this architecture under real world conditions confirms its viability. The system maintained continuous data flow, while randomized audits uncovered no evidence of data alteration. Moreover, the low power demands of LoRaWAN considerably extend device battery life, reducing maintenance burdens on cold-chain personnel. Collectively, these findings attest that an IoT-DLT-based cold-chain is not merely a theoretical enhancement but a practical, scalable solution that can significantly reduce vaccine wastage, shorten response times to excursions, and strengthen overall logistical resilience.

Moving from pilot to widespread implementation will require coordinated investment and standardization. National governments and international health agencies should prioritize the deployment of sensor networks and supporting infrastructure recognizing that the savings gained by reducing vaccine loss can outweigh initial outlays. At the same time, industry bodies such as WHO and UNICEF must promulgate common data formats, communication protocols, and response procedures, ensuring interoperability across diverse platforms and simplifying integration into existing supply chain management systems. Clear guidelines on alert thresholds, data privacy safeguards, and audit workflows will be essential to embed these technologies smoothly into standard operating procedures.

Equally important is the human dimension of digital transformation. Supply chain managers and healthcare workers need training not only in operating IoT devices but also in interpreting the resulting data and trusting automated alerts. Building confidence in digital information requires familiarity and consistent exposure; when users understand how readings are generated and verified on the ledger, they are more willing to act on the system's recommendations. Previous studies have confirmed that limited technical training and low data literacy often undermine cold-chain management, leading to errors and reduced responsiveness to temperature excursions (Gebretnsae et al., 2022; Gelaw et al., 2023; Geneti et al., 2024). Early pilot programs and simulation-based workshops in similar contexts have shown that short, scenario-driven exercises can significantly improve user confidence and accuracy when responding to alerts. Well-documented pilot projects that quantify the number of prevented excursions and preserved doses will provide compelling evidence for broader implementation, beginning at central warehouses and progressively extending to peripheral clinics.

To our knowledge, this study is among the first to operationalize a unified cold-chain monitoring architecture that integrates IoT sensing, LoRaWAN communication, and a feeless DAG-based ledger (IOTA), demonstrating how these three technologies can jointly address visibility, connectivity, and data-integrity challenges within a single framework.

Finally, the integration of cold-chain telemetry into routine decision-making meetings will ensure that data drive continuous improvement. By reviewing performance metrics alongside logistics plans, program leaders can identify patterns such as routes prone to temperature spikes or seasonal risks and apply predictive analytics to anticipate and prevent problems. This creates a feedback loop where growing historical datasets enhance AI-driven optimization capabilities, turning vaccine delivery from reactive monitoring into proactive orchestration.

In conclusion, the digital cold-chain system we have described can transform vaccine delivery. By providing real-time tracking, secure data, providing transparency and smart logistics, it ensures every vaccine is publicly and carefully monitored from production to patient. While this shift requires investment, teamwork, and common standards, the rewards are clear, which are fewer wasted doses, stronger public trust, and more lives saved. The evidence is strong digitalizing this asset and upgrading to a digital cold chain isn't just helpful also it's essential.

Declarations

Competing Interests The author(s) has no competing interests to declare that are relevant to the content of this manuscript.

References

Acharya, K. P., & Phuyal, S. (2025). *The unsung virtue of thermostable anti-rabies vaccine. Open Veterinary Journal, 15*(5), 1864.

Agrawal, P., & Narain, R. (2018). Digital supply chain management: An Overview. *IOP Conference Series: Materials Science and Engineering, 455*(1), 012074 (IOP Publishing). https://doi.org/10.1088/1757-899X/455/1/012074

Alfaqiyah, E., Alzubi, A., Aljuhmani, H. Y., & Öz, T. (2025). How industry 4.0 technologies enhance supply chain resilience: The interplay of agility, adaptability, and customer integration in manufacturing firms. *Sustainability, 17*(17), 7922.

Ali, Y., & Khan, H. U. (2023). IoT platforms assessment methodology for COVID-19 vaccine logistics and transportation: A multi-methods decision-making model. *Scientific Reports, 13*(1), 17575 (Nature Publishing Group). https://www.nature.com/articles/s41598-023-44966-y

Alshaikhli, M., Elfouly, T., Elharrouss, O., Mohamed, A., & Ottakath, N. (2022). Evolution of internet of things from blockchain to IOTA: A survey. *IEEE Access, 10*, 844–866. https://ieeexplore.ieee.org/abstract/document/9662390

Ashok, A., Brison, M., & LeTallec, Y. (2017). Improving cold chain systems: Challenges and solutions. *Vaccine, 35*(17), 2217–2223. https://www.sciencedirect.com/science/article/pii/S0264410X16307307

Balfaqih, M., Balfagih, Z., Lytras, M. D., Alfawaz, K. M., Alshdadi, A. A., & Alsolami, E. (2023). A blockchain-enabled IoT logistics system for efficient tracking and management of high-price shipments: A resilient, scalable and sustainable approach to smart cities. *Sustainability, 15*(18), 13971 (Number: 18) (Multidisciplinary Digital Publishing Institute). https://www.mdpi.com/2071-1050/15/18/13971

Bigliardi, B., Filippelli, S., Petroni, A., & Tagliente, L. (2022). The digitalization of supply chain: a review. *Procedia Computer Science, 200*, 1806–1815. https://www.sciencedirect.com/science/article/pii/S1877050922003908

Bonilla, V., Campoverde, B., & Yoo, S. G. (2023). A systematic literature review of lo-RaWAN: Sensors and applications. *Sensors, 23*(20), 8440 (Number: 20) (Multi-disciplinary Digital Publishing Institute). https://www.mdpi.com/1424-8220/23/20/8440

Büyüközkan, G., & Göçer, F. (2018). Digital supply chain: Literature review and a proposed framework for future research. *Computers in Industry, 97*, 157–177. https://www.sciencedirect.com/science/article/pii/S0166361517304487

Crnjac Milić, D., Dujmenović, I., & Peko, M. (2023). An approach to the application of the internet of things in logistics. *Tehnički glasnik, 17*(1), 134–140 (Sveučilište Sjever). https://hrcak.srce.hr/292493

Dash, S., Ghugar, U., Godavarthi, D., & Mohanty, S. N. (2024). HCSRL: Hyperledger composer system for reducing logistics losses in the pharmaceutical product supply chain using a blockchain-based approach. *Scientific Reports, 14*(1), 13528 (Nature Publishing Group). https://www.nature.com/articles/s41598-024-61654-7

de Carvalho Silva, J., Rodrigues, J. J. P. C., Alberti, A. M., Solic, P., & Aquino, A. L. L. (2017). LoRaWAN—A low power WAN protocol for internet of things: A review and opportunities. In *2017 2nd International multidisciplinary conference on computer and EnergyScience (SpliTech)* (pp. 1–6). https://ieeexplore.ieee.org/abstract/document/8019271

Elngar, A. A., Thiyaneswaran, B., Anguraj, K., Kumarganesh, S., Sagayam, K. M., & Muthmainnah. (2023). IOT based smart cold chain temperature monitoring with alert system for vaccination container directed to universities and schools. *AIP Conference Proceedings, 2736*(1), 050001. https://doi.org/10.1063/5.0170641

Erassa, T. E., Behailu Balcha, B., Wolde Facha, F., Simegn, M., & Bogino, E. A. (2023). Vaccine cold chain management and associated factors in public health facilities and district health offices of Wolaita Zone, Ethiopia. *Journal of Multidisciplinary Healthcare, 16*, 75–84 (Dove Medical Press). https://doi.org/10.2147/JMDH.S385466

Ergetie, F. S., Kassaw, A. T., & Sendekie, A. K. (2023). Vaccine cold chain management practices in primary health centers providing an expanded immunization program in Northwest Ethiopia: self-reported and actual practice observational study. *Frontiers in Public Health, 11*, 1194807. https://doi.org/10.3389/fpubh.2023.1194807/full

Feltrin, L., Buratti, C., Vinciarelli, E., De Bonis, R., & Verdone, R. (2018). LoRaWAN: Evaluation of link- and system-level performance. *IEEE Internet of Things Journal, 5*(3), 2249–2258. https://ieeexplore.ieee.org/abstract/document/8344411

Garcia-Valtanen, P., Yeow, A. E., Mekonnen, Z. A., Whelan, D. M., Santos, R., Al-Delfi, Z.,Rodrigues, S., Gavan, P., Howard, K., Masavuli, M. G., et al. (2025). Thermostable unit solid dose formulations for subcutaneous administration of DNA vaccines. *Molecular Therapy Nucleic Acids, 36*(3).

Gaynor, M., Gillespie, K., Roe, A., Crannage, E., & Tuttle-Newhall, J. (2024). Blockchain applications in the pharmaceutical industry. *Blockchain in HealthcareToday, 7*. https://doi.org/10.30953/bhty.v7.298. https://www.ncbi.nlm.nih.gov/pmc/articles/PMC11073477/

Gebretnsae, H., Hadgu, T., Ayele, B., Gebre-Egziabher, E., Woldu, M., Tilahun, M., Abraha, A., Wubayehu, T., & Medhanyie, A. A. (2022). Knowledge of vaccine handlers and status of cold chain and vaccine management in primary health care facilities of tigray region, northern ethiopia: Institutional based cross-sectional study. *PLoS ONE, 17*(6), e0269183.

Gelaw, A., Belyhun, Y., Wondimeneh, Y., Kokeb, M., Dagnew, M., Amare, A., Mulu, M., Alemayehu, M., & Gelaw, B. (2023). Knowledge and associated factors of healthcare workers on measles vaccine and cold chain management at health institutions in Gondar, Ethiopia. *Asian Pacific Journal of Tropical Medicine, 16*(1), 26–32.

Geneti, L., Shallo, S. A., Yebasa, M. A., & Daba, D. B. (2024). Health workers' knowledge and practices toward vaccine cold chain management and its associated factors in a resource limited setting of sheger, Oromia, Ethiopia: A multicenter cross-sectional study. *BMC Pediatrics, 24*(1), 786.

Goodarzian, F., Navaei, A., Ehsani, B., Ghasemi, P., & Muñuzuri, J. (2023). Designing an integrated responsive-green-cold vaccine supply chain network using Internet-of-Things: Artificial intelligence-based solutions. *Annals of Operations Research, 328*(1), 531–575. https://doi.org/10.1007/s10479-022-04713-4

Habazin, J., Bajor, I., Bajec, P., & Rožić, T. (2025). A review of artificial intelligence applications in cold chain and reverse logistics. *Promet-Traffic & Transportation, 37*(6), 1409–1440.

Halim, A. H. A., Halim, M. H. A., Usman, S., & Daud, S. M. (2021). Implementation of IoT and blockchain for temperature monitoring in Covid19 vaccine cold chain logistics. *Open International Journal of Informatics, 9*(1), 78–87 (Number: 1). https://oiji.utm.my/index.php/oiji/article/view/4

Hanson, C. M., George, A. M., Sawadogo, A., & Schreiber, B. (2017). Is freezing in the vaccine cold chain an ongoing issue? A literature review. *Vaccine, 35*(17), 2127–2133. https://www.sciencedirect.com/science/article/pii/S0264410X16309471

Haque, E. U., Abbasi, W., Almogren, A., Choi, J., Altameem, A., Rehman, A. U., & Hamam, H. (2024). Performance enhancement in blockchain based iot data sharing using lightweight consensus algorithm. *Scientific Reports, 14*(1), 26561.

Hasanat, R. T., Arifur Rahman, M., Mansoor, N., Mohammed, N., Rahman, M. S., & Rasheduzzaman, M. (2020). An IoT based real-time data-centric monitoring system for vaccine cold chain. In *2020 IEEE east-west design & test symposium (EWDTS)* (pp. 1–5). ISSN: 2472-761X. https://ieeexplore.ieee.org/abstract/document/9225047

Hosangadi, D. et al. (2021). Supporting use of thermostable vaccines during public health emergencies. *Vaccine, 39*(45), 6562–6570. https://pmc.ncbi.nlm.nih.gov/articles/PMC8575557/

Hu, H., Xu, J., Liu, M., & Lim, M. K. (2023). Vaccine supply chain management: An intelligent system utilizing blockchain, IoT and machine learning. *Journal of Business Research, 156*, 113480. https://www.sciencedirect.com/science/article/pii/S0148296322009456

Ibrahim, D. M. (2019). Internet of things technology based on LoRaWAN revolution. In *2019 10th International conference on information and communication systems (ICICS)* (pp. 234–237). ISSN: 2573-3346. https://ieeexplore.ieee.org/abstract/document/8809176

Jiang, S., & Wen-yan Song, Z.-l. Z. (2023). A real-time surveillance system for vaccine cold chain based on internet of things technology. *Journal of Information Processing Systems, 19*(3), 394–406. https://doi.org/10.3745/JIPS.04.0279

Jiang, S., Jia, S., & Guo, H. (2024). Internet of things (IoT)-enabled framework for a sustainable vaccine cold chain management system. *Heliyon, 10*(7) (Elsevier). https://www.cell.com/heliyon/abstract/S2405-8440(24)04941-7

Jordieres (2024). IoT-IoTA MicroPython firmware for ESP32-based RuuviTag data acquisition. https://github.com/jordieres/IoT-IoTA_PSI_2024. Accessed 17 June 2025.

Kartoglu, U., & Milstien, J. (2014). Tools and approaches to ensure quality of vaccines throughout the cold chain. *Expert Review of Vaccines, 13*(7), 843–854 (Taylor & Francis). https://doi.org/10.1586/14760584.2014.923761

Kartoglu, U., & Ames, H. (2022). Ensuring quality and integrity of vaccines throughout the cold chain: The role of temperature monitoring. *Expert Review of Vaccines, 21*(6), 799–810 (Taylor & Francis). https://doi.org/10.1080/14760584.2022.2061462

Katoch, R. (2022). IoT research in supply chain management and logistics: A bibliometric analysis using vosviewer software. Materials Today:Proceedings 56, 2505–2015. https://www.sciencedirect.com/science/article/pii/S2214785321057163

Kitamura, T., Bouakhasith, V., Phounphenghack, K., Pathammavong, C., Xeuatvongsa, A., Norizuki, M., Okabayashi, H., Mori, Y., Machida, M., & Hachiya, M. (2018). Assessment of temperatures in the vaccine cold chain in two provinces in Lao People's Democratic Republic: A cross-sectional pilot study. *BMC Research Notes, 11*(1), 261. https://doi.org/10.1186/s13104-018-3362-1

Kristensen, D. D., Lorenson, T., Bartholomew, K., & Villadiego, S. (2016). Can thermostable vaccines help address cold-chain challenges? Results from stakeholder interviews in six low- and middle-income countries. *Vaccine, 34*(7), 899–904. https://www.sciencedirect.com/science/article/pii/S0264410X16000189

Kumar, N. M., Dash, A., & Singh, N. K. (2018). Internet of things (IoT): An opportunity for energy-food-water nexus. In *2018 International conference on power energy, environment and intelligent control (PEEIC)* (pp. 68–72). https://ieeexplore.ieee.org/document/8665632

Kumar, S., Raut, R. D., Priyadarshinee, P., Mangla, S. K., Awan, U., & Narkhede, B. E. (2024). The impact of IoT on the performance of vaccine supply chain distribution in the COVID-19 context. *IEEE Transactions on Engineering Management, 71*,13123–13133. https://ieeexplore.ieee.org/abstract/document/9760292

Kumru, O. S., Joshi, S. B., Smith, D. E., Middaugh, C. R., Prusik, T., & Volkin, D. B. (2014). Vaccine instability in the cold chain: Mechanisms, analysis and formulation strategies. *Biologicals, 42*(5), 237–259. https://linkinghub.elsevier.com/retrieve/pii/S1045105614000487

Lam, H., & Tang, V. (2023). Digital transformation for cold chain management in freight forwarding industry. *International Journal of Engineering Business Management, 15*, 18479790231160856.

Lavric, A., & Popa, V. (2017). Internet of things and LoRa™ low-power wide-area networks: A survey. In *2017 International symposium on signals, circuits and systems (ISSCS)* (pp. 1–5). https://ieeexplore.ieee.org/abstract/document/8034915

Liu, L., Zhang, X., Xu, X., Lin, X., Zhao, Y., Zou, L., Wu, Y., & Zheng, H. (2021). Development of low-temperature eutectic phase change material with expanded graphite for vaccine cold chain logistics. *Renewable Energy, 179*, 2348–2358. https://www.sciencedirect.com/science/article/pii/S0960148121011010

Łukasiewicz, K. (2019). Digital competences in supply chain management. *Zeszyty Naukowe Szkoły Głównej Gospodarstwa Wiejskiego w Warszawie. Ekonomika i Organizacja Logistyki, 4*(4), 85–96 (Gospodarstwa Wiejskiego w Warszawie). https://www.ceeol.com/search/article-detail?id=889699

Makhdoom, I., Abolhasan, M., & Ni, W. (2018). Blockchain for IoT: The challenges and a way forward. https://opus.lib.uts.edu.au/handle/10453/128083

Mohsin, A., & Yellampalli, S. S. (2017). IoT based cold chain logistics monitoring. In *2017 IEEE international conference on power, control, signals and instrumentation engineering (ICPCSI)* (pp. 1971–1974). https://ieeexplore.ieee.org/document/8392059/

Oliveira, R. M. J. (2024). Transformação digital nas cadeias de suprimentos: benefícios, desafios e inovações tecnológicas. *Aracê 6*(3), 4583–4598 (Number: 3). https://periodicos.newsciencepubl.com/arace/article/view/1159

Onyeaka, H., Akinsemolu, A., Miri, T., Nnaji, N. D., Duan, K., Pang, G., Tamasiga, P., Khalid, S., Al-Sharify, Z. T., & Ugwa, C. (2025). Artificial intelligence in food system: Innovative approach to minimizing food spoilage and food waste. *Journal of Agriculture and Food Research, 21*, 101895.

Ordieres-Mere, J., & Ortega-Mier, M. A. (2024). Challenges in industry 5.0: Human behavior integration. In A. Hamrol, M. Grabowska, & M. Hinz (Eds.), *Advances in manufacturing IV* (pp. 183–197). Springer Nature Switzerland.

PAHO/WHO. (2021). *Manufacturing, safety and quality control of vaccines*. PAHO/WHO Pan American Health Organization. https://www.paho.org/en/documents/manufacturing-safety-and-quality-control-vaccines

Pajić, V., Andrejić, M., & Chatterjee, P. (2024). Enhancing cold chain logistics: A framework for advanced temperature monitoring in transportation and storage. *Mechatronics and Intelligent Transportation Systems, 3*, 16–30.

Pambudi, N. A., Sarifudin, A., Gandidi, I. M., & Romadhon, R. (2022). Vaccine cold chain management and cold storage technology to address the challenges of vaccination programs. *Energy Reports, 8*, 955–972. https://www.sciencedirect.com/science/article/pii/S2352484721014785

Prayudi, A., Hakim, O. S., Zainuddin, M. A., Sukaridhoto, S., & Budiarti, R. P. N. (2024). Private blockchain-based platform for cool box truck based on LoRa communication protocol. In *2024 IEEE international symposium on consumer technology (ISCT)* (pp. 378–384). ISSN: 2159-1423. https://ieeexplore.ieee.org/abstract/document/10791246

Pullo, S., Pareschi, R., Piantadosi, V., Salzano, F., & Carlini, R. (2024). Integrating IOTA's tangle with the internet of things for sustainable agriculture: A proof-of-concept study on rice cultivation. *Informatics, 11*(1), 3 (Number: 1) (Multidisciplinary Digital Publishing Institute). https://www.mdpi.com/2227-9709/11/1/3

Quintero, C. (2019). Will the internet of things lead to the next currency revolution? [Editorial]. *IEEE Potentials, 38*(2), 4–8. https://ieeexplore.ieee.org/abstract/document/8658091

Raut, R., Shrestha, R., Adhikari, A., Fatima, A., & Naeem, M. (2025). Revolutionizing veterinary vaccines: Overcoming cold-chain barriers through thermostable and novel delivery technologies. *Applied Microbiology, 5*(3), 83.

Redondo, G., & Coutinho, C. (2024). Monitoring solution for cold chain logistic transport based on LoRa technology. In *2024 International symposium on sensing and instrumentation in 5G and IoT Era (ISSI)* (Vol. 1, pp. 1–5). https://ieeexplore.ieee.org/abstract/document/10720504.

Rejeb, A., Keogh, J. G., & Treiblmaier, H. (2019). Leveraging the internet of things and blockchain technology in supply chain management. *Future Internet, 11*(7), 161 (Number: 7) (Multidisciplinary Digital Publishing Institute). https://www.mdpi.com/1999-5903/11/7/161

Ren, T., Ren, J., Matellini, B., Tammas-Williams, S., & Ouyang, W. (2021). The trend of modern cold chain management: Characteristics, challenges and opportunities of vaccine logistics. In *2021 6th International conference on transportation information and safety (ICTIS)* (pp. 669–673). https://ieeexplore.ieee.org/abstract/document/9798659

Rhee, E., & Lee, J. (2024). Improved DAG in blockchain tangle for IOTA. *Indonesian Journal of Electrical Engineering and Computer Science, 34*(2), 806–813 (Number: 2). https://ijeecs.iaescore.com/index.php/IJEECS/article/view/36442

Salunkhe, P. G., & Nerkar, R. (2016). IoT driven smart system for best cold chain application. In *2016 International conference on global trends in signal processing, information computing and communication (ICGTSPICC)* (pp. 64–67). https://ieeexplore.ieee.org/abstract/document/7955270

Sarkar, S., Akshatha, K., Saurabh, A., Samanvitha, B., & Sarwar, M. F. (2022). IoT enabled cold supply chain monitoring system. In *2022 IEEE 3rd global conference for advancement in technology (GCAT)* (pp. 1–6). https://ieeexplore.ieee.org/abstract/document/9972137

Shabandri, B., & Maheshwari, P. (2019). Enhancing IoT security and privacy using distributed ledgers with IOTA and the tangle. In *2019 6th International conference on signal processing and integrated networks (SPIN)* (pp. 1069–1075). https://ieeexplore.ieee.org/abstract/document/8711591

Sharmila, B. S., Kumar, P., Garg, A. K., & Nair, S. (2022). Blockchain powered vaccine efficacy for pharma sector. *Computational and Mathematical Methods in Medicine, 2022*(1), 4862742. https://doi.org/10.1155/2022/4862742

Shashi, M. (2022). Digitalization of pharmaceutical cold chain systems using IoT digital enabler. *International Journal of Engineering and Advanced Technology, 11*.

Shvaika, D. I., Shvaika, A. I., & Artemchuk, V. O. (2024). Advancing IoT interoperability: Dynamic data serialization using things board. *Journal of Edge Computing, 3*(2), 126–135.

Silvano, W. F., & Marcelino, R. (2020). Iota tangle: a cryptocurrency to communicate internet-of-things data. *Future Generation Computer Systems, 112*, 307–319. https://www.sciencedirect.com/science/article/pii/S0167739X19329048

Singh, R., Dwivedi, A. D., & Srivastava, G. (2020). Internet of things based blockchain for temperature monitoring and counterfeit pharmaceutical prevention. *Sensors, 20*(14), 3951 (Number: 14) (Multidisciplinary Digital Publishing Institute). https://www.mdpi.com/1424-8220/20/14/3951

Song, J. C., Demir, M. A., Prevost, J. J., & Rad, P. (2018). BLOCKCHAIN DESIGN FOR TRUSTED DECENTRALIZED IoT networks. In *2018 13th annual conference on system of systems engineering (SoSE)* (pp. 169–174). https://ieeexplore.ieee.org/abstract/document/8428720

Taghipour, A., Lu, X., Derradji, M., & Sow, A. D. (2022). The impact of digitalization on supply chain management: A literature review. In *Proceedings of the 12th International Conference on Information Communication and Management', ICICM '22* (pp. 75–78). Association for Computing Machinery, New York, NY. https://doi.org/10.1145/3551690.3551702

Talbot, A., de Koning-Ward, T. F., & Layton, D. (2025). Left out in the cold—Inequity in infectious disease control due to cold chain disparity. *Vaccine, 45*, 126648. https://www.sciencedirect.com/science/article/pii/S0264410X24013306

Ullo, S., Gallo, M., Palmieri, G., Amenta, P., Russo, M., Romano, G., Ferrucci, M., Ferrara, A., & De Angelis, M. (2018). Application of wireless sensor networks to environmental monitoring for sustainable mobility. In *2018 IEEE international conference on environmental engineering (EE)* (pp. 1–7). https://ieeexplore.ieee.org/document/8385263

Vargis, B. K., Alam, M. S., Upreti, K., Raut, R. D., Kumar, N., & Jalil, S. Z. A. (2022). Scoping analysis of leveraging IoT with blockchain for monitoring and ensuring efficacy of vaccine cold chains. In *2022 6th International Conference on Intelligent Computing and Control Systems (ICICCS)* (pp. 795–803). ISSN: 2768-5330. https://ieeexplore.ieee.org/abstract/document/9788216

Venable, J. R., Pries-Heje, J., & Baskerville, R. L. (2017). Choosing a design science research methodology. In *Proceedings of the Australasian conference on information systems (ACIS)*. Association for Information Systems (AIS), Hobart. https://aisel.aisnet.org/acis2017/112

Verma Pargaien, A., Pargaien, S., Adhikari, M., Maan, M., Sharma, S., & Joshi, H. (2021). The role of IOT for monitoring the wastage of vaccines due to poor cold chain management. In *2021 Fifth international conference on I-SMAC (IoT in social, mobile, analytics and cloud) (I-SMAC)* (pp. 78–86). ISSN: 2768-0673. https://ieeexplore.ieee.org/abstract/document/9640679

Villafranca, A., Tasic, I., Gallegos, V., Gimenez, A., Rego, J. O., Fernandez, J. A., & Cano, M.-D. (2025). Comparing blockchain and dag technologies for smart agriculture traceability in terms of efficiency and latency. *Simulation Modelling Practice and Theory, 142*, 103131.

WHO (2020). Why optimized cold-chains could save a billion COVID vaccines. In *Section: News and Stories*. https://www.unep.org/news-and-stories/story/why-optimized-cold-chains-could-save-billion-covid-vaccines

Yauba, S., Sobngwi, J., Jude, N., Tracy, B., Kobela, M., Charles, N., Hermelle, E., Marius, V., Julius, S., Alain, B., Marcellin, N., Baku, A., Marianne, M., Mike, B., Kamga, D., Robinson, M., & Divine, N. (2017). Temperature monitoring in the vaccine cold chain in Cameroon. *Journal of Vaccines & Vaccination, 09.*

Yong, B., Shen, J., Liu, X., Li, F., Chen, H., & Zhou, Q. (2020). An intelligent blockchain-based system for safe vaccine supply and supervision. *International Journal of Information Management, 52*, 102024. https://www.sciencedirect.com/science/article/pii/S0268401219304505

Zichichi, M., Ferretti, S., & D'Angelo, G. (2020). A distributed ledger based infrastructure for smart transportation system and social good. In *2020 IEEE 17th Annual consumer communications & networking conference (CCNC)* (pp. 1–6). ISSN: 2331-9860. https://ieeexplore.ieee.org/document/9045640

AI-Powered Maintenance Strategies in Transportation

Johan Wideberg

Abstract Artificial intelligence (AI) is reshaping maintenance for conventional, electric (EV), and autonomous vehicles (AV). By leveraging on-board sensors and the Internet of Vehicles (IoV), AI enables a shift from reactive repairs to predictive strategies. Machine learning (ML) and deep learning (DL) models now support continuous health monitoring. These models utilize data from diverse sources, including Digital Twins (DTs) and low-latency V2X networks, to detect faults early. Recent studies (Hossain et al. in Measurement 253, 2025) report up to 95% fault-detection accuracy for conventional vehicle subsystems under controlled benchmarks. Similarly, diagnostics for AV perception show high reliability in specific test scenarios. In the EV domain, simulation-based evaluations (Hu et al. in Energy Convers Manag 300, 2024; Kermansaravi et al. in Energy Rep 13:5535–5550, 2025) indicate potential energy efficiency improvements of 15–20% and battery lifespan extensions of 10–15% compared to baseline methods. Additionally, AI-enabled control strategies in heavy-duty fleets may reduce operating costs by 31.4–40.5%, as observed in optimized microgrid case studies (Hu et al. in Ad Hoc Net 146, 2023; Kumar and Prabhansu in Future Batter 7:100087, 2025). Unlike broad technological overviews, this chapter presents a novel Task–Data–AI–KPI mapping. This framework connects maintenance objectives to specific data requirements and algorithmic choices. It situates these strategies within a layered infrastructure architecture—spanning edge sensors to cloud-based digital twins—to demonstrate their impact on key performance indicators (KPIs) such as availability and lifecycle costs.

Keywords AI-driven transportation maintenance · Vehicle health monitoring · Predictive maintenance for electric and autonomous vehicles · Internet of vehicles and connected diagnostics · Digital twin-enabled fleet optimization

J. Wideberg (✉)
Transportation Engineering Group, Escuela Técnica Superior de Ingeniería, Universidad de Sevilla, Seville, Spain
e-mail: wideberg@us.es

A. Crespo Márquez et al. (eds.), *Digital Maintenance and Asset Digitalization*, Engineering Asset Management Review 5,
https://doi.org/10.1007/978-3-032-21502-4_13

1 Introduction

1.1 Defining Vehicle Health Monitoring (VHM) and Fault Diagnosis

Vehicle health monitoring (VHM) and fault diagnosis systems are integral to the safe and reliable operation of modern automobiles. VHM aims to ensure that a vehicle runs smoothly and dependably, continuously assessing its performance and condition. Complementing this, fault diagnosis involves the precise identification and localization of any issues or problems within the vehicle's various subsystem. These intelligent and advanced systems are crucial for detecting potential faults before they escalate into full-blown failures, thereby playing a vital role in ensuring the safety of occupants and the reliability of transportation on the road. in the benchmark of Hossain et al. (2025) for engine and brake faults in conventional vehicles.

The increasing complexity of modern automotive systems, encompassing intricate mechanical, electrical, and computational components, necessitates diagnostic methods that go beyond traditional approaches. Older methods, which often rely on static thresholds and simplistic decision rules, prove insufficient in providing the flexibility and accuracy required to detect and prevent future faults, particularly in advanced vehicles like electric vehicles (EVs) and autonomous vehicles (AVs) Vehicles equipped with such outdated fault detection systems may fail to identify issues accurately and in a timely manner, leading to compromised safety and suboptimal performance.

This chapter differentiates itself from recent surveys by providing a cross-modal synthesis that unifies maintenance architectures across conventional, electric, and autonomous fleets. Its primary novelty lies in a strict KPI-oriented framing, establishing a quantitative traceability between specific AI techniques (e.g., Deep Learning, Reinforcement Learning) and measurable outcomes in reliability and cost reduction, thereby bridging the gap between theoretical algorithms and industrial deployment. Unlike prior reviews (e.g., Hossain et al., 2025; Saki & Soori, 2026), it provides a cross-modal synthesis that connects diagnostic accuracy, predictive-maintenance models, and sustainability metrics within a unified analytical framework. It also outlines the evolving hierarchy from component-level fault detection to fleet-level optimization, thereby clarifying AI's systemic contribution to next-generation maintenance engineering.

1.2 Shift from Reactive to Predictive and Proactive Maintenance Paradigms

Historically, maintenance practices in the transportation sector have largely been reactive, addressing vehicle failures only after they occurred. This traditional approach, however, has significant drawbacks. Research indicates that reliance on poorly designed VHM techniques can lead to a substantial increase in maintenance expenses, potentially by as much as 40% Furthermore, decreased failure cycles of automotive components often result in unanticipated malfunctions, generating unexpected downtime that disrupts transport operations (Hossain et al., 2025).

The advent of AI-driven approaches is fundamentally transforming these maintenance practices, shifting the paradigm from reactive repair to predictive and proactive strategies This evolution enables the early detection of potential faults, thereby significantly reducing the likelihood of unexpected breakdowns and lowering overall maintenance costs. This transformation is not merely an incremental improvement; it represents a fundamental paradigm shift driven by compelling economic necessity and advanced technological capability. The significant financial and operational pain points associated with traditional reactive maintenance, such as increased costs and unexpected downtime, are directly addressed by AI's technical capacity for highly accurate early fault detection. For instance, AI-driven fault diagnosis can achieve up to 95% accuracy in conventional vehicles and 99% reliability in autonomous vehicles for early detection. The sheer magnitude of potential cost savings and the enhancement in reliability, marked by reduced downtime, strongly incentivize the adoption of AI. This makes AI integration not just a beneficial upgrade but a critical business imperative for a rapidly growing and increasingly complex industry. This profound shift extends its impact beyond individual vehicle owners and fleet managers, influencing the entire supply chain for parts and services, potentially fostering new business models like "maintenance-as-a-service" and necessitating significant re-skilling of the technical workforce (Hossain et al., 2025; Hu et al., 2024; Saki & Soori, 2026).

1.3 The Necessity of AI in Addressing the Complexity of Modern Transportation Systems

The global automotive sector is experiencing staggering growth, projected to reach a valuation of USD 9 trillion by 2030, with the worldwide vehicle population expected to double in the next two decades. This rapid expansion underscores an escalating need for sophisticated and efficient maintenance solutions. The increasing intricacy of modern vehicles, from conventional internal combustion engine vehicles (CVs) to advanced electric (EVs) and autonomous vehicles (AVs), presents challenges that traditional diagnostic methods are ill-equipped to handle (Hossain et al., 2025).

Artificial intelligence algorithms, particularly those rooted in machine learning (ML) and deep learning (DL) techniques, possess an unparalleled ability to process and analyse massive amounts of data collected from diverse sensor arrays and other sources This capability allows them to detect subtle patterns, anomalies, and correlations that are indicative of faults or impending failures—a level of discernment largely unattainable by conventional methods The interconnected and multidisciplinary nature of modern vehicular systems, which increasingly rely on integrated solutions spanning mechanical, electrical, and computational domains, further demands the holistic and adaptive problem-solving capabilities that AI can provide (Hossain et al., 2025; Saki & Soori, 2026).

2 State-of-the-Art AI Techniques for Transportation Maintenance

The landscape of transportation maintenance is being profoundly reshaped by artificial intelligence techniques that target vehicle health monitoring (VHM), fault diagnosis, and maintenance decision support. Rather than presenting AI methods in isolation, this section reviews machine learning (ML), deep learning (DL), and complementary intelligent techniques in terms of how they enable early fault detection, estimation of critical states such as State of Charge (SoC) and State of Health (SoH), remaining useful life (RUL) prediction, and optimisation of energy management and routing (Hossain et al., 2025; Hu et al., 2024; Saki & Soori, 2026).

For each family of methods, three aspects that are central to maintenance: (i) data requirements (sensor types, labels, historical operating data), (ii) deployment constraints (on-board/edge versus cloud, real-time requirements, computational resources), and (iii) operational KPIs that are directly affected (fault-detection accuracy, false-alarm rate, downtime, energy consumption, and cost). This task-oriented perspective links the methodological discussion in this section to the modality-specific applications in the following section and the enabling infrastructure in the technology stack.

2.1 Machine Learning (ML) Paradigms

Machine learning, a subset of AI, empowers machines to learn automatically and improve their functionality from data without explicit programming. The process typically involves two crucial stages: a training phase where a model learns from empirical data, and a testing phase where the trained model generates predictions.

Supervised Learning: This ML paradigm is highly effective in fault classification due to its accuracy in detecting and isolating faults. Its application has been demonstrated in complex systems such as vehicle power transmission systems and autonomous vehicle controllers common algorithms within this category include Decision Trees (DT), Support Vector Machines (SVM), K-Nearest Neighbors (KNN), Random Forests (RF), Artificial Neural Networks (ANN), and Multilayer Perceptrons (MLP). However, a significant limitation of supervised models is their heavy reliance on large, meticulously labeled datasets, which are often impractical and costly to obtain in real-world vehicle fault diagnosis scenarios across diverse vehicle models and operational conditions (Hossain et al., 2025; Hu et al., 2024; Saki & Soori, 2026).

Unsupervised Learning: In contrast, unsupervised learning approaches offer the advantage of automatic feature extraction and reduced human intervention, making them suitable for handling large datasets and non-stationary sensor faults, particularly in autonomous vehicles For instance, K-Means clustering is utilized to identify fault patterns within unlabeled datasets, proving highly valuable for predictive maintenance in modern vehicles Despite these advantages, unsupervised methods may encounter difficulties with feature similarity and shift-variant properties, potentially leading to misclassification (Hossain et al., 2025; Yamini et al., 2025).

Reinforcement Learning (RL): This paradigm excels at real-time adaptive decision-making, making it particularly relevant for dynamic energy optimization in electric vehicles RL-based control has demonstrated superior performance in EV energy optimization, achieving a vehicle range of 310 miles, significantly surpassing the 186–215 miles achieved by other optimization algorithms such as Grey Wolf Optimizer (GWO), Social Spider Algorithm (SSA), and Multi-Verse Optimizer (MVO). It also boasts 92% energy efficiency, compared to 80–87% for other methods, and substantially reduced charging and computational times (Hu et al., 2023, 2024). Despite its considerable potential for optimizing real-time fault prediction and maintenance strategies, RL is often hindered by long training times, high computational costs, and the inherent challenge of defining appropriate reward functions for complex vehicle dynamics (Hossain et al., 2025; Hu et al., 2024).

Prominent Algorithms in ML: Specific ML algorithms have shown notable success in transportation maintenance. Support Vector Machines (SVM) are often preferred for addressing unbalanced datasets in steering actuator fault diagnosis and multi-sensor systems fault identification within autonomous vehicles Random Forests (RF) have achieved a 92% classification accuracy in brake fault detection and an impressive 94.47% prediction accuracy in air brake systems for heavy commercial vehicles. For energy management systems, standard RL approaches like Q-learning and SARSA are widely used due to their adaptability and effectiveness in optimizing fuel and battery management across various driving cycles Furthermore, Particle Swarm Optimization (PSO) and Genetic Algorithms (GA) are frequently employed as powerful optimization algorithms in various vehicular contexts (Hossain et al., 2025; Kermansaravi et al., 2025; Khosravi et al., 2025; Watanabe, 2022).

2.2 *Deep Learning (DL) Architectures*

Deep Learning, a sophisticated and rapidly evolving field within machine learning, has yielded impressive results in automotive fault diagnosis by automatically learning the most informative and discriminative features from high-dimensional, multimodal data sources such as sensor readings, imagery, and time-series data.

Key Architectures: Prominent DL architectures include Convolutional Neural Networks (CNNs), Recurrent Neural Networks (RNNs), Long Short-Term Memory (LSTM) networks, Multilayer Perceptrons (MLPs), and Deep Neural Networks (DNNs).

Applications: CNNs, for example, are crucial components in the perception systems of autonomous vehicles, where they analyze visual inputs in real-time to detect objects, recognize traffic signs, and identify lane markings LSTM networks have been effectively utilized to diagnose electromechanical conversion chain faults in electric vehicles based on various sensor data Deep Neural Networks (DNNs) have demonstrated the ability to accurately identify faults within the dynamic models of autonomous vehicles.

Advantages and Challenges: DL models possess a remarkable capacity to capture complex non-linear relationships and subtle patterns within data, enabling them to identify anomalies and fault signatures that are often difficult to detect with traditional methods They offer superior accuracy, with some applications achieving up to 99.5% However, the success of DL models is heavily contingent on the availability of large volumes of high-quality labeled data, which can be a significant challenge to acquire in real-world automotive environments. Moreover, these models are computationally intensive, often requiring specialized hardware accelerators like graphics processing units (GPUs) for efficient training and inference.

To mitigate challenges such as data scarcity and expedite the training process, techniques like transfer learning and data augmentation are increasingly employed.

2.3 *Complementary Intelligent Techniques*

Beyond the core ML and DL paradigms, several other intelligent techniques play a crucial role in enhancing transportation maintenance systems.

Fuzzy Logic (FL): Fuzzy Logic is particularly effective in handling the inherent uncertainty and imprecision often found in battery data, such as fluctuations in State of Charge (SoC) or temperature Fuzzy Logic Controllers (FLCs) and Adaptive Neuro-Fuzzy Inference Systems (ANFIS) combine human-like reasoning with mathematical control to manage energy distribution, offering an interpretable control solution well-suited for stable hybrid systems. Their robustness against variations in battery behaviour and external conditions makes them reliable for real-time applications.

Bayesian Networks (BNs): Bayesian Networks are utilized to model temporal dependencies and uncertainties within complex vehicle systems, particularly for prognostics and health management (PHM) applications. While computationally lightweight for certain tasks, their accuracy may be constrained by their reliance on predefined rules and models rather than adaptive learning Dynamic Bayesian Networks (DBNs) are specifically employed for diagnosis and prognosis in autonomous vehicles.

Genetic Algorithms (GA): Genetic Algorithms are powerful optimization tools. They are employed for the optimal regulation of electric vehicle charging and discharging ranges, as well as the dynamic configuration of hydrogen energy cycles within micro-grids In the context of heavy-duty trucks, GAs are used to identify optimal driving profiles that effectively balance environmental sustainability (e.g., CO_2 emissions) with economic efficiency (operational costs). The NSGA-II algorithm, an efficient multi-objective genetic algorithm, is specifically used to find optimal solutions in complex scenarios.

Optimization Algorithms: Beyond GAs, various optimization algorithms are crucial for balancing multiple objectives in transportation systems. For instance, Particle Swarm Optimization (PSO) is used to enhance energy efficiency in dynamic scenarios. These algorithms are fundamental for achieving goals such as minimizing power drawn from the main grid, sustaining electric vehicle charge levels, and ensuring the satisfaction of EV owners.

The selection of an AI technique for transportation maintenance is not a "one-size-fits-all" decision; rather, it represents a strategic trade-off dictated by specific application requirements, data availability, and computational constraints. Supervised machine learning, while offering high accuracy, demands meticulously labelled data, a resource often scarce in real-world scenarios. Unsupervised learning can process unlabelled data but may be prone to misclassification. Reinforcement learning provides real-time adaptability but incurs significant computational costs and requires extensive training data. Similarly, deep learning delivers superior accuracy for complex data but is computationally intensive, whereas Fuzzy Logic, while simpler and more interpretable, may not achieve the same level of precision as more complex ML or DL models. This inherent diversity in capabilities and limitations means that different AI methods are optimal for different vehicular contexts. For example, an embedded system with limited onboard resources might favour simpler ML algorithms or Fuzzy Logic for real-time processing, while a cloud-based system with access to vast datasets could leverage the power of Deep Reinforcement Learning for comprehensive analysis. The optimal selection of AI models, therefore, depends critically on the specific vehicle's computational resources, the imperative for real-time processing, and a careful balance between accuracy, latency, and power consumption. This understanding leads to the development of integrated hybrid frameworks, where multiple AI approaches are combined to leverage their respective strengths and mitigate their individual weaknesses. Such an approach suggests a future where maintenance systems are not monolithic but rather modular and adaptive, composed of various AI components operating in concert to achieve holistic optimization.

3 AI-Driven Maintenance Across Diverse Transportation Modalities

The application of AI in transportation maintenance is not uniform; it is tailored to the unique characteristics and operational demands of different vehicle types. This demonstrates a clear evolutionary path from component-specific fault detection in conventional vehicles to complex system-level optimization in electric and autonomous vehicles, ultimately culminating in multi-objective fleet and grid management for broader sustainability.

3.1 Conventional Vehicles (CVs)

Recent advancements in vehicle health monitoring for conventional vehicles have predominantly focused on leveraging AI and data-driven techniques to significantly enhance the accuracy and reliability of fault detection across various vehicle subsystems.

Engine Performance: For monitoring engine performance, a combination of model-based techniques, machine learning (ML), and deep learning (DL) approaches provides highly accurate results, although they can be computationally intensive. ML and DL methods such as Decision Trees (DT), Support Vector Machines (SVM), K-Nearest Neighbours (KNN), Random Forests (RF), Artificial Neural Networks (ANN), and Multilayer Perceptrons (MLP) are particularly effective at processing high-dimensional datasets and uncovering intricate patterns indicative of faults hybrid approaches, which combine techniques like the analytic hierarchy process with neural networks, further enhance the accuracy of engine fault diagnosis (Table 1).

4 Enabling Technologies and Infrastructure for AI Maintenance Systems

The effectiveness and scalability of AI-driven maintenance in transportation are heavily reliant on a sophisticated ecosystem of enabling technologies and robust infrastructure.

Table 1 Mapping of maintenance tasks to data, AI techniques, and KPIs"

Task	Vehicle type	Data sources	AI techniques	Primary KPIs
Early brake fault detection	CVs and heavy-duty	Wheel speed, pressure, temperature	Random forest (RF), support vector machines (SVM)	Classification accuracy (%) false positive rate (events per 1000 km) mean time to failure (MTTF, hours)
Battery SoH estimation	EVs	Voltage, current, temperature, cycling history	LSTM, deep neural networks (DNN), ANFIS	SoH mean absolute error (MAE, %) range capacity loss (% per year) remaining useful life (Cycles)
Perception health monitoring	AVs	Camera/ LiDAR/radar diagnostics, fault flags	CNNs, sensor-fusion DNNs, Bayesian networks	Decision Accuracy (% correct classifications) missed hazard rate (events per million miles) latency (ms)
Fleet maintenance scheduling	Heavy-duty	Telematics + workshop logs	Gradient boosted trees, reinforcement learning	Unplanned downtime (hours/year) maintenance cost ($ per vehicle-km) fleet availability (%)

4.1 Advanced Sensor Technology and Multi-sensor Fusion

Sensors are fundamental electronic devices that detect physical attributes, such as pressure or acceleration, and convert them into electrical signals or other readable outputs for control systems They form the bedrock of data acquisition in vehicle health monitoring (VHM) A transformative role in VHM and fault diagnosis is played by the integration of advanced sensors, the Internet of Things (IoT), AI, and multi-sensor fusion (Hu et al., 2024).

Multi-sensor fusion is not merely about collecting more data; it is about creating a more robust and reliable representation of a vehicle's state by overcoming the inherent limitations of individual sensors. While individual sensors can be affected by noise or provide only a limited perspective of the vehicle's condition, multi-sensor fusion combines inputs from diverse sensor types. For instance, in autonomous vehicles, this could involve LIDAR, RADAR, cameras, and ultrasonic sensors; in conventional vehicles, it might include temperature, pressure, gas, position, speed, mass air flow, and torque sensors; and in electric vehicles, it encompasses motor, battery, charging, inverter, and transmission sensors. This integration significantly enhances fault scanning accuracy while simultaneously reducing the impact of noise. By providing a more comprehensive and reliable data input, sensor fusion directly improves the effectiveness of AI algorithms, as the performance of AI models is inherently tied to the quality of the data they are trained on. This approach is crucial for mitigating the "garbage in, garbage out" problem, especially in safety–critical applications where diagnostic precision is paramount (Fig. 1).

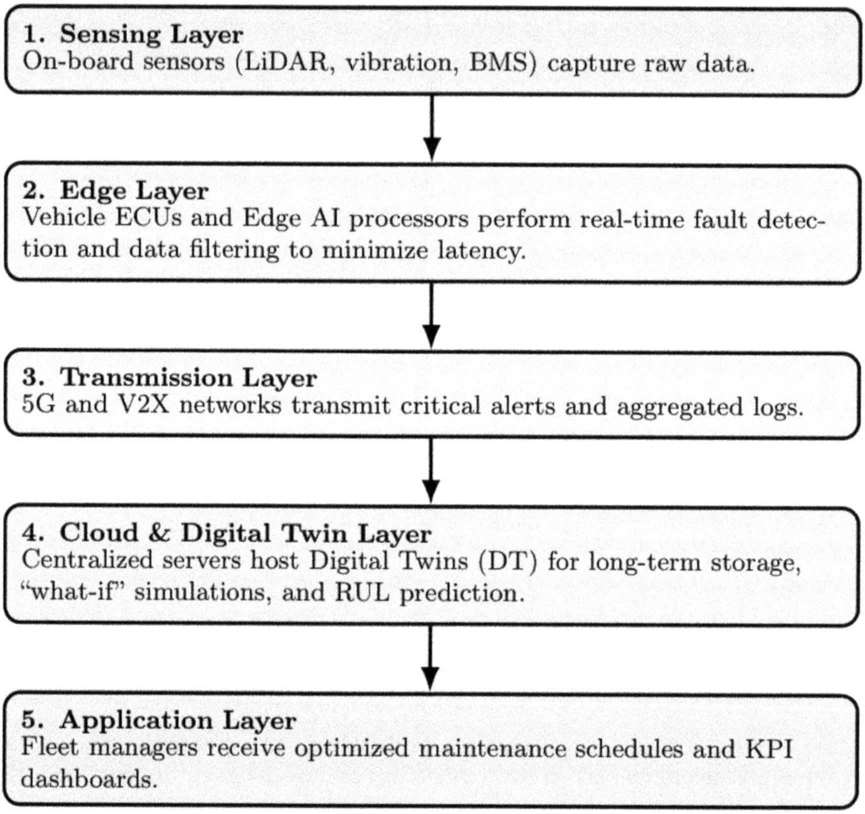

Fig. 1 The layered AI-enabled maintenance architecture. This diagram illustrates the data flow from physical assets (sensors) through the Edge and Cloud layers, culminating in digital twin applications for fleet-level decision making

4.2 Internet of Things (IoT) and Internet of Vehicles (IoV)

The Internet of Things (IoT) enables the continuous collection of data from various vehicle systems, which is then sent for analysis, adding significant dynamism to intelligent networks IoT is emerging as a transformative technology, offering substantial advancements in real-time monitoring, data acquisition, and predictive maintenance across the automotive sector.

IoT and IoV transform vehicles from isolated machines into connected data-generating nodes within a dynamic, intelligent network, enabling fleet-wide and ecosystem-level maintenance strategies. Historically, vehicle diagnostics were largely performed locally, with limited external connectivity However, IoT and IoV integrate sensors and communication technologies such as Wi-Fi, Zigbee, Bluetooth, and 4G/5G cellular networks to continuously transmit data for analysis. This enables real-time monitoring, data acquisition, and predictive maintenance across entire fleets It also facilitates remote diagnosis and over-the-air software updates, simplifying maintenance procedures and enhancing vehicle safety and reliability. This connectivity shifts the focus of maintenance from individual vehicle events to a centrally managed fleet operation. Fleet managers can gain comprehensive insights into the health and performance of their entire fleet, implement proactive maintenance strategies, and optimize logistics. This leads to significant cost savings and improved operational efficiency across the transportation sector.

IoT-based vehicle fault diagnosis systems leverage knowledge bases, ontologies, and deductive or inductive reasoning to provide high-level reasoning and inquiry responses to non-expert users These systems also collect and analyse multi-variable data using wireless sensor networks, such as Zigbee technology, for accurate state estimation and intelligent fault prediction The Internet of Vehicles (IoV) extends the principles of IoT to vehicular networks, creating virtual models of vehicles and traffic systems. This allows for real-time monitoring, predictive analysis, and informed decision-making through detailed, multidimensional simulations.

4.3 Edge and Cloud Computing Architectures

A novel conceptual framework for vehicle health monitoring (VHM) integrates sensors, IoT, AI, and big data analytics to enhance capabilities across all vehicle types. This framework is designed to address challenges related to heterogeneous data integration, efficiency, and real-time processing within dynamic automotive environments.

The hybrid approach of edge and cloud computing is essential for balancing the conflicting demands of real-time responsiveness and comprehensive, large-scale data analysis in AI-driven transportation maintenance. The problem arises because real-time fault detection requires extremely low latency, yet complex AI models and the vast datasets they process demand significant computational power Edge computing addresses this by processing data locally at the vehicle level or within nearby infrastructure, thereby minimizing latency and ensuring real-time fault analysis. This enables fast and immediate responses for detected anomalies, such as alerting a driver or initiating preventive actions Edge AI, by processing data locally, can significantly reduce latency and improve responsiveness while conserving network bandwidth by transmitting only the most critical data to centralized cloud systems. Conversely, cloud computing provides large-scale storage and powerful computational resources essential for extensive data analysis. Cloud platforms facilitate large-scale predictive maintenance across entire fleets and enable the sharing of diagnostic insights. The optimal strategy, therefore, is a hybrid approach: edge computing handles immediate, critical tasks requiring rapid response, while cloud computing manages complex, non-time-critical analysis, long-term data storage, and fleet-wide predictive modelling. This distributed architecture ensures both safety through real-time response and efficiency through comprehensive analysis, making AI-driven maintenance practical and scalable across diverse operational scenarios.

4.4 Digital Twin (DT) Technology

Digital Twin (DT) technology involves creating digital replicas of physical systems, which significantly enhances the entire lifecycle of complex items, systems, and processes In the automotive industry, DTs are particularly crucial for improving the design, construction, and operation of electric vehicles (EVs), contributing to safer, more comfortable, and more enjoyable driving experiences.

Digital Twin technology acts as a central nervous system for AI-driven maintenance, providing a holistic, real-time, and predictive virtual replica that bridges the gap between physical reality and analytical intelligence. Digital twins provide a virtual representation of a vehicle or subsystem that supports monitoring, simulation, and prediction. By integrating sensor data, digital twins can estimate condition in near real time and support predictive maintenance decisions. As noted in Kermansaravi et al. (2025) and Li et al. (2018), digital twins enable "what-if" analyses that test operational scenarios and their implications for health. This capability is valuable for electric and autonomous vehicles, where interactions between software, hardware, and environment can be complex. Hybrid approaches that combine physics-based and data-driven models can improve fault detection and RUL estimates. Overall, digital twins support adaptive maintenance through continuous updating of models and plans. Ultimately, DTs provide a powerful platform for AI to operate, facilitating proactive maintenance, optimized resource utilization, and continuous improvement throughout the vehicle's entire lifecycle. They transform raw data into actionable intelligence within a dynamic, interactive framework.

DTs enable comprehensive digital lifecycle analysis, which enhances battery management efficiency through optimal models for State of Charge (SoC) and State of Health (SoH) assessments. They are crucial for predictive diagnostics and overall performance optimization. Furthermore, DTs allow for simulating vehicle behaviour in a wide variety of scenarios, aiding in safety testing and design improvement. They are also essential tools for fleet management, enabling route optimization, efficient charging session scheduling, and accurate maintenance demand prediction.

4.5 Vehicle-to-Everything (V2X) Communication and 5G Networks

Vehicle-to-Everything (V2X) communication, encompassing Vehicle-to-Vehicle (V2V) and Vehicle-to-Infrastructure (V2I) interactions, is a revolutionary system that significantly enhances both safety levels and system reliability in transportation.

V2V Communication: V2V technology enables vehicles to share critical operating information—such as speed, position, acceleration status, and real-time road conditions—live through their system networks. This capability allows vehicles to identify future threats proactively and collaboratively make decisions, thereby minimizing safety risks and improving overall traffic flow efficiency V2V communication also facilitates cooperative fault diagnosis, where vehicles can jointly analyse potential errors. For example, if one vehicle detects an irregularity in its braking system, it can share this information via V2V communication with surrounding vehicles, allowing nearby vehicles to modify their driving decisions and prevent potential hazards.

5G Networks: The advent of 5G networks is a critical enabler for advanced V2X communication. 5G significantly advances wireless communications by boosting capacity, reliability, and speed while drastically reducing latency. This high-performance network is vital for electric vehicles (EVs), as it facilitates seamless component communication, enables self-navigating functions, and supports the autonomous exchange of vast amounts of traffic data The integration of 5G with Digital Twin (DT) technology further optimizes traffic resource management and enhances real-time traffic data prediction.

V2X communication, enabled by 5G, extends AI-driven maintenance beyond individual vehicles to a collaborative, network-wide intelligence, fostering collective safety and efficiency. Single-vehicle maintenance is constrained by onboard sensing and computing. With V2X connectivity, vehicles can share status updates and diagnostic insights, enabling cooperative or fleet-level maintenance. 5G networks provide bandwidth and latency characteristics that support real-time alerts and high-frequency data exchange. In Ranjan et al. (2025), V2X is described as a key enabler of distributed digital twins and cooperative diagnostics. This connectivity supports fleet-level health monitoring and faster response to emerging issues. Overall, V2X and 5G contribute to a connected maintenance ecosystem that improves coordination and reliability across fleets. This approach could lead to predictive maintenance for entire road segments or traffic patterns, not just individual vehicles, with profound implications for accident prevention, traffic flow optimization, and overall system resilience.

Gearbox: Vibration monitoring remains one of the most widely used methods for gearbox fault diagnosis. Analysis in both the time domain (e.g., Root Mean Square, RMS value) and frequency domain (e.g., Fourier Transform) is employed to detect anomalies and identify characteristic fault frequencies. Furthermore, meshless techniques are being developed to enable online condition-based monitoring, leading to quicker diagnosis.

Brake Systems: Learning-based fault identification schemes have shown remarkable accuracy in detecting brake faults. For instance, Random Forest (RF) algorithms have achieved a 92% classification accuracy in this domain, outperforming other methods such as Naïve Bayes, KNN, SVM, and DT. When applied to air brake systems in heavy commercial vehicles, DT and RF have demonstrated a prediction accuracy of 94.47%

Suspension: For suspension systems, clustering-based approaches combined with Fisher discriminant analysis are utilized for residual analysis, proving suitable for online monitoring. Additionally, observer-based techniques are employed to detect faults by analysing observer residuals.

Tire Monitoring: Tire monitoring benefits from observer-based and learning-based approaches, which offer high accuracy and adaptability. Actuator-redundancy-based methods and soft computing approaches provide robust solutions for real-time fault detection. Cost-effective and reliable alternatives for practical applications include indirect tire pressure monitoring, model-based, and signal-based methods.

Quantifiable Impact: AI-driven fault diagnosis in conventional vehicles has achieved up to 95% accuracy in the early detection of mechanical failures, which directly contributes to reducing maintenance costs and preventing potentially catastrophic failures.

4.6 Electric Vehicles (EVs)

The increasing prevalence of electric vehicles necessitates advanced monitoring and fault diagnosis techniques to ensure enhanced performance, safety, and environmental sustainability. Research in this area focuses heavily on model-based approaches, signal processing methods, AI, and ML (Kanagamalliga et al., 2025; Kumar & Prabhansu., 2025; Li et al., 2018).

Battery Management Systems (BMS): Battery Management Systems (BMS) are essential for optimizing battery use, extending driving range, and improving EV performance. Advanced BMS increasingly use AI to estimate State of Charge (SoC) and State of Health (SoH) more accurately than conventional methods (Hu et al., 2024; Kermansaravi et al., 2025). Machine-learning models (e.g., neural networks and SVMs) can combine temperature, voltage, and current signals to predict battery behaviour over time. These estimates support proactive decisions such as recalibration or replacement and can improve safety.

AI-based diagnostics can also detect anomalies (e.g., thermal runaway risk or cell imbalance) at an early stage. Signal-processing methods, including wavelet-based approaches, can reduce noise and improve the reliability of monitoring. Overall, AI strengthens BMS through improved estimation, fault detection, and energy-use optimisation, including charging recommendations based on usage patterns.

Electric Motor and Powertrain Fault Diagnosis: Long Short-Term Memory (LSTM) networks are effectively used to diagnose electromechanical conversion chain faults in EVs based on various sensor data Hybrid approaches, which combine signal-based analysis with AI techniques such as mixed clustering, have been developed for onboard health monitoring of EV propulsion systems.

AI-based Energy Management Strategies and Charging Optimization: In EVs, energy management is central to range and efficiency. AI can optimise the allocation of energy across the battery, regenerative braking, and auxiliary loads. Reinforcement learning has been used to adapt strategies based on real-time conditions (Hu et al., 2024; Kermansaravi et al., 2025).

AI can also optimise charging by forecasting user behaviour, demand, and grid conditions. Smart charging can schedule timing and power to reduce costs and mitigate grid constraints. Studies report that AI-based charging strategies can improve efficiency and reduce computation time compared with traditional optimisation (Hu et al., 2024). Reported accuracy improvements (e.g., ~ 97% vs. ~ 80 to 87%) should be interpreted in the context of the specific dataset and evaluation setup.

4.7 Autonomous Vehicles (AVs)

Autonomous vehicles represent a rapidly evolving technology that promises to transform the transportation industry. Various fault diagnosis methods are employed to identify anomalies in AVs, ranging from traditional model-based approaches to advanced machine learning and deep learning techniques.

Perception System Health: The reliability of perception systems is paramount for AV safety. Sensor fusion and AI-based prediction achieve an impressive 99% reliability in real-time decision-making, significantly enhancing operational safety and passenger confidence Support Vector Machines (SVM) have been specifically utilized for multi-sensor systems fault identification in Avs.

Fault Diagnosis in Steering Actuators and Control Systems: Advanced SVM algorithms are applied to address issues of unbalanced datasets in steering actuator fault diagnosis, ensuring robust performance Deep Neural Networks (DNNs) have demonstrated the ability to accurately identify faults in dynamic models of autonomous vehicles Furthermore, hybrid data analysis schemes, integrating fuzzy Proportional-Integral-Derivative (PID) control, combine sensor monitoring, anomaly detection, and actuator fault diagnosis for comprehensive system health assessment.

Real-time Decision-making: For real-time decision-making and control, model-predictive control combined with sliding mode observers is employed for fault detection and reconstruction in longitudinal control Digital twin-driven techniques, coupled with adaptive extended Kalman filters, are used to infer the size of faults within AV systems.

4.8 Heavy-Duty and Commercial Fleets

AI is also making significant inroads into the management and maintenance of heavy-duty and commercial fleets, offering substantial economic and environmental benefits (Sampaio et al., 2025; Watanabe, 2022; Yalavarthy et al., 2025).

Optimization for Fuel Efficiency and Emissions Reduction: Artificial intelligence, specifically Artificial Neural Networks (ANN) and Genetic Algorithms (GA), is applied to truck emissions reduction. This involves creating predictive models that integrate CO2 emissions with operational costs These models identify optimal vehicle driving profiles—such as a weight of 49.67 tons and a speed range of 31.00–36.61 km/h—to achieve a balance between environmental sustainability and economic efficiency.

Predictive Maintenance Strategies: Machine learning (ML) and the Internet of Things (IoT) are extensively utilized to monitor the health of fleet vehicles. These systems predict potential failures before they occur, which significantly reduces downtime and repair costs while simultaneously improving overall fleet reliability Sensors installed in vehicles continuously collect data on critical metrics like engine performance and tire pressure for analysis by ML algorithms.

Quantifiable Impact: AI models applied to heavy-duty truck operations have yielded significant cost reductions, ranging from 31.4 to 40.5%, reflecting substantial savings in both operational expenses and environmental costs.

AI's application in transportation maintenance reveals a clear evolutionary path from component-specific fault detection in conventional vehicles to complex system-level optimization in electric and autonomous vehicles, culminating in multi-objective fleet and grid management for broader sustainability. In conventional vehicles, AI primarily enhances the accuracy of fault detection for isolated components like engines, brakes, and gearboxes. This focus is on identifying and addressing individual component failures. As the technology progresses to electric vehicles, AI's role expands to system-level optimization, particularly for battery management (State of Charge, State of Health, lifespan) and overall energy management, which are central to EV performance This involves managing intricate interdependencies within the vehicle's power ecosystem. For autonomous vehicles, AI becomes critical for ensuring the reliability of perception systems and enabling real-time decision-making in highly dynamic and safety–critical environments, often involving multi-sensor fusion Here, the focus is on maintaining the integrity of the vehicle's "senses" and "brain." Finally, AI extends its reach to fleet-wide economic and environmental optimization, as seen in heavy-duty trucks, and even to grid-level energy management for EV charging and hydrogen storage within microgrids. This demonstrates AI's capacity for macro-level control and balancing diverse, often competing, objectives across an entire operational ecosystem. This progression underscores how AI is not merely about fixing a single part, but about optimizing the entire operational ecosystem, from individual vehicle health to fleet efficiency and grid stability. This implies that future transportation maintenance systems will be highly integrated, with data flowing seamlessly from individual components to fleet management centres and potentially even smart city infrastructure, all orchestrated by AI for holistic optimization.

5 Quantifiable Benefits and Transformative Impact of AI in Transportation Maintenance

The benefits of AI in transportation maintenance are best understood through their quantitative impact on operational key performance indicators (KPIs) such as fault-detection performance, maintenance cost, component lifetime, safety, efficiency, and environmental footprint. Importantly, these gains are reported for specific datasets, vehicle types, and operating conditions, and should be interpreted as case-study evidence rather than universal guarantees. This section synthesises representative results from recent studies and relates them to maintenance tasks across CVs, EVs, AVs, and heavy-duty fleets.

5.1 *Improvements in Fault Detection Accuracy*

AI-driven fault diagnosis significantly enhances the precision and timeliness of identifying issues across vehicle types. In conventional vehicles, supervised ML models applied to engine, brake, and gearbox data have achieved fault-detection accuracies up to approximately 95% in early detection of mechanical failures under benchmark conditions (Hossain et al., 2025). For example, Random Forest classifiers have reached 92% classification accuracy in brake fault detection and 94.47% prediction accuracy in air brake systems in heavy commercial vehicles (Hossain et al., 2025). In AVs, sensor-fusion architectures and AI-based perception health monitoring report real-time decision performance on the order of 99% correct decisions in simulated and controlled driving scenarios, improving the robustness of perception and control pipelines (Hossain et al., 2025; Luo et al., 2025). For EVs, AI-based battery and powertrain diagnostics use ML/DL models to identify incipient faults and abnormal degradation patterns, thereby reducing missed detections and false alarms compared with threshold-based methods (Hu et al., 2024; Kermansaravi et al., 2025). In some studies, deep neural networks and LSTM models have achieved fault-classification accuracies exceeding 95% on experimental datasets of EV drive systems (Hossain et al., 2025; Kermansaravi et al., 2025). These improvements provide a foundation for the cost, availability, and safety benefits discussed below.

5.2 *Maintenance Cost Reduction*

The economic implications of AI-enabled maintenance are substantial at both vehicle and fleet level. At the individual vehicle level, early detection of faults reduces the probability of catastrophic failures and unplanned roadside breakdowns, which are typically associated with high direct repair costs and secondary losses due to downtime. While poorly designed VHM strategies can increase maintenance expenses by up to 40% (Hossain et al., 2025), well-calibrated AI-based monitoring and predictive maintenance can reduce both the frequency and severity of interventions.

At fleet level, AI models applied to heavy-duty truck operations have yielded total cost reductions in the range of 31.4–40.5%, reflecting combined savings in fuel consumption, maintenance, and emissions-related penalties when optimal eco-driving profiles and maintenance strategies are implemented (Kumar & Prabhansu, 2025). In the context of EV-microgrid systems, AI-driven hybrid control strategies for hydrogen-integrated microgrids report annual financial benefits on the order of USD 468000, together with significant energy and emissions savings (Hu et al., 2023). These case studies illustrate how AI shifts maintenance from a cost centre to a lever for economic optimisation.

5.3 Component Lifespan Extension

AI is pivotal in extending the service life of key vehicle components by aligning maintenance actions with the actual condition of assets. For EV batteries, AI-driven SoH estimation and intelligent charge-control strategies have been shown to prolong battery lifespan by approximately 10–15% in accelerated ageing tests and simulation-based studies (Hu et al., 2024; Kermansaravi et al., 2025). Prognostics and health management frameworks that use ML/DL models or Bayesian networks to estimate RUL can schedule maintenance only when necessary, avoiding both premature replacement and over-extended operation (Hossain et al., 2025; Khosravi et al., 2025).

Similar logic applies to mechanical subsystems such as brakes, suspension, and steering, where AI-based fault detection reduces the likelihood of operating components under severe defect conditions, thereby mitigating accelerated wear. Across fleets, these effects aggregate into higher asset utilisation, lower capital expenditure on replacements, and more predictable planning of overhaul activities.

5.4 Enhancements in Operational Safety

Safety is a central motivation for AI-enabled maintenance, especially in AVs and high-occupancy public transport. For CVs, AI-based early detection of engine and brake faults help prevent loss-of-power events, brake fade, or wheel lock scenarios that could precipitate accidents (Hossain et al., 2025). For AVs, the reliability of perception and decision-making is directly tied to safety outcomes: AI-based perception systems and health monitoring frameworks report real-time decision reliability close to 99% in benchmarked environments, thus reducing the probability of unsafe control actions under sensor faults or environmental disturbances (Hossain et al., 2025; Kanagamalliga et al., 2025; Luo et al., 2025).

In addition, AI contributes to safety via advanced driver-assistance systems (ADAS), real-time hazard detection, and V2X-enabled cooperative awareness.

Predictive analytics can identify high-risk patterns in driving behaviour or environmental conditions, allowing preventive interventions such as adaptive speed recommendations, targeted inspections, or dynamic maintenance scheduling.

5.5 Overall System Efficiency

AI-driven solutions foster a more efficient transportation ecosystem by optimising energy management across vehicles and infrastructure. In EVs, AI-based energy management systems and charge–discharge strategies can improve effective vehicle mileage by more than 24% relative to baseline control strategies in mixed urban and extra-urban cycles (Kermansaravi et al., 2025). Deep and reinforcement learning approaches to EV energy optimisation have reported up to 310 miles of achievable range, compared with 186–215 miles for alternative meta-heuristic optimisers such as Grey Wolf Optimizer, Social Spider Algorithm, and Multi-Verse Optimizer (Hu et al., 2023, 2024). In the same studies, energy efficiency reached around 92%, versus 80–87% for competing methods, with reduced charging times (1.5 h vs. 2.0–2.5 h) and much lower computational effort (Hu et al., 2024).

At system level, AI-controlled microgrids and V2G/V2H schemes can conserve over 12,600 MWh of energy annually and avoid more than 8800 tons of CO_2 emissions in representative scenarios (Hu et al., 2023). Grid-aware charging optimisation further reduces peak loads and associated infrastructure costs. In urban networks, AI-based traffic management and eco-routing algorithms shorten travel times, reduce idling, and smooth traffic flow, indirectly lowering fuel/energy use and wear on components.

5.6 Contributions to Environmental Sustainability

The environmental benefits of AI-enabled maintenance arise from a combination of improved energy efficiency, extended component lifetimes, and reduced emissions at both vehicle and system level. As noted above, AI-driven microgrids and EV energy-management strategies can significantly reduce CO_2 emissions and energy consumption (Hu et al., 2023, 2024; Kermansaravi et al., 2025). Eco-routing and eco-driving profiles generated for heavy-duty trucks, for example, balance operating speed, payload, and terrain to minimise fuel use while satisfying service requirements (Kumar & Prabhansu, 2025).

Beyond direct environmental metrics, AI-enabled maintenance supports wider sustainability goals by improving reliability and availability of public transport services, thereby making modal shifts away from private car use more attractive. It also underpins new service models such as “maintenance-as-a-service” and more sustainable asset-management strategies.

Overall, the quantitative evidence from recent studies suggests that AI can deliver meaningful improvements across multiple KPIs when carefully matched to maintenance tasks, data availability, and deployment constraints. The following tables summarise selected case-study results and provide a task–tech–KPI mapping to guide practical deployment decisions (Table 2).

6 Conclusion

Artificial Intelligence (AI), Machine Learning (ML), and Deep Learning (DL) technologies have fundamentally revolutionized vehicle health monitoring and fault diagnosis, enabling a profound shift from reactive repair to predictive and proactive maintenance across conventional, electric, and autonomous vehicle types.

This review has highlighted significant advancements driven by AI, including superior fault-detection accuracy, such as up to 95% in conventional vehicles, and 99% decision accuracy in autonomous vehicle perception systems. These algorithmic improvements translate into enhanced operational reliability, reducing unexpected downtime and maintenance costs, with AI-driven optimization in heavy-duty trucks yielding savings ranging from 31.4 to 40.5%. Furthermore, AI has contributed to improved energy efficiency, notably a 15–20% enhancement in electric vehicles, and extended component lifespans, with EV batteries seeing a 10–15% increase in longevity. The synergistic integration of AI with advanced sensors, the Internet of Things (IoT), Digital Twins (DT), and high-speed communication networks has underpinned these achievements, creating a robust and intelligent maintenance ecosystem.

While challenges related to data quality, computational demands, cybersecurity, and model interpretability ("black box" problem) persist, ongoing research is actively developing innovative solutions. These include the development of hybrid AI models, federated learning for privacy-preserving data utilization, and Explainable AI (XAI) techniques to enhance transparency and trust. The critical importance of addressing ethical considerations, fostering public acceptance, and developing adaptive regulatory frameworks has also been emphasized as essential for widespread and responsible deployment.

The transformative potential of AI extends far beyond operational efficiency, contributing significantly to enhanced transportation safety, reduced environmental impact through optimized energy use and emissions, and increased accessibility of reliable transportation options by embracing these advanced techniques and fostering cross-disciplinary collaboration among academia, industry, and government, the automotive industry can achieve higher reliability, improved safety, and reduced operational costs. This collective effort will ultimately shape a more sustainable and intelligent future for transportation.

Table 2 Quantified benefits of AI in transportation maintenance (selected case studies)

Metric	Vehicle/system	Quantified value	Units	Context/scenario	Source
Fault-detection accuracy (CVs)	Conventional vehicles (engine, brakes, gearbox)	Up to ≈ 95	%	Supervised ML models for early mechanical fault detection in powertrain and brake systems, using experimental and in-vehicle datasets	Hossain et al. (2025)
Fault-detection performance (AV perception)	Autonomous vehicles	≈ 99	% correct decisions	Sensor-fusion and AI-based perception health monitoring in simulated and controlled driving scenarios	Hossain et al. (2025), Luo et al. (2025) and Kanagamalliga et al. (2025)
EV energy-efficiency improvement	Electric vehicles	15–20	%	AI-optimised battery and thermal management in EV driving cycles relative to baseline strategies	Hu et al. (2024) and Kermansaravi et al. (2025)
EV battery lifespan extension	Electric vehicles	10–15	%	AI-based SoH estimation and charge-control strategies in accelerated ageing tests and simulations	Hu et al. (2024) and Kermansaravi et al. (2025)
EV range increase (RL-based EMS)	Electric vehicles	Up to 310 (vs. 186–215)	Miles	Reinforcement-learning energy-management controller compared with meta-heuristic optimisers (GWO, SSA, MVO)	Hu et al. (2023, 2024)
EV charging-time reduction (RL-based)	Electric vehicles	1.5 vs. 2.0–2.5	Hours	Fast-charging strategy controlled by RL vs. conventional methods	Hu et al. (2024)
EV computational-time reduction (RL-based)	EV energy-management optimisation	≈ 1200 vs. 25,000–32,000	Seconds	RL-based optimisation vs. other meta-heuristics on representative drive cycles	Hu et al. (2024)
Fleet-level cost reduction	Heavy-duty trucks	31.4–40.5	%	ANN + GA-based eco-driving and maintenance optimisation for long-haul truck operations	Kumar and Prabhansu (2025)
Microgrid energy conservation	EV–microgrid system	> 12,600	MWh/year	AI-driven hybrid control for hydrogen-integrated microgrid with V2G	Hu et al. (2023)

(continued)

Table 2 (continued)

Metric	Vehicle/system	Quantified value	Units	Context/scenario	Source
Microgrid CO_2 emission reduction	EV–microgrid system	> 8,800	t CO_2/year	Same case as above	Hu et al. (2023)
Microgrid annual financial benefit	EV–microgrid system	≈ 468,000	USD/year	Same case as above	Hu et al. (2023)
EV mileage improvement (AI-based EMS)	Electric vehicles	> 24	%	AI-based energy-management system compared with baseline controllers on mixed driving cycles	Kermansaravi et al. (2025)

Declarations

Competing Interests The author(s) has no competing interests to declare that are relevant to the content of this manuscript.

List of Acronyms

AV	Autonomous vehicle
BMS	Battery management system
CNN	Convolutional neural network
CV	Conventional vehicle (internal combustion engine vehicle)
DL	Deep learning
DT	Digital twin
EMS	Energy management system
EV	Electric vehicle
GA	Genetic algorithm
IoT	Internet of things
IoV	Internet of vehicles
KPI	Key performance indicator
LSTM	Long short-term memory
ML	Machine learning
PHM	Prognostics and health management
PSO	Particle swarm optimisation
RL	Reinforcement learning
RUL	Remaining useful life
SVM	Support vector machine
SoC	State of charge
SoH	State of health
V2G	Vehicle-to-grid
V2H	Vehicle-to-home
V2I	Vehicle-to-infrastructure
V2V	Vehicle-to-vehicle
V2X	Vehicle-to-everything

References

Hossain, M. N., Rahman, M. M., & Ramasamy, D. (2025). Advances in intelligent vehicular health monitoring and fault diagnosis: Techniques, technologies, and future directions. *Measurement, 253*, 117618.

Hu, P., Chu, X., Lv, L., Zuo, K., Ni, T., Wang, T., & Shen, Z. (2023). An efficient and secure data collection scheme for predictive maintenance of vehicles. *Ad Hoc Networks, 146*, 103157.

Hu, J., Lin, Y., Li, J., Hou, Z., Chu, L., Zhao, D., Zhou, Q., Jiang, J., & Zhang, Y. (2024). Performance analysis of AI-based energy management in electric vehicles: A case study on classic reinforcement learning. *Energy Conversion and Management, 300*, 117964.

Kanagamalliga, S., Rajalingam, S., Karthik, R., & Jerome R. K. A. (2025). Analyzing the impact of AI-powered energy optimization in electric vehicles. *Procedia Computer Science, 260*, 1009–1016.

Kermansaravi, A., Refaat, S. S., Trabelsi, M., & Vahedi, H. (2025). AI-based energy management strategies for electric vehicles: Challenges and future directions. *Energy Reports, 13*, 5535–5550.

Khosravi, M., Behzadi, A., Duwig, C., & Sadrizadeh, S. (2025). AI-driven hybrid control for hydrogen-integrated microgrids: Probabilistic energy management with vehicle-to-grid. *International Journal of Hydrogen Energy, 146*, 149994.

Kumar, N., & Prabhansu. (2025). Next-generation battery energy management systems in electric vehicles: An overview of artificial intelligence. *Future Batteries, 7*, 100087.

Li, L., Lin, Y. L., Zheng, N. N., Wang, F.-Y., Liu, Y., Cao, D., Wang, K., & Huang, W. L. (2018). Artificial intelligence test: A case study of intelligent vehicles. *Artificial Intelligence Review, 50*(3), 441–465.

Luo, Z., He, T., Lv, Z., Zhao, J., Zhang, Z., Wang, Y., Yi, W., Lu, S., He, K., & Liu, H. (2025). Insights into transportation CO_2 emissions with big data and artificial intelligence. *Patterns, 6*(4), 101186.

Ranjan, R., Kulkarni, K., & Musharraf, M. (2025). Potential of explanations in enhancing trust—What can we learn from autonomous vehicles to foster the development of trustworthy autonomous vessels? *Ocean Engineering, 325*(4), 120753.

Saki, S., & Soori, M. (2026). Artificial intelligence, machine learning and deep learning in advanced transportation systems: A review. *Multimodal Transportation, 5*(1), 100242.

Sampaio, A. R. de S., Franco, D. G. de B., Zukowski Junior, J. C., & Spada, A. B. D. (2025). Artificial intelligence applied to truck emissions reduction: A novel emissions calculation model. *Transportation Research Part D: Transport and Environment, 138*, 104533.

Watanabe, N. A. (2022). Man-and-wife coupling and need for artificially intelligent heavy vehicle technology in *The Long, Long Trailer*. In *Autonomous and connected heavy vehicle technology* (pp. 161–182). Elsevier.

Yalavarthy, U. R. S., Kumar, N. B., Babu, A. R. V., Narasipuram, R. P., & Padmanaban, S. (2025). Digital twin technology in electric and self-navigating vehicles: Readiness, convergence, and future directions. *Energy Conversion and Management: X, 26*, 100949.

Yamini, E., Zarnoush, M., Jalilvand, M., Zolfaghari, S. M., Esmaeilion, F., Taklifi, A., Astiaso Garcia, D., & Soltani, M. (2025). Integration of emerging technologies in next-generation electric vehicles: Evolution, advancements, and regulatory prospects. *Results in Engineering, 25*, 104082.

Organizational Maturity, Strategy, and Operational Excellence

Maturity Models in Asset Management, Paving the Way for Digital Transformation

Fernando Jesús Guevara Carazas and Carmen Elena Patiño Rodríguez

Abstract The pursuit of digital transformation entails a range of challenges across various domains, with asset management being no exception. In this context, the evaluation of asset management process maturity constitutes a critical foundation for enabling a successful digital transformation. This chapter offers a comprehensive review of maturity assessment models relevant to asset management within the framework of operational excellence. It examines the key requirements involved and proposes an assessment model intended to support the systematic planning and monitoring of actions necessary to achieve excellence in asset management as part of the broader digital transformation agenda. Accordingly, this chapter introduces a novel visual maturity model designed to support continuous improvement and facilitate comprehensive digital readiness assessment.

Keywords Asset management maturity models · Operational excellence in asset-intensive organizations · Digital transformation readiness assessment · Excellence map for organizational maturity

1 Introduction

In the current industrial landscape, characterized by digital transformation, globalization, and increasing operational complexity, achieving operational excellence is no longer optional—it is essential. Companies are expected not only to maintain efficiency and quality, but also to adapt quickly to changes and innovate continuously. Within asset-intensive sectors, such as manufacturing, transportation, exploitation

F. J. Guevara Carazas (✉)
Universidad Nacional de Colombia, Medellín, Colombia
e-mail: fjguevarac@unal.edu.co

C. E. Patiño Rodríguez
Industrial Engineering Department, Engineering Faculty, Universidad de Antioquia, Medellín, Colombia
e-mail: elena.patino@udea.edu.co

A. Crespo Márquez et al. (eds.), *Digital Maintenance and Asset Digitalization*, Engineering Asset Management Review 5,
https://doi.org/10.1007/978-3-032-21502-4_14

of resources, and utilities, the asset management function plays a pivotal role in delivering this excellence.

However, a digital transformation process oriented towards operational excellence cannot be achieved without understanding the current state of an organization's operational maturity. Evaluating maturity systematically enables organizations to identify gaps, prioritize improvement actions, and track progress. When integrated with digital maintenance strategies and asset digitalization initiatives, maturity assessment provides a robust foundation for deploying technologies such as CMMS, EAM systems, and IoT platforms more effectively (Crespo, 2022; da Silva & de Souza, 2022).

This chapter presents a structured approach for evaluating the maturity of maintenance processes within the framework of operational excellence. It focuses on the use of diagnostic tools, maturity models, and visual instruments—like the "Excellence Map"—to support systematic and transparent implementation. Unlike traditional maturity models, this proposal embeds PDCA logic within a continuous visual framework tailored to asset management processes, thereby not only reinforcing continuous improvement through the PDCA cycle but also facilitating strategic alignment with the organization's broader digitalization initiatives.

Additionally, the latest version of ISO 55000 of 2024 highlights the need to assess the maturity status for asset management, so this chapter contributes to the path of specific improvements in search of operational excellence. (Gaitán, 2007; Gibson, 2000; Vidal, 2013; Yanez et al., 2022).

2 Operational Excellence in the Digital Age: Integrating Asset Management and Maturity Models

In the era of digital transformation, organizations are facing increasing demands to improve performance, manage complexity, and respond to dynamic environments. Within this context, Operational Excellence (OE) and Asset Management (AM) have become two key paradigms for achieving sustained value creation. The ISO 55000 standard defines asset management as the "coordinated activity of an organization to realize value from assets," emphasizing the balance between performance, risk, and cost over the asset lifecycle. (ISO, 2024).

Operational Excellence and Asset Management are not isolated concepts; rather, they are complementary frameworks that, when integrated, enable organizations to achieve higher levels of maturity, resilience, and strategic alignment. In this stage of the chapter explores the evolution of OE in light of Asset Management principles, highlighting the role of maturity models, continuous improvement, and the enabling function of digital technologies.

2.1 Origin and Evolution of Operational Excellence (EO)

The foundational ideas of operational excellence emerged in the late eighteenth century, when Adam Smith proposed new methods to maximize production efficiency, and, around the same period, Frederick Taylor introduced the first principles of management. Later, by the end of the nineteenth century, the concept of value in processes—closely linked with cost reduction as a sign of efficiency—gained relevance and helped shape the modern interpretation of operational excellence (Jaeger et al., 2014).

In the twentieth century, the central research question shifted toward how to achieve excellence. As a result, various methodologies began to emerge, such as Total Quality Management (TQM), Lean Manufacturing, and Six Sigma, along with other approaches aimed at enhancing organizational performance, including Just-In-Time (JIT) and Single Minute Exchange of Die (SMED). Notably, all these approaches were grounded in the KAIZEN cycle—Plan, Do, Check, Act (PDCA)—as a response to the growing need for continuous improvement (Jaeger et al., 2014).

Thus, historically, the concept of excellence has been closely tied to process efficiency and quality. Consequently, contemporary quality models are also referred to as excellence models.

Since 2008, studies on operational excellence have increasingly focused on identifying the key factors required to effectively manage excellence. In response to this need, several authors have emphasized the existence of enablers or organizational capabilities that drive and support operational processes (Jaeger et al., 2014). In this context, six essential factors for achieving long-term operational success have been proposed (Alcaide, 2016):

(a) Strategy,
(b) Operations and organizational structure,
(c) Performance management,
(d) Competencies and skills,
(e) Culture and leadership,
(f) Information systems and technologies.

This author discusses an excellence-driven approach focused on strategy, performance improvement, and excellence enablers, which in turn address various operational challenges related to people, technology, and processes. Similarly, various institutions have developed assessment models that evaluate the areas or factors an organization should prioritize in order to achieve excellence, as will be discussed later in this chapter.

However, one of the key questions that must be addressed is: What does excellence mean? According to Doeleman et al. (2014), there may be more than thirty validated definitions of the concept, each influenced by the context in which it was developed. Therefore, it becomes essential to examine some of the definitions that the concept of excellence has adopted over the years.

Campbell et al. (2010) states that "*Operational Excellence is achieved when best practices are properly aligned with the outcomes and needs of the organization.*"

In this regard, companies striving for excellence must select and adopt the set of methodologies, methods, and tools recognized as best practices in their industry, as part of their business strategy. Typically, such organizations begin with a quality management system that enables them to understand their processes and the needs of stakeholders, ultimately reaching a level of organizational autonomy that allows for continuous improvement across all organizational dimensions (Carvalho et al., 2017).

According to Duggan (2018), "*When each and every employee can see the flow of value to the customer and fix that flow before it breaks down, that's where operational excellence begins.*" From this perspective, it is inferred that at such a point, the organization no longer needs to focus on executing day-to-day operations, but rather on developing strategic activities that drive business growth. Operational excellence thus becomes a strategic approach to developing operations and delivering reliable, timely, and high-quality goods and/or services.

As a result of the aforementioned arguments, it can be stated that Operational Excellence is a measurable attribute that an organization can achieve, and it is closely linked to its competitiveness and the performance of its business processes (Miranda, 2016). Furthermore, it is evident that the concept of excellence encompasses all activities and functions within an organization—from strategy, vision, values, and culture to each of the processes, activities, and tasks required to carry out operations (González et al., 2015; Rosemann, 2010).

2.2 *Operational Excellence Process*

As we have seen, various authors present a wide range of steps or processes for achieving operational excellence. This section provides a general overview of the procedures outlined in different bibliographic sources. In this regard, Banna (2019) identifies ten principles for achieving operational excellence:

(a) Respect for every individual,
(b) Lead with humility,
(c) Pursue perfection,
(d) Scientific thinking,
(e) Focus on process,
(f) Ensure quality at the source,
(g) Create value from process flow,
(h) Systems thinking,
(i) Constancy of purpose, and
(j) Create value for the customer.

On the other hand, we find proposals for a four-step operational excellence model, structured as a continuous cycle: identifying organizational needs, understanding best practices, selecting alternative practices aligned with those needs, and defining and implementing a suitable model. It is noteworthy that both authors emphasize the importance of stakeholder empowerment and participation throughout the process (Ojha, 2015).

Regardless of the specific approach, different authors argue that the path toward achieving operational excellence generally begins with a thorough understanding of the organization's current state in terms of its processes, strategies, and goals. This is followed by the clear and measurable definition of objectives, which serves as the foundation for establishing strategies and an action plan that enables incremental progress through stages defined by the organization (Banna, 2019; Campbell, 2010; Carvalho et al., 2017).

2.3 *Maturity Models for Excellence in Asset Management*

Models for measuring excellence serve as general frameworks that establish the foundations, principles, and approaches an organization must adopt to achieve continuous improvement. Most of these models share a common characteristic: they enable the evaluation of performance and the identification of process weaknesses and threats that must be managed. Typically, they are used as diagnostic, risk analysis, or benchmarking tools, providing valuable information that should be integrated into the organization's business plans.

The first excellence models—also known as quality models—emerged in the 1980s in response to growing concern among Western organizations about the superior performance of Japanese companies. At that time, the Deming Prize and its underlying model already existed, embodying the philosophy applied by Eastern industries to enhance process performance. Many countries attempted to replicate this philosophy without accounting for cultural particularities, leading to several failed implementations of quality tools and approaches borrowed from Eastern contexts.

In reaction to these challenges, the Malcolm Baldrige model was developed to address the general conditions of Western enterprises. Shortly thereafter, in 1991, a group of European companies followed a similar path, establishing the European Foundation for Quality Management (EFQM) (Moeller, 2001) and its corresponding Excellence Award. As these programs evolved, evidence supporting the effectiveness of their excellence-oriented approaches demonstrated their potential to improve organizational performance (Carvalho et al., 2017; Correia et al., 2021).

Over the years, new models have emerged in response to contemporary perspectives on operational excellence. These models tend to differ in the naming and weighting of assessment criteria, the way results are categorized, and the level of detail and analysis applied to various subcategories (Alcaide, 2016). Table 1 presents some of the most frequently cited models in the literature, according to Yanez et al. (2022).

Regarding the application of these models, several relevant aspects can be highlighted: EFQM and MBM are most frequently applied in service sectors, healthcare institutions, universities, and government agencies (Thürer et al., 2018), (Rusjan, 2005). In contrast, BPMM and OMG-BPMM are applied across various industries,

Table 1 Characterization of excellence models

Model	Definition	Levels	Autor
BPMM (Business process maturity model)	This model serves as a guide for how organizations evolve based on the development of their business processes. It considers maturity as the degree to which an organization has explicitly and consistently implemented its business processes	(a) Initial (b) Defined (c) Predictable (d) Managed (e) Optimized	Fisher (2004)
CMMI (Capability maturity model integration)	This model contains the essential elements of effective processes and outlines a path for improvement from immature to disciplined, high-quality, and effective processes. It considers maturity as the degree to which processes are documented, managed, measured, controlled, and continuously improved	(a) Initial (b) Managed (c) Defined (d) Quantitatively managed (e) Optimized	CMMI Institute LLC (2020)
EFQM (European foundation for quality management excellence model)	This model is a framework based on results orientation, customer focus, leadership and consistency, process and fact management, people development and involvement, continuous improvement and innovation, mutually beneficial partnerships, and corporate social responsibility	(a) Top level (b) Second level (c) Third level	Moeller (2001)
FAA-ICMM (Federal aviation administration integrated capability maturity model)	This model removes redundancies between the FAA and ICMM models, integrating best practices into a common reference model with a unified structure and terminology, applicable across disciplines	(a) Performed (b) Managed (c) Defined (d) Quantitatively managed (e) Optimized	Looy and Poels (2011)
ISO (15504—9004)/IEC (Organizational maturity model—OMM)	Includes lifecycle definitions described in terms of process purpose and outcomes, along with an architecture describing relationships between processes, making it suitable for assessing process capability	(a) Incomplete (b) Performed (c) Managed (d) Established (e) Predictable (f) Optimized	ISO (2020)

(continued)

Table 1 (continued)

Model	Definition	Levels	Autor
Malcolm baldrige model (MBM)	A tool for evaluating, improving, and planning processes. This model is results-oriented, emphasizing the development of policies for business alignment and focusing on all key business processes, areas, and activities	(a) Leadership (b) Strategic planning (c) Stakeholder and market focus (d) Measurement, analysis, and knowledge management (e) Workforce engagement (f) Process management (g) Organizational performance results	National Institute of Standars of Technology (2020)
OMG-BPMM (Business process maturity model—OMG)	This model provides a roadmap based on best practices to guide the evolution from poorly defined and inconsistent tasks to stable unit-level practices, ultimately achieving statistically managed processes	(a) Initial (b) Managed (c) Standardized (d) Predictable (e) Optimized	Gardiner et al. (2008)
PEMM (Process and enterprise maturity model)	Considers two dimensions: processes and the organization. It states that companies must possess or develop organizational capabilities in leadership, culture, expertise, and governance	(a) Reliable and predictable process (b) Process with superior results (c) High-performance process replicable in other areas (d) Best-in-class process with internal and external reach	Hammer and Company (2007)

particularly within multinational corporations (Oakland, 2008). PEMM, on the other hand, is generally used by medium-sized enterprises due to its simplicity, whereas the CMMI model is typically implemented in software development companies (Chrissis et al., 2012). Finally, ISO standards represent one of the most widely applicable models across different sectors and organizations of various sizes (Pérez, 2014).

It is also important to emphasize that some models share structural elements. This is the case with BPMM and OMG-BPMM, both of which incorporate aspects related to process capability and organizational maturity levels. Process capability refers to the ability to control variations in actual outcomes, predict process costs and performance, and effectively achieve and enhance specific results. This is accomplished through institutionalization—i.e., the implementation of policies, standards, and organizational structures that support routine-based practices (Correia et al., 2021).

Maturity, in this context, is a metric used to assess organizational competencies, particularly those related to management practices.

Similarly, Henriquez (2023) proposes a Maturity Model designed to assess the implementation status of OE in firms operating in emerging economies, given its increasing relevance within the Industry 4.0 context. The study empirically validates 23 critical OE variables through interviews with managers and operations experts across 49 organizations from multiple sectors, ultimately consolidating five maturity levels: basic, beginner, developing, innovative, and champion. using the CMMI model as a basis.

Aras and Büyüközkan (2023) present a comprehensive literature study revealing a substantial rise in the development and application of digital Maturity Models. Their review identifies 497 documents supported by more than 20,000 referenced sources, underscoring the growing academic and industrial emphasis on assessing digital transformation. The bibliometric analysis indicates that publications on digital maturity have increased steadily since 2018, driven primarily by conference papers, while the most influential thematic clusters revolve around digital transformation, digital maturity, digitalization, and Industry 4.0. Furthermore, the thematic mapping confirms the consistent evolution of these clusters, highlighting the central role of Maturity Models in structuring transformation initiatives across multiple sectors.

It is worth noting that although the models presented in Table 1 were developed by different authors or institutions and are designed for diverse application contexts, they all share core criteria that emphasize leadership, control, and continuous improvement. Accordingly, Table 2 presents the most salient characteristics of each of the previously discussed models (Alcaide, 2016; Pérez-Mergarejo et al., 2014; Röglinger et al., 2012).

It is observed that most of the reviewed models do not provide a specific roadmap outlining the practices or actions required to progress toward higher levels of excellence. Additionally, they employ terminology and definitions whose adaptation process may prove complex in certain organizational contexts.

In this regard, after identifying improvement opportunities in the existing excellence models, this chapter proposes a methodological development for assessing the maturity level of an organizational process. The model consists of a quantitative method with moderate application complexity, a visual tool for representation, and an intuitive guide that facilitates the pursuit of excellence in a generic manner across any type of organization.

3 Methodological Development

In alignment with ISO 55000:2024, an asset management system must incorporate, in its decisions, plans, and activities, elements of continuous improvement and strong governance as essential foundations for achieving operational excellence. This part of the chapter presents three sections designed to establish a step-by-step process for implementing the proposed excellence model.

Table 2 Comparative analysis of mayor maturity models

Maturity model	Positive criteria	Opportunities for improvement
MBM	Provides methodological elements to conduct indicator-based analyses Focus on business sustainability and management excellence Applicable across all sectors	May involve the identification of a relatively larger number of indicators compared to other methodologies
EFQM	Does not require consultancy (unless certification is pursued) Applicable across all sectors International recognition Considers leadership and people-related management aspects	Abstract concepts complicate implementation Requires a significant amount of time Award eligibility requires accreditation by a certified consultant
BPMM	Applicable across all sectors Provides a detailed roadmap for guiding maturity assessment International recognition Evaluates both process capability and maturity	Too general Extensive and complex Does not address the critical role of Information Technology (IT) in Business process management (BPM)
PEMM	Applicable across all sectors Identifies essential characteristics for high-performance processes and organizations Does not require consultancy International recognition	Overly general, increasing subjectivity during assessment Lack of available procedures for practical implementation
ISO Standards	Applicable across all sectors Covers most functional areas of an organization (e.g., management, HR, production, engineering, and quality) International recognition	High level of generality results in few specific guidelines for implementation in certain industries or domains In the case of ISO 9004, lacks guidance on prioritizing areas for implementation
CMMI (Capability maturity model integration)	Provides a step-by-step guide for improvement based on maturity and capability levels (as compared to ISO standards) Strong international reputation	May be overly detailed for some organizations Requires significant investment for full implementation Nearly exponential growth in the number of areas, practices, time, resources, and costs Limited applicability

The first section introduces the methodology, which begins with the characterization of the internal process targeted for improvement and concludes with change management. The second section presents the excellence matrix designed for the model, as well as the necessary calculations for its construction once the reader begins implementation. Finally, the third section introduces the roadmap to excellence, a graphical resource that allows the organization to identify the current state of the process and the future steps required to progress along the path to excellence.

3.1 *Defining the Process Flow*

Figure 1 illustrates the implementation process of this proposed methodology, aimed at deploying an operational excellence strategy. Organizations seek to initiate their path toward excellence as part of their asset management efforts. The first step involves characterizing the internal process (activities, roles, responsibilities, resources) in order to determine whether there are foundational leadership capabilities that can effectively manage change.

Subsequently, the external context is analysed to identify regulations, standards, or policies applicable to the business (Fernández, 2002). These results help define appropriate criteria for constructing the excellence matrix, as detailed in the following section of this chapter. An initial assessment is then conducted to determine the current maturity level of excellence within the organization and to locate its position on the excellence roadmap, which is introduced in the subsequent stage.

Finally, change management enables the organization to make informed decisions regarding its maturity level, process transformations, and changes in its external environment, thereby fostering continuous improvement.

3.2 *Design of the Excellence Matrix*

Based on the definition of the organization's specific conditions and business context, the work streams (i) that the organization must develop are identified. Each work stream is assigned a set of evaluation criteria (k) that must be fulfilled at each of the five maturity levels (j). Table 5 presents the proposed maturity levels derived from the literature review (see Table 1) and the conceptual framework discussed previously (Campbell et al., 2011).

The evaluation scale shown in Table 3 corresponds to a continuous ratio scale ranging from 0 to 100 points, evenly distributed across the five maturity levels (j), with the objective of ensuring a standardized and impartial measurement system that enables comparisons between levels or organizations. A score of 0 represents a complete lack of awareness or fulfillment of the requirements at the "innocence" level, while a score of 100 reflects a state of excellence.

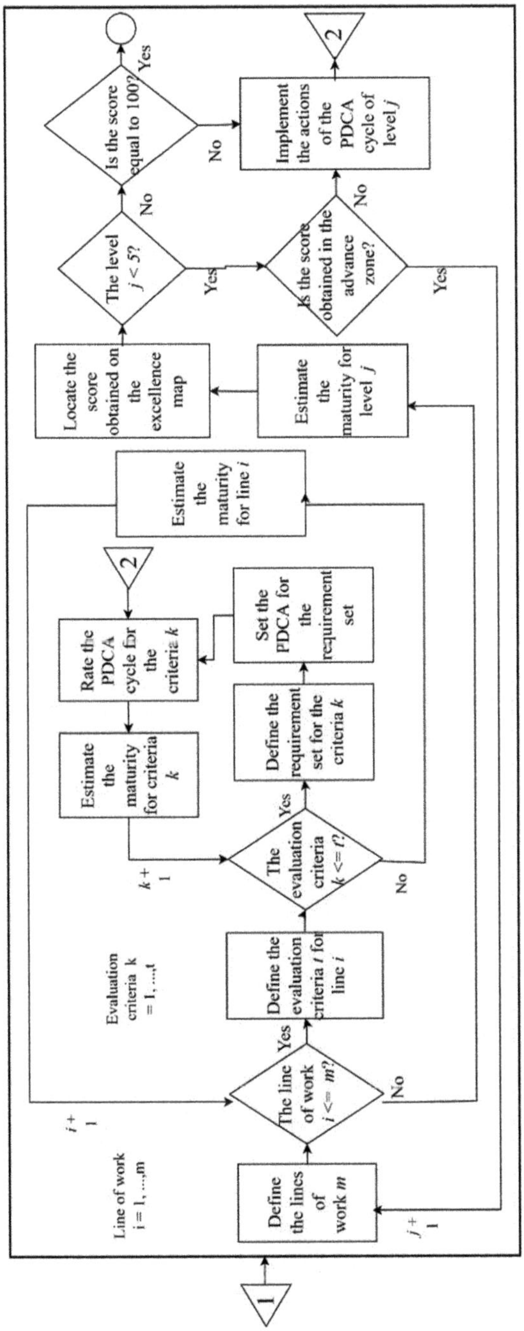

Fig. 1 Operational excellence implementation process

Table 3 Maturity levels (j)

Level (*j*)	Description	Characteristics	Range
Innocence	There is a lack of awareness regarding the implications, characteristics, or criteria of best practices	There may be some improvements oriented toward better practices	$0 < \text{level} < 20$
Awareness	The characteristics and benefits of best practices are understood	Minor improvements are implemented and aligned with some requirements	$20 \leq \text{level} < 40$
Understanding	The criteria, characteristics, and benefits of standards and methodologies aimed at excellence are well understood	There is good control over best practices, which are in the process of being extended organization-wide	$40 \leq \text{level} < 60$
Competence	The organization can demonstrate that it systematically and consciously meets the relevant requirements established in leading standards and methodologies	Requirements are fulfilled in alignment with the organization's objectives and operational context	$60 \leq \text{level} < 80$
Excellence	The organization can demonstrate the use of leading practices and achieves maximum value from the management of its processes and resources	Its objectives are fully aligned with the strategic goals of the organization and its operational context	$80 \leq \text{level} < 100$

Adapted from (Quintero, 2010; Yanez et al., 2022)

Subsequently, for each criterion *k* within the Innocence level, the corresponding activities are developed within the Deming cycle to fulfill criterion *k*. This serves as the basis for evaluating the first maturity level, as illustrated in Fig. 2

To assess the first maturity level, each of the activities listed within the Deming cycle is assigned a score *E,* based on the evaluation scale presented in Table 4, in order to meet the criteria *k* of the Innocence level for each of the defined work streams.

The scores for subsequent evaluations must be independent of previous assessments. This means that lower scores—even a score of zero—may be assigned in comparison to historical results, in order to ensure that processes are continually improved.

In general, the score obtained for each Deming cycle associated with work stream *i,* at maturity level *j,* and criterion *k*, is denoted as MC_{ijk}. The target score for each work stream is denoted as ML_{ij}. Thus, the score for each work stream is calculated as the sum of the scores obtained in its specific Deming cycles, while the total score for the maturity level corresponds to the sum of the scores across all work streams *i.* Table 5 details the calculations required to quantify the proposed maturity model.

To evaluate the Innocence level, if the results indicate that the organization has achieved more than 80% of the expected performance at this level—i.e., a score

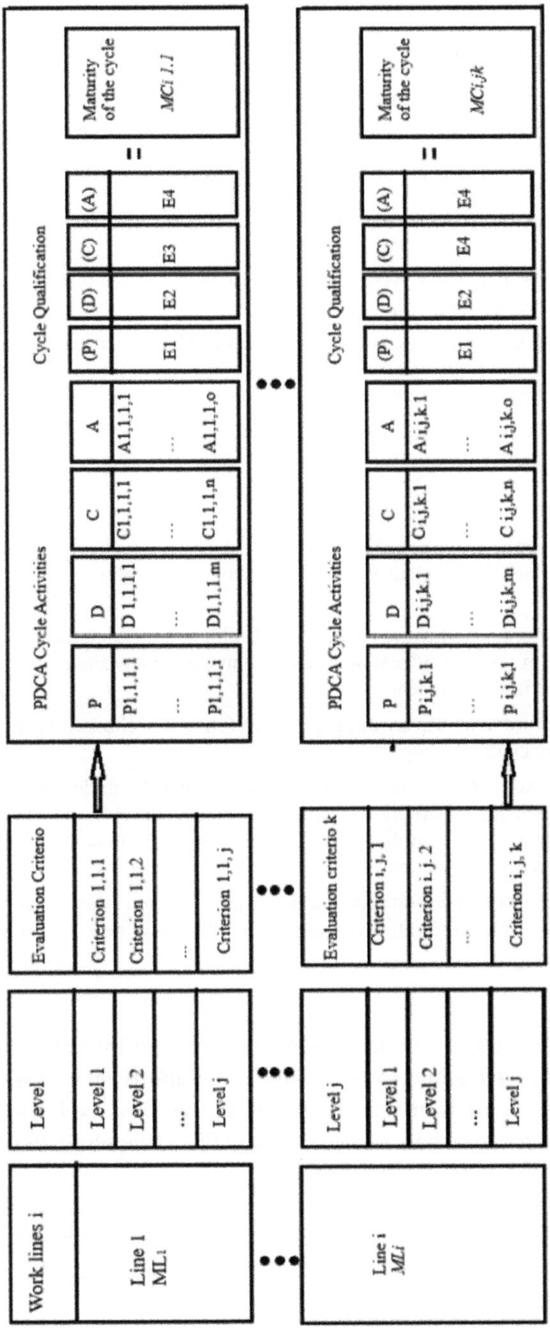

Fig. 2 Conceptual design of the excellence matrix

Table 4 Evaluation criteria

Description	E
The implementation of activities adds value to the organization and promotes continuous improvement. An effective communication plan is in place, fostering a sense of ownership and autonomy among all individuals involved in the process	10
Activities are effectively implemented and based on best practices applicable to the context, indicating proper process control	9
Activities are implemented as part of a standardized process with appropriate risk management. These activities generate significant benefits for the organization (economic, time, environmental, regulatory, cultural)	8
The implementation of best practices yields beneficial results in meeting the criterion, implying a developed level of leadership	7
The activities, methods, methodologies, and/or procedures used to execute the planned actions are appropriate for fulfilling the criterion. This suggests an understanding of the characteristics and benefits of best practices, along with evidence of improvement actions	6
The planned activities enable more effective fulfillment of the criterion (resource management, outcomes); in other words, **no alternative set of activities** exists that would fulfill the criterion more effectively. This implies a strong understanding of the process and best practices applicable to its context	5
At most, 95% of the planned activities are adequate for meeting the evaluated criterion, and a clear schedule (deliverables, defined dates, priorities, and responsibilities) is in place for execution	4
At least 80% of the planned activities are adequate for fulfilling the evaluated criterion. There is clear evidence of resource allocation (financial, human, time, technology, environment) to support its achievement	3
At least 60% of the planned activities are adequate for fulfilling the criterion. There is some evidence of resource allocation to support the criterion	2
At least 40% of the planned activities are adequate for the evaluated criterion. Some stakeholder needs are met, and the criterion is partially fulfilled. However, there are activities in execution that do not contribute to fulfilling the criterion, indicating partial unawareness of best practice implications	1
None of the planned activities are adequate for fulfilling the evaluated criterion. However, there is some level of execution, indicating complete unawareness of the implications of best practices	0

higher than 16 points (80% of the maximum score for the Innocence level)—it is necessary to construct the Deming cycle for the next maturity level (Awareness) and assess the organization's performance according to this new level. This process is repeated until the organization fails to meet at least 80% of the score for the evaluated maturity level.

However, if at any point the obtained score exceeds 80% of the maximum expected score of the matrix (80 points), it can be concluded that the organization is in a state of excellence, and it is therefore time to make strategic decisions regarding the process or the business, based on changes in the external environment.

The adoption of an 80% threshold is justified insofar as it reflects the point at which organizational practices exhibit demonstrable capability, reduced process variability,

Table 5 Measurement of variables

Maturity	Formula	Parameters
(C) Deming cycle	$MC_{i,j,k} = FC_1 * \sum_{q=1}^{4} E_q$ (1) $FC_1 = \frac{MT_{max}}{n} * \frac{1}{4E_{max}}$ (2)	• ***i*** is the line of work, where $i = 1,2,3, 4\ldots. n$ • ***j*** is the maturity level of each line of work • ***k*** is the evaluation criterion for each level ***j*** of each line of work ***i*** • $\boldsymbol{FC_1}$ is a criterion correction factor • ***q*** is the rating of each component of the PDCA cycle • $\boldsymbol{E_q}$ is the score obtained in the cycle q; $0 \le E_q \le E_{max}$ For the calculation of $\boldsymbol{FC_1}$, • $\boldsymbol{MT_{max}}$ is the maximum score expected from the complete excellence matrix • $\boldsymbol{E_{max}}$. is the maximum score for each component of the PDCA cycle • ***n*** is the total number of criteria in the matrix
Line of work (ML)	$ML_{i,j} = \sum_{k=1}^{k} MC_{i,j,k}$(3)	$\boldsymbol{MC_{i,j,k}}$ is the score obtained for each criterion k for the level j, from the line of work ***i***
Excellence level (NE)	$NE = \sum_{i=1}^{n} ML_{i,j}$(4)	***NE*** is the score obtained from the matrix

and a stable pattern of implementation. This level of attainment is consistent with the evaluative logic of ISO management system standards, wherein a high proportion of systematic conformity is interpreted as evidence of operational reliability, sustained performance, and an advanced degree of managerial maturity.

It is important to note that the score obtained in the evaluation of the Excellence Matrix is not necessarily cumulative, since the assessment begins from zero in each evaluation cycle. Therefore, it is possible that future assessments result in lower maturity scores, indicating opportunities for improvement in change management and in the sustainability of the implemented actions.

The frequency of evaluation of the Excellence Matrix must be defined by the organization, considering the minimum period required for the execution of activities. This decision should consider variables such as organizational culture, administrative, financial, and technical capacity, growth plans, and the leadership level of key roles, among others.

3.3 Excellence Map

The Excellence Map is a tool that enables the graphical representation of the maturity level and progress a company may have in relation to the partial or full achievement of the criteria defined according to its specific characteristics and business conditions (Yanez et al., 2022). The following section presents each of the components that constitute the proposed Excellence Map.

The first feature of the Excellence Map is organizational competencies, which include leadership, control, and continuous improvement. It is worth emphasizing that these competencies must be developed by a company in order to implement operational excellence processes.

Thus, leadership is positioned within the domain of social processes, where a certain level of influence is achieved to meet organizational objectives (Serrano, 2017). Control, in turn, must ensure that the organization's objectives are met and that coherence and consistency are maintained across organizational actions to guide the company toward fulfilling its mission. Continuous improvement, meanwhile, is a transversal competency across all organizational areas and is grounded in the measurement and feedback of process performance (see Fig. 3).

Note that the progress lines for each competency are not entirely continuous, nor do they originate from the same starting point. This is intentional, as it reflects the idea that different competencies emerge progressively as maturity levels advance,

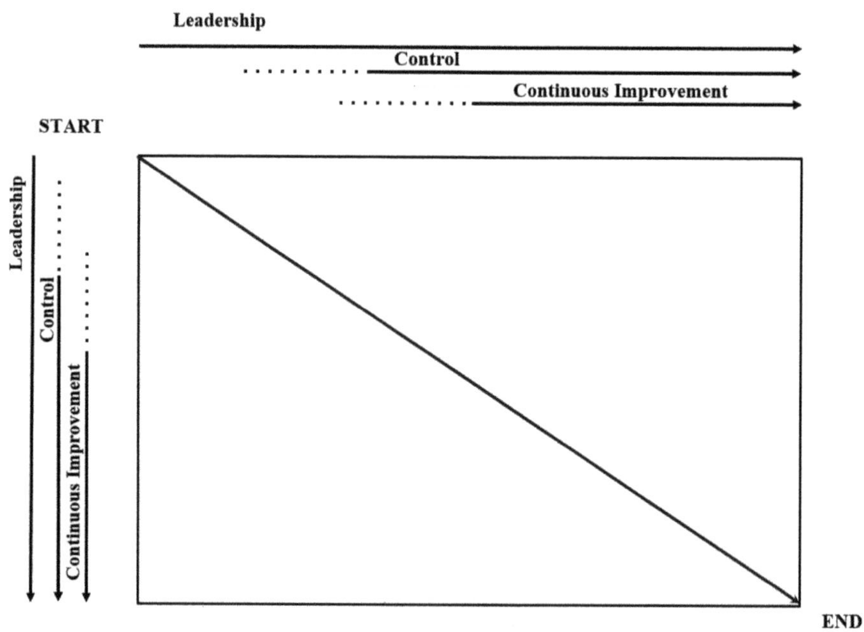

Fig. 3 Localization of organizational competencies

responding to the evolving needs of change processes. In this context, leadership is the fundamental competency required in all processes targeted for improvement.

The second feature of the map consists of the performance tracking lines, as illustrated in Figs. 4 and 5. At the bottom of the map, two arrows are shown pointing in opposite directions. The first arrow (Reliability and Execution) starts on the left side and ends on the right side. Its left-to-right direction indicates process growth in terms of maturity level, perception, and organizational competencies. Excellence is associated with high execution of activities necessary to meet organizational objectives, while reliability may be compromised in processes with low levels of maturity.

The second arrow (Costs plannig) originates on the right side and ends on the left. Its right-to-left direction suggests that as maturity levels decrease, the execution of unplanned actions and the consumption of resources are expected to increase, due to the lack of well-developed organizational competencies

The fourth characteristic considered in the Excellence Map is the perception level of management. Each perception level is represented by a straight, diagonal, dashed line, as illustrated in Fig. 6. Together, these lines reflect the company's gradual transformations throughout its journey on the Excellence Map, viewed from the perspective of standards, regulations, and the specific conditions of the business.

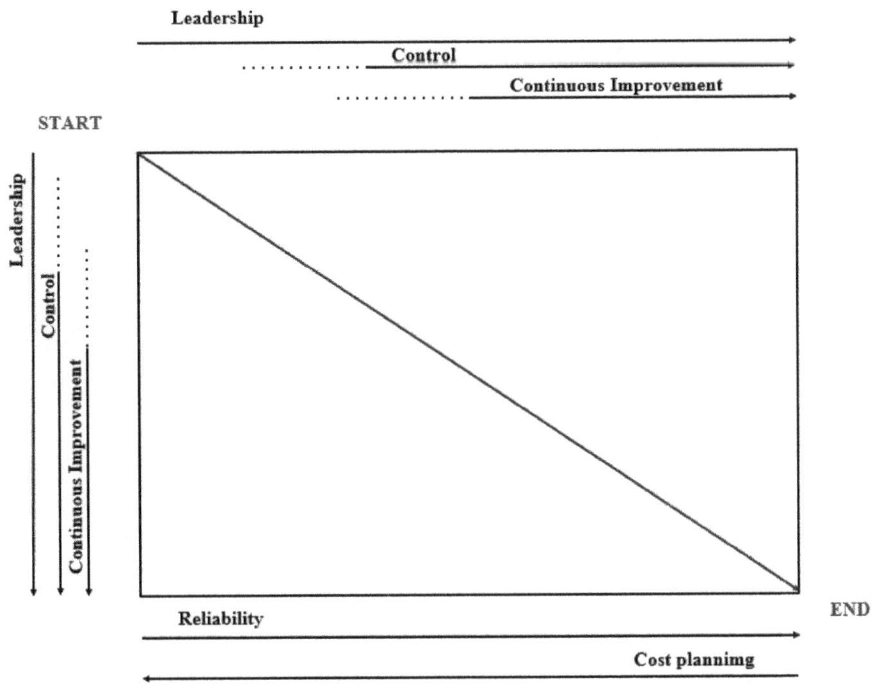

Fig. 4 Performance monitoring

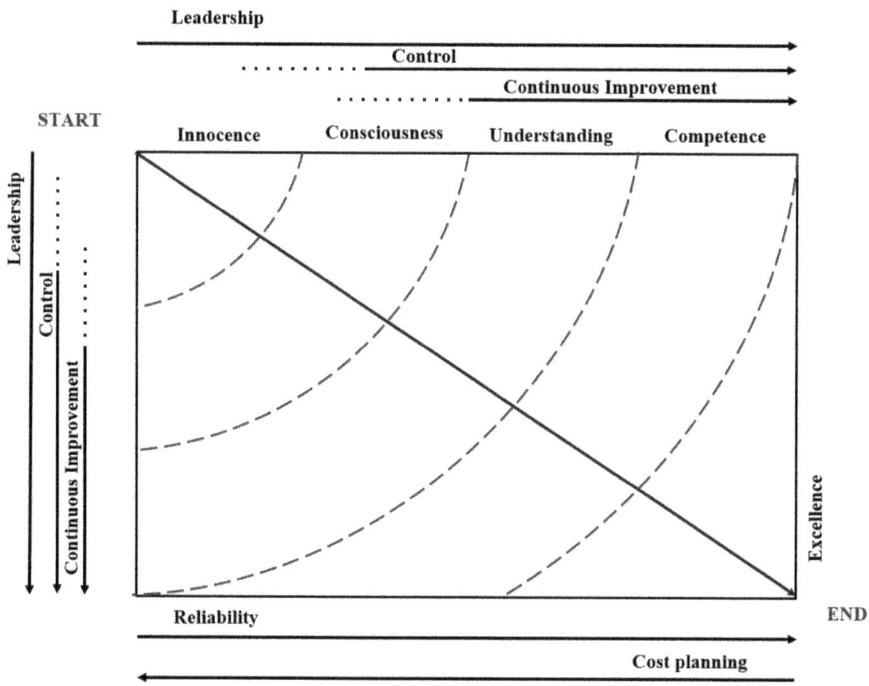

Fig. 5 Maturity levels

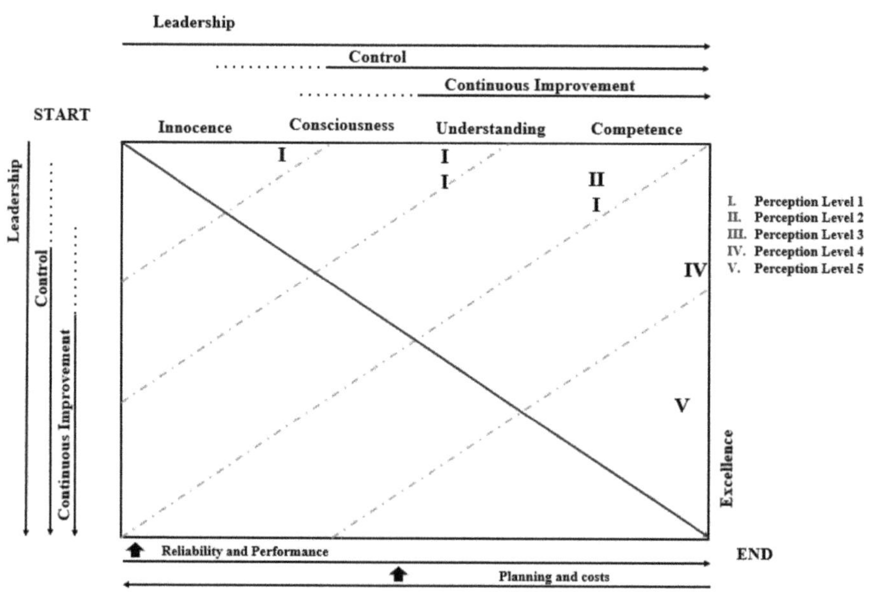

Fig. 6 Level of management perception

As with the maturity sectors, the perception bands have a directional flow indicating a higher degree of development. This progression begins at the top-left vertex and concludes at the highest maturity level in the bottom-right area.

It is important to emphasize that perception is not solely an internal matter; it requires external agents who ensure proper compliance with the guidelines established by each organization in its pursuit of excellence, in order to determine whether the stated perception level is appropriate.

A detailed analysis of the matrix reveals that maturity levels and management perception levels are not biased or misaligned. This means that as a maturity level approaches its peak (i.e., when the score for the current level exceeds 90% of the total expected score), and the organization is preparing to transition to a higher level of awareness, the next level of management perception begins to exhibit some of its characteristic traits. These transitional areas are referred to as advancement zones, as shown in Fig. 7. Within these zones, best practices emerge that represent the fulfillment of the objectives defined for each maturity level.

The final advancement zone is referred to as the "great leap" zone, which occurs when the score for the Competence level exceeds 90% of its expected total. This indicates that the company, organization, or business unit is fully prepared for the highest level of maturity development and can, at that point, be considered to be in a state of Excellence.

Best practices are represented using lowercase letters and refer to the activities that the organization should be carrying out to advance in both maturity level and management perception, see Fig. 8.

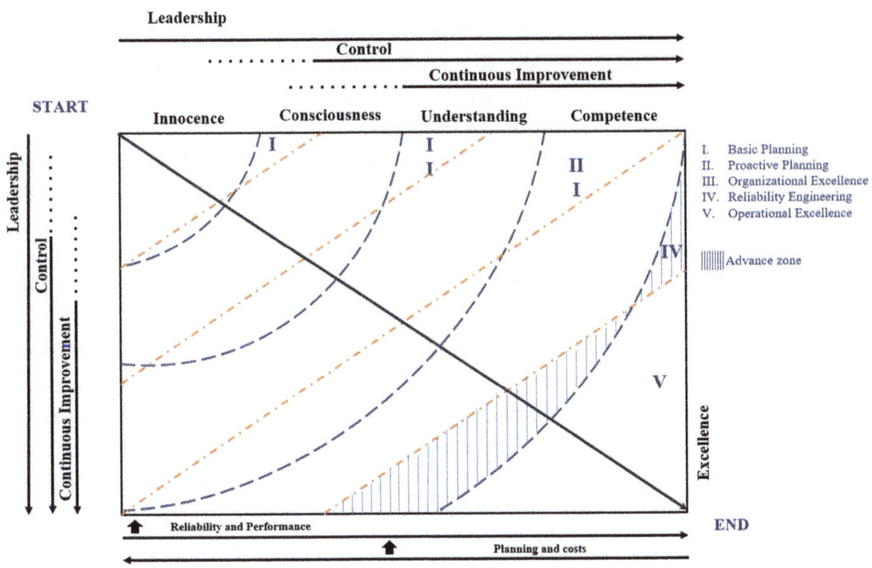

Fig. 7 Advance zone

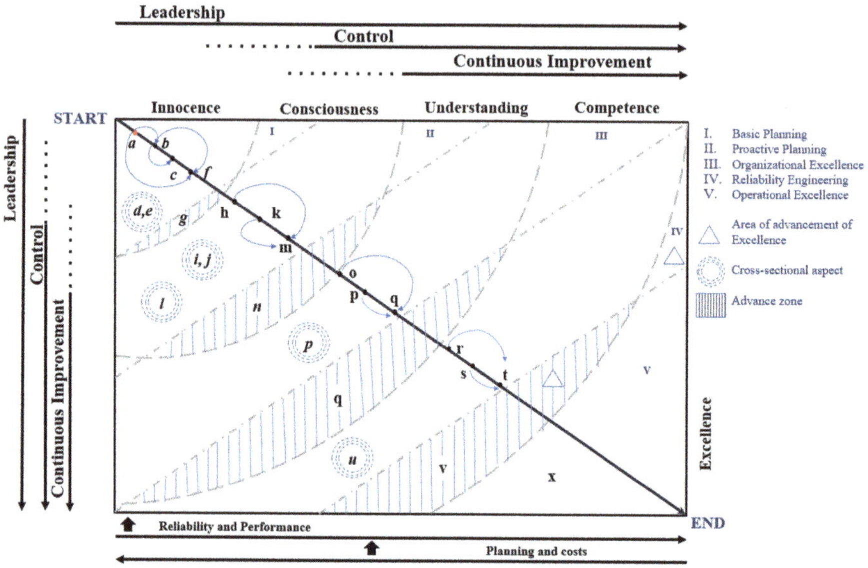

Fig. 8 Excellence map

To locate the result of the Excellence Matrix evaluation within the proposed diagram, the equation of a straight line is used (Table 5). In this case, the value of the horizontal axis "x" corresponds to the score obtained from the evaluation, projected onto the slope of the diagonal of the Excellence Map on which it will be plotted. The vertical axis "y" represents the evaluation result itself(Table 6). Consequently, coordinates are obtained along the diagonal of the Excellence Map, where each point (in Table 6) reflects both the score achieved and its corresponding position within the maturity levels, as illustrated in Fig. 9.

The final element of the Excellence Map is changes management. The path toward excellence involves significant transformations across the entire organization—from strategic planning to the most operational activities—in order to meet the previously defined requirements. As the organization progresses through the maturity levels, it will be required to make critical decisions regarding its internal processes, which may be influenced by external contextual conditions.

For example, the organization may need to redefine its organizational structure to appropriately assign responsibilities, especially in excellence-related processes; adapt the workforce to align with business strategies; implement new processes; or deploy training and employee engagement methodologies, among others. Likewise, during its journey toward excellence, the company may be impacted by external environmental changes, such as the adoption of emerging technologies, economic crises, shifts in consumer behavior, the threat of new competitors, or strategic mergers and alliances.

Table 6 Components of excellence map

Letter	Element
a	Work prioritization
b	Planning and scheduling
c	Work execution
d	Information system
e	Equipment history
f	KPI management
g	Preventive maintenance
h	Condition monitoring
i	Internal benchmarking
j	Technical competencies
k	Root cause analysis
l	Materials management
m	Equipment improvement
n	Predictive maintenance
o	Integration (Operations and maintenance)
p	External benchmarking
q	TPM (Total productive maintenance)
r	Risk-based inspection (RBI)
s	Life cycle cost (LCC)
t	RCM (Reliability centered maintenance)
u	Equipment standardization
v	RAM (Reliability, availability, and maintainability analysis)
x	Asset management

Thus, the proposed model serves as a strategic tool to support decision-making and influence tactical and operational outcomes within a VUCA (Volatile, Uncertain, Complex, and Ambiguous) world.

3.4 Strengths and Limitations of the Proposed Model

The development of this proposal emerges from the need for a robust tool aligned with the core concepts of ISO 55000 asset management, capable of determining an organization's maturity level—particularly in the face of major transitions such as the digital transformation of integrated asset management. Accordingly, one of the method's principal strengths lies in its explicit alignment with ISO 55000 and its foundations centered on value creation within organizations, including financial

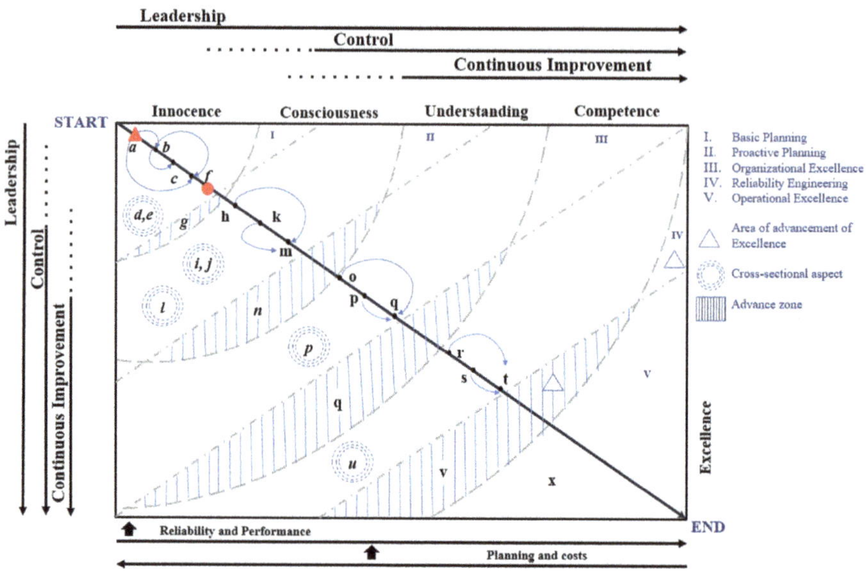

Fig. 9 Location of score in the excellence matrix

performance, maintenance effectiveness, reliability, and risk reduction, among other dimensions.

Furthermore, the method is inherently scalable, demonstrating the ability to adapt and adjust to any implementation scenario without compromising its capacity to assess maturity levels, regardless of the context or type of organization under evaluation. This scalability is reinforced by its conceptual soundness, methodological clarity, and innovative visual nature expressed through the Excellence Map.

Among its limitations, the model still requires further validation, and only through repeated application across diverse contexts will it be possible to consolidate its standing as a robust evaluation tool in the pursuit of operational excellence. Finally, successful implementation demands objectivity and prior expertise from evaluators to minimize subjectivity in scoring throughout the assessment process.

4 Model Application

The evaluation method was implemented in an organization dedicated to the collection and disposal of solid waste. For the pilot application, the organization's management selected the maintenance management process associated with the Solid Waste Collection and Compaction Trucks (SWCCT), as this process was considered critical to fulfilling the organization's mission. Moreover, delays or non-compliance in this area exposed the organization to significant fines imposed by public-service regulatory bodies.

In this pilot study, leadership capabilities were not formally managed, as they had only been preliminarily recognized. The external context was assessed using a SWOT-based methodology that incorporated stakeholder inputs and benchmarking against comparable organizations in the sector. This analysis revealed several threats, including frequent administrative turnover, scope deviations in operational activities, extended execution times, and a heavy reliance on external contractors.

The method's implementation demonstrated its practical utility in identifying organizational capabilities, diagnosing maturity gaps, and structuring targeted improvement actions. The characterization phase revealed leadership competencies at intermediate levels, clarified operational workloads, and exposed functional misalignments that had previously gone unrecognized.

Through the application of the Excellence Matrix and the subsequent development of the Excellence Map, nineteen evaluation criteria across six work streams were assessed, enabling the organization to determine its baseline maturity level and isolate priority areas for intervention. Overall, the case study offered empirical evidence of the model's capacity to support systematic diagnosis, guide decision-making, and align operational improvements with emerging digital-transformation requirements.

Beyond its immediate value as a maturity-assessment instrument, the model contributed to evaluating the organization's digital readiness by demonstrating how leadership, governance, process capabilities, and continuous-improvement mechanisms shaped the adoption of digital technologies. Its structured logic and visual outputs provided a diagnostic foundation for planning and monitoring digital-transformation initiatives, thereby enabling a more coherent integration of data-driven processes, advanced analytics, and Industry 4.0 technologies into asset-management systems. As such, the model strengthened decision-making at both operational and strategic levels and positioned the organization to transition more effectively toward digitally enabled excellence.

5 Conclusions

Digital transformation, within the framework of asset management, is closely aligned with the goals of achieving OE. In this regard, it is essential to have a well-structured model to measure the level of maturity that an organization possesses or is progressively acquiring throughout the process. Therefore, this chapter has presented the results of a comprehensive review of various bibliographic sources to define the concept of operational excellence and to illustrate how this concept has undergone several transformations throughout history, influenced by prevailing thinking models and production systems of each era. Nonetheless, its core remains rooted in the continuous evolution of the Deming cycle across all organizational areas through the application of best practices.

The implementation of an excellence model requires, as a priority, the development of leadership capabilities that enable the organization to communicate and foster commitment toward the achievement of organizational objectives. Among these capabilities, the ability to consolidate a clear vision of the desired outcomes and to guide organizational personnel toward a collective effort in accomplishing process goals is particularly relevant.

Implementing an improvement plan in an organization begins with assessing its initial condition or point of departure, in order to determine the resources needed to achieve the objectives defined by an operational excellence strategy. The methodology proposed herein serves as a structured companion to this process, defining incremental goals step by step. This methodology evaluates maturity, plans corresponding actions, and monitors their implementation, while simultaneously measuring the maturity of involved processes in light of the complete progression of each improvement cycle. This comprehensive approach provides added value compared to other methodologies reviewed in the literature. Furthermore, it ensures that planning efforts are fully aligned with organizational goals and future projections, thereby promoting continuity and long-term sustainability of actions.

The in-depth literature review revealed that, in many cases, existing methodologies are developed for individual actions and often lack integration, resulting in misalignments between corporate strategies set by top management and the daily activities carried out at all organizational levels.

Consequently, the main added value of the proposed methodology lies in the incorporation of a visual tool—referred to as the Excellence Map. This tool enables personnel at any organizational level to visualize the maturity status of the organization and identify the key activities that should be prioritized to contribute to the achievement of corporate objectives. In doing so, it supports the projection of the organization's vision and future plans.

Moreover, this chapter offers substantive contributions to the domains of operational excellence and asset management. It introduces a novel, quantitative, and visually oriented Excellence Matrix that enhances an organization's ability to assess its asset-management maturity with improved diagnostic rigor and transparency. It also integrates the foundational principles of operational excellence, the PDCA continuous-improvement cycle, and the governance requirements of ISO 55000:2024 into a coherent methodological architecture, thereby strengthening the organization's capacity to progress systematically through successive maturity stages.

6 Limitations and Pathways for Future Development

The conceptual character of this study constitutes its principal limitation, as the proposed Maturity Model has not yet been subjected to systematic empirical validation. Accordingly, future research should implement the model across multiple industrial settings to assess its reliability, scalability, and contextual robustness, as well as its capacity to integrate with emerging digital-twin–based assessment architectures.

Additional avenues for advancement include the exploration of AI-enabled maturity evaluation, data-driven operational monitoring, and advanced analytical techniques, all of which may enhance the model's diagnostic accuracy and further align it with the broader trajectory of organizational digital transformation.

References

Alcaide. (2016). *Estudio Comparado de Modelos de Excelencia Operacional Con el Apoyo de Juicio de Experto y Desarrollo de un Modelo Maestro Para su Aplicación Industrial* (pp. 1–79). Thesis available in: https://riunet.upv.es/server/api/core/bitstreams/618ffd49-e4ef-463e-a6a6-3ca6b1986240/content

Aras, Büyüközkan. (2023). Digital transformation journey guidance: a holistic digital maturity model based on a systematic literature review. *Systems*, *11*, 213, https://doi.org/10.3390/systems11040213

Banna. (2019). *The 10 principles of operational excellence.* Available in: https://blog.kainexus.com/improvement-disciplines/operational-excellence/the-10-principles-of-operational-excellence

Brocke, & Rosemann. (2010). *Handbook on business process management* (Vol. 1). https://doi.org/10.1007/978-3-642-00416-2

Campbell, Andrew, & McGlynn. (2010). *Asset management excellence: Optimizing equipment life-cycle decisions* (2nd ed.). Mechanical Engineering.

Carvalho, Sampaio, Rebentisch, Saraiva. (2017). Operational excellence as a means to achieve an enduring capacity to change–Revision and evolution of a conceptual model. *Procedia Manufacturing*, *13*, 1328–1335. https://doi.org/10.1016/j.promfg.2017.09.109

Chrissis, Konrad, Shrum. (2012). *Desarrollo y Gestión de Requerimientos. CMMI® Guía para la integración de procesos y la mejora de productos.* SBN: 9788499610788 Editorial: Editorial Universitaria Ramón Areces. Madrid-España.

CMMI Institute LLC. (2020). CMMI & CMMC. [Online] Available at: https://cmmiinstitute.com

Correia, Carvalho, Campbell-Allen, & Sampaio. (2021). *A new approach to organisational excellence for small and medium enterprises: The QOE-SME model. Total Quality Management & Business Excellence, 32*(11–12), 1359–1383. https://doi.org/10.1080/14783363.2020.1718490

Crespo Marquez. (2022). *Digital maintenance management: Guiding digital transformation in maintenance* (1st ed.). Springer. https://doi.org/10.1007/978-3-030-97660-6

da Silva, & de Souza. (2022). Modeling a maintenance management framework for asset management based on ISO 55000 series guidelines. *Journal of Quality in Maintenance Engineering*, *28*, 915–937. https://doi.org/10.1108/JQME-08-2020-0082

Doeleman, ten Have, Ahaus. (2014). Empirical evidence on applying the European foundation for quality management excellence model, a literature review. *Total Quality Management & Business Excellence*, *25*(5–6), 439–460. https://doi.org/10.1080/14783363.2013.862916

Duggan. (2018). *8 principles to achieve operational excellence* (pp. 1–11). [Online]Available at: https://www.processexcellencenetwork.com/lean-six-sigma-business-performance/articles/8-operational-excellence-principles-to-grow-your-b

Fernández. (2002). Dirección estratégica: una síntesis. *Investigaciones Europeas de Dirección y Economía de La Empresa*, *8*(1), 13–38. ISSN 1135-2523

Fisher. (2004). The business process maturity model A practical approach for identifying opportunities for optimization. *BP Trends.* [Online] Available at: https://bptrends.info/wp-content/publicationfiles/10-04%20ART%20BP%20Maturity%20Model%20-%20Fisher.pdf

Gaitán Rebollo. (2007). Diseño de un Modelo de Gestión de la calidad Basado en los Modelos de Excelencia y el Enfoque de Gestión por Procesos. Thesis Available at: https://manglar.uninorte.edu.co/bitstream/handle/10584/86/32884145.pdf

Gardiner, Weber, Curtis (2008). Business process maturity model (BPMM) version 1.0. Business Process Trends, (June), 496.

Gibson. (2000). Assessing ergonomics maturity level. In *Proceedings of the human factors and ergonomics association*, (Vol. 44), Issue 28578–28579. https://doi.org/10.1177/154193120004402846

González, Melo, & Limón. (2015). The organizational climate and its relationship to the quality of public health services: Design of a theoretical model. *Estudios Gerenciales, 31*(134), 8–19. https://doi.org/10.1016/j.estger.2014.08.003

Hammer and Company. (2007). *Process and enterprise maturity model—(PEMMTM).* Available at: http://www.hammerandco.com/pemm.htm

Henriquez, Muñoz-Villamizar, & Santos. (2023). Key factors in operational excellence for Industry 4.0: an empirical study and maturity model in emerging countries. *Journal of Manufacturing Technology Management, 34*(5), 771–792. https://doi.org/10.1108/JMTM-09-2022-0330

International Organization for Standardization (ISO). (2024). ISO 55000:2024 Asset management—Overview, principles and terminology.

Jaeger, M., & Sihn. (2014). Development of an assessment framework for operations excellence (OsE), based on the paradigm change in operational excellence (OE). *Procedia CIRP.* https://doi.org/10.1016/j.procir.2014.01.062

Miranda. (2016). Aplicación de un modelo de excelencia operacional en las organizaciones. Caso: Empresa CANELSA. Thesis—UNMSM. Available at: https://core.ac.uk/download/323349595.pdf

Moeller. (2001). The EFQM excellence model. German experiences with the EFQM approach in health care. *International Journal for Quality in Health Care, 13*(1), 45–49. https://doi.org/10.1093/intqhc/13.1.45

National Institute of Standars of Technology. (2020). Baldrige Performance Excellence Program.

Oakland, T. (2008). The relationship between business excellence and performance—An empirical study using Kanji's leadership excellence model. *Total Quality Management and Business Excellence, 19*(7–8), 733–749. https://doi.org/10.1080/14783360802159402

Ojha. (2015). Operational excellence for sustainability of Nepalese industries. *Procedia Social and Behavioral Sciences, 189*, 458–464. https://doi.org/10.1016/j.sbspro.2015.03.196

Pérez-Mergarejo, Pérez-Vergara, & Rodríguez-Ruíz. (2014). Modelos de madurez y su idoneidad para aplicar en pequeñas y medianas empresas. *Igeniería Industrial ISSN 1815-5936., 35*(2), 146–158. Available at: https://www.redalyc.org/pdf/3604/360433597004.pdf

Quintero. (2010). Estructuración y desarrollo de la matriz de excelencia en la empresa Confipetrepol S.A.SOM. *Universidad industrial de Santander.* Thesis Available in: https://noesis.uis.edu.co/items/c85bfe1c-30db-46d3-801e-151f618f7d3e

Röglinger, Pöppelbuß, & Becker. (2012). Maturity models in business process management. *Business Process Management Journal, 18*(2), 328–346. https://doi.org/10.1108/14637151211225225

Rusjan. (2005). Usefulness of the EFQM excellence model: Theoretical explanation of some conceptual and methodological issues. *Total Quality Management and Business Excellence, 16*(3), 363–380. https://doi.org/10.1080/14783360500053972

Serrano. (2017). Management skills and virtues: A road to excellence. *Estudios Gerenciales, 33*(143), 208–216. https://doi.org/10.1016/j.estger.2017.03.004

Thürer, Tomašević, Stevenson, Fredendall, & Protzman. (2018). On the meaning and use of excellence in the operations literature: A systematic review. *Total Quality Management and Business Excellence, 0*(0), 1–28. https://doi.org/10.1080/14783363.2018.1434770

Looy, & Poels. (2011). Defining business process maturity. A journey towards excellence. *Total Quality Management and Business Excellence, 22*(11), 1119–1137. https://doi.org/10.1080/14783363.2011.624779

Vidal, & Soto. (2013). Principios de la RSC en los modelos de excelencia. *Tourism & management studies, book of proceedings—Tourism and management studies international conference Algarve 2012* (Vol. 4) ISBN 978-989-8472-25. ESGHT-University of the Algarve, Portugal.

Yanez, Macias, ClavijoMesa, Patiño-Rodriguez, & Guevara-Carazas. (2022). Excellence model for the maintenance area in heavy-duty Truck Company. *IFAC-Papers on Line*, *55*(19), 163–168. https://doi.org/10.1016/j.ifacol.2022.09.201

Knowledge Engineering for Fusion Systems: Ontological Integration and Semantic Reasoning in Practice

Mohammed Anouar Amzert, Antonio Sanchez Membrieves, Juan Fernández Salas, and Manuel Chiachio Ruano

Abstract This chapter presents a knowledge-driven framework for enhancing maintenance management in complex fusion facilities, with a specific focus on the IFMIF-DONES project. The approach leverages semantic technologies, including a domain-specific OWL ontology and graph databases, to address the limitations of traditional maintenance methods. We detail the practical application of this framework, from ontology development and system architecture to rule-based reasoning using SPARQL. The chapter demonstrates how this semantic approach facilitates data integration, enhances decision traceability, and enables adaptive maintenance planning through practical use cases. The performance of the ontology is demonstrated using SPARQL, highlighting its effectiveness in querying and reasoning over complex maintenance data. This work underscores the value of semantic technologies in creating more intelligent, transparent, and efficient maintenance systems for safety–critical environments.

Keywords Ontology-based maintenance management · Semantic knowledge graphs for industrial systems · Rule-based semantic reasoning · Knowledge engineering for safety–critical facilities · Intelligent decision support in fusion infrastructure

M. A. Amzert (✉) · A. Sanchez Membrieves · M. Chiachio Ruano
Andalucian Research Institute in Data Science and Computational Intelligence (DaSCI), University of Granada, Granada, Spain
e-mail: ma.amzert@go.ugr.es

A. Sanchez Membrieves
e-mail: e.sanchezantonio@go.ugr.es

M. Chiachio Ruano
e-mail: mchiachio@go.ugr.es

J. Fernández Salas
Quantia Consultancy & Engineering S.L., Granada, Spain
e-mail: juanfdez@ugr.es

A. Crespo Márquez et al. (eds.), *Digital Maintenance and Asset Digitalization*, Engineering Asset Management Review 5,
https://doi.org/10.1007/978-3-032-21502-4_15

1 Introduction

Maintenance in large-scale scientific infrastructures is far from a routine technical task. In environments such as fusion research facilities—most notably IFMIF-DONES-, maintenance becomes a strategic, knowledge-intensive process that must coordinate personnel, remote handling systems, safety protocols, and scheduling constraints under demanding operational conditions. Ensuring continuity and safety in such settings requires not only technical expertise but also a structured understanding of the relationships and dependencies that govern every maintenance action.

Traditional maintenance management systems primarily focus on data recording and task tracking. While effective for procedural management, these systems often fall short when faced with the **complex, interdependent, and dynamic nature** of fusion environments. As summarized in Table 1, existing approaches are often siloed and reactive, struggling to navigate the immense data complexity and dynamic interdependencies inherent in such cutting-edge environments. While prior work has demonstrated the value of semantic technologies in nuclear and fusion maintenance (Wallbridge & Lowe, 2014, 2; Fortineau & Paviot, 2012, 2; Telnov & Korovin, 2019, 2), most efforts have focused on either static ontological modeling or data-level knowledge graph construction. On the other hand, recent work have increasingly focused on building comprehensive knowledge graphs for nuclear fusion energy (Loreti, 2025, 2), optimizing maintenance for safety–critical systems (Diao et al., 2024, 2), and addressing the specific logistics and maintenance challenges of the IFMIF-DONES project (Arranz, 2025, 2).

This chapter unveils a transformative semantic framework designed to revolutionize maintenance management. By harnessing the power of ontologies and graph databases. Following the classic definition of ontology as a "formal and explicit specification of a shared conceptualization" (Gruber, 1993, 2), we suggest that maintenance itself can be represented within such a structure. We present a practical, intelligent solution that moves beyond conventional limitations, enabling proactive decision-making and unparalleled operational efficiency in the most demanding of industrial landscapes.

Figure 1 illustrates this conceptual model. A maintenance activity is not just an isolated task. It takes place in a specific location, involves a defined set of resources, is subdivided into smaller operations, and is governed by contextual rules. Capturing this information in a formal ontology allows us to describe maintenance processes with clarity and precision, creating a shared language that supports knowledge integration, semantic querying, and advanced reasoning.

Despite progress in semantic modeling for nuclear and fusion maintenance, several critical questions remain unresolved:

(1) How can maintenance knowledge be represented in a way that is both formally consistent and practically usable during operational decision-making?
(2) How can this representation support both semantic reasoning and high-performance querying?

Table 1 Detailed comparison with traditional maintenance management methods with established and state-of-the-art approaches

Dimension	Traditional methods (CMMS/EAM/ relational DB)	State-of-the-art (digital twins/early ontologies)	Proposed semantic framework
Data integration	**Limited and manual**: data from different systems (Faila et al., 2025, 3)	**Improved but incomplete**: early semantic approaches demonstrated integration within a specific domain	**Semantic and automated**: designed for future integration with CMMS and digital twins
Reasoning and inference	**Procedural and implicit**: logic is hard-coded in application software	**Rule-based but limited**: early systems introduced rule-based reasoning (e.g., using SWRL (Fortineau et al., 2014, 3), but often faced limitations in expressiveness and performance	**Hybrid and multi-layered**: implements a powerful hybrid reasoning strategy using both SWRL for ontological consistency and SPARQL for complex querying and rule-based validation
Decision traceability	**Opaque and log-based**: decision logic is buried within application code or documented in text-based logs	**Improved but fragmented**: ontologies provide a clearer model, but the reasoning path can still be difficult to follow if not explicitly designed for traceability. (Lemaignan et al., 2006, 3)	**Transparent and verifiable**: every piece of data, rule, and relationship is an explicit part of the knowledge graph. SPARQL queries provide a clear, auditable path from a conclusion back to the source data and logical rules that produced it
Query expressiveness	**Structured (SQL)**: limited to querying explicit data in tables	**Domain-specific queries**: querying is often limited to the specific scope of the ontology	**Graph-centric (SPARQL and cypher)**: the dual-database architecture allows for both semantic (SPARQL) and pattern-matching (Cypher) queries
Adaptability and flexibility	**Rigid and brittle**: the relational schema is difficult to change	**More flexible but still constrained**: ontologies are more flexible than relational schemas. (Karray et al., 2011, 4)	**Dynamic and extensible**: the knowledge graph can be easily extended by adding new concepts, relationships, and instances without any schema downtime

(3) How can automated reasoning be leveraged to detect conflicts, ensure safety compliance, and support adaptive re-planning in dynamic maintenance environments?

To address these questions, this work introduces a comprehensive framework with the following contributions:

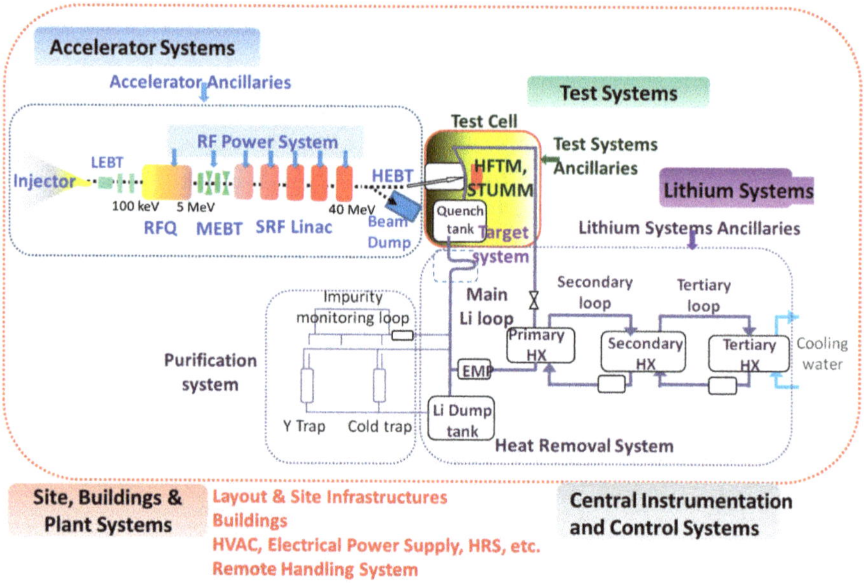

Fig. 1 Schematic viewchart of IFMIF-DONES systems (Zsákai & Muñoz, 2019, 1)

- A domain-specific ontology for fusion facility maintenance, providing a formal, shared conceptualization of maintenance activities.
- A dual-instantiation methodology, deploying the ontology on both RDF (GraphDB) and property graph (Neo4j) databases to leverage the unique advantages of each.
- A hybrid reasoning approach, combining the declarative power of SWRL with the expressive, data-driven capabilities of SPARQL for dynamic and adaptive maintenance logic.
- Validation through a practical use case from the IFMIF-DONES facility, demonstrating the framework's effectiveness in a real-world scenario.

2 Ontology Development and Knowledge Representation

The practical application of this ontology lies in its ability to define a common vocabulary and logical structure for maintenance-related information, thereby facilitating data integration, consistency, and formal reasoning.

The ontology models various elements crucial for maintenance operations, including concepts (classes), relations (object and data properties), and logical constraints (axioms). Key concepts within the ontology (as presented in Fig. 2) encompass entities such as Equipment,

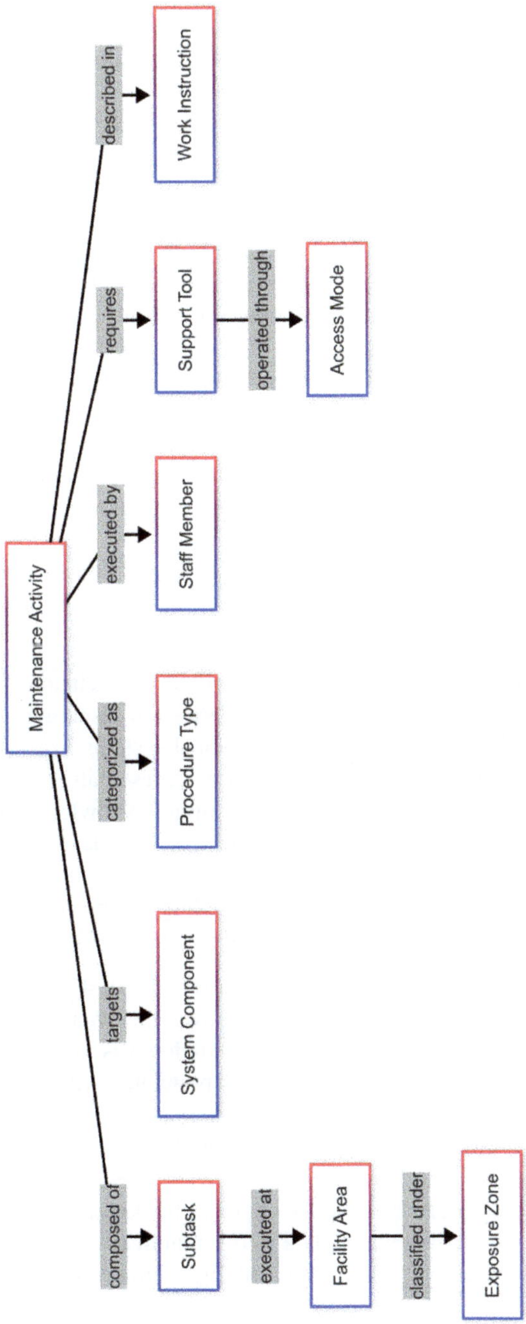

Fig. 2 Principal entities and relations defined in the maintenance ontology

MaintenanceTask, FailureMode, SparePart, Personnel, and Location. For instance, *Equipment* classes can represent specific components of the IFMIF-DONES facility, like AcceleratorSystemComponent or LithiumSystemComponent. MaintenanceTask classes define different types of maintenance activities, such as PreventiveMaintenance or CorrectiveMaintenance.

Relations, or properties, are used to define connections between these concepts.

Object properties link instances of classes, such as *hasTask* connecting an *Equipment* instance to a *MaintenanceTask* instance, or *requiresPart* linking a *MaintenanceTask* to a *SparePart*. Data properties assign literal values to class instances, for example, *hasMaintenanceDate* for a *MaintenanceTask* or *hasSerialNumber* for an *Equipment*. These relationships are crucial for capturing the intricate interdependencies within the maintenance landscape, allowing for a holistic view of the facility's operational state and maintenance needs.

Formal constraints are also integrated into the ontology to ensure semantic validity and structural coherence. These constraints help maintain the consistency of the knowledge base, preventing contradictory information and ensuring that the modeled data accurately reflects the real-world maintenance processes. For example, a constraint might ensure that a CorrectiveMaintenance task is always associated with a FailureMode.

The development of this ontology, while rooted in formal logic, was driven by the practical need to support real-world maintenance scenarios. It provides a structured framework that allows for:

- **Enhanced Data Integration**: By providing a unified schema, the ontology enables seamless integration of maintenance data from disparate sources, overcoming the fragmentation often found in traditional systems.
- **Improved Knowledge Discovery**: The explicit representation of relationships and constraints allows for the discovery of implicit knowledge and complex patterns that would be difficult to identify in unstructured data.
- **Foundation for Automated Reasoning**: The formal nature of the ontology lays the groundwork for rule-based reasoning, enabling automated inferences and decision support for maintenance planning and execution.

The resulting ontology comprises a comprehensive set of 41 classes, 50 object properties, and 40 data properties, designed to cover the breadth of the maintenance planning. While a detailed quantitative breakdown is beyond the scope of this chapter, the underlying knowledge graph was populated with a dataset of over 1000 triples, representing a significant volume of maintenance data. This provides a rich foundation for the reasoning and querying capabilities described in subsequent sections.

In essence, the ontology serves as the backbone of the knowledge representation system, transforming raw maintenance data into semantically rich, interconnected information that can be effectively utilized for intelligent maintenance management.

3 System Architecture and Implementation

The practical realization of the proposed semantic framework for maintenance management involves a multi-layered system architecture designed to transform raw maintenance data into a functional, intelligent knowledge base. This section focuses on the applied aspects of this architecture, detailing how the conceptual ontology is implemented and integrated with graph databases to support real-world maintenance operations.

At its foundation, the system relies on an ontology-driven knowledge graph that represents the semantic and operational logic of maintenance activities. Developed in OWL 2 with Protégé (Sivakumar & Arivoli, 2011, 3), the ontology defines core domain concepts, relationships, and constraints. Figure 3 illustrates the general process of the implementation.

The system architecture begins with the **Data Acquisition and Pre-processing layer**, where heterogeneous maintenance data including sensor readings, maintenance logs, and planning documents are ingested from various sources. This raw data undergoes a crucial cleaning and transformation process to correct inconsistencies and standardize formats. The output of this layer is structured and semi-structured

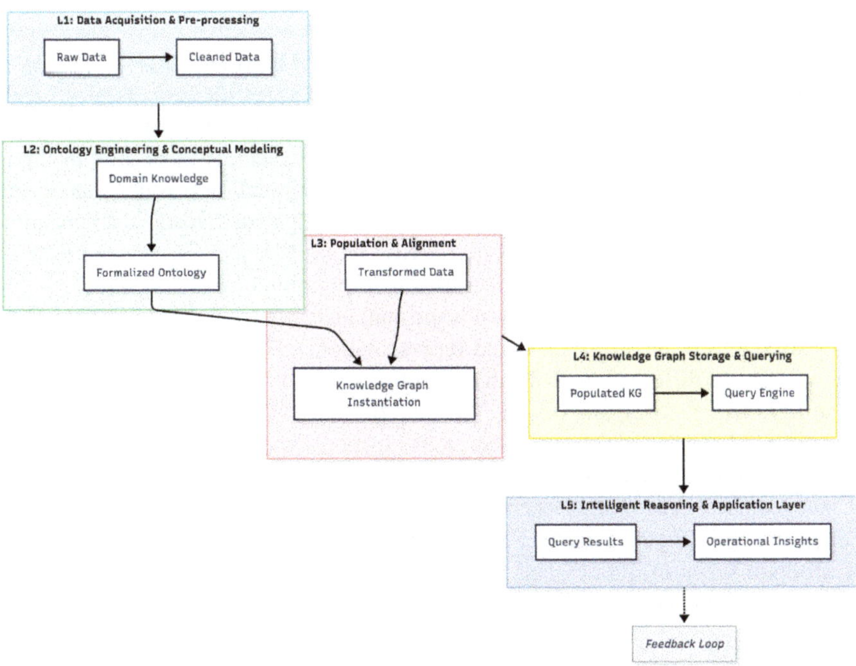

Fig. 3 Conceptual representation of the proposed multi-layer semantic framework integrating ontology modeling, hybrid reasoning, and dual graph database deployment for maintenance management

maintenance data, from which relevant features are extracted to facilitate subsequent semantic modeling.

Following this, the **Ontology Engineering and Conceptual Modeling layer** is responsible for constructing the ontology. This involves an extensive knowledge elicitation process, drawing insights from subject-matter experts, technical documentation, and system design blueprints. Key domain entities such as *MaintainableItem, MaintenanceTask, Personnel, WorkOrder, Tool,* and *RadiationZone* are represented as OWL classes. Their interrelations are captured through well-typed object properties like *requiresTool, performedBy, hasRadiationClassification,* and *isPartof*. The class hierarchy is meticulously structured to reflect both taxonomic relationships (e.g., Component is a subclass of *MaintainableItem*) and part-whole dependencies defined by the Plant Breakdown Structure (PBS), which organizes facility components into structured levels for engineering and maintenance management.

Logical axioms are formally specified within Protégé to enforce critical domain rules and constraints, ensuring the logical consistency and integrity of the knowledge base. These include disjointness axioms (e.g., *Manager* and *Engineer* roles are mutually exclusive), cardinality constraints (e.g., each maintenance task must be assigned to at least one responsible personnel), and property restrictions (e.g., tools used for maintenance must be available). These practical constraints are vital for maintaining data quality and enabling reliable automated reasoning.

To translate the formal ontology into an effective knowledge graph, the system incorporates a **Knowledge Graph Population and Alignment layer**. This layer converts the conceptual framework into a machine-interpretable format using OWL 2 and RDF (Beckett & Mcbride, 2003, 4) standards. Real-world entities, such as specific maintainable items, maintenance procedures, or facility zones, are instantiated and linked to their conceptual categories. This population process transforms the abstract conceptual model into a tangible knowledge base, ready for reasoning and querying. The process is integrated across multiple stages of the workflow to ensure the practical feasibility and seamless incorporation of real-world data.

A key aspect of the implementation is the dual instantiation path, supporting both RDF-based and property graph-based representations. This means the ontology is deployed on two different graph database platforms: GraphDB (Kiryakov et al., 2005, 5) (an RDF triple store), and Neo4j (Webber, 2020) (a property graph model). This integration allows for exploring the strengths of both types of databases, providing flexibility in data storage, querying, and performance optimization for various maintenance scenarios. The practical benefits of this dual approach include enhanced interoperability, allowing the system to leverage the specific advantages of each database for different types of queries and data relationships, and improved scalability for handling large and complex maintenance datasets.

In summary, the system architecture is designed for practical application, ensuring that the semantic framework can effectively ingest, model, store, and manage complex maintenance data. The integration with GraphDB and Neo4j provides a robust and flexible foundation for enabling advanced reasoning and querying capabilities, ultimately leading to more intelligent and adaptive maintenance management within fusion-based facilities.

4 Rule-Based Reasoning and Performance Demonstration (SPARQL)

Beyond the foundational ontology population and knowledge graph deployment, the semantic enrichment of the knowledge base is achieved through a sophisticated integration of rule-based reasoning mechanisms. This section focuses on the practical application of SPARQL (Prud'hommeaux & Seaborne, 2008, 5) (SPARQL Protocol and RDF Query Language) for materializing derived facts, enforcing complex operational logic, and demonstrating the performance of the ontology in supporting intelligent reasoning within the maintenance management framework.

While SWRL (Horrocks et al., 2004, 5) (Semantic Web Rule Language) can be used for inferring implicit knowledge, its inherent limitations, such as lack of support for negation as failure, aggregation functions, direct modification of the knowledge base, or complex temporal constructs, necessitate the use of more expressive querying capabilities. Therefore, this framework primarily leverages SPARQL queries, executed within the GraphDB SPARQL engine, to materialize derived knowledge, enforce scheduling consistency, and capture advanced operational logic. This approach allows for dynamic adaptation during maintenance execution, as the state of the knowledge base is continuously updated, enabling SPARQL queries to dynamically adjust execution plans and data values. This aligns with modern rule-based approaches for synthesizing operating procedures in nuclear facilities (Song, 2020, 7) and using knowledge graphs for failure information fusion to enhance reliability (Xing & Boring, 2024, 7; Zhang, 2024, 7).

SPARQL queries are instrumental in addressing practical maintenance challenges, such as:

- **Detecting Invalid Task Sequences**: By querying for patterns that represent logical inconsistencies or violations of predefined operational workflows. For example, a SPARQL query can identify if a maintenance task is scheduled to begin before its prerequisite tasks are completed.
- **Enforcing Procedural Constraints**: Ensuring that specific resources are available before a task can be initiated, or that certain environmental conditions are met. This can involve checking the availability of specialized tools, qualified personnel, or safe radiation levels before approving a maintenance operation.
- **Dynamic Adaptation**: The continuous update of the knowledge base during maintenance operations allows SPARQL queries to dynamically adjust execution plans and data values. This enables real-time decision support and adaptive maintenance strategies.

The process of transforming IFMIF-DONES maintenance domain knowledge into formally encoded reasoning logic primarily utilizes SPARQL for complex rules. This involves a close examination of structured data sources, human-driven knowledge elicitation from subject-matter experts, and the distillation of domain-specific rules and constraints. Rules with negation, filters, temporal aspects, or those requiring multiple conditions are assigned to the SPARQL formalization track.

For instance, to detect overlapping tasks that are not yet completed, a SPARQL query can be constructed as follows:

```
PREFIX : <http://example.org/ontology#>
CONSTRUCT {
   ?task1 :conflictsWith ?task2 .
} WHERE {
   ?task1 :startTime ?start1 ;
      :endTime ?end1 ;
      :hasTaskProgress ?prog1 .
   ?task2 :startTime ?start2 ;
      :endTime ?end2 ;
      :hasTaskProgress ?prog2 .
   FILTER (?task1 != ?task2)
   FILTER (
     (?start1 <= ?end2 && ?end1 >= ?start2) &&
     (?prog1 != :Completed && ?prog2 != :Completed)
   )
}
```

This query identifies pairs of distinct tasks that overlap in scheduled time and are either ongoing or scheduled to begin (i.e., not yet ended). The CONSTRUCT clause allows for the creation of new knowledge (e.g.,*:conflictsWith* relationship) based on the inferred overlap, which can then be used for further analysis or alerts within the maintenance system.

4.1 Performance Assessment

The performance of the framework was evaluated to demonstrate its practical applicability and effectiveness. Rather than focusing on quantitative benchmarks, the assessment centered on the semantic completeness and qualitative performance of the system in addressing real-world maintenance scenarios. The effectiveness of the framework was measured by its ability to correctly answer a series of competency questions (CQs), which were designed in collaboration with domain experts to reflect complex, practical information needs. The correctness of the inferences and the relevance of the query results were validated by these experts, confirming the framework's utility. The integration of the ontology with GraphDB, optimized for RDF triple stores, played a crucial role in enabling efficient SPARQL query execution.

The tests were conducted on a standard server configuration, and the results, presented in Figs. 4 and 5, demonstrate that the framework can handle complex queries with response times suitable for interactive decision support.

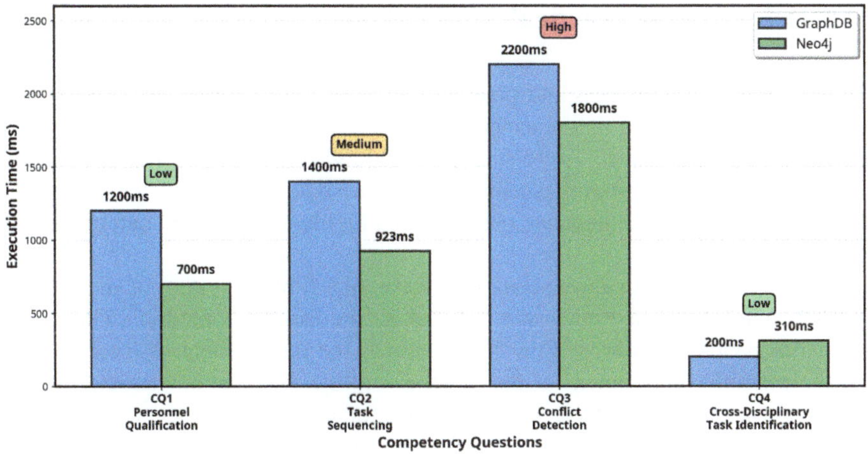

Fig. 4 Comparative analysis of GraphDB and Neo4j query execution times of the queries samples

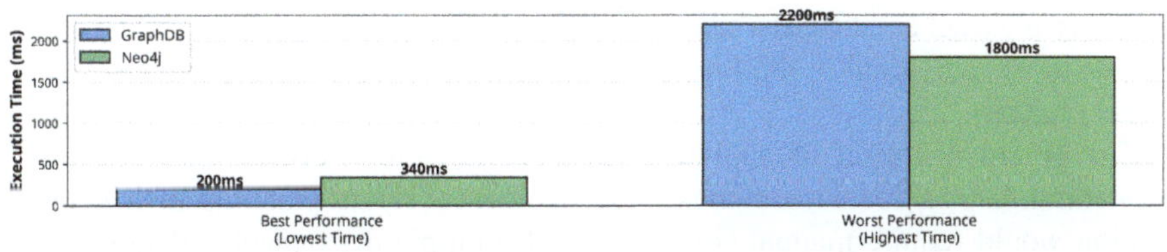

Fig. 5 Comparative analysis of GraphDB and Neo4j query best and worst case execution time performance on the overall competency queries

Key performance indicators included query response times for various levels of complexity, the ability to handle large volumes of maintenance data, and the accuracy of inferred knowledge. The results demonstrated that SPARQL, when applied to the well-structured ontology and knowledge graph, provides a powerful and efficient mechanism for querying and reasoning over maintenance data. This efficiency is critical for real-time decision support and adaptive maintenance planning in a dynamic environment.

For example, queries involving complex joins across multiple classes and properties, or those requiring filtering based on temporal conditions, showed acceptable response times, validating the practical applicability of the framework. The ability to quickly retrieve information about equipment status, personnel availability, historical maintenance records, and potential conflicts significantly enhances the operational efficiency of the maintenance team. The performance assessment confirmed that the chosen approach, centered on SPARQL for querying and reasoning, effectively supports the demanding requirements of fusion facility maintenance management.

5 Use Cases and Practical Applications

To validate the effectiveness and practical utility of the proposed semantic framework, several real-world maintenance scenarios within the IFMIF-DONES facility were used as case studies. These scenarios highlight how the integrated ontology and SPARQL-based reasoning capabilities enhance data integration, decision traceability, and adaptive maintenance planning in a highly complex and safety–critical environment.

One prominent application scenario involves the lithium system of the IFMIF-DONES, a novel engineering system critical for the facility's operation. One of the key maintenance activities within this system is the replacement of the Hot Trap and the monthly replacement of the target assembly. This last is characterized by several constraints that underscore its relevance for advanced maintenance planning: the management of significant radiological inventories, the frequency of intervention, and the necessity of hybrid handling strategies combining manual and remote operations due to the activation levels of the involved components. The instantiation of this task using our built ontology hierarchy is represented in Fig. 6, this diagram is not merely a schematic but a semantically enriched model where each node corresponds to an individual in the knowledge base and each edge represents a defined object property.

The practical impact of applying the semantic framework to this scenario is substantial. In traditional maintenance management systems, planning such an intervention would require manual consultation of multiple disconnected data sources: equipment databases for component specifications, personnel databases for qualification records, radiation safety documentation for zone classifications, and procedural manuals for handling requirements. This fragmented approach is time-consuming, error-prone, and lacks the ability to automatically validate constraints or detect conflicts. For example, manually verifying that assigned personnel possess the required certifications for working in specific radiation zones, while also checking their availability and current workload, could take several hours and still risk oversight.

With the semantic framework, this entire validation process is automated through SPARQL queries that traverse the knowledge graph, checking all relevant constraints in seconds. The framework can automatically identify qualified personnel, verify their radiation dose limits, check tool availability, validate task sequencing, and detect potential scheduling conflicts. This automation not only reduces planning time from hours to minutes but also significantly enhances safety by ensuring that all regulatory and procedural constraints are systematically verified. Furthermore, the framework's ability to trace decision rationale through the explicit representation of relationships provides full transparency and accountability, which is essential for regulatory compliance in safety–critical environments.

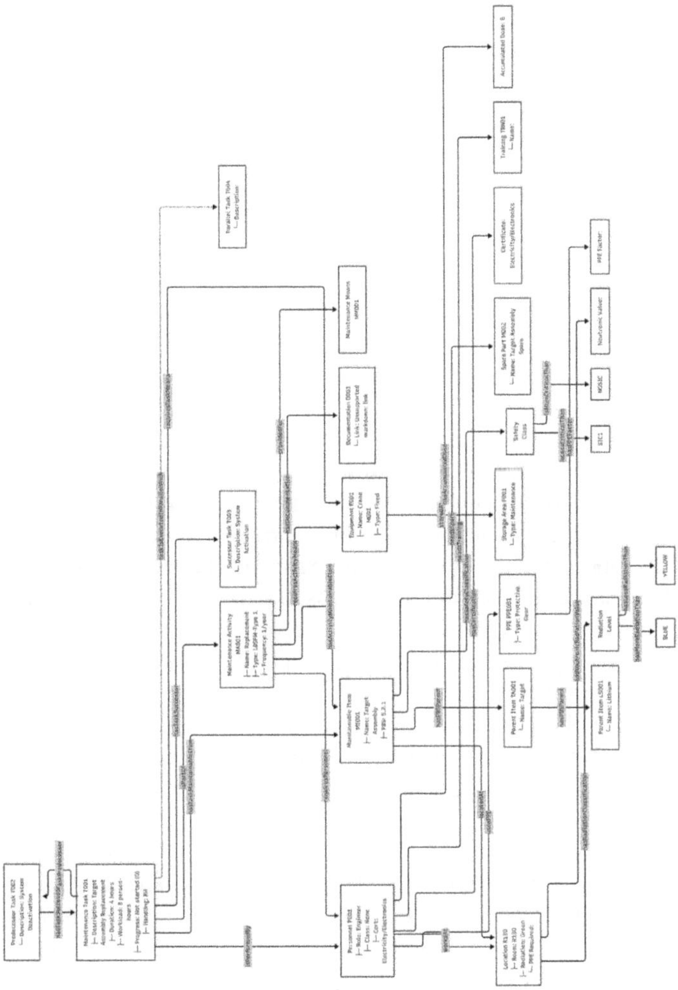

Fig. 6 Instantiation of the target assembly replacement workflow within the ontology, illustrating task decomposition, resource dependencies, safety constraints, and semantic relationships across maintenance entities

The framework's ability to formally structure all relevant information including maintainable items, maintenance tasks, personnel, equipment, documentation, locations, and handling methods into a unified semantic layer is critical for consistent interpretation and reasoning in such complex operations.

5.1 Competency Questions and Practical Querying

The framework's practical utility was further demonstrated through a set of competency questions (CQs) derived from typical maintenance scenarios. These CQs serve as benchmarks for evaluating the expressive power and performance of SPARQL in a practical context. Some examples are shown in Table 2.

These examples illustrate how SPARQL queries, leveraging the rich semantic connections within the knowledge graph, enable maintenance engineers to retrieve highly specific and context-aware information that would be challenging to obtain from traditional, siloed databases. The ability to semantically trace, combine, and infer information across multiple dimensions confirms the practical utility of the ontology for intelligent planning, validation, and decision support in high-risk maintenance environments.

Following the examples above, Fig. 7 provides a compact, visual summary of how the ontology and knowledge graph cover the set of CQs used to validate the framework. The matrix breaks down coverage by CQ into the main ontology elements required to answer each question: classes, object properties, data properties, and axioms/constraints, and annotates query complexity and the number of multi-hop joins required. At a glance, CQ1 is simple (1 class, 0 object properties, 4 data properties; low complexity, 0 joins) while CQ3 is the most demanding (4 classes, 3 object properties, 7 data properties; high complexity, 3 + joins), showing where the reasoning and traversal demands concentrate. CQ2 and CQ4 occupy intermediate positions (CQ2: 3 classes/3 object props/6 data props/medium/2 joins; CQ4: 2 classes/1 object prop/3 data props/low/1 join). The lower panel provides coverage summary statistics (5 unique classes; 5 unique object properties; 12 unique data properties) and the figure's legend clarifies optional elements (asterisked items). Importantly, all CQs were validated against the IFMIF-DONES knowledge graph, which confirms practical applicability while also exposing gaps and extension points: the visualization highlights which CQs demand additional object properties, deeper join paths, or new axioms, thereby guiding targeted ontology enrichment and query optimization in future work.

Table 2 Set of chosen competency questions adopted for the validation of ontology scope, data integration, and decision-support capabilities in the proposed semantic framework

Competency question (CQ)	Description	Relevance to maintenance	SPARQL query
CQ1	Personnel expertise and availability	Which available personnel possess expertise in 'Vacuum, cryogenics' and have an accumulated radiation dose below a certain threshold?	PREFIX : <http://www.semanticweb.org/fusion-maintenance-ontology#> SELECT *?personnelUID ?areaOfKnowledge ?availability ?accumulatedDose WHERE {* *?personnel a :Personnel ; :hasPersonnelUID ?personnelUID ; :hasAreaOfKnowledge* "Vacuum, cryogenics" ; *:hasPersonnelAvailability* "true"^^xsd:boolean ; *:hasAccumulatedDoze ?accumulatedDose .* FILTER (*?accumulatedDose* < 10) . } ORDER BY *?personnelUID*
CQ2	Task assignment and location safety	Identify all tasks assigned to personnel with a specific skill set that are to be performed in locations requiring personal protective equipment (PPE) and having an 'orange' radiation classification	PREFIX : <http://www.semanticweb.org/fusion-maintenance-ontology#> SELECT DISTINCT *?taskUID ?personnelUID ?locationName ?radiationClassification* WHERE { ?task a *:MaintenanceTask* ; *:hasTaskUID ?taskUID* ; *:isPerformedBy* ?personnel *. ?personnel* a *:Personnel ; :hasPersonnelUID* ?personnelUID ; *:hasAreaOfKnowledge* "Metrology, Control, Instrumentation" ; *:worksAt* ?location. *?task :worksAt ?location . ?location* a *:Location ; :requiresPPE* "true"^^xsd:boolean ; *:hasRadiationClassification* ns:Orange ; *:hasLocationName ?locationName ; :hasRadiationClassification* ?radiationClassification . BIND("Orange" AS ?radiationClassification) } ORDER BY ?taskUID

(continued)

Table 2 (continued)

Competency question (CQ)	Description	Relevance to maintenance	SPARQL query
CQ3	Equipment utilization and maintenance history	Retrieve the maintenance history for a given piece of equipment, including the types of maintenance performed, the personnel involved, and the duration of each activity	PREFIX : <http://www.semanticweb.org/fusion-maintenance-ontology#> SELECT ?activityName ?activityUID ?maintenanceType ?personnelUID ?taskDuration WHERE { ?MaintenanceMeans a :MaintenanceMeans ; :hasMeansName "EquipmentX" . ?activity :hasActivityMaintainableItem ?equipment ; :hasMaintenanceActivityName ?activityName ; :hasMaintenanceActivityUID ?activityUID ; :hasMaintenanceType ?maintenanceType ; :requiresPersonnel ?personnel . ?personnel :hasPersonnelUID ?personnelUID . OPTIONAL { ?activity :hasTask ?task . ?task :hasTaskDuration ?taskDuration . } } ORDER BY ?activityUID

CQ4	Cross-disciplinary task identification	Identifying tasks that are associated with personnel having diverse skill sets. This will test the ability to query for multiple property values for a single entity and then link those entities to tasks	PREFIX :
			<http://www.semanticweb.org/fusion-maintenance-ontology#>
			SELECT DISTINCT ?taskUID
			?personnelUID ?areaOfKnowledge1
			?areaOfKnowledge2
			WHERE {
			?task a :MaintenanceTask ;
			:hasTaskUID ?taskUID ;
			:isPerformedBy ?personnel .
			?personnel a :Personnel ;
			:hasPersonnelUID ?personnelUID ;
			:hasAreaOfKnowledge ?areaOfKnowledge1 ;
			:hasAreaOfKnowledge ?areaOfKnowledge2 .
			FILTER (?areaOfKnowledge1 !=
			?areaOfKnowledge2) .
			FILTER (
			(?areaOfKnowledge1 = "Mechanics" &&
			?areaOfKnowledge2 = "Electricity,
			Electronics, including RF") ||
			(?areaOfKnowledge1 = "Electricity,
			Electronics, including RF" &&
			?areaOfKnowledge2 = "Mechanics")
			)
			}
			ORDER BY ?taskUID ?personnelUID

6 Dynamic Adaptation and Decision Support

The framework supports dynamic adaptation during maintenance execution. For instance, if a personnel member's accumulated radiation dose exceeds a predefined limit, the system can identify alternative qualified personnel for their currently assigned tasks in high-radiation areas. Similarly, it can detect anomalies in task

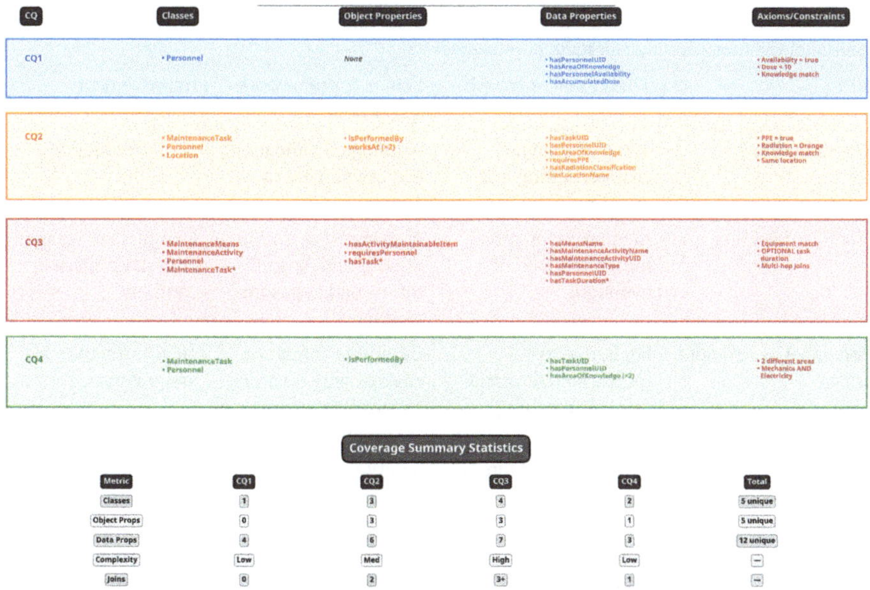

Fig. 7 Competency question coverage matrix showing the systematic mapping of four SPARQL queries to their corresponding ontology components (classes, object properties, data properties) and semantic constraints. Each row details the ontology elements utilized, axioms applied, and query complexity metrics (join operations)

durations, identifying maintenance tasks whose actual duration significantly deviates from their estimated duration, considering factors like handling method and location radiation levels. This proactive identification of deviations allows for timely intervention and adjustment of maintenance plans.

Furthermore, the framework aids in optimizing resource allocation or high priority maintenance activities by suggesting optimal assignments of available personnel and equipment to minimize overall completion time, taking into account skills, certifications, and current assignments. This capability is crucial for maintaining the high availability targets of facilities like IFMIF-DONES.

Some performance benefits of these capabilities, compared with traditional maintenance planning approaches, are summarized in Table 3, which highlights substantial reductions in planning time and personnel assignment errors, improvements in safety compliance, and efficiency gains enabled by semantic reasoning and automated constraint validation.

In essence, the practical applications of this semantic framework extend beyond mere data storage and retrieval. It provides a powerful tool for intelligent decision-making, enabling maintenance teams to proactively manage complex operations, ensure safety compliance, optimize resource utilization, and adapt to dynamic operational conditions within fusion facilities.

Table 3 Comparative performance analysis metrics for the proposed semantic framework versus traditional maintenance management approaches

KPI	Traditional approach	Semantic framework (proposed)	Improvement
Planning time	4–6 h of manual cross-checking and coordination	Automated validation and assignment in < 10 min	> 95% reduction
Conflict detection	Manual, error-prone; high likelihood of oversight	Automated detection of temporal, spatial, safety, and exposure conflicts	Complete coverage; eliminates missed conflicts
Personnel assignment errors	High, due to fragmented data and manual matching	Eligibility inference ensures only qualified and available personnel are assigned	100% reduction in assignment errors
Safety compliance	Safety verified through manual checklists after planning	Safety rules enforced automatically during planning	Higher assurance and fewer revision cycles
Query execution efficiency	Relational joins slow significantly with deeper relationships	Graph traversal optimized for multi-relation queries	30–60% faster query execution
Knowledge reuse	Expertise must be re-interpreted for each new planning cycle	Domain rules, constraints, and classifications persist and apply consistently across cases	Knowledge consistency preserved over time

7 Conclusion

Our semantic framework provides a powerful new approach to maintenance management in complex fusion facilities. By leveraging ontologies, graph databases, and SPARQL, it enables the creation of intelligent, adaptive, and efficient maintenance systems.

However, several technical and methodological challenges should be acknowledged. First, the ontology development process required extensive domain knowledge acquisition and iterative validation with experts, underscoring the difficulty of balancing semantic richness with operational simplicity. Additionally, ontology alignment with existing standards (e.g., ISO 15926, EMMO) remains a non-trivial task, particularly when extending the model to other domains or integrating with legacy systems.

The scalability of the framework has been demonstrated on a representative but not exhaustive dataset; further testing will be necessary to evaluate performance with the full-scale data of the IFMIF-DONES facility on databases. Finally, ontology maintenance represents a long-term commitment, requiring sustained effort to ensure consistency and alignment with the evolving facility structure and operational procedures.

Future work will focus on integrating real-time data streams and machine learning techniques to enhance the framework's predictive capabilities, as well as exploring advanced graph-based methods for maintenance data analysis. In addition, we plan to expand the ontology to cover a broader range of maintenance scenarios and enable seamless integration with external facility management systems.

Acknowledgements This work has been carried out within the framework of the EUROfusion Consortium, funded by the European Union via the Euratom Research and Training Programme (Grant Agreement No 101052200—EUROfusion). Also, this work has received funding under the project PLEC2024-011195, reference MICIU/AEI/https://doi.org/10.13039/501100011033, and by the FEDER and UE. Views and opinions expressed are, however, those of the author(s) only and do not necessarily reflect those of the European Union or the European Commission. Neither the European Union nor the European Commission can be held responsible for them.

References

Arranz, F. (2025). Logistics and maintenance: current status in the IFMIF DONES project. In J. Chiachio, J. A. Garrido, & T. Lehmann (Eds.), *Nuclear fusion* (Vol. 65, No. 12 (09)). https://doi.org/10.1088/1741-4326/ade16c

Beckett, D., & Mcbride, B. (2003). RDF/XML syntax specification. In *W3C working draft*, Sep 05, 2003.

Diao, X., Zhao, Y., Vaddi, P., & Pietryskowski, M. (2024). Multiple aspects maintenance ontology-based intelligent maintenance optimization framework for safety-critical systems. *Artificial Intelligence for Engineering Design Analysis and Manufacturing, 01.* https://doi.org/10.1017/S0890060423000215

Faila, L., Rossoni, M., & Colombo, G. (2025). Ontology-based product lifecycle management: Insights from a proof-of-concept implementation. *IEEE Access* (10). https://doi.org/10.1109/ACCESS.2025.3621327

Fortineau, V., & Paviot, T. (2012). SWRL as a rule language for ontology-based models in power plant design. In *9th International conference on product lifecycle management (PLM)* (Montreal).

Fortineau, V., Fiorentini, X., Paviot, T., Sidney, L., & Lamouri, S. (2014). Expressing formal rules within ontology-based models using SWRL: An application to the nuclear industry. *International Journal of Product Lifecycle Management, 7.* https://doi.org/10.1504/IJPLM

Gruber, Thomas, R. (1993). A translation approach to portable ontology specifications. *Knowledge Acquisition.*

Horrocks, I., Patel-Schneider, & Peter, F. (2004). SWRL: A semantic web rule language combining OWL and RuleML. In *W3C submission, proposed rule language extending OWL DL and Lite.*

Karray, H., Chebel-Morello, B., & Zehrouni, N. (2011). A formal ontology for industrial maintenance. *Terminology & Ontology: Theories and Applications, TOTh Conference, 7*(5), 1–20. https://doi.org/10.3233/AO-2012-0112

Kiryakov, A., Ognyanov, D., & Manov, D. (2005). OWLIM—A pragmatic semantic repository for OWL. In *Proceedings of the 2005 international workshop on description logics (DL2005) OWLIM later became Ontotext's GraphDB.*

Lemaignan S., Siadat A., & Dantan, J. Y. (2006). MASON: A proposal for an ontology of manufacturing domain. *IFAC Workshop Distributed International Systems* (7). https://doi.org/10.1109/DIS.2006.48

Loreti, A. (2025). In K. Chen, R. George, R. Firth, A. Agnello, & S. Tanaka (Eds.), *Automated construction of a knowledge graph of nuclear fusion energy for effective elicitation and retrieval of information.* arXiv, (04). https://doi.org/10.48550/arXiv.2504.07738

Prud'hommeaux, E., & Seaborne, A. (2008). SPARQL query language for RDF. In *W3C Recommendation.*

Sivakumar, R., & Arivoli, P. (2011). Reducing the complexities in the cognition of ontology knowledge representation. *International Journal of Information Sciences and Techniques (IJIST), 12.*

Song, M. (2020). Model-based and rule-based synthesis of operating procedures for planning severe accident management strategies. In A. Gofuku & M. Lind (Eds.), *Progress in nuclear energy* 123 (May). https://doi.org/10.1016/j.pnucene.2020.103318

Telnov, V., & Korovin, Y. (2019). 9th international conference on product lifecycle management (PLM). *Nuclear Energy and Technology.*

Wallbridge, S., & Lowe, A. J. (2014). An ontological approach to knowledge management for sustainable nuclear decommissioning. *International Journal of Nuclear Knowledge Management (IJNKM).*

Webber, J. (2020). *Neo4j user conference.* Episode neo4j originated from Neo Technology circa. A personal history of neo4j.

Xing, J., & Boring, R. L. (2024). Enhancing nuclear power plant operations: An ontology for conditional tasks. In P. Liu & P. Tang (Eds.), *Computing in civil engineering 2023* (Vol. 8). https://doi.org/10.1061/9780784485231.071

Zhang, Y. (2024). A knowledge graph-based failure information fusion method for enhancing reliability in sustainable systems. *Sustainability, 16*(12) (H. Yang & D. Han (Eds.)). https://doi.org/10.3390/su162310651.

Zsákai, A., & Muñoz, A. (2019). IFMIF-DONES systems engineering approach. *Fusion Engineering and Design.*

www.ingramcontent.com/pod-product-compliance
Ingram Content Group UK Ltd.
Pitfield, Milton Keynes, MK11 3LW, UK
UKHW020320200926
475648UK00006B/14
9783032215017